Ellis, Barbara W.

Taylor's guide to perennials :
more than 600 flowering and
foliage plants, including ferns
and ornamental grasses

Taylor's Guides to Gardening

Barbara W. Ellis

FRANCES TENENBAUM, Series Editor

Taylor's Guide to

Perennials

MORE THAN 600 FLOWERING AND FOLIAGE PLANTS,
INCLUDING FERNS AND ORNAMENTAL GRASSES

HOUGHTON MIFFLIN COMPANY
BOSTON · NEW YORK

Visit our Web site: www.houghtonmifflinbooks.com.

Taylor's Guide is a registered trademark of Houghton Mifflin Company.

Library of Congress Cataloging-in-Publication Data
Ellis, Barbara W.
Taylor's guide to perennials : more than 600 flowering and
foliage plants, including ferns and ornamental grasses /
Barbara W. Ellis.
     p. cm. — (Taylor's guide to gardening)
    ISBN 0-395-98363-0
    1. Perennials. I. Title: Perennials. II. Title. III. Series.
SB434 .E47 2001
635.9'32 — dc21   00-033436

Cover photograph by Jerry Pavia Photography, Inc.
Drawings by Steve Buchanan
Book design by Anne Chalmers
Typefaces: Minion, News Gothic

Printed in Singapore
TWP 10 9 8 7 6 5 4 3 2

❧ Contents

✿ Introduction

❦ THE PERENNIAL GARDEN

The saying that variety is the spice of life also applies to perennials. The fact that most perennials are long-lived and reliable is just a small part of their appeal. Perennials mark the progress of the season whether you garden in sun or shade, rich soil or poor. Well-grown plants provide a better show each year, and since many perennials need dividing regularly, they also offer an opportunity for sharing the joys of gardening with friends and neighbors through divisions. Perennials also bring a deeply satisfying characteristic to a garden: change. A perennial garden changes from day to day, week to week, and month to month. In a garden featuring a well-chosen variety of plants, perennials provide a parade of ever-changing color and form from early spring right up to the first killing frost of fall. Some add color beyond the end of the growing season in the form of stray flowers that appear after frost and seed heads that stand through winter. Evergreen perennials add green or sometimes burgundy or purple to the winter landscape.

This book is designed to help gardeners sample the amazing variety of perennials available and determine which ones to add to their beds and borders. It contains information on hundreds of perennials. Both the photographs and the individual entries appear in alphabetical order by botanical name — *Coreopsis, Corydalis, Crambe,* and so forth. See the index if you need to locate a plant by its common name. The photographs are accompanied by captions that summarize essential information about the plants and give page numbers for the text entries where they are covered in more detail. The text entries include descriptions of outstanding species and cultivars, corresponding page references to the photographs, and a How to Grow section for each genus. The How to Grow information covers site and soil requirements as well as essential growing information: Do you need to divide the plants frequently to keep them vigorous? Do they spread quickly or slowly? What are the best methods for propagation?

🌾 DECIDING WHAT TO GROW

Perennials offer such a wealth of shapes, sizes, and colors, it's hard to even begin figuring out which of them to plant and where to plant them. Fortunately, there's a simple rule you can use to guide your choices that will keep you on the path toward a successful planting: always match the plant to the site. In other words, when selecting plants to grow, use your garden's sun, soil, and weather conditions to guide your choices. Plants selected because they thrive in the conditions available in your yard inevitably will perform better — and have fewer problems with pests and diseases — than ones that have to struggle to survive. And what could be better than a garden filled with plants that are thriving — and thriving in the conditions that exist already?

If you are not already familiar with the conditions your garden has to offer, take time to learn more about the site before selecting plants. First, study the sun and shade pattern in your yard on a typical day. Perennials that require full sun need a site that offers at least 8 hours of direct sun per day. Perennials that need light or partial shade need either good light all day or sun for part of the day and shade the rest. Sites that receive direct sun for a few hours in the morning or afternoon and dappled shade the rest of the day will keep many perennials happy. Dappled shade cast by trees with high branches is ideal for growing a wide variety of plants, provided those trees are deep-rooted species like oaks. (Few plants can compete with the dense mat of surface roots produced by most maples.) The best sites for a shade garden offer good light all day long. Some dappled or direct sun during the day is a bonus. A site with deep all-day shade, such as one shaded by evergreens, isn't suitable, and even shade-loving plants won't succeed there. As you examine sites, keep in mind that you may decide to adjust the location of the garden depending on the conditions available, especially if your goal is to grow a particular group of plants.

Sun-loving Achillea *species, commonly known as yarrows, grow in a wide range of soils. They thrive in average to poor, well-drained conditions, tolerate dry and sandy soil, and also grow well in sites that offer moist, rich soil, provided it is well drained.*

Also dig a few test holes to find out about the soil. Is it damp, heavy clay? Rich and loamy? Sandy? You can improve any soil by adding organic matter and using some of the techniques mentioned in "Preparing the Soil" (page 7), but starting out with perennials that thrive in the existing conditions is almost always the best course of action. For example, yarrows (*Achillea* spp.) will grow well right from the start in a site with poor, dry soil, and they'll perform even better if the soil is amended with organic matter. Delphiniums (*Delphinium* spp.) planted on the same site will fail without herculean soil-building efforts and extensive care through the season.

In any site, if you want to experiment, plant the majority of the garden with perennials that prefer the conditions available, but leave some room for plants that only tolerate them. For example, fill a shady site with hostas, ferns, and epimediums, then experiment with perennials that prefer brighter conditions — astilbes, columbines, and hardy geraniums. Plant them in the brightest spots and see how they do. Even if they don't perform up to expectations, the garden will look fine because most of it is planted with shade-loving selections.

Taking the "match the plant to the site" rule one step further, it stands to reason that the best gardens are made up of plants that all thrive in similar conditions. Preparing the soil in an entire bed and then filling it with plants that will be happy there is a much more practical approach to gardening than trying to satisfy each plant individually — especially if their needs are diverse. So, once you know what kind of site you have to work with, start a list of perennials that will thrive there as it is. Also make a list of plants that will grow there with some site modification — such as double digging to provide deeper, richer, more well drained soil. Use this book to get your list started, but also consult neighborhood gardeners and look at public plantings in your area for more ideas.

Hardiness

Throughout this book, you'll find hardiness zones listed for each species, along with the USDA Plant Hardiness Zone Map on pages 466–67. The map lists zones from coldest, Zone 1, to warmest, Zones 10 and 11, and the plant information in this book lists a range for each species. In each range, the first zone listed indicates the northern limit of hardiness, while the second gives a guideline for how much heat a plant can tolerate. For example, peach-leaved bellflower *(Campanula persicifolia)*, hardy from Zones 3 to 7, is fairly cold tolerant — it withstands Zone 3 winters, with

Peach-leaved bellflower (Campanula persicifolia), hardy to Zone 3, is a very cold-tolerant species, but it struggles in heat and humidity. As a result, it doesn't grow well south of Zone 7.

average annual minimum temperature of –30° to –40°F. It is not as forgiving of heat and doesn't grow well in the hot summers characteristic of areas south of Zone 7.

Gardeners vary in the way in which they use hardiness information. Some stick to plants that fall within their zones, an approach that gives good insurance that the majority of perennials will reappear year after year. Others look at hardiness as a challenge and continually experiment with the hardiness limits of the plants they grow. Techniques for experimenting with the cold hardiness of a plant include growing it in a protected site (at the base of a south-facing wall, for example) or providing extra winter protection in the form of a protective layer of evergreen boughs or salt hay placed over the plants in late fall after the soil has frozen. To experiment with heat tolerance, look for cool sites — spots with morning sun and afternoon shade are cooler than those in morning shade and afternoon sun, for example. Ensuring that soil remains evenly moist also can make the difference between success and failure with a particular plant. Sometimes good soil drainage is the key to overwintering a particular perennial successfully, and trying a plant you have failed with in past years in a new site at the top of a rock wall or in a raised bed, for example, may make all the difference.

☙ BUYING PLANTS

Perennials can be expensive, but if you take time to inspect and compare plants — and choose carefully — you can make sure you get the most for your money. Loading up at the local garden center is an easy way to fill your yard with perennials, but unless you take along a list of plants selected to match your site, it's easy to be swept away by all the tempting choices that may or may not be suitable for your site. (Avoid sidewalk displays at home centers and discount stores, where plants receive minimal care and often are stressed by heat and drought.) Well-grown perennials will have dense crowns with healthy-looking stems and leaves. Early in the season, the plants may be quite small, but if you look closely you should be able to see shoots coming up or a healthy crown with sprouting buds. Later in the season, container-grown perennials should be lush and full, again with healthy-colored leaves that show no evidence of scorched or brown leaf edges or signs of disease such as black or brown spots or moldy or powdery patches. Plants starved for nutrients typically have yellowed lower leaves or yellow patches between veins. Check under the leaves for signs of pests (wear glasses if you need them for reading!) such as aphids, spider mites, or whiteflies. Tip a plant out of its pot to see if the roots are excessively crowded. Plants that are not yet blooming are generally a better buy than those already in flower. They recover from transplanting more quickly because they can direct energy to growing roots rather than to supporting flowers.

Don't hesitate to pay a little more for good-size, high-quality specimens because they fill in faster and look attractive much more quickly than sickly, bargain-basement ones. Also remember that most perennials are long-lived plants, and that makes them good long-term garden investments. It's worth spending a little extra to buy topnotch cultivars. If you are just starting out, leave choice, newly introduced ones to the experts: they are notoriously expensive simply because propagators haven't had time to produce enough plants to go around yet. Instead, concentrate on classic older cultivars. Add new cultivars to your garden after they've been offered for a few seasons and the price comes down.

Finally, when comparing prices, pay attention to the size of plant you are buying. Pot size is an obvious place to start comparing prices, but also look at the size of the plant in the pot. (Read the ordering information in catalogs to determine and compare plant size.) Be sure to read descriptions on plant labels or accompanying displays, which should include size at maturity. Many perennials never reach their full size until they're planted in the garden. Hostas are a case in point: the largest cultivars are especially notorious for looking puny in containers — container culture tends to dwarf the leaves and the size of the clumps and diminish the colors. It also adversely affects the color and patterning of the leaves. With good soil and room to spread, the plants will be transformed after a few seasons in the garden.

Buying Native Plants

Many popular perennials are native to North America, and native species are identified as such in this book. Do not add perennials to your garden by digging them from the wild yourself, and buy them only from a reputable nursery that sells nursery-propagated, not wild-collected, plants. Also avoid plants described as nursery grown because these may have been wild-collected and then grown at the nursery for a year or two. The end result is the same: individuals who collect wild plants decimate natural areas, and buying collected plants puts money in their pockets. Nursery-propagated plants will look uniform and healthy, while wild-collected ones often have a just-potted-up look, with an off-center crown and broken or wilted leaves or stems. The plants often are large when compared to the size of the pots but are not root bound. Other signs of wild-collected plants include weeds in the pots and unusually cheap prices for the size of the plants offered. If in doubt, ask the owners where the plants came from; shop elsewhere if you receive an unsatisfactory response. Plant sales sponsored by local native plant societies, conservation associations, and botanical gardens are other good sources for native plants. They offer propagated plants or specimens rescued from areas that are about to be developed.

❦ PREPARING THE SOIL

Whether you are starting a new perennial garden or reworking an existing one, devote some time to improving your soil — before you bring the plants home. Every time you add a new perennial or move one from another part of the garden, take time to work compost, leaf mold, or other organic matter into the soil. You may want to work in a balanced organic fertilizer at the same time. Having a soil test done will tell you whether your soil lacks fertility or if you should be routinely taking steps to adjust pH.

Improving the soil is a continuing process you should think about throughout the year, not just once at planting time. Ideally, the longer

---

WORK WHEN THE SOIL IS RIGHT

Whenever you work the soil, be it to dig a new bed or incorporate organic matter, take a minute to test for moisture before you dig. Working soil when it is either too wet or too dry will damage it, so always squeeze a handful of soil from the site before you start digging or tilling. If it makes a ball that holds together tightly after you open your hand, it is too wet. Wait a day or so and check again before you dig. If the soil is dust-dry, give the site a good soaking, then test again the next day. Ideally, the soil should hold together when you first open your hand but crumble easily when you tap it with a finger.

you tend a garden and care for the soil in it, the richer the soil gets and the wider the variety of plants you can grow in it. Loose, well-drained soil that remains evenly moist, is rich in organic matter, and has a slightly acid to neutral pH will satisfy the widest variety of perennials. The best way to develop or maintain great garden soil is to add organic matter regularly. Organic matter improves soil drainage and also holds nutrients in the soil for plants to use. Spreading a layer of compost over the garden (or at least around the plants) is a great way to get organic matter into the soil. Your mulching and feeding practices also can help build great soil. Organic mulches such as shredded bark and chopped leaves add vital organic matter, albeit more slowly than compost does. Mulch also protects the soil from erosion by wind or water and compaction by rain (raindrops pounding down on bare soil exert considerable force).

If you are starting a new garden, try to prepare the soil the season *before* you plant to give it time to settle. Late fall, when the air is cool and crisp, is a great time to prepare new garden beds for spring planting. (After digging, mulch them to protect the soil over winter.) If you can't wait to plant, prepare the soil, water the site thoroughly to help it settle, and then wait a day or so before planting.

After you have prepared a bed, stay off the soil as much as possible. Half of the volume of good garden soil is pore space — about half of that consists of small pores that hold water, and about half consists of larger pores that hold air once the soil drains after a rain. Walking, sitting, kneeling, or standing on soil compresses soil pores, thus reducing the amount of large pores that hold air (which plant roots need in order to grow) and impeding soil drainage. Compacting the soil also simply makes it more difficult for roots to penetrate. Walk around garden beds or lay down stepping stones if you are inclined to cut through them.

Double Digging and Single Digging

Double digging is a classic soil preparation technique that loosens and improves the soil to about 2 feet, or the depth of two shovels. It ensures good drainage, allows you to work plenty of organic matter into the soil, and encourages plants to grow deep, wide-spreading roots. To double dig, spread organic matter such as compost over the site, then dig a 1-foot-wide trench along one edge of the planting area. Pile the removed soil on a tarp or in a wheelbarrow. Spread a 1-inch layer of compost or other organic matter over the bottom of the trench, then work it into the soil with a garden fork. Next, dig another trench next to the first, turning the soil into the previous trench. Add more organic matter to the bottom of the new trench and fork it in. Continue this process until you reach the other end of the planting area, then fill the last trench with the soil you removed from the first one.

If your soil is good, or if you simply don't have the time to double dig, single digging is a good alternative. To single dig, spread compost over the site, and then turn the soil over to a shovel's depth, working in the compost as you go.

Raised Beds

Raised beds are an option for sites with poor soil or for areas that are too wet. You can build a raised bed directly on top of the ground, but tilling or digging the site as deeply as you can first encourages deeper roots and helps water percolate down into the soil. Incorporate a couple of inches of compost or chopped leaves into the soil as you work. Then install landscape ties or sides consisting of rock or brick and fill the bed with topsoil mixed with compost. Water thoroughly to settle the soil, top it off, and you're ready to plant. For plantings on slopes, building terraces into the side of the slope is an ideal option. Use landscape ties or stones to hold the lower edges of the terraces, which carve level planting sites out of the slope. Like raised beds, terraces create well-drained, deeply prepared soil on a site that otherwise would be difficult to plant successfully.

❧ PLANTING PERENNIALS

Once the soil is prepared, you're ready to plant. If you've purchased plants at a garden center, set them in a cool, shady, protected site until you're ready to move them to the garden. If you've ordered them through the mail, unpack them promptly. Water plants that are still in their pots whenever the soil surface dries out. Keep bare-root ones packed in the material in which they were shipped, moistening it if necessary. If they were shipped without anything covering their roots, soak them in lukewarm water for an hour or so and then pot them up or heel them in by placing them in a protected spot with their roots covered with damp soil or compost. Ideally, plant as soon as you can after they arrive.

A cool, cloudy, or even rainy day is the best time to plant — or transplant — perennials. To plant a pot-grown plant, dig a hole large enough to accommodate the roots, and tip the plant out of its pot. If the plant has roots that wind around the inside of the pot, use a knife to score them on each side to encourage the roots to extend out into the surrounding soil. Set container-grown plants at the same depth at which they were growing in the pot, or position them slightly higher to allow for settling. Then refill and water thoroughly.

Soak bare-root plants in water for a couple of hours before planting, then dig a hole large enough to make it easy to spread out the roots. If bare-root plants have sprouted, cut back top growth by about one-third to give them a better chance to recover from the transplant shock. Set them with the crown of the plant — where the roots meet the buds or top growth — at the soil surface, and hold them in place while you refill the hole with soil. Water each plant thoroughly.

With both container-grown and bare-root perennials, if the weather is warm or windy, cover new plants with burlap, bushel baskets, or spun-bonded row covers for a few days to help them recover.

❦ CARE THROUGH THE SEASONS

Spring is the busiest time in the garden as plants re-emerge from their winter dormancy. In addition to planting new perennials, other important activities include dividing established ones, as well as weeding and fertilizing. Winter coverings of evergreen boughs or other protective coverings also need to be removed. From late spring into summer, garden tasks include mulching, staking, deadheading, cutting back, watering, and pest control — along with the still-essential task of keeping weeds at bay. Late summer and fall usher in another round of planting and dividing, plus cutting back plants when they stop blooming, watering if the weather is dry, and more weeding. In late fall, cut plants back for the winter, and after the soil freezes, provide protection for those that may not be hardy by covering them with evergreen boughs, salt hay, or straw. From fall through winter, also keep an eye out for winter weeds, which germinate in fall and set seeds by spring or early summer. Pulling them up on warm winter days gives you a reason to be out in the garden and also keeps them from getting a foothold. Here's a rundown of essential garden chores.

Deadheading
This is a simple technique that involves nothing more than removing flowers after they have faded either by pinching them off between your thumb and forefinger or by clipping them off with pruning shears. Dead-

Like other rudbeckias, Rudbeckia hirta 'Indian Summer' self-sows if spent flowers are not removed as they fade. Seedheads left on the plants also add winter interest and provide food for the birds.

heading prevents plants from spending energy to set seed and directs that energy to overall growth. It also keeps the garden looking neat and encourages many plants to rebloom later in the season. Plants with an abundance of small flowers can be deadheaded by shearing. To shear a plant, cut it back by one-third to one-half with hedge clippers or garden shears. Many gardeners don't deadhead perennials bearing seed heads that feed the birds and add interest in winter, such as coneflowers (*Echinacea* spp. and *Rudbeckia* spp.). If you want a plant to self-sow, leave at least some of the flowers on the plant to set seed.

Dividing

Division is both a propagation technique and a technique used to rejuvenate perennials or control their spread. Good candidates for division include clumps that have died out or become woody in the center, ones that are overcrowded and blooming less, and plants that have spread too far and are threatening to overtake their neighbors. See the individual entries for recommendations on when to divide. Cool, rainy, or overcast weather is best for dividing plants, because it reduces stress on the plants. Newly divided plants have reduced root systems and have trouble supplying top growth with water until the roots begin growing again. Cutting the top growth back by about half helps divisions recover more quickly.

To divide a plant, dig the clump with a spade or a garden fork starting about 6 inches or more from the outside edge of the clump. Dig all the way around it, then lift the plant out of the hole. (If the plant you are dividing is very large or heavy, divide it into smaller, manageable pieces while it is still in the hole.) Separate small plants with fibrous roots into pieces with your fingers. Use a sharp knife or shears to cut apart plants with woody or dense crowns or rhizomes. Cut apart large clumps with a spade or force them apart with two garden forks placed back to back. Ornamental grasses are so dense and woody that a mattock or an ax is required to divide them. If you have difficulty deciding where to cut, wash the soil off the roots with a stiff stream of water from the hose before dividing. While the plants are out of the ground, make sure the roots do not dry out. Cover them with mulch, loose soil, or a piece of plastic if they are going to be out of the ground for more than a few minutes.

Discard old, woody growth and replant the youngest, most vigorous portions of the clumps. And always amend the soil with compost or other organic matter before you replant. To create good-size clumps within a season or two, plant three to five pieces together, spaced as you would new plants. Don't overcrowd, or you'll defeat the purpose of dividing. Water new divisions deeply. If the weather is sunny, shade them with bushel baskets, cardboard boxes propped up on sticks, or burlap for a few days. Plant extra divisions elsewhere in the garden or give them away to friends. If the individual plants are small or you don't have a spot prepared for them, pot them up (use commercial potting soil, not garden soil), water, and hold them in a shady, protected location.

Feeding

Most perennials growing in soil that is well supplied with organic matter don't need to be fertilized throughout the growing season. Give all your perennials a spring feeding with very well rotted manure, compost, or a balanced organic fertilizer. Spread it on the surface of the soil around plants, but under any mulch layer, and keep it away from plant stems.

Then replace the mulch. If you have fresh manure available, spread it in late fall—again keeping it away from plant stems—so there is plenty of time for it to rot over winter.

Mulching

A layer of organic mulch such as compost, shredded bark, or chopped leaves on your garden not only controls weeds, it also improves the soil by adding vital organic matter. Mulch also benefits soil by holding in moisture, keeping it cool, and protecting it from erosion by wind and rain. Your choice of mulches depends on where you live. Shredded bark is available nearly everywhere, but pine needles are commonly available only in some regions. Most gardeners have a ready supply of chopped leaves — pick them up off the lawn in a bagging lawn mower or chop them in a shredder. Compost has the advantage of improving the soil and adding some nutrients at the same time. If you don't have enough of it to mulch the entire garden, spread a thin layer around your plants and top it with a more readily available mulch such as shredded bark. *Never* use peat moss as mulch, because it forms an impenetrable crust on the soil. Plants that demand perfect drainage are best left unmulched, but if you do choose to mulch, consider pea gravel, granite chips, or limestone chips, which are commonly used to mulch rock gardens.

The best time to mulch a garden is late spring or early summer, when most perennials are up and the soil has had a chance to warm up a bit. Spread a 2- to 3-inch layer over the soil, but keep the mulch away from plant stems. For best results, feather out the thickness of the mulch as you get closer to plant crowns or stems, keeping the mulch 1 to 2 inches away from the stems. Some gardeners remove and compost mulch in late fall, as part of fall cleanup, and replace it each spring. Other gardeners leave mulch on their garden year round, although mulch can encourage rodents to spend the winter dining on the crowns of your plants. Apply winter mulches, which are designed to protect marginally hardy plants over winter, after the ground has frozen completely. Evergreen boughs are a good choice, but weed-free straw or salt hay is also effective. Don't use anything that will hold moisture around the crowns. Remove winter mulch in late winter or early spring.

Pinching

This technique encourages branching and denser, shorter, more compact growth. To pinch a plant, use your thumb and forefinger to snap off the tip of each shoot just above a set of leaves. If the growth is too hard to remove with your fingers, use pruning or garden shears. Pinching a plant often results in more, although smaller, flowers and is best used on bushy, multistemmed plants. It won't work on plants with unbranched stems (such as lilies) or basal foliage (such as daylilies).

Staking

There are several effective methods for staking plants, and the methods you choose will vary depending on the type of plant and its size. Whichever method you choose, always stake plants early in the season, before they need support. Staking plants after they have already flopped over is generally a futile effort, and the end result is an unattractive, hog-tied effect.

For plants with tall stems, such as delphiniums, staking each stem individually is often the best approach. Bamboo stakes are effective and relatively unobtrusive. Metal stakes covered with green plastic work well, too. You'll need stakes at least a foot longer than the plants will be at maturity, so that you can drive them solidly into the ground. Install the stakes *before* the flower stalks are much more than a foot high. Take care not to drive them into the crowns of the plants. As the stems grow, tie them to the stakes with yarn, old shoelaces, strips of nylon stockings, or soft string. Don't tie them too tightly, or you'll constrict the stems. The stems should be able to move slightly. Figure-eight ties — around the stake, crossing over in the center, and around the stem — work best.

Stakes and string are an effective method for supporting clump-forming plants such as peonies. Again, you'll need stakes that are slightly longer than the plants are high. Pound them into the ground around each clump, then wind string around the outside of the stakes and through the center of the clump to form a spider web–type pattern. Add another tier of string, if necessary, as the plant grows. As the plant's stems grow up through the string, the string that crosses the center will provide support to stems through the center of the clump.

"Pea brush," "brushy twigs," and "pea stakes" are all terms used to describe another traditional staking method that is suitable for smaller, lighter-weight plants such as catmint (*Nepeta* spp.). Cut well-branched twigs from shrubs, ideally with a fairly straight section at the bottom, and push them into the soil around the clumps. You can break the tips of the twigs and point them toward the center of the clump to provide added support. Keep in mind that twigs from some shrubs will root when stuck back in the garden, so cut them several weeks before you need them and leave them in the sun. Even then, watch for leaves or other evidence that you've accidentally added a shrub to your garden.

Several commercial staking systems are available, too — hoops, stakes that link together, and individual supports for flower stems. Have a variety of options on hand — both traditional and commercial — so you can stake plants quickly and easily.

Transplanting

Whether you have perennials growing in a spot that doesn't make them happy, colors that clash, or plants that simply are too large for the space available, transplanting is the technique to solve the problem. Cool, cloudy, or even rainy weather is the best time to move plants from one place to another. To minimize damage to the roots, start digging about 6 inches or so from the outside edge of the clump. Dig all the way around the clump, then lift the plant out of the hole. Then dig another hole in the new location, plop the plant in place, fill the hole, firm the soil, and water. Most plants can be transplanted from one place to another in the garden anytime the soil can be worked. Don't try it with plants described as difficult to divide, however. Be sure to set the plant at the same depth at which it was growing. If the weather promises to be cloudy for a few days, you're all finished. If it's going to be sunny, shade the plant by propping burlap or a bushel basket over it for a few days.

Watering

Watering is a simple, straightforward task, but you'll grow a healthier, more trouble-free garden if you observe two basic rules. The first is, when you need to water, water deeply. Moisten at least the top 6 inches of soil. This encourages plants to develop deep roots and improves drought tolerance. The second rule is to put the water directly on the soil rather than up in the air. Lawn sprinklers can cover large areas, but much of the water evaporates before it hits the ground. Water on the foliage — especially if you water late in the day and the plants are wet overnight — can lead to foliar diseases. Soaker hoses are a very efficient way to water: spread them each time you need to water, or install them at the beginning of the season and cover them up with mulch. Keep the ends exposed so it's easy to connect them up to the water supply when you need to.

FOILING INSECTS AND OTHER PESTS

Matching each plant to an appropriate site and building healthy soil will allow you to circumvent most problems with pests and diseases. Get in the habit of watching plants closely for signs of problems. Look under leaves for signs of infestations, and know which plants need regular watering or feeding to keep them healthy. Keep in mind that plants that need dividing regularly may exhibit signs that can be mistaken for a disease, such as weak, spindly growth.

On the whole, perennials present few problems once they're planted out in the garden. Most diseases are fairly easy to control, especially if you spot them in the early stages. Pick off leaves that have yellow, brown, or black spots or blotches as they appear. Root and crown rots, commonly caused by poor soil drainage, are best dealt with by siting plants properly and improving the soil. Below, you'll find information on some of the most common pests you may encounter and safe, organic ways to control them.

APHIDS. These are tiny green, black, brown, or reddish, pear-shaped, soft-bodied insects. Some have wings. Look for them clustered on buds, shoots, and undersides of leaves where they suck plant juices, causing stunted or deformed blooms and leaves. They also exude a sticky substance called honeydew, which produces a shiny coating on leaves and supports the growth of black sooty mold fungus. Aphids also transmit plant viruses. To control them, encourage or introduce natural predators, including lacewings and ladybugs. Pinch off and destroy infested plant parts, or knock the pests off plants with a strong spray of water. Spray serious infestations with insecticidal soap or pyrethrins.

BEETLES. While some of these hard-shelled, oval to oblong insects are beneficial in the garden, others are pests, especially Japanese beetles, which are metallic-looking green insects with coppery brown wings; the larvae are brown-headed white grubs. Beetles chew holes in leaves, stems, and flowers during the growing season. The larvae of some kinds feed on roots. To control them, handpick adult beetles early in the morning and drop them into a container of soapy water. Apply parasitic nematodes to the soil to control grubs. You also can apply spores of milky disease to lawns to control Japanese beetle grubs. Treat seriously infested plants with neem, pyrethrins, or rotenone.

CATERPILLARS. These soft-bodied, wormlike creatures have several pairs of legs and smooth, hairy, or spiny bodies. Adults are moths or butterflies. They chew holes in leaves, flowers, fruit, and shoots through the growing season. To control, handpick and destroy them. (Wear gloves to prevent possible skin irritation.) Or leave them alone or move them to other plants — many caterpillars are the larvae of butterflies that most gardeners welcome to their gardens. The larvae of swallowtail butterflies, for example, feed on parsley, dill, and other related plants.

CUTWORMS. Gardeners seldom see these plump, smooth, brown, gray, or green, 1-inch-long caterpillars, but their presence is evident when they chew through the stems of seedlings and transplants near the soil line. The larvae are active only at night and are most troublesome in spring. The adults are brown or grayish moths. Prevent damage by surrounding stems with cardboard collars extending 2 inches above and below the soil line. Apply parasitic nematodes to the soil around the base of young plants.

LEAFHOPPERS. Adult leafhoppers are small, greenish, wedge-shaped, soft-bodied insects that hop quickly when disturbed. Nymphs look similar to the adults but lack wings. Both feed on stems and the undersides of leaves. They suck plant juices, causing discoloration and stunted or distorted growth. The tips and sides of affected leaves may turn yellow or brown and curl upward. Leafhoppers exude sticky honeydew on leaves and also transmit plant diseases. Use a strong spray of water to wash nymphs off plants. Spray serious infestations with insecticidal soap or pyrethrins; use rotenone or sabadilla as a last resort.

MITES. Often called spider mites, these very tiny, golden, red, or brown spiderlike pests spin fine webs around leaves or between leaves and stems. They suck plant juices from leaves, producing a light-colored stippling on leaf surfaces. Whole leaves become pale and dry and may drop. Rinsing or spraying leaves frequently with water can suppress mite populations. Pollen- and nectar-rich plants attract natural predators, such as ladybugs and lacewings. Spray serious infestations with insecticidal soap, superior oil, neem, or pyrethrins.

PLANT BUGS. Adult plant bugs are fast-moving, oblong, flattened insects, ¼ to ⅓ inch long. Four-lined plant bugs are greenish yellow and have four black stripes on the back. The wingless nymphs are reddish with black dots. Tarnished plant bugs are greenish to brownish and have brown or black mottling on the back. Nymphs are smaller and pale yellow with black dots; they lack wings. Plant bugs suck plant juices, causing sunken, brown or black spots on leaves and deformed leaves, buds, and shoots. Handpick adults and nymphs in early morning (while they are still sluggish) and drop them in a container of soapy water. Grow pollen- and nectar-rich plants to attract natural predators. Treat serious infestations with neem, sabadilla, or rotenone. To prevent damage to future crops, clean up garden debris in fall and spring to remove overwintering sites for adults.

SLUGS AND SNAILS. These are gray, tan, or black, slimy, soft-bodied mollusks. Snails have a hard outer shell and may be up to 1½ inches long. Slugs lack shells; they may be ⅛ inch to 6 inches or more in length. Both leave slime trails on leaves and rasp large holes in leaves, stems, and fruit; they may completely devour seedlings. Slugs are usually most active at night and in damp places; snails are less dependent on moisture. Trap slugs and snails under fruit rinds, cabbage leaves, or boards set on the soil, or in shallow pans of beer set into the soil surface; check traps daily and destroy pests. If slugs or snails are a major problem, eliminate mulches and garden debris; these materials provide ideal hiding places. Use barriers of copper screen or sheeting to repel slugs and snails. Plant ground covers to attract ground beetles and other predators.

WHITEFLIES. Sometimes called "flying dandruff," adult whiteflies are tiny flies with white powdery wings. They cluster on the undersides of leaves and fly up in great numbers when disturbed. Both the adults and the tiny, flattened larvae suck plant juices through the season outdoors and all year indoors. Infested plants look yellow, sickly, and stunted. As they feed, whiteflies exude a sticky honeydew that supports the growth of black sooty mold. Inspect greenhouse plants carefully for whiteflies before bringing the plants home. Spray serious infestations with insecticidal soap, superior oil, pyrethrins, or rotenone.

☙ PROPAGATING PERENNIALS

Perennials can be propagated by a variety of techniques, but simply digging and dividing the clumps is by far the most common technique used to accomplish this satisfying garden task. Dividing yields good-size plants very quickly, and many perennials need to be divided regularly anyway to keep them vigorous and/or in bounds. Division is an asexual, or vegetative, propagation technique, which means dividing a clump of perennials yields exact replicas of the parent plant. Other asexual techniques commonly used to propagate perennials include growing plants from cuttings (either shoot cuttings or root cuttings) and mound layering. Asexual techniques are the propagation methods of choice if you are propagating a particular cultivar and want an exact replica of the parent plant. They also yield full-size plants much faster than growing plants from seeds — a sexual propagation technique. Starting from seeds, on the other hand, often is the only option for acquiring rare or unusual species. However, many popular perennials are hybrids, and seed-grown plants do not resemble their parents. (There are perennial cultivars that do come true from seeds, meaning they resemble their parents.) See below for more on specific propagation techniques. For more on division, see "Dividing" on page 11.

Perennials that spread by sending out suckers, runners, or offsets are especially easy to propagate — essentially by division, since all that is required is severing the connection to the parent plant and potting up or transplanting the new one. Suckers, which arise from root tissue below ground or stem tissue at the base of the plant, may appear close to the parent plant or as much as several feet away. Runners are horizontal shoots that grow along the soil surface and often root at the nodes (the points where leaves emerge from the stem), yielding self-supporting new plants. Encourage runners to take root by pinning them to the ground with a U-shaped piece of wire or to a pot of moist growing mix sitting near the parent plant. An offset is a type of side shoot or branch that develops from the base of the main stem and establishes its own root system. To propagate from any of these structures, wait until the new plants have formed their own roots before severing their connection to the parent plant and digging them up.

Cuttings

Cuttings offer a fast, easy way to propagate a wide range of perennials. You'll find recommendations for the best seasons to collect cuttings in the individual plant entries. Before collecting cuttings, fill small pots with a moistened rooting medium such as a 50-50 mix of perlite and vermiculite or peat moss and perlite. Also set up a system for maintaining high humidity around the cuttings so they don't dry out before they can establish a new root system. Consider a wooden or wire frame draped with plastic, large clear-plastic sweater boxes, or an old aquarium with a piece of glass over the top.

Gather cuttings early in the day, while the stems are full of moisture. Cuttings from wilted or water-stressed plants are not likely to root well, so if the weather has been dry, water on the day before gathering cuttings. Take cuttings from strong-looking growth, with leaves that have fully expanded and growth that has hardened a bit. Avoid spindly shoots or ones that are growing very rapidly. To judge if the growth is at the best stage for collecting, try bending one of the plant's stems firmly. If it snaps off cleanly, it's a good time to collect cuttings. Growth that just bends over is too soft, while growth that crushes or partially breaks is old and may be slow to root. Snip off shoots with a sharp, clean pair of pruning or garden shears. Make sure each shoot has at least two nodes (the joints where the leaves or leaf pairs emerge from the stem). Collect cuttings in a plastic bag to prevent them from drying out, and keep them out of direct sun. As soon as you have all the cuttings you need, take them indoors and prepare them for planting. If you can't plant them immediately, wrap them in a moist paper towel and keep them in the plastic bag in a cool, shady spot until you are ready for them.

Use a sharp, clean pair of shears or a utility knife to trim each shoot to its final cutting size — 2- to 4-inch-long cuttings are ideal. Whenever possible, trim each cutting so there are at least two nodes left, and make the bottom cut just *below* a node. Trim the leaves off the bottom half of

Rooting Softwood Cuttings

LEAF NODE
AT BOTTOM
OF CUTTING

STICK CUTTING
HALFWAY INTO
MEDIUM

the cutting, and remove any flowers or flower buds. Use a pencil to poke a hole in the growing medium, then insert the cutting about halfway into the medium, to just below the lowest leaves. Push the medium back around the stem to support the cutting. Repeat with the remaining cuttings, spacing them 1 to 4 inches apart. The cuttings shouldn't touch, so if the leaves are large, either space the cuttings farther apart or trim their leaves slightly (by no more than one-half). A 4-inch pot will usually hold several cuttings. Different plants root at different rates, so it's best to use separate pots for each different species or cultivar. Label each pot with the name of the plant and the date. After planting, water thoroughly.

Set the cuttings in a warm (65° to 75°F) spot in the sweater box or other enclosure you prepared. The growing medium should be a steady 70° to 75°F, so ideally use a heated propagating mat. Good light, but not direct sun, is also essential. Outdoors, set covered cuttings at the base of a north-facing wall or in a spot that's lightly shaded all day by trees or shrubs. Cuttings also root well under fluorescent lights.

If condensation doesn't build up on the inside of the propagation enclosure within a day, water again thoroughly. Otherwise, leave the cuttings covered and water only when the condensation thins or disappears; don't let the pots sit in water. Remove the cover for an hour or so two or three times a week to allow some air circulation around the leaves. To discourage diseases, immediately remove any dropped leaves or obviously dead cuttings. Most soft-stemmed plants start rooting in 2 to 5 weeks. Once you see the cuttings producing new growth, tug lightly on the stems. When the cuttings feel firmly anchored in the medium, they are ready to transplant to individual pots. Gradually remove or open the enclosure over a period of a few days to increase ventilation and to decrease humidity. This will help the new growth harden off and reduce the chance of wilting.

Move the rooted cuttings into pots filled with moistened potting soil. Lightly tap the base of each pot against a hard surface two or three times to settle the mix around the roots, then water thoroughly. Set potted cuttings in a shady spot and mist them a few times with a hand sprayer daily for 2 or 3 days. Then move them to their preferred light conditions and water and fertilize as usual.

Mound Layering

Mound layering is a handy technique for propagating shrubby plants such as artemisias, lavenders, and thymes. Mound-layer plants in spring by piling roughly 3 to 5 inches of crumbly, sandy soil or finely shredded bark mulch — ideally mixed with a handful or two of compost — over the center of the plant. Leave 3 to 4 inches of each shoot tip exposed. Work the soil or mulch around the stems with your fingers to eliminate air pockets. Water carefully just after mounding (a strong spray of water will wash away the soil or mulch) and over the next few months as needed to keep the mound from drying out. Add more soil or mulch if rains wash part of the mound away. In late summer to early fall, pull away some of the soil or mulch with your fingers to see if roots have formed along the covered parts of the stems. If there are few or no roots, leave the mound in place and check it again in spring. If the shoots look well rooted, pull away more of the mound and snip off the rooted stems near the original soil level. Plant well-rooted stems directly into the garden or move them into individual pots. In some cases, the parent plant may produce new growth from the roots after this process. If it isn't growing in a highly visible spot, you may want to leave it in place for a season after removing the mound, to see if it sprouts again. If it is too prominent, just dig it out, work a few handfuls of compost into the site, and replant the spot with one or more of the rooted stems.

Root Cuttings

A number of perennials are easy to propagate by root cuttings, including bear's breeches (*Acanthus* spp.) and purple coneflowers (*Echinacea purpurea*). In general, gather root cuttings in late winter to early spring, when the soil has thawed and dried out enough to be dug. (See the individual plant entries for the best season to collect them.) To gather root cuttings from small plants, dig up the whole plant, rinse the soil off the roots, take your cuttings, and replant. With larger plants, collect cuttings by digging carefully around the base of the plant to expose the roots, then collect the cuttings with a clean, sharp knife or pruning shears.

For plants with relatively fine roots, cut off whole roots, then snip them into 2-inch sections. Where the roots are thick or fleshy, select pencil-thick roots and gather 2- to 3-inch-long sections. Like stem cuttings, root cuttings must be planted right-side up. To keep track of which is which, on each thick or fleshy cutting, make a straight cut on the end that was closest to the crown of the plant and a sloping cut at the other end. Place gathered cuttings in a plastic bag to keep them from drying out until you are ready to prepare and plant them.

Plant the root cuttings in pots filled to just below the rim with a moistened mix of equal parts peat moss and perlite, and set the pots in a

cold frame or a cool, bright room. To plant, lay thin-rooted cuttings horizontally on the surface of the mix, spaced about 1 inch apart, and cover
them with an additional ½ inch of mix. Insert thicker cuttings vertically
into the mix or soil, with the flat end of the cuttings pointing upward.
Space them about 2 inches apart, with the tops even with or just below
the surface. Water to settle the medium around the roots. Keep the medium evenly moist but not wet (covering pots loosely with plastic is a good
idea). Root cuttings often produce top growth before their new roots are
established. Wait until you can see roots through the pots' drainage holes
before transplanting to individual pots or to a nursery bed. Transplant
the young plants to the garden in the fall if they are large enough, or leave
them in a cold frame or nursery bed for an extra growing season.

Starting Seeds

Without doubt, growing perennials from seeds takes more patience than
starting annuals, but starting from seeds is often the best way to acquire
an unusual species or raise large quantities of plants. Late winter to midspring is the busiest time for sowing annual seeds, and many perennials
can be sown at that time. However, midsummer also is a great time to
sow perennials. In fact, for some, midsummer sowing is essential because
the seeds must be sown as soon as they are ripe to ensure adequate germination. For example, spring-blooming wildflowers such as Virginia
bluebells *(Mertensia virginica)* and bleeding hearts *(Dicentra* spp.) produce seeds that are quick to dry out and must be planted when still quite
fresh in order to get good germination. For other perennials, summer
sowing yields sturdy young plants that can stay outside through the winter and be transplanted in spring the following year as blooming-size
plants. Some perennial seeds germinate best when sown outdoors in fall,
either in pots or in a nursery bed. Sowing outdoors in fall and even into
winter provides the chilling period, or the periods of alternating warm
and cold temperatures, that these seeds may need to start sprouting.
You'll usually see seedlings emerge the following spring, although some
seeds may take 2 or even 3 years to germinate.

The easiest way to grow many hardy perennials from seeds is to sow
them in pots and set them outdoors for germination. In this case, sow
them just as you would pots to be germinated indoors, then top off the
pots with a ¼- to ½-inch layer of fine, washed gravel; the small pebbles
sold for use in aquariums usually work well. This layer keeps the mix
from drying out quickly, and it also helps prevent mosses from developing and smothering your seedlings. Also add a plastic label (wooden ones

SPREAD SEEDS OUT OVER SOWING MEDIUM TO PREVENT OVERCROWDING

FOR OUTDOOR SOWING, MULCH POTS WITH FINE GRAVEL.

OUTDOORS, SINK POTS TO THE RIM IN SOIL OR SET IN A PROTECTED LOCATION.

Starting Seeds Outdoors

rot quickly) marked with the seed name and sowing date. Set the pots in a cold frame, or sink them to their rims in a nursery bed or a protected spot in the garden. Cover them with a piece of fine-mesh hardware cloth to keep mice and other animals from digging in the pots. Natural rainfall will take care of most of the watering, but you will need to water during dry spells. While some perennials will germinate in a few weeks, it may take months for others to appear.

Indoors, sow perennial seeds as you would annuals in late winter or early spring. Fill containers with moist seed-starting mix, and press the seeds into the surface or cover them with the amount of mix recommended on the packet. A few plants germinate more reliably if the seeds are scarified before they are sown — baptisias (*Baptisia* spp.), for example. To scarify seeds, nick the seed coat gently with a razor blade or utility knife (don't damage the embryo inside). Another option is to rub the seeds on a piece of sandpaper or a nail file. Still another option is to soak the seeds in hot, but not boiling, water for 12 to 24 hours.

Label each pot with the name of the seed and the sowing date. Cover the containers with sheets of clear plastic suspended on a wire frame or with molded plastic "domes" sold for this purpose. Put covered containers under fluorescent lights. Remove the coverings once the seedlings emerge. The seeds of a few perennials — columbines (*Aquilegia* spp.), for example — benefit from a brief chilling period before they're germinated. Sow these plants in pots, place each pot in a plastic bag, close the bag loosely, and set it in the refrigerator for the recommended amount of time. After that, germinate them at the recommended temperature. Keep the pots evenly moist but not wet until seedlings emerge.

Whether sown indoors or out, once your seedlings emerge, remove any covers to allow good air circulation, and give them plenty of light. Most seedlings will need transplanting only once before you move them out into the garden. When the first pair of true leaves have developed (after the first "seed" leaves), transplant indoor- or outdoor-grown seedlings into individual 2- to 4-inch pots. Use a growing medium that's somewhat coarser — with more perlite and/or vermiculite — than the seed-starting mix. Moisten the growing mix and the pots of seedlings before transplanting. Next, tip the whole clump of seedlings and roots into one hand. Holding one seedling by a leaf (not the stem), use a pencil or a plant label to separate its roots from the others. Then use the pencil or plant label to make a hole in the center of the new container. Lower the seedling into the hole, so the point where the roots join the stem is even with the top of the growing mix. Gently push the moist mix around the roots until the mix supports the seedling. Don't press the soil down around the seedling; just lightly tap the bottom of the pot once or twice on your work surface to settle the mix around the roots. Add a little more mix, if needed. Water as soon as possible after transplanting. Keep the pots evenly moist, and start feeding seedlings once they have begun growing again. Use a liquid houseplant fertilizer, diluted to half its regular strength. Feed once a week for 3 to 4 weeks. After that, use the fertilizer full strength every 10 to 14 days until the seedlings are ready for transplanting into the garden.

Before moving seedlings to the garden, gradually expose them to the outdoors. This process, called hardening off, minimizes transplanting stress by helping them withstand drying winds, sun, and fluctuating temperatures and thus eases the plants' transition into the garden. About a week before you're ready to move seedlings to the garden, set them outdoors for a few hours in a shaded location that is protected from wind. Leave them out for a few more hours each day, and gradually move them into a more exposed location. Keep them well watered during this process. The night before you transplant, leave them out all night.

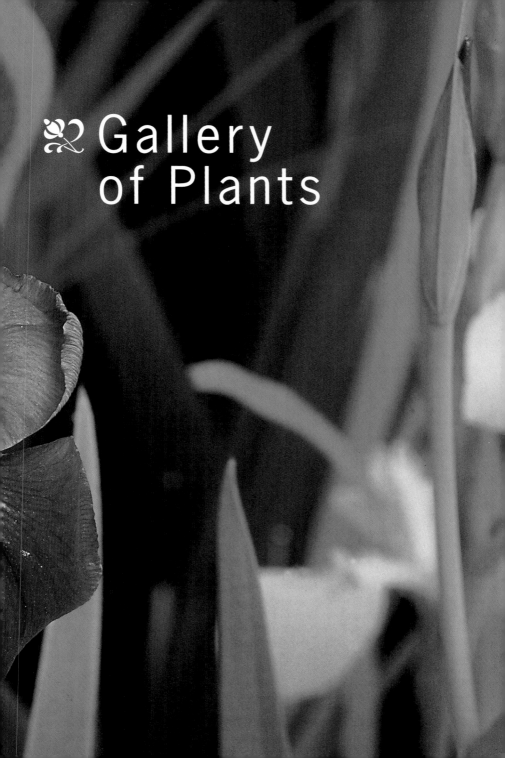

❧ Gallery
of Plants

Acanthus mollis
Common Bear's Breech
SIZE: 2½ feet to 5 feet

Full sun or light shade

Evenly moist, well-drained soil

Produces spiny-toothed leaves topped by erect
spikes of purple-and-white flowers in late
summer

Zones 7 to 10

P. 229

Acanthus spinosus
Spiny Bear's Breech
SIZE: 2½ to 5 feet

Full sun or light shade

Evenly moist, well-drained soil

Handsome mounds of spiny-margined leaves
topped by racemes of purple-and-white
flowers from late spring to midsummer

Zones 5 to 10

P. 230

▲*Achillea* 'Coronation Gold'
Yarrow

SIZE: 3 to 3½ feet

Full sun

Average to poor well-drained soil

Bears ferny leaves and 4- to 5-inch-wide mustard yellow flowers on erect stems all summer

Zones 3 to 9

P. 230

▼*Achillea millefolium* 'Paprika'
Yarrow

SIZE: 2 feet

Full sun

Average to poor well-drained soil

Features ferny leaves and flat-topped orangered flower clusters from early to late summer

Zones 3 to 9

P. 231

Achillea ptarmica 'The Pearl'
Sneezewort
SIZE: 1 to 3 feet
Full sun
Average to poor well-drained soil
Narrow, lance-shaped leaves and loose sprays of
    buttonlike double white flowers from early
    to late summer
Zones 2 to 9
P. 231

Achillea tomentosa
Woolly Yarrow
SIZE: 1 foot
Full sun
Very well drained, average to poor soil
Low mounds of woolly gray-green leaves and
    clusters of yellow flowers from early sum-
    mer to fall
Zones 3 to 7
P. 231

Aconitum carmichaelii
Azure Monkshood

SIZE: 3 to 5 feet

Partial or dappled shade; afternoon shade in
    areas with hot summers

Rich, moist, well-drained soil

Bears spikes of rich violet-blue blooms from
    late summer through fall

Zones 3 to 7

P. 232

Aconitum napellus
Common Monkshood

SIZE: 3 to 4 feet

Partial or dappled shade; afternoon shade in
    areas with hot summers

Rich, moist but well-drained soil

Produces showy clusters of dark blue-violet
    flowers in mid- to late summer

Zones 3 to 8

P. 233

▲*Acorus calamus* 'Variegata'

Variegated Sweet Flag

S I Z E : 3 to 4 feet

Full sun or partial shade

Rich, constantly moist to wet soil or standing
water

Forms handsome clumps of strap-shaped leaves
striped lengthwise with cream and white

Zones 4 to 11

P. 233

▼*Acorus gramineus* 'Oborozuki'

Grassy-leaved Sweet Flag

S I Z E : 12 inches

Full sun or partial shade

Rich, constantly moist to wet soil or standing
water

Cultivar of an evergreen to semievergreen
species with clumps of glossy, grasslike
leaves

Zones 5 to 11

P. 233

Actaea alba
Doll's Eyes, White Baneberry
SIZE: 2 to 4 feet

Partial shade

Average to rich, evenly moist soil

Native wildflower with fluffy racemes of white flowers in late spring and early summer followed by clusters of white berries

Zones 3 to 7

P. 234

Actaea rubra
Red Baneberry, Snakeberry
SIZE: 2 to 4 feet

Partial shade

Average to rich, evenly moist soil

Native wildflower with fluffy clusters of flowers in late spring and early summer followed by showy clusters of round red berries

Zones 3 to 7

P. 234

Adenophora confusa
Common Ladybells
SIZE: 2 to 2½ feet
Full sun to partial shade
Rich, moist, well-drained soil
Bears loose panicles of bell-shaped purple-blue
    flowers for 3 to 4 weeks in early summer
Zones 3 to 8
P. 235

Adiantum pedatum
Northern Maidenhair Fern
SIZE: 1 to 1½ feet
Partial shade
Moist, well-drained, slightly acid soil
Produces clumps of lacy, branched fronds with
    shiny black stems
Zones 2 to 8
P. 235

Aegopodium podagraria 'Variegata'
Bishop's Weed

SIZE: 1 to 2 feet

Partial to full shade

Thrives in any soil, but poor, dry soil is best

Vigorous to invasive foliage plant grown for its three-part leaves with irregular creamy white margins

Zones 4 to 9

P. 236

Agastache cana
Wild Hyssop, Hummingbird Mint

SIZE: 2 to 3 feet

Full sun or very light shade

Rich, well-drained soil

Bears aromatic leaves and loose 1-foot-long spikes of pink or rose-purple flowers from late summer to fall

Zones 5 to 10

P. 237

Agastache foeniculum
Anise Hyssop

SIZE: 3 to 5 feet

Full sun or very light shade

Rich, well-drained soil

Bears anise-scented leaves and spikes of blue
flowers with violet bracts from midsummer
to fall

Zones 6 to 10

P. 237

Ajania pacifica
Gold-and-silver Chrysanthemum

SIZE: 1 foot

Full sun

Poor to average, well-drained soil

Mounding perennial with handsome silver-
edged leaves and clusters of golden buttonlike flowerheads in fall

Zones 5 to 9

P. 237

▲*Ajuga genevensis* 'Pink Beauty'

Geneva Bugleweed

SIZE: 6 to 12 inches

Light to partial shade; tolerates full sun to full shade

Well-drained, moist, average to rich soil

Moderately spreading species with dense spikes of pink flowers in spring

Zones 4 to 8

P. 238

▼*Ajuga pyramidalis* 'Metallica Crispa'

Pyramid Bugleweed, Upright Bugleweed

SIZE: 4 to 6 inches

Light to partial shade; tolerates sun or shade

Average to rich, moist, well-drained soil

Moderate spreader with crinkled dark green or metallic bronze-purple leaves and short spikes of purple-blue flowers

Zones 3 to 8

P. 239

Ajuga reptans 'Catlin's Giant'
Common Bugleweed, Carpet Bugleweed

SIZE : 4 to 6 inches

Light to partial shade; tolerates sun or shade

Average to rich, well-drained, moist soil

Fast-spreading species with large spoon-shaped
leaves and spikes of violet-blue flowers in
late spring

Zones 3 to 9

P. 239

Alchemilla alpina
Alpine Lady's Mantle

SIZE : 6 to 8 inches

Partial shade; partial to full shade in areas
where summers are hot

Rich, moist, well-drained soil

Mounding species with deeply lobed leaves
edged with silver hairs and loose sprays of
yellow-green flowers in summer

Zones 3 to 7

P. 240

Alchemilla mollis
Common Lady's Mantle
SIZE: 1 to 2 feet

Partial shade; partial to full shade in areas
where summers are hot

Rich, moist, well-drained soil

Mounding species with handsome, pleated
leaves and frothy clusters of chartreuse
flowers from late spring to early summer

Zones 4 to 7

P. 240

Amsonia hubrectii
SIZE: 2 to 3 feet

Sun or partial shade

Average, moist, well-drained soil

Native species forming handsome clumps of
narrow leaves that turn golden in fall; bears
very pale blue flowers in summer

Zones 5 to 9

P. 241

▲ *Amsonia tabernaemontana*
Willow Blue Star
S I Z E : 1 to 3 feet
Sun or partial shade
Average, moist, well-drained soil
Native species with lance-shaped leaves and
    clusters of star-shaped flowers in spring and
    early summer
Zones 3 to 9
P. 241

▼ *Anaphalis margaritacea*
Pearly Everlasting
S I Z E : 2 to 3 feet
Full sun to partial shade
Average to rich, moist, fairly well drained soil
Bears papery white flowers from midsummer to
    fall and attractive gray-green leaves with sil-
    very edges
Zones 4 to 8
P. 241

Anchusa azurea 'Loddon Royalist'

Italian Alkanet, Italian Bugloss

SIZE: 3 feet

Full sun to light shade

Rich, well-drained, moist soil

Produces showy, loose clusters of deep blue
   flowers in early summer

Zones 3 to 8

P. 242

Anemone canadensis

Meadow Anemone

SIZE: 6 to 8 inches

Partial shade

Light, rich, moist soil

Native wildflower with single white flowers
   from late spring to early summer

Zones 3 to 7

P. 244

Anemone × hybrida 'Alba'

Japanese Anemone, Hybrid Anemone

SIZE: 2½ to 5 feet

Full sun or partial shade; afternoon shade in areas with hot summers

Rich, moist, well-drained soil

In late summer and early fall bears clusters of long-stalked white flowers above low mounds of foliage

Zones 4 to 8

P. 244

Anemone sylvestris

Snowdrop Anemone

SIZE: 1 to 1½ feet

Partial shade

Light, rich, moist soil

Vigorous species bearing single white 2-inch-wide flowers in spring

Zones 3 to 8

P. 244

Anemone tomentosa 'Robustissima'

Grape-leaved Anemone

SIZE: 3 feet

Full sun or partial shade; afternoon shade in areas with hot summers

Rich, moist, well-drained soil

Bears loose umbels of pale pink flowers from late summer to fall

Zones 4 to 8

P. 244

Angelica archangelica

Archangel, Wild Parsnip

SIZE: 6 feet

Partial shade; tolerates full shade

Rich, deep, moist soil

Produces mounds of bold leaves topped by large clusters of tiny greenish yellow flowers from early to midsummer

Zones 4 to 9

P. 245

Angelica gigas

SIZE : 3 to 6 feet

Partial shade; tolerates full shade

Rich, deep, moist soil

Bears rounded clusters of tiny purple flowers
  on purplish red stems in late summer and
  early fall

Zones 4 to 9

P. 245

Antennaria dioica

Pussytoes

SIZE : 2 to 4 inches

Full sun to very light shade

Average, well-drained soil; tolerates poor soil
  and hot or dry locations

Bears gray-green leaves and fluffy clusters of
  white or pale pink flowers in early summer

Zones 4 to 8

P. 246

▲*Anthemis sancti-johannis*
Golden Marguerite
SIZE: 2 to 3 feet

Full sun

Very well drained poor to average soil

Bears fernlike gray-green leaves and small buttonlike orange daisies all summer

Zones 4 to 9

P. 247

▼*Anthemis tinctoria*
Golden Marguerite
SIZE: 1½ to 2½ feet

Full sun

Very well drained, poor to average soil

Bears fernlike leaves and yellow to cream-colored daisy flowers from summer to fall

Zones 3 to 7

P. 247

Anthriscus sylvestris
'Ravenswing'

SIZE: 2½ to 3 feet

Full sun or partial shade

Average to rich well-drained soil

Produces clumps of lacy, fernlike purple-black
leaves topped by lacy white flowers in late
spring and early summer

Zones 6 to 10

P. 247

Aquilegia caerulea
Rocky Mountain Columbine

SIZE: 1½ to 3 feet

Full sun or partial shade; dappled or afternoon
shade in hot climates

Rich, evenly moist, well-drained soil

Native wildflower bearing blue-and-white flowers from late spring to midsummer

Zones 3 to 8

P. 249

Aquilegia canadensis
Wild Columbine

S I Z E : 1 to 3 feet

Full sun or partial shade; dappled or afternoon
 shade in hot climates

Rich, evenly moist, well-drained soil

Native wildflower with racemes of nodding
 red-and-yellow flowers from midspring to
 midsummer

Zones 3 to 8

P. 249

Aquilegia chrysantha
Golden Columbine, Yellow Columbine

S I Z E : 3 to 4 feet

Full sun or partial shade; dappled or afternoon
 shade in hot climates

Rich, evenly moist, well-drained soil

Southwestern native with pale to golden yellow
 flowers from late spring to late summer

Zones 3 to 9

P. 249

Aquilegia flabellata f. *pumila* 'Alba'

Dwarf Fan Columbine

SIZE: 6 to 8 inches

Full sun or partial shade; dappled or afternoon shade in hot climates

Rich, evenly moist, well-drained soil

Compact species with blue-green leaves and long-spurred white flowers in early summer

Zones 3 to 9

P. 249

Aquilegia Long-spurred hybrid

Long-spurred Hybrid Columbine

SIZE: 2 to 2½ feet; dwarf types 4 to 15 inches

Full sun or partial shade; dappled or afternoon shade in hot climates

Rich, evenly moist, well-drained soil

Showy flowers from late spring to midsummer in a mix of solid colors and bicolors

Zones 3 to 9

P. 249

Aquilegia vulgaris
'Nora Barlow'
European Columbine
SIZE: 1½ to 3 feet

Full sun or partial shade; dappled or afternoon
shade in hot climates

Rich, evenly moist, well-drained soil

Bears pale green and red pomponlike double
flowers in late spring and early summer

Zones 3 to 8

P. 250

Arabis caucasica
Wall Rock Cress
SIZE: 6 to 10 inches

Full sun or light shade

Average, well-drained soil; tolerates heat,
drought, and poor, dry soil

Spreading species with gray-green leaves and
racemes of fragrant white flowers in spring

Zones 4 to 8

P. 251

▲*Armeria maritima*

Sea Pink, Common Thrift

SIZE: 6 to 8 inches

Full sun

Poor to average, well-drained soil

Produces low tufts of grassy leaves topped by round flower clusters in shades of pink or white in early summer

Zones 3 to 8

P. 252

▼*Artemisia absinthium* 'Lambrook Silver'

Wormwood

SIZE: 2½ feet

Full sun

Average, well-drained soil

Vigorous, shrubby cultivar forming mounds of aromatic, deeply divided silvery gray leaves

Zones 3 to 9

P. 253

Artemisia ludoviciana 'Silver King'

White Sage, Western Mugwort
SIZE: 2 to 4 feet
Full sun
Average, well-drained soil
Fast-spreading foliage plant grown for its silver-
white leaves
Zones 3 to 9
P. 253

Artemisia 'Powis Castle'

SIZE: 2 to 3 feet
Full sun
Average, well-drained soil
Shrubby perennial forming billowing clumps of
feathery, aromatic, silver-gray foliage
Zones 5 to 8
P. 253

Artemisia schmidtiana 'Nana'

Silvermound Artemisia

SIZE: 1 to 2 feet

Full sun

Average, well-drained soil

Mounding foliage plant with feathery, soft-textured silver-gray leaves

Zones 3 to 7

P. 253

Aruncus aethusifolius

Dwarf Goat's Beard

SIZE: 8 to 12 inches

Partial or dappled shade

Rich, evenly moist soil

Clump-forming species with ferny leaves and plumes of creamy white flowers from early to midsummer

Zones 4 to 8

P. 254

Aruncus dioicus
Goat's Beard

SIZE: 3 to 6 feet
Partial or dappled shade
Rich, evenly moist soil
Shrubby native wildflower with featherlike
    leaves and creamy white plumelike flowers
    from early to midsummer
Zones 3 to 7
P. 255

Arundo donax 'Variegata'
Giant Reed

SIZE: 10 to 25 feet
Full sun
Average, moist but well-drained soil
Ornamental grass forming spreading clumps of
    white-striped leaves that usually fade to
    green as they age
Zones 6 to 10
P. 255

Asarum europaeum
European Wild Ginger
S I Z E : 6 to 8 inches
Partial to full shade
Rich, evenly moist soil
Ground-covering evergreen with glossy leaves
 and insignificant red-brown flowers in late
 spring
Zones 4 to 8
P. 256

Asarum shuttleworthii
Mottled Wild Ginger
S I Z E : 3 to 9 inches
Partial to full shade
Rich, evenly moist soil
Native wildflower with dark green evergreen
 leaves often mottled with silver and
 insignificant purple-brown flowers in early
 summer
Zones 5 to 9
P. 256

Asclepias incarnata
Swamp Milkweed
SIZE: 3 to 5 feet

Full sun

Rich, moist to wet soil; also grows in well-drained conditions

Native wildflower producing flat-topped clusters of pale to deep rose pink flowers in midsummer and early fall

Zones 3 to 8

P. 257

Asclepias tuberosa
Butterfly Weed
SIZE: 2 to 3 feet

Full sun

Average, well-drained soil; thrives in poor, dry conditions

Shrubby native wildflower bearing rounded clusters of bright orange or orange-red flowers in midsummer

Zones 3 to 9

P. 257

Aster alpinus
Alpine Aster
SIZE : 6 to 12 inches
Full sun; best in areas with cool summers
Rich, well-drained, moist soil
Bears solitary flower heads from early to mid-summer in violet purple to lavender, pink, and white
Zones 2 to 7
P. 259

Aster × frikartii
Frikart's Aster
SIZE : 2 to 3 feet
Full sun
Rich, well-drained, moist soil
Bears loose sprays of lavender-blue flower heads from midsummer through fall
Zones 5 to 8
P. 260

Aster lateriflorus
Calico Aster, Starved Aster
SIZE: 2 to 4 feet

Full sun

Average to very poor soil

Native wildflower producing clouds of starry white to pale lavender flower heads from midsummmer to fall

Zones 3 to 8

P. 260

Aster novae-angliae 'Purple Dome'
New England Aster, Michaelmas Daisy
SIZE: 1½ feet

Full sun

Rich, well-drained, moist soil

Mounding cultivar of a native wildflower with deep purple flowers with yellow centers in fall

Zones 3 to 8

P. 260

Aster novae-belgii
New York Aster, Michaelmas Daisy
SIZE: 1 to 4 feet
Full sun
Rich, well-drained, moist soil
Much hybridized native wildflower bearing
   showy clusters of lavender-blue, white, ruby
   red, pink, or purple flower heads in fall
Zones 3 to 8
P. 260

Aster tataricus 'Jindai'
Tartarian Aster
SIZE: 4 to 5 feet
Full sun
Rich, well-drained, moist soil
Dwarf cultivar of a very tall, robust, strong-
   stemmed aster with large clusters of laven-
   der-blue flower heads from mid- to late fall
Zones 2 to 8
P. 261

Astilbe chinensis var. *davidii*
Chinese Astilbe

SIZE: 4 to 6 feet

Partial shade; also tolerates considerable sun

Rich, constantly moist, well-drained soil

Vigorous selection with erect panicles of pinkish purple flowers in late summer

Zones 4 to 8

P. 261

Astilbe hybrid 'Fanal'
Hybrid Astilbe

SIZE: 2 to 3 feet

Partial shade or sun in the morning and shade
in the afternoon

Rich, constantly moist, well-drained soil

Bears plumy blood red flowers in early summer
above mounds of fernlike leaves

Zones 3 or 4 to 8

P. 262

Astilbe hybrid 'Peach Blossom'
Hybrid Astilbe

SIZE: 2 to 3 feet

Partial shade or sun in the morning and shade in the afternoon

Rich, constantly moist, well-drained soil

Bears plumy pink flowers in late spring and early summer above mounds of fernlike leaves

Zones 3 or 4 to 8

P. 262

Astrantia major
Masterwort

SIZE: 1 to 3 feet

Partial or dappled shade; full sun

Rich, moist soil

Bears branched stems of buttonlike flower clusters, each with a ruff of papery bracts in early and midsummer

Zones 4 to 7

P. 263

▲*Athyrium filix-femina*
Lady Fern, European Lady Fern

SIZE: 2 to 3 feet

Partial to full shade

Rich, evenly moist, well-drained soil

Spreading fern forming mounds of handsome, thrice-cut fronds

Zones 4 to 8

P. 264

▼*Athyrium niponicum* var. *pictum*
Japanese Painted Fern

SIZE: 1 to 1½ feet

Partial to full shade

Rich, moist, well-drained soil

Vigorous, spreading fern with twice-cut fronds variously marked with silver or gray and maroon-purple midribs

Zones 4 to 9

P. 264

Aubrieta × cultorum

Aubrieta, Rock Cress

SIZE: 2 inches

Full sun

Average, well-drained soil

Mat-forming perennial bearing single or double flowers in shades of pink and purple in spring

Zones 4 to 7

P. 265

Aurinia saxatilis

Basket-of-gold, Cloth-of-gold, Gold Dust

SIZE: 8 inches

Full sun

Average, well-drained soil

Mounding perennial with gray-green leaves and dense clusters of small yellow flowers in spring

Zones 4 to 8

P. 265

Baptisia alba
White Wild Indigo
SIZE: 2 to 3 feet

Full sun

Rich, moist, well-drained soil; tolerates poor,
  sandy, or dry soil

Southeastern native wildflower with racemes of
  white flowers in early summer

Zones 4 to 9

P. 266

Baptisia australis
Blue False Indigo, Plains False Indigo
SIZE: 3 to 5 feet

Full sun

Rich, moist, well-drained soil

Robust species with handsome blue-green
  leaves and erect clusters of dark blue flowers
  in early summer

Zones 3 to 9

P. 266

Begonia grandis ssp. *evansiana*

Hardy Begonia

SIZE: 2 to 2½ feet

Partial to full shade

Rich, moist, well-drained soil

Bears wing-shaped leaves and graceful, arching clusters of pink flowers in late summer

Zones 5 or 6 to 10

P. 267

Belamcanda chinensis

Blackberry Lily, Leopard Flower

SIZE: 2 to 4 feet

Full sun

Average to somewhat rich, well-drained, moist soil

Bears sword-shaped leaves, orange or yellow spotted flowers in summer, and blackberry-like seed heads

Zones 5 to 9

P. 268

▲*Bergenia cordifolia*
Heart-leaved Bergenia
SIZE: 1 to 2 feet

Partial to dappled shade

Well drained, humus-rich, moist soil

Bears leathery leaves and rose pink to rose-red flowers in late winter and early spring

Zones 3 to 8

P. 269

▼*Boltonia asteroides* 'Snowbank'
Boltonia
SIZE: 4 to 5 feet

Full sun

Rich, well-drained, evenly moist soil

Bears masses of small white-petaled daisies from late summer to fall

Zones 3 to 9

P. 270

Brunnera macrophylla
Siberian Bugloss
SIZE: 1 to 1½ feet
Partial to full shade
Rich, evenly moist soil
Forms mounds of heart-shaped leaves and
    bears clusters of tiny blue flowers in mid- to
    late spring
Zones 3 to 8
P. 271

Calamagrostis × acutiflora
Feather Reed Grass
SIZE: 2 to 6 feet
Full sun to light shade
Average to rich, well-drained, moist soil
Ornamental grass with arching leaves and erect
    panicles of flowers in mid- to late summer
Zones 5 to 9
P. 271

Calamintha grandiflora
Large-flowered Calamint
SIZE: 1½ feet

Full sun or partial shade

Average, moist, well-drained soil; tolerates poorer soil

Bushy perennial bearing aromatic leaves and loose clusters of small pink flowers in summer

Zones 5 to 9

P. 272

Caltha palustris
Marsh Marigold
SIZE: 1 to 1½ feet

Full sun

Rich, constantly moist to boggy soil

Native wildflower bearing clusters of waxy, golden yellow flowers in spring

Zones 3 to 7

P. 273

▲*Campanula carpatica*
Carpathian Harebell

SIZE: 8 to 12 inches

Full sun to partial shade

Gritty, moist, cool, well-drained soil

Bears masses of cup-shaped blue, violet, or white flowers over a long season from late spring through summer

Zones 3 to 8

P. 274

▼*Campanula cochleariifolia*
Spiral Bellflower, Fairies' Thimbles

SIZE: 3 to 6 inches

Full sun to partial shade

Gritty, moist, cool, well-drained soil

Creeping, mat-forming species with nodding lilac-blue to white flowers in summer

Zones 5 to 7

P. 274

Campanula glomerata
Clustered Bellflower

SIZE: 1 to 2 feet

Full sun to partial shade

Average to rich, moist but well-drained soil; tolerates wet soil

Rhizomatous species with rounded clusters of violet, white, or lavender-blue flowers from early to midsummer

Zones 3 to 8

P. 274

Campanula lactiflora
Milky Bellflower

SIZE: 3 to 5 feet

Full sun to partial shade

Average to rich, moist but well-drained soil

Bears branched clusters of bell-shaped white or lavender-blue flowers from early to late summer

Zones 3 to 7

P. 274

Campanula latifolia
Great Bellflower

SIZE: 4 to 5 feet

Full sun to partial shade

Average to rich, moist but well-drained soil

Vigorous, fast-spreading species with clusters of white, violet, or lilac-blue flowers in summer

Zones 3 to 7

P. 275

Campanula persicifolia
Peach-leaved Bellflower

SIZE: 1 to 3 feet

Full sun to partial shade

Average to rich, moist but well-drained soil

Clump-forming species bearing racemes of flowers from early to midsummer in shades of blue and white

Zones 3 to 7

P. 275

Campanula portenschlagiana
Dalmatian Bellflower

SIZE: 4 to 6 inches

Full sun to partial shade

Gritty, moist, cool, well-drained soil

Mounding, fast-spreading species with panicles
    of violet purple flowers from late spring to
    early summer

Zones 4 to 8

P. 275

Campanula poscharskyana
Serbian Bellflower

SIZE: 6 to 12 inches

Full sun to partial shade

Gritty, moist, cool, well-drained soil

Vigorous to invasive species with loose panicles
    of starry pale blue flowers in early summer

Zones 3 to 7

P. 275

Campanula rotundifolia
Bluebell, Harebell
SIZE: 5 to 12 inches
Full sun to partial shade
Gritty, moist, cool, well-drained soil
Dainty bellflower with round leaves and nodding pale- to violet-blue or white flowers on slender stems in summer
Zones 2 to 7
P. 276

Cardamine pratensis
Lady's Smock, Cuckoo Flower
SIZE: 1 to 1½ feet
Partial to full shade
Very rich, evenly moist soil
Bears panicles of lilac, purple, or white 1/2- to 1-inch-wide flowers in late spring
Zones 5 to 8
P. 276

Carex elata 'Aurea'
Bowles' Golden Sedge

SIZE: 1½ to 2 feet

Full sun or partial shade; shade and moist soil in areas with hot summers

Rich, moist, well-drained soil; also grows in wet soil

Deciduous sedge forming dense clumps of arching golden yellow leaves

Zones 5 to 9

P. 277

Carex morrowii 'Gold Band'
Sedge

SIZE: 16 to 20 inches

Full sun or partial shade

Rich, moist, well-drained soil

Evergreen sedge forming clumps of leaves with creamy white margins

Zones 5 to 9

P. 277

Carex siderosticha 'Variegata'
Sedge

SIZE: 8 to 12 inches

Full sun or partial shade

Rich, moist, well-drained soil; also grows in wet soil

Deciduous sedge forming mounds of strap-shaped white-margined leaves

Zones 6 to 9

P. 278

Caryopteris × clandonensis
Bluebeard, Blue-mist Shrub, Blue Spirea

SIZE: 2 to 3 feet

Full sun or very light shade

Loose, well-drained soil

Shrubby perennial with aromatic leaves and clusters of blue flowers from late summer to early fall

Zones 4 to 9

P. 279

▲ *Catanache caerulea*
Cupid's Dart
SIZE: 1½ to 2 feet

Full sun or very light shade

Average, well-drained soil

Bears grassy leaves and solitary lilac-blue flower heads atop wiry stems from midsummer to fall

Zones 3 to 8

P. 279

▼ *Centaurea dealbata*
Persian Centaurea
SIZE: 2 to 3 feet

Full sun

Average to rich, well-drained, evenly moist soil

Bears pink thistlelike flower heads with conelike bases in summer

Zones 3 or 4 to 8

P. 280

Centaurea macrocephala
Globe Centaurea, Giant Knapweed
SIZE: 3 to 5 feet
Full sun
Average to rich, well-drained, evenly moist soil
Bears yellow flower heads in mid- and late
    summer that have prominent brown cone-
    like bases
Zones 3 to 7
P. 280

Centaurea montana
Mountain Bluet
SIZE: 1½ to 2 feet
Full sun
Average to rich, well-drained, evenly moist soil
Vigorous to weedy perennial with rich blue
    flower heads in early summer
Zones 3 to 8
P. 281

▲*Centranthus ruber*

Valerian, Jupiter's Beard

SIZE: 1 to 3 feet

Full sun

Poor to average, well-drained soil

Woody-based perennial with rounded clusters
    of small red, pink, or white flowers from late
    spring through late summer

Zones 4 to 8

P. 281

▼*Cerastium tomentosum*

Snow-in-summer

SIZE: 6 to 10 inches

Full sun

Poor to average, very well drained soil

Vigorous, mat-forming species with silver-gray
    leaves and clusters of white flowers in late
    spring and early summer

Zones 2 to 7

P. 282

Ceratostigma plumbaginoides
Plumbago, Leadwort
SIZE: 6 to 12 inches

Full sun; tolerates partial shade

Rich, evenly moist, well-drained soil

Fast-spreading species with showy clusters of brilliant blue flowers from summer to fall and orange or red fall foliage color

Zones 5 to 9

P. 283

Chamaemelum nobile
Roman Chamomile
SIZE: 6 to 12 inches

Full sun

Light, well-drained soil; thrives in sandy soil

Mat-forming perennial with threadlike leaves and small white daisylike flowers in summer

Zones 6 to 9

P. 283

Chasmanthium latifolium
Northern Sea Oats
SIZE: 2 to 3 feet
Partial shade
Rich, moist, well-drained soil
Native grass with bamboolike leaves and
    drooping green seed heads in midsummer
    that ripen to brown
Zones 5 to 9
P. 284

Chelidonium majus
'Flore Pleno'
Greater Celandine
SIZE: 1½ to 2 feet
Partial shade; tolerates sun or shade
Rich, well-drained soil; tolerates any soil
Brittle-stemmed plant with loose umbels of
    bright yellow flowers in summer
Zones 5 to 8
P. 284

Chelone lyonii
Pink Turtlehead
SIZE: 1 to 3 feet
Partial shade or full sun
Deep, rich, moist soil
Native wildflower with tubular, two-lipped pur-
ple-pink flowers from late summer to fall
Zones 3 to 8
P. 285

Chelone obliqua
Rose Turtlehead
SIZE: 1½ to 2 feet
Partial shade or full sun
Deep, rich, moist soil
Native wildflower with two-lipped dark pink or
purple-pink flowers from late summer to
fall
Zones 5 to 9
P. 285

▲*Chrysanthemum* hybrids

Mum, Hardy Fall Mum, Garden Mum

SIZE: 1 to 5 feet

Full sun

Average to rich, well-drained soil

Late summer to fall flowers in many forms in shades of bronze, purple, yellow, mauve, red, and white

Zones 4 or 5 to 9

P. 286

▼*Chrysogonum virginianum*

Green-and-gold, Goldenstar

SIZE: 6 to 8 inches

Full sun or partial shade

Rich, moist, well-drained soil

Spreading perennial with heart-shaped leaves and starry yellow flower heads from spring to early summer

Zones 5 to 8

P. 288

Cimicifuga racemosa
Black Snakeroot, Black Cohosh
SIZE: 4 to 7 feet
Partial to dappled shade; full sun in the North
Rich, evenly moist soil
Produces mounds of deeply cut leaves topped
    by branched racemes of tiny white flowers
    in midsummer
Zones 3 to 8
P. 288

Clematis integrifolia
SIZE: 2 feet
Full sun to partial shade
Cool, rich, well-drained soil
Mounding perennial bearing bell-shaped blue-
    violet flowers in summer
Zones 3 to 7
P. 290

Convallaria majalis
Lily-of-the-valley
SIZE: 6 to 9 inches

Partial shade; tolerates full sun to full shade

Evenly moist, rich soil

Vigorous, ground-covering perennial with one-
sided racemes of fragrant white bells in
spring

Zones 2 to 8

P. 290

Coreopsis auriculata
Mouse-ear Coreopsis
SIZE: 1 to 2 feet

Full sun or partial shade

Average to rich well-drained soil

Mounding species with solitary yellow-orange
flowers from late spring to summer

Zones 4 to 9

P. 291

Coreopsis lanceolata
Lance-leaved Coreopsis

SIZE: 1 to 2 feet
Full sun
Average to rich well-drained soil
Bears lance-shaped leaves and solitary golden yellow flowers from late spring to midsummer
Zones 3 or 4 to 9
P. 292

Coreopsis rosea
Pink Coreopsis

SIZE: 1 to 2 feet
Full sun or partial shade
Average to rich well-drained soil
Bears needlelike leaves and small rosy pink flowers with yellow centers from summer to early fall
Zones 4 to 8
P. 292

Coreopsis verticillata 'Moonbeam'

Thread-leaved Coreopsis

SIZE: 1 to 2 feet

Full sun

Average to rich well-drained soil

Bears threadlike leaflets and pale to golden yellow daisy flowers in summer

Zones 3 to 9

P. 292

Corydalis flexuosa 'Blue Panda'

Blue Corydalis

SIZE: 1 foot

Full sun to partial shade; best in areas with cool summers

Rich, well-drained soil

Bears glaucous leaves and racemes of sky blue flowers from late spring to summer

Zones 6 to 8

P. 293

Corydalis lutea
Yellow Corydalis
SIZE: 1½ feet
Full sun to partial shade
Average to rich, well-drained soil
Bears ferny bluish green leaves and yellow flowers from midspring to early fall
Zones 5 to 8
P. 293

Corydalis ochroleuca
SIZE: 1 foot
Full sun to partial shade
Rich, well-drained soil
Produces mounds of ferny leaves topped by racemes of white flowers with yellow throats from spring to summer
Zones 6 to 8
P. 294

Crambe cordifolia
Giant Kale, Colewort
SIZE: 6 to 8 feet
Full sun; tolerates partial shade
Deep, rich, well-drained soil; tolerates poor soil
Bears airy panicles of tiny white flowers from
     late spring to early summer
Zones 6 to 9
P. 294

Crambe maritima
Sea Kale
SIZE: 2½ feet
Full sun; tolerates partial shade
Deep, rich, well-drained soil; tolerates poor soil
Bears rounded blue-green leaves and dense 2-
     foot-wide racemes of tiny white flowers in
     early summer
Zones 6 to 9
P. 294

▲*Cynara cardunculus*

Cardoon

SIZE: 2 to 5 feet

Full sun

Well-drained, average to rich soil

Forms clumps of large deeply cut gray-green
leaves and purple flower heads from early
summer to fall

Zones 6 or 7 to 9

P. 295

▼*Darmera peltata*

Umbrella Plant

SIZE: 4 feet

Full sun or partial shade

Rich, constantly moist to boggy soil

Native perennial with 2-foot-wide leaves, red in
fall, and rounded clusters of flowers in late
spring

Zones 5 to 9

P. 296

Delosperma nubigerum
Ice Plant

S I Z E : 2 to 3 inches

Full sun

Very well drained soil; tolerates heat and poor, dry soil

Creeping, mat-forming plants with orange-red flowers in summer

Zones 6 to 9

P. 296

Delphinium
Elatum Group Pacific Hybrids
Delphinium

S I Z E : 4 to 6 feet

Full sun to partial shade; afternoon shade in areas with hot summers

Very rich, well-drained soil

Hybrids that produce dense spikes of single, semidouble, or double flowers in early and midsummer

Zones 3 to 7

P. 297

Dendranthema weyrichii

SIZE: 1 foot

Full sun

Rich, moist, well-drained soil

Forms mounds of five-lobed leaves topped with white or pink, yellow-centered daisies in late summer and fall

Zones 3 to 8

P. 298

Deschampsia cespitosa
Tufted Hair Grass

SIZE: 2 to 4 feet

Full sun or partial shade

Average moist garden soil; tolerates heavy soils and boggy conditions

Ornamental grass forming dense clumps of foliage topped by cloudlike spikelets of flowers from early to late summer

Zones 4 to 9

P. 299

Dianthus alpinus
Alpine Pinks

SIZE : 3 to 6 inches

Full sun

Well-drained dry to evenly moist soil

Mounding, much-hybridized species with flowers in shades of pink, white, and red in late
spring or early summer

Zones 3 to 8

P. 300

Dianthus deltoides
Maiden Pinks

SIZE : 6 to 12 inches

Full sun

Well-drained dry to evenly moist soil

Mat-forming, much-hybridized species with
single blooms from early to midsummer in
shades of pink, red, and white

Zones 3 to 9

P. 300

▲*Dianthus gratianopolitanus* 'Tiny Rubies'

Cheddar Pinks

SIZE: 4 inches

Full sun

Well-drained dry to evenly moist soil

Compact, mat-forming pink with tiny rose pink flowers on 4-inch plants

Zones 3 to 9

P. 300

▼*Dianthus* hybrids

Allwood Pink

Allwood Pinks

SIZE: 8 to 18 inches

Full sun

Well-drained dry to evenly moist soil

Hybrids with flowers in shades of pink, red, and white in spring and summer

Zones 4 or 5 to 8

P. 300

▲*Dianthus* hybrids 'Bath's Pink'

Hybrid Pink

SIZE: 10 inches

Full sun

Well-drained dry to evenly moist soil

Bears soft pink blooms with fringed petals from spring to summer

Zones 3 to 9

P. 301

▼*Dianthus plumarius* hybrid

Cottage Pinks, Border Pinks, Grass Pinks

SIZE: 1 to 2 feet

Full sun

Well-drained dry to evenly moist soil

Mounding pinks with fragrant flowers from spring to early summer in shades of pink, red, and white

Zones 3 to 9

P. 301

Dicentra eximia
Fringed Bleeding Heart
SIZE: 1½ feet
Light to full shade
Moist, rich, well-drained soil
Native wildflower with fernlike leaves and pendent, heart-shaped pink or white flowers from spring to fall
Zones 3 to 9
P. 302

Dicentra spectabilis
Common Bleeding Heart
SIZE: 1½ to 2½ feet
Light to full shade
Moist, rich, well-drained soil
Bears arching racemes of dangling, heart-shaped flowers in shades of pink and white in spring
Zones 2 to 9
P. 302

Dictamnus albus var. *purpureus*
Gas Plant

SIZE: 1½ to 3 feet

Full sun or light shade

Rich, well-drained soil

Bears dark green leaves and racemes of purple-pink dark-veined flowers from late spring to early summer

Zones 3 to 8

P. 303

Digitalis grandiflora
Yellow Foxglove

SIZE: 3 to 4 feet

Full sun or partial shade

Rich, evenly moist, well-drained soil

Bears racemes of tubular pale yellow flowers in midsummer that have brown veins on the inside

Zones 3 to 8

P. 304

Digitalis lutea

SIZE: 3 to 4 feet

Full sun or partial shade

Rich, evenly moist, well-drained soil

Bears racemes of tubular pale yellow flowers
from early to midsummer

Zones 3 to 8

P. 304

Digitalis × mertonensis

Strawberry Foxglove

SIZE: 3 feet

Full sun or partial shade

Rich, evenly moist, well-drained soil

Bears racemes of tubular flowers in late spring
and early summer in shades of pink and
white

Zones 3 to 8

P. 304 I

Digitalis purpurea
Common Foxglove

SIZE: 2 to 6 feet

Full sun or partial shade

Rich, evenly moist, well-drained soil

Bears racemes of tubular flowers in early summer in shades of rose-purple, white, pink, and creamy yellow

Zones 4 to 8

P. 304

Disporum flavens
Fairy Bells

SIZE: 2½ feet

Partial shade

Rich, moist, well-drained soil

Bears small clusters of tubular, pendent, pale yellow flowers in early spring

Zones 4 to 9

P. 305

Dodecatheon meadia
Common Shooting Star
SIZE: 1 to 1½ feet
Full sun or partial shade
Rich, moist, well-drained soil
Native clump-forming wildflower bearing clusters of magenta-pink or white flowers in mid- and late spring
Zones 4 to 8
P. 306

Dryopteris filix-mas
Male Fern
SIZE: 2 to 3 feet
Partial shade
Rich, moist, well-drained soil
Native fern forming large spreading clumps of erect fronds
Zones 4 to 8
P. 307

Echinacea purpurea
Purple Coneflower
SIZE: 2 to 4 feet
Full sun
Well-drained, average soil
Native wildflower with purple-pink daisylike flower heads from early to midsummer with pincushion-like centers
Zones 3 to 9
P. 308

Echinops ritro
Small Globe Thistle
SIZE: 2 feet
Full sun
Poor to average, well-drained soil
Bears spiny, thistlelike leaves and round, spiny, silvery blue flower heads in mid- to late summer
Zones 3 to 9
P. 309

Epimedium grandiflorum
Long-spurred Epimedium
SIZE: 8 to 12 inches

Partial to full shade

Rich, evenly moist soil

Produces mounds of handsome leaves and showy racemes of spring flowers in white, yellow, pink, and purple

Zones 4 to 8

P. 310

Epimedium × rubrum
Red-flowered Epimedium
SIZE: 8 to 12 inches

Partial to full shade

Rich, evenly moist soil

Produces mounds of leaves flushed with red when young and red and pale yellow spring flowers

Zones 4 to 8

P. 311

▲*Epimedium* × *versicolor*

Bicolor Epimedium

SIZE : 12 inches

Partial to full shade

Rich, evenly moist soil

Vigorous hybrid species with evergreen to
semievergreen leaves and pinkish red-and-
yellow flowers in spring

Zones 4 to 8

P. 311

▼*Erigeron* hybrid 'Foersters Liebling'

Hybrid Erigeron

SIZE : 1½ to 2 feet

Full sun or light shade

Rich, well-drained, evenly moist soil

Bears daisylike flowers in early to midsummer
with yellow centers and reddish pink ray
florets

Zones 5 to 8

P. 312

Eryngium amethystinum
Amethyst Sea Holly
SIZE: 2 feet

Full sun

Average, well-drained soil; tolerates heat, drought, and poor soil

Bears stalks of round, metallic blue flower heads with spiny silvery bracts from mid- to late summer

Zones 3 to 8

P. 313

Eryngium bourgatii
Mediterranean Sea Holly
SIZE: 1 to 2 feet

Full sun

Average, well-drained soil; tolerates heat, drought, and poor soil

Bears clusters of rounded gray-green flowers from mid- to late summer, each with a star-like ruff of bracts

Zones 5 to 9

P. 314

Eryngium yuccifolium
Rattlesnake Master

SIZE: 2 to 4 feet

Full sun

Average, well-drained soil; thrives in rich, moist, well-drained conditions

Native wildflower with sword-shaped leaves and clusters of whitish green flower heads from midsummer to fall

Zones 4 to 8

P. 314

Eupatorium coelestinum
Hardy Ageratum, Mistflower

SIZE: 2 to 3 feet

Full sun or partial shade

Average to rich soil

Native wildflower with fluffy, flat-topped clusters of lilac-blue flowers from late summer to fall

Zones 5 to 9

P. 315

▲*Eupatorium fistulosum* 'Gateway'

Hollow Joe-Pye Weed

SIZE: 5 to 10 feet

Full sun or partial shade

Average to rich soil

Native wildflower with black stems and large rounded clusters of pink flowers in mid-summer

Zones 3 to 8

P. 315

▼*Euphorbia amygdaloides* var. *robbiae*

Wood Spurge, Robb's Spurge

SIZE: 1½ to 2 feet

Partial to full shade

Evenly moist, rich soil; also tolerates dry shade

Produces mounds of shiny, evergreen leaves and greenish yellow flowers from midspring to early summer

Zones 6 to 9

P. 316

Euphorbia characias ssp. *wulfenii*

SIZE: 3 to 4 feet

Full sun to partial or light shade

Loose, poor to average, well-drained soil

Evergreen gray-green foliage and rounded clusters of chartreuse flowers from spring to summer

Zones 7 to 10

P. 316

Euphorbia dulcis 'Chameleon'

SIZE: 1 foot

Full sun to partial or light shade

Loose, poor to average, well-drained soil

Rhizomatous species with purple-maroon foliage and yellow-green flowers in early summer

Zones 4 to 9

P. 316

Euphorbia griffithii 'Fireglow'
Griffith's Spurge

SIZE: 2 to 3 feet

Light shade; tolerates full sun in northern zones

Evenly moist, rich soil

Mounding plant with dark green leaves, red in fall, and clusters of showy scarlet-orange flowers

Zones 4 to 8

P. 316

Euphorbia polychroma
Cushion Spurge

SIZE: 1 to 2 feet

Full sun to partial or light shade

Loose, poor to average, well-drained soil

Compact, mounding species with green leaves and bright yellow-green flowers in early to late spring

Zones 4 to 9

P. 317

Festuca glauca 'Elijah Blue'
Blue Fescue
SIZE: 12 inches

Full sun to partial shade

Moist, well-drained soil

Ornamental grass forming evergreen mounds
of pale silvery blue leaves

Zones 4 to 9

P. 318

Filipendula rubra
Queen-of-the-prairie
SIZE: 6 to 8 feet

Full sun or light shade

Average to rich, moist, well-drained soil; grows
in boggy soil

Native wildflower producing fluffy clusters of
pink flowers from early to midsummer

Zones 3 to 9

P. 319

Filipendula ulmaria
Meadowsweet, Queen-of-the-meadow
SIZE: 3 to 6 feet

Full sun or light shade

Average to rich, moist but well-drained soil;
    grows in boggy soil

Produces mounds of leaves topped by showy
    clusters of white flowers in summer

Zones 3 to 9

P. 319

Foeniculum vulgare
'Purpureum'
Bronze Fennel
SIZE: 5 to 6 feet

Full sun

Average to rich, moist but well-drained soil

Produces large, cloudlike mounds of threadlike,
    airy-textured bronze-purple leaves topped
    by yellow flowers from mid- to late summer

Zones 4 to 9

P. 320

Fragaria vesca
Alpine Strawberry, Fraise de Bois

SIZE: 6 to 12 inches

Full sun or light shade

Rich, moist, well-drained soil

Bears evergreen to semievergreen leaves, white
  flowers from late spring into summer, and
  edible red fruit

Zones 5 to 9

P. 320

Gaillardia × grandiflora
Blanket Flower

SIZE: 2 to 3 feet

Full sun

Average to rich, well-drained soil; tolerates
  poor, dry soil

Bears showy flower heads in combinations of
  reds, maroons, oranges, and yellows from
  early summer to fall

Zones 3 to 8

P. 321

▲*Galium odoratum*
Sweet Woodruff
SIZE: 6 to 8 inches

Partial to deep shade

Rich, well-drained soil

Creeping perennial with dainty clusters of starry white flowers from late spring to summer

Zones 4 to 8

P. 322

▼*Gaultheria procumbens*
Wintergreen, Checkerberry
SIZE: 4 to 6 inches

Partial shade

Moist, acid to neutral soil

Native evergreen shrublet with glossy, aromatic leaves, white or pale pink flowers in summer, and red berries

Zones 3 to 8

P. 322

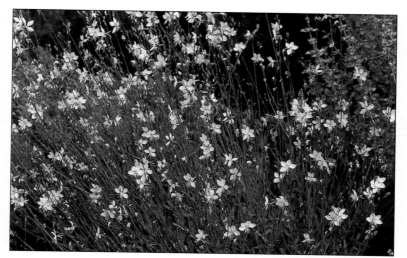

▲*Gaura lindheimeri*
White Gaura

SIZE: 3 to 5 feet

Full sun

Moist, well-drained soil

Shrubby native wildflower with airy panicles of small white to pink flowers from early summer to fall

Zones 5 to 9

P. 323

▼*Gentiana andrewsii*
Bottle Gentian, Closed Gentian

SIZE: 1 to 2 feet

Full sun; afternoon shade in areas with warm summers

Well-drained, evenly moist soil

Native wildflower producing clusters of tubular dark blue flowers in late summer

Zones 3 to 7

P. 324

Gentiana septemfida

Crested Gentian

SIZE: 6 to 8 inches

Full sun; afternoon shade in areas with warm
summers

Well-drained, evenly moist soil

Low-growing gentian with clusters of blue to
purple-blue trumpets with white throats in
late summer

Zones 3 to 8

P. 324

Geranium clarkei 'Kashmir White'

Clark's Geranium

SIZE: 1½ feet

Full sun or partial shade; afternoon shade in
areas with hot summers

Rich, evenly moist, well-drained soil

Cultivar of a mounding, fast-spreading species
with deeply cut leaves and white flowers
from late spring to early summer

Zones 4 to 8

P. 325

Geranium endressii
Endres Cranesbill
SIZE: 1½ feet

Full sun or partial shade; afternoon shade in
  areas with hot summers

Rich, evenly moist, well-drained soil; tolerates
  drought

Mounding to sprawling species bearing pale
  pink flowers in spring; blooms all summer
  in areas with cool summers

Zones 4 to 8

P. 326

Geranium hybrid
'Ann Folkard'
SIZE: 2 feet

Full sun or partial shade; afternoon shade in
  areas with hot summers

Rich, evenly moist, well-drained soil

Scrambling, spreading hybrid with yellow-
  green leaves and magenta flowers from midsummer to fall

Zones 5 to 9

P. 326

Geranium hybrid 'Johnson's Blue'

SIZE: 1½ feet

Full sun or partial shade; afternoon shade in
areas with hot summers

Rich, evenly moist, well-drained soil

Bears lavender-blue 1½- to 2-inch-wide flowers
in early summer on mounding plants

Zones 5 to 9

P. 326

Geranium macrorrhizum 'Ingwersen's Variety'

Bigroot Geranium

SIZE: 1½ feet

Full sun or shade; afternoon shade in areas with
hot summers

Rich, evenly moist, well-drained soil; tolerates
drought

Cultivar of a mounding, vigorously spreading
species with aromatic leaves and pink to
purplish pink flowers in spring

Zones 3 to 8

P. 326

Geranium × magnificum
Showy Geranium

SIZE: 2 feet

Full sun or partial shade; afternoon shade in areas with hot summers

Rich, evenly moist, well-drained soil

Bears deeply lobed leaves and violet flowers with darker veins in midsummer

Zones 4 to 8

P. 327

Geranium × oxonianum
'Claridge Druce'

SIZE: 1½ to 3 feet

Full sun or partial shade; afternoon shade in areas with hot summers

Rich, evenly moist, well-drained soil

Vigorous hybrid with grayish green leaves and rose pink flowers from spring to fall

Zones 4 to 8

P. 327

Geranium sanguineum var. *striatum*
Bloody Cranesbill

SIZE: 4 to 6 inches

Full sun or shade; afternoon shade in areas with hot summers

Rich, evenly moist, well-drained soil; tolerates drought

Mounding selection with lacy leaves, red in fall, and pale pink flowers from spring to summer

Zones 3 to 8

P. 328

Geranium sylvaticum
Wood Cranesbill

SIZE: 2½ to 3 feet

Partial shade

Rich, evenly moist, well-drained soil

Bushy, clump-forming species with deeply cut leaves and violet-blue flowers in early to midspring

Zones 3 to 8

P. 328

Geum chiloense 'Mrs. J. Bradshaw'

Geum, Avens

SIZE: 1½ to 2 feet

Full sun

Average to rich, evenly moist, well-drained soil

Clump-forming plant with deeply lobed leaves
and saucer-shaped red flowers in summer

Zones 4 to 7 or 8

P. 328

Geum rivale

Water Avens, Indian Chocolate

SIZE: ½ to 2 feet

Full sun

Average to rich, evenly moist, well-drained soil

From late spring to midsummer bears pendent,
bell-shaped flowers with purple-pink petals
and red-brown sepals

Zones 3 to 8

P. 329

Geum triflorum
Prairie Smoke, Purple Avens
SIZE : 1½ feet

Full sun

Average to rich, evenly moist, well-drained soil

Native wildflower with ferny leaves, creamy-
petaled flowers with long purple bracts, and
plumy, silvery pink seedpods

Zones 1 to 7

P. 329

Gillenia trifoliata
Bowman's Root, Indian Physic
SIZE : 2 to 4 feet

Partial shade

Rich, moist, well-drained soil

Native wildflower with bronzy green leaves and
loose clusters of starry flowers from late
spring to early summer

Zones 4 to 8

P. 330

▲*Gypsophila paniculata*
Baby's Breath
SIZE: 2 to 4 feet

Full sun or very light shade

Rich, evenly moist, very well drained soil

Shrubby perennial bearing cloudlike panicles of tiny white or pink flowers from mid- to late summer

Zones 3 to 9

P. 331

▼*Gypsophila repens*
Creeping Baby's Breath
SIZE: 4 to 8 inches

Full sun or very light shade

Rich, evenly moist, very well drained soil

Mat-forming plant with loose clusters of pink or white flowers from early to midsummer

Zones 4 to 8

P. 331

Hakonechloa macra 'Aureola'

Hakone Grass

SIZE: 1½ to 2 feet

Partial shade

Rich, evenly moist, well-drained soil

Mounding ornamental grass with stunning green-and-yellow-striped leaves

Zones 5 to 9

P. 331

Helenium autumnale 'Brilliant'

Common Sneezeweed

SIZE: 2 to 3 feet

Full sun

Rich, evenly moist, well-drained soil

Cultivar of a native wildflower bearing orange-bronze daisylike flowers from late summer to fall

Zones 3 to 8

P. 332

Helenium autumnale 'Butterpat'
Common Sneezeweed

SIZE: 2 to 3 feet

Full sun

Rich, evenly moist, well-drained soil

Cultivar of a native wildflower bearing yellow
daisylike flowers with brown centers from
late summer to fall

Zones 3 to 8

P. 332

Helianthus angustifolius
Swamp Sunflower

SIZE: 4 to 8 feet

Full sun; tolerates light shade

Average, moist, well-drained soil

Native wildflower with clusters of yellow flower
heads with purple to brown centers from
early to midfall

Zones 6 to 9

P. 333

Helianthus divaricatus
Woodland Sunflower

SIZE: 2 to 6 feet
Full sun; tolerates light shade
Average, moist, well-drained soil
Native wildflower with yellow flower heads
    midsummer to midfall
Zones 3 to 8
P. 334

Helianthus maximiliani
Maximillian Sunflower

SIZE: 4 to 10 feet
Full sun
Average, moist, well-drained soil; grows in wet
    soil
Native wildflower bearing clusters of yellow
    flowers with brown centers from late sum-
    mer to fall
Zones 3 to 8
P. 334

Helianthus salicifolius
Willow-leaved Sunflower

SIZE: 3 to 7 feet

Full sun

Average, moist, well-drained soil

Native wildflower with clusters of golden yellow flowers from early to midfall

Zones 3 or 4 to 8
P. 334

Helictotrichon sempervirens
Blue Oat Grass

SIZE: 2 to 4 feet

Full sun to light shade

Poor to average, well-drained soil

Clump-forming ornamental grass with gray-
blue leaves and spikes of yellow oatlike seed
heads in early summer

Zones 4 to 9
P. 335

Heliopsis helianthoides 'Light of Loddon'

Oxeye

SIZE: 3 to 6 feet

Full sun or partial shade

Average to rich soil; tolerates dry conditions

Cultivar of a native wildflower with bright yellow flower heads from midsummer to early fall

Zones 4 to 9

P. 336

Helleborus foetidus

Stinking Hellebore

SIZE: 1½ to 2 feet

Light to full shade

Rich, evenly moist, well-drained soil

Shrubby species with deeply cut leaves and clusters of nodding green flowers from midwinter to early spring

Zones 5 or 6 to 9

P. 337

Helleborus × hybridus
Lenten Rose
SIZE: 1 to 1½ feet
Light to full shade
Rich, evenly moist, well-drained soil
Bears evergreen leaves and flowers in shades of
cream, green, purple, and mauve from late
winter to early spring
Zones 4 to 9
P. 337

Hemerocallis hybrid
'Gentle Shepherd'
Hybrid Daylily
SIZE: 2 to 3 feet
Full sun or light shade
Average to rich, well-drained, evenly moist soil
Semievergreen diploid hybrid bearing rounded
white flowers with green throats in summer
Zones 3 to 10
P. 339

Hemerocallis hybrid 'Little Grapette'

Hybrid Daylily

SIZE: 2 feet

Full sun or light shade

Average to rich, well-drained, evenly moist soil

Reblooming miniature cultivar with small grape purple blooms in midsummer

Zones 3 to 10

P. 339

Heuchera × brizoides 'Firebird'

Hybrid Coral Bells

SIZE: 6 inches

Partial shade

Rich, evenly moist, well-drained soil

Bears low mounds of leaves topped by clusters of tiny scarlet flowers from late spring to early summer

Zones 4 to 8

P. 341

▲ *Heuchera* hybrid 'Pewter Veil'

Hybrid Heuchera

SIZE: 1 foot

Partial shade

Rich, evenly moist, well-drained soil

Mounding foliage plant with silvery dark-veined leaves blushed purple and tiny greenish flowers in early summer

Zones 4 to 8

P. 341

▼ *Heuchera micrantha* 'Palace Purple'

SIZE: 1 to 1½ feet

Partial shade

Rich, evenly moist, well-drained soil

Cultivar of a mound-forming native species with metallic bronze-red leaves and greenish white flowers

Zones 4 to 8

P. 341

× *Heucherella alba* 'Bridget Bloom'
Foamy Bells
SIZE: 1 to 1½ feet
Sun or partial shade
Light, rich, moist but well-drained soil
Bears low mounds of foliage and airy panicles of white flowers from late spring to fall
Zones 5 to 8
P. 342

Hibiscus coccineus
Scarlet Rose Mallow, Swamp Rose Mallow
SIZE: 5 to 10 feet
Full sun or very light shade
Rich, well-drained soil; thrives in wet to boggy soil
Native, woody-based wildflower with lacy leaves and showy red flowers from summer to fall
Zones 6 to 11
P. 343

▲*Hibiscus moscheutos* 'Disco Belle'

Common Rose Mallow,
Common Mallow

SIZE: 2 to 2½ feet

Full sun or very light shade

Rich, well-drained soil

Cultivar of a native perennial with very showy
9-inch-wide white flowers in summer

Zones 5 to 10

P. 343

▼*Hosta* 'Francee'

SIZE: 20 to 22 inches

Light to full shade

Rich, evenly moist soil

Bears dark green heart-shaped leaves with
white margins and handsome lavender
flowers in summer

Zones 3 to 8

P. 345

Hosta 'Ginkgo Craig'

SIZE: 10 inches

Light to full shade

Rich, evenly moist soil

Bears clumps of lance-shaped dark green leaves
edged in white; lavender flowers in late
summer

Zones 3 to 8

P. 345

Hosta 'Great Expectations'

SIZE: 20 to 22 inches

Light to full shade

Rich, evenly moist soil

Bears yellow leaves with blue-green edges and
gold to creamy white centers; white flowers
in early summer

Zones 3 to 8

P. 345

Hosta plantaginea
August Lily
SIZE: 2 to 2½ feet
Light to full shade
Rich, evenly moist soil
Bears clumps of heart-shaped green leaves and
showy racemes of very fragrant white flow-
ers in late summer
Zones 3 to 8
P. 346

Hosta tokudama
'Flavocircinalis'
SIZE: 1½ feet
Light to full shade
Rich, evenly moist soil
Bears clumps of heavily puckered blue-green
leaves with irregular yellow-green margins
Zones 3 to 8
P. 346

▲*Houttuynia cordata* 'Chameleon'

SIZE: 6 inches to 1 foot
Full sun or partial shade
Average to rich soil
Vigorous to very invasive plant with leaves variegated with red, pink, and green; small white flowers in summer

Zones 3 to 9

P. 347

▼*Iberis sempervirens*

Perennial Candytuft,
Common Candytuft
SIZE: 6 to 12 inches
Full sun or very light shade
Average, well-drained soil
Bears evergreen leaves and rounded clusters of tiny white flowers in midspring

Zones 3 to 9

P. 348

Inula ensifolia
Sword-leaved Inula
SIZE: 1 to 2 feet
Full sun
Rich, moist, well-drained soil
Bears lance-shaped leaves and small clusters of
golden yellow daisylike flowers in mid- to
late summer
Zones 4 to 9
P. 349

Inula helenium
Elecampane
SIZE: 3 to 6 feet
Full sun
Rich, moist, well-drained soil
Robust herb with ovate, toothed leaves and yel-
low flowers from mid- to late summer
Zones 5 to 8
P. 349

▲*Iris* bearded hybrids

Bearded Iris

SIZE: 8 to 27 inches

Full sun

Average to rich, well-drained soil

Bears strap-shaped leaves and showy flowers in late spring or early summer

Zones 3 through 9

P. 350

▼*Iris cristata*

Crested Iris

SIZE: 4 to 8 inches

Partial to full shade

Rich, evenly moist, well-drained, slightly acid soil

Native wildflower bearing lavender-blue or white flowers in late spring

Zones 3 to 9

P. 350

▲*Iris ensata*

Japanese Iris

SIZE: 2½ to 3 feet

Full sun to partial shade

Rich, moist, well-drained, acid soil

Produces grasslike leaves and early to midsummer flowers in violets, purples, lavenders, whites, and pinks

Zones 4 to 9

P. 351

▼*Iris* Louisiana hybrids

Louisiana Iris

SIZE: 1½ ft to 5 feet

Full sun to partial shade

Very rich, constantly moist to wet, acid soil

Hybrid irises bearing flowers in midspring to early summer in purples to blue-black, blues, reds, and violets

Zones 6 to 11; some cultivars to Zone 4

P. 351

Iris pseudacorus
Yellow Flag
SIZE: 3 to 4 feet

Full sun or light shade

Evenly moist, well-drained to constantly wet soil or in standing water

Produces clumps of sword-shaped leaves and bright yellow flowers in early summer

Zones 4 to 9

P. 351

Iris sibirica
Siberian Iris
SIZE: 1 to 3 feet

Full sun to light shade

Evenly moist, well-drained or constantly wet soil

Produces handsome clumps of grassy leaves and early summer flowers in violets, purples, white, and yellow

Zones 2 to 9

P. 351

Iris versicolor
Blue Flag
SIZE: 2 to 2½ feet

Full sun

Constantly moist soil or standing water

Native wildflower bearing blue-violet or purple
    flowers in early to midsummer

Zones 2 to 9

P. 352

Kirengeshoma palmata
Yellow Wax Bells
SIZE: 3 to 4 feet

Partial shade

Rich, evenly moist, acid soil

Bears palmately lobed leaves and pale yellow
    waxy-textured flowers in late summer and
    early fall

Zones 5 to 8

P. 353

Knautia macedonica

SIZE: 2 to 2½ feet

Full sun

Average to rich well-drained soil

Clump-forming perennial bearing purple- to maroon-red flower heads from mid- to late summer

Zones 4 to 8

P. 353

Kniphofia uvaria

Common Torch Lily

SIZE: 2 to 4 feet

Full sun

Average to rich, evenly moist, well-drained soil

Produces clumps of grassy leaves and spikes of red-orange and yellow flowers from early to late summer

Zones 5 to 9

P. 354

Lamium galeobdolon 'Hermann's Pride'
Yellow Archangel

SIZE: 2 feet

Partial to full shade

Average to rich, moist, well-drained soil

Bears attractive silver-streaked leaves and
    whorls of yellow flowers in summer

Zones 4 to 8

P. 355

Lamium maculatum 'Beacon Silver'
Spotted Deadnettle

SIZE: 8 to 10 inches

Partial to full shade

Average to rich, moist, well-drained soil

Bears silver leaves with green margins and
    whorls of pink flowers in summer

Zones 3 to 8

P. 355

Lathyrus latifolius
'White Pearl'

Everlasting Pea, Perennial Pea

SIZE: 5 to 6 feet

Full sun or light shade

Rich, well-drained soil

Climbing species with blue-green leaves and
racemes of white flowers in summer to early
fall

Zones 5 to 9

P. 356

Lathyrus vernus

Spring Vetchling

SIZE: 1 to 1½ feet

Full sun or light shade

Rich, well-drained soil

Clumping species bearing racemes of purple-
blue flowers in spring

Zones 5 to 9

P. 356

Lavandula angustifolia
'Munstead'

Common Lavender, English Lavender

SIZE: 2 to 3 feet

Full sun; tolerates very light shade

Poor to rich, very well drained soil

Evergreen shrub with aromatic gray-green
 leaves and spikes of tiny fragrant lavender
 purple flowers in summer

Zones 5 to 9

P. 357

Lavatera thuringiaca

Tree Mallow, Tree Lavatera

SIZE: 5 to 6 feet

Full sun

Average, well-drained soil

Shrubby perennial bearing funnel-shaped pink
 flowers in summer either singly or in loose
 clusters

Zones 6 or 7 to 9

P. 357

Lespedeza thunbergii 'White Fountain'

Bush Clover

SIZE: 6 feet

Full sun

Average, well-drained soil

Bears arching, pendent racemes of white flowers from late summer to fall

Zones 4 to 8

P. 358

Leucanthemum × superbum

Shasta Daisy

SIZE: 1 to 4 feet

Full sun

Average to rich, well-drained soil

Bears single, semidouble, or double white daisies from early summer to early fall

Zones 3 or 4 to 8

P. 359

Leucanthemum vulgare
Oxeye Daisy

SIZE: 1 to 3 feet

Full sun

Average to rich, well-drained soil

Weedy, vigorous species bearing white, yellow-centered daisies in late spring and early summer

Zones 3 to 8

P. 359

Lewisia cotyledon

SIZE: 8 to 12 inches

Light shade

Fairly rich, very well drained acid to neutral soil

Bears mounds of evergreen leaves and flowers from spring to summer in pink, white, cream, and yellow

Zones 6 to 8

P. 360

Liatris punctata
Dotted Blazing Star
SIZE: 6 to 14 inches

Full sun

Average to rich, well-drained soil; tolerates dry soil

Native wildflower bearing dense spikes of small rosy purple flower heads in late summer

Zones 2 to 8

P. 361

Liatris spicata
Spike Gayfeather
SIZE: 2 to 5 feet

Full sun

Average to rich, well-drained to evenly moist soil

Native wildflower bearing densely packed spikes of pinkish purple flower heads from mid- to late summer

Zones 3 to 9

P. 361

Ligularia stenocephala 'The Rocket'

SIZE: 5 to 6 feet

Light to partial shade

Very rich, constantly moist soil

Produces low clumps of large toothed leaves topped by racemes of lemon yellow flower heads in late summer

Zones 4 to 8

P. 362

Limonium latifolium

Sea Lavender

SIZE: 1 to 2½ feet

Full sun or partial shade

Average to rich, well-drained soil

Bears airy clusters of tiny pale lavender to bluish purple flowers in late summer

Zones 3 to 9

P. 363

Linaria purpurea
'Canon J. Went'
Purple Toadflax

SIZE: 3 feet

Full sun

Light, average to rich, well-drained soil

Bears airy racemes packed with tiny pink flowers from early summer to fall

Zones 5 to 8

P. 363

Linum flavum
Golden Flax, Yellow Flax

SIZE: 1 to 1½ feet

Full sun to partial shade

Average to rich, light, well-drained soil

Woody-based perennial bearing clusters of funnel-shaped yellow flowers in summer

Zones 4 to 7

P. 364

Linum perenne
Perennial Flax
SIZE: 1 to 1½ feet

Full sun to partial shade

Average to rich, light, well-drained soil

Wiry-stemmed plant with panicles of rich blue
  flowers from early to midsummer

Zones 4 to 8

P. 364

Liriope muscari 'Big Blue'
Big Blue Lilyturf
SIZE: 8 to 10 inches

Partial to full shade

Rich, well-drained soil

Bears evergreen leaves and spikes of tiny violet
  purple or white flowers above the leaves in
  fall

Zones 6 to 9

P. 364

Lobelia cardinalis
Cardinal Flower
SIZE: 2 to 4 feet
Light to partial shade
Rich, constantly moist soil
Native wildflower bearing erect racemes of
scarlet flowers in summer and early fall

Zones 2 to 9

P. 366

Lobelia siphilitica
Great Blue Lobelia
SIZE: 2 to 4 feet
Light to partial shade
Rich, constantly moist soil
Native wildflower bearing dense racemes of
blue flowers from late summer to fall

Zones 4 to 8

P. 366

Lupinus Russell hybrids
Lupine
SIZE: 2½ to 3 feet

Full sun

Average to rich, well-drained soil

Bears densely packed spikes of flowers in early and midsummer in purple, violet, yellow, pink, red, and white

Zones 3 or 4 to 8

P. 367

Lychnis × arkwrightii
Arkwright's Campion
SIZE: 1½ to 2 feet

Full sun or partial shade

Light, average to rich, well-drained soil

Bears clusters of starry orange-red flowers in early to midsummer

Zones 4 to 8

P. 369

Lychnis chalcedonica
Jerusalem Cross, Maltese Cross
S I Z E : 3 to 4 feet
Full sun or partial shade
Light, average to rich, well-drained soil
Bears rounded clusters of starry scarlet flowers
  with deeply notched petals in early to mid-
  summer
Zones 4 to 8
P. 369

Lychnis coronaria
Rose Campion, Mullein Pink, Dusty Miller
S I Z E : 2½ to 3 feet
Full sun or partial shade
Light, average to rich, well-drained soil
Bears rosettes of woolly silver-gray leaves and
  branched clusters of magenta-pink or white
  flowers in mid- to late summer
Zones 4 to 8
P. 369

Lysimachia clethroides

Gooseneck Loosestrife

SIZE: 3 feet

Full sun or partial shade

Rich, well-drained, evenly moist soil

Fast-spreading species bearing dense, curved racemes of white flowers from mid- to late summer

Zones 3 to 9

P. 370

Lysimachia nummularia 'Aurea'

Creeping Jenny

SIZE: 2 to 4 inches

Full sun or partial shade

Rich, well-drained, evenly moist soil

Mat-forming perennial with rounded golden yellow leaves and solitary yellow flowers in summer

Zones 4 to 9

P. 370

▲ *Lysimachia punctata*
Whorled Loosestrife

SIZE: 3 feet

Full sun or partial shade

Rich, well-drained, evenly moist soil

Bears erect stems with whorls of yellow flowers
   in early summer

Zones 4 to 8

P. 370

▼ *Lythrum virgatum*
Wand Loosestrife

SIZE: 2 to 3 feet

Full sun

Moist soil; extremely invasive in wetlands

Spikelike racemes of purple-red flowers from
   early to late summer

Zones 3 to 8

P. 371

Macleaya cordata
Plume Poppy
SIZE: 7 to 8 feet

Full sun

Average, moist, well-drained soil

Rhizomatous perennial with gray- to olive green leaves and plumes of tiny creamy flowers from mid- to late summer

Zones 4 to 9

P. 372

Malva alcea 'Fastigiata'
Hollyhock Mallow
SIZE: 2½ to 3 feet

Full sun

Average to moderately rich, well-drained soil

Bears clusters of funnel-shaped rose pink flowers with notched petals from early summer to fall

Zones 4 to 9

P. 373

Malva sylvestris 'Zebrina'
Tree Mallow, Cheeses
SIZE: 2 to 3 feet
Full sun
Average to moderately rich, well-drained soil
Bears white to pale pink flowers striped with dark pink from late spring or early summer to fall
Zones 4 to 8
P. 373

Matteuccia struthiopteris
Ostrich Fern
SIZE: 2 to 6 feet
Partial shade
Rich marshy or wet soil; also evenly moist, well-drained conditions
Large native fern forming bold, vase-shaped clumps of twice-cut fronds
Zones 2 to 6
P. 374

Mazus repens

SIZE: 2 inches

Full sun or partial shade

Average to somewhat rich, moist, well-drained
    soil

Mat-forming species bearing small clusters of
    purple flowers with yellow and white spots
    from late spring to summer

Zones 5 to 8

P. 374

Melissa officinalis 'Variegata'
Variegated Lemon Balm

SIZE: 2 to 4 feet

Full sun; tolerates partial shade

Poor to average, well-drained soil

Herb bearing lemon-scented, gold-splashed
    leaves and spikes of small pale yellow to
    white flowers in summer

Zones 4 to 10

P. 375

Mertensia pulmonarioides
Virginia Bluebells, Virginia Cowslip
SIZE: 1 to 2 feet

Sun or shade

Rich, evenly moist, well-drained soil

Produces mounds of bluish green leaves and
    pink flower buds in spring opening into
    nodding blue bells

Zones 3 to 9

P. 376

Miscanthus sinensis
Eulalia, Japanese Silver Grass
SIZE: 3 to 9 feet

Full sun

Average, moist, well-drained soil

Ornamental grass forming vase-shaped clumps
    of foliage topped by plumy purplish flowers
    from summer to fall

Zones 4 to 9

P. 377

Miscanthus sinensis 'Zebrinus'

Zebra Grass

SIZE: 3 to 9 feet

Full sun

Average, moist, well-drained soil

Ornamental grass with striped foliage topped by plumy purplish flowers from summer to fall

Zones 4 to 9

P. 377

Mitchella repens

Partridge Berry, Twin Berry, Running Box

SIZE: 1 to 2 inches

Dappled or partial shade

Rich, evenly moist, well-drained, acid soil

Mat-forming native wildflower with glossy leaves, small white flowers in early summer, and red berries

Zones 4 to 9

P. 377

Molinia caerulea
Purple Moor Grass
SIZE : 1 to 4 feet
Full sun to partial shade
Poor to average, moist, well-drained soil
Ornamental grass forming mounds of linear
    leaves topped by airy spikes of purplish
    flowers in early to midsummer
Zones 4 or 5 to 9
P. 378

Monarda didyma
'Cambridge Scarlet'
Bee Balm, Bergamot, Oswego Tea
SIZE : 2 to 4 feet
Full sun or light shade
Rich, evenly moist, well-drained soil
Rhizomatous native perennial with aromatic
    leaves and whorls of scarlet flowers from
    mid- to late summer
Zones 4 to 8
P. 379

▲*Monarda didyma* 'Prairie Night'

Bee Balm, Bergamot, Oswego Tea

SIZE: 2 to 4 feet

Full sun or light shade

Rich, evenly moist, well-drained soil

Mildew-resistant cultivar of a native perennial with lilac-purple flowers from mid- to late summer

Zones 4 to 8

P. 379

▼*Monarda fistulosa*

Wild Bergamot

SIZE: 3 to 5 feet

Full sun or light shade

Average to rich moist to slightly dry soil

Native species with aromatic, mildew-resistant leaves and lavender-pink flowers from mid- to late summer

Zones 3 to 9

P. 379

Myosotis sylvatica 'Ultramarine'

Forget-me-not,
Woodland Forget-me-not

SIZE: 5 to 12 inches

Full sun or light shade

Well-drained, moist soil

Bears gray-green leaves and clusters of tiny
saucer-shaped flowers in spring and early
summer

Zones 5 to 9

P. 380

Nepeta × faassenii

Nepeta, Catmint

SIZE: 1 to 2 feet

Full sun or light shade

Average to dry, well-drained soil

Produces mounds of aromatic gray-green
leaves and spikes of lavender-blue flowers
from early summer to fall

Zones 3 or 4 to 8

P. 381

Nepeta sibirica
Siberian Catnip

SIZE: 3 feet
Full sun or light shade
Average to dry, well-drained soil
Bears lance-shaped dark green leaves and
racemes of lavender-blue flowers in sum-
mer
Zones 3 to 9
P. 382

Nipponanthemum nipponicum
Nippon Daisy

SIZE: 2 feet
Full sun
Average, very well drained soil
Shrubby perennial with dark green leaves and
white, yellow-centered daisylike flowers in
fall
Zones 5 to 9
P. 383

Oenothera caespitosa
Tufted Evening Primrose
SIZE: 4 to 8 inches

Full sun

Poor to average, well-drained soil

Bears fragrant white flowers in summer that open at sunset, change to pink, and die the following morning

Zones 4 to 8

P. 383

Oenothera fruticosa
Common Sundrops
SIZE: 1 to 3 feet

Full sun

Poor to average, well-drained soil

Bears racemes of deep yellow flowers from late spring through summer

Zones 4 to 8

P. 384

▲*Oenothera macrocarpa*

Ozark Sundrops, Missouri Evening Primrose

SIZE: 6 inches

Full sun

Poor to average, well-drained soil

Perennial with trailing stems that bears solitary yellow flowers from late spring to fall

Zones 5 to 8

P. 384

▼*Oenothera speciosa*

Showy Evening Primrose

SIZE: 1 foot

Full sun

Poor to average, well-drained soil

Fast-spreading plant with solitary, cup-shaped white or pink flowers from early summer to fall

Zones 5 to 8

P. 384

Omphalodes verna

Blue-eyed Mary, Creeping Forget-me-not

SIZE: 8 inches

Partial shade

Rich, moist, well-drained soil; tolerates dry soil

Mounding perennial with racemes of small bright blue flowers in spring

Zones 6 to 9

P. 385

Onoclea sensibilis

Sensitive Fern

SIZE: 1 to 3 feet

Full sun to shade

Moist, well-drained soil; also constantly wet to dry soil

Native, fast-spreading fern with roughly triangular, featherlike fronds

Zones 2 to 10

P. 386

Ophiopogon planiscapus 'Nigrescens'

SIZE: 8 inches

Full sun or partial shade

Rich, moist, well-drained soil

Bears grassy, nearly black leaves and racemes of small bell-shaped purplish white flowers

Zones 6 to 10

P. 386

Opuntia compressa

Hardy Cactus

SIZE: 4 to 12 inches tall

Full sun

Fairly rich, sandy, very well drained soil

Native wildflower with rounded pads and yellow flowers, often with red centers, in late spring to early summer

Zones 4 or 5 to 9

P. 387

Oreganum vulgare 'Aureum'

Golden Oregano

SIZE : 1 to 3 feet

Full sun

Poor to somewhat rich, well-drained soil

Bears aromatic golden-yellow leaves and sprays
of tiny white or purplish pink flowers in
summer

Zones 5 to 9

P. 388

Osmunda cinnamomea

Cinnamon Fern

SIZE : 3 feet

Partial shade

Rich, evenly moist, well-drained soil to constantly wet conditions

Native fern forming bold clumps of twice-cut
fronds and tall cinnamon brown fertile
fronds in late spring

Zones 2 to 10

P. 389

Osmunda regalis
Royal Fern, Flowering Fern

SIZE: 5 to 6 feet

Partial shade

Rich, evenly moist, well-drained soil to constantly wet conditions

Produces clumps of twice-cut fronds with spores borne on brown tassel-like frond tips

Zones 2 to 10

P. 389

Pachysandra procumbens
Allegheny Spurge

SIZE: 1 foot

Partial to full shade

Average to rich, evenly moist soil

Native wildflower with white flowers in spring and semievergreen leaves marked with maroon as the season progresses

Zones 5 to 9

P. 390

Pachysandra terminalis 'Variegata'
Japanese Spurge
SIZE: ½ to 1 foot
Partial to full shade
Average to rich, evenly moist soil
Bears evergreen leaves marked in white and tiny creamy white flowers in early summer
Zones 4 to 9
P. 390

Paeonia hybrid 'Miss America'
Common Garden Peony
SIZE: 1 to 3 feet
Full sun
Average to rich well-drained soil
Semidouble early-season cultivar with white petals and gold stamens in late spring
Zones 3 to 8
P. 391

Paeonia hybrids mixed
Common Garden Peony
SIZE: 1½ to 3 feet

Full sun

Average to rich well-drained soil

Bears single, semidouble, or double flowers in
late spring in shades of red, pink, and white

Zones 3 to 8

PP. 391–392

Paeonia tenuifolia
Fernleaf Peony
SIZE: 2 feet

Full sun

Average to rich well-drained soil

Bears finely divided, fernlike leaves and single
ruby red flowers from mid- to late spring

Zones 3 to 8

P. 392

Panicum virgatum
Switch Grass
S I Z E : 3 to 8 feet

Full sun

Rich, evenly moist, well-drained soil

Native prairie grass forming clumps of fine-
textured leaves topped by silvery or pinkish
flowers

Zones 5 to 9

P. 392

Papaver croceum
Iceland Poppy, Arctic Poppy
S I Z E : 1 to 2 feet

Full sun

Average to rich, evenly moist, well-drained soil

Bears showy flowers in spring and early summer in hot oranges, reds, and pinks plus
pastels

Zones 2 to 8

P. 394

Papaver orientale
Oriental Poppy
SIZE: 2 to 4 feet

Full sun

Average to rich, evenly moist, well-drained soil

Bears large, showy red-orange flowers with purple-black centers for a few weeks in early
summer

Zones 3 to 7

P. 394

Papaver orientale cultivar
Oriental Poppy
SIZE: 2 to 4 feet

Full sun

Average to rich, evenly moist, well-drained soil

Bears low mounds of foliage and large, showy
rose-pink flowers for a few weeks in early
summer

Zones 3 to 7

P. 394

Patrinia scabiosaefolia

SIZE: 3 to 7 feet

Full sun or partial shade

Average to rich, moist but well-drained soil

Bears low mounds of leaves and branched clusters of tiny yellow flowers in late summer and fall

Zones 4 to 8

P. 395

Pennisetum alopecuroides 'Moudry'

Fountain Grass

SIZE: 2 to 3 feet

Full sun; tolerates light shade

Average to rich, well-drained soil

Reseeding ornamental grass with mounds of leaves topped by black-purple flower heads in midsummer

Zones 5 or 6 to 9

P. 395

Penstemon barbatus
Common Beardtongue, Beardlip Penstemon

SIZE: 1½ to 4 feet

Full sun to partial shade

Rich, very well drained, evenly moist soil

Native wildflower bearing panicles of tubular red flowers tinged pink from early summer to fall

Zones 4 to 9

P. 396

Penstemon digitalis
'Husker Red'

SIZE: 2 to 4 feet

Full sun to partial shade; tolerates heat and humidity

Rich, very well drained, evenly moist soil

Native wildflower with maroon-red leaves and panicles of white flowers tinged pink from early to late summer

Zones 2 to 8

P. 396

Penstemon hirsutus var. *pygmaeus*

SIZE: 4 inches

Full sun to partial shade

Rich, very well drained, evenly moist soil

Native wildflower with evergreen leaves and clusters of tubular- to funnel-shaped white flowers in summer

Zones 3 to 9

PP. 396–397

Penstemon hybrid 'Sour Grapes'

Hybrid Penstemon, Hybrid Beardtongue

SIZE: 1½ to 2 feet

Full sun to partial shade

Rich, very well drained, evenly moist soil

Bears bunched clusters of tubular to bell-shaped purple-blue flowers with purple and white throats from midsummer to fall

Zones 6 or 7 to 10

P. 397

▲*Penstemon pinifolius*

SIZE : 1 to 1½ feet

Full sun to partial shade

Rich, very well drained, evenly moist soil

Evergreen subshrub with needlelike leaves and
loose racemes of scarlet tubular flowers in
summer

Zones 4 to 10

P. 397

▼*Perovskia atriplicifolia*

Russian Sage

SIZE : 3 to 5 feet

Full sun

Very well drained poor to average sandy or
loamy soil

Subshrub with aromatic leaves and panicles of
small violet-blue flowers from late summer
to fall

Zones 4 or 5 to 9

P. 398

Persicaria affinis
Himalayan Knotweed
SIZE: 10 inches

Full sun or partial shade

Average to rich, evenly moist soil

Mat-forming evergreen with spikes of tiny cup-shaped rose-red flowers from midsummer to fall

Zones 3 to 8

P. 399

Persicaria bistorta
Bistort, Snakeweed
SIZE: 2½ feet

Full sun or partial shade

Average to rich, evenly moist soil

Semievergreen species with bottlebrush-like spikes of small pink bell-shaped flowers from early summer to fall

Zones 3 to 8

P. 399

▲*Petasites japonicus* var. *giganteus*

SIZE: 3½ feet

Partial to full shade

Rich, constantly moist soil

Rhizomatous species producing clumps of large leaves and conelike white or yellowish flower heads in early spring

Zones 5 to 9

P. 399

▼*Phlomis russeliana*

Jerusalem Sage

SIZE: 3 feet

Full sun or light shade

Average to rich, well-drained soil

Bears erect stems with dense whorls of butter yellow hooded flowers from late spring to early fall

Zones 4 to 9

P. 400

Phlomis tuberosa

SIZE: 4 to 5 feet

Full sun

Average to rich, well-drained soil

Bears erect stalks with whorls of purplish pink flowers in summer

Zones 5 to 8

P. 401

Phlox bifida

Cleft Phlox, Sand Phlox

SIZE: 6 to 8 inches

Full sun

Average to rich, well-drained soil

Produces mounds of needlelike leaves and fragrant lavender to white flowers with cleft petal ends in spring

Zones 4 to 8

P. 402

Phlox divaricata
Wild Blue Phlox, Woodland Phlox

SIZE: 10 to 14 inches

Light to full shade

Rich, evenly moist, well-drained soil

Native woodland wildflower with clusters of
    fragrant lavender, pale violet, or white flow-
    ers in spring

Zones 3 to 9

P. 402

Phlox maculata
'Miss Lingard'
Wild Sweet William, Meadow Phlox

SIZE: 2 to 3 feet

Full sun or partial shade

Rich, deeply prepared, evenly moist soil

Bears glossy leaves and clusters of fragrant
    white flowers in early to midsummer

Zones 4 to 8

P. 403

Phlox maculata 'Rosalinde'
Wild Sweet William, Meadow Phlox
SIZE: 2 to 3 feet
Full sun or partial shade
Rich, deeply prepared, evenly moist soil
Bears glossy leaves and clusters of fragrant rose pink flowers in early to midsummer
Zones 4 to 8
P. 403

Phlox paniculata
Garden Phlox
SIZE: 3 to 4 feet
Full sun or partial shade
Rich, deeply prepared, evenly moist soil
Bears rounded clusters of fragrant flowers in summer to early fall in pinks, purples, lilacs, and white
Zones 3 to 8
P. 403

▲*Phlox stolonifera*
Creeping Phlox

SIZE: 4 to 6 inches

Light to full shade

Rich, evenly moist, well-drained soil

Native woodland wildflower bearing loose clusters of pink, lilac-blue, and white flowers in spring

Zones 3 to 8

P. 403

▼*Phlox subulata*
Moss Phlox, Creeping Phlox, Moss Pink

SIZE: 2 to 6 inches

Full sun

Average to rich, well-drained soil

Bears evergreen, needlelike leaves and masses of flowers in mid- to late spring in shades of lavender, purple, pink, and white

Zones 2 to 9

P. 403

Physalis alkekengi
Chinese Lantern
SIZE: 2 to 3 feet

Full sun or partial shade

Average, well-drained, evenly moist soil

Fast-spreading species with creamy white flowers in midsummer followed by showy red-orange "lanterns"

Zones 5 to 8

P. 404

Physostegia virginiana
Obedient Plant, False Dragonhead
SIZE: 3 to 4 feet

Full sun to partial shade

Average, evenly moist soil

Rhizomatous perennial bearing spikes of two-lipped lilac- to rose pink flowers from midsummer to early fall

Zones 3 to 9

P. 405

Platycodon grandiflorus
Balloon Flower
S I Z E : 1 to 2 feet

Full sun or light shade

Average to rich, well-drained soil

Bears attractive blue-green leaves and clusters
in purples, blues, pink, and white from early
to midsummer

Zones 3 to 8

P. 405

Polemonium caeruleum
Jacob's Ladder, Greek Valerian
S I Z E : 1 to 3 feet

Full sun or partial shade

Rich, well-drained, evenly moist soil

Native wildflower bearing clusters of bell-
shaped lilac-blue flowers in early summer

Zones 4 to 7

P. 406

Polemonium reptans
Creeping Jacob's Ladder

SIZE: 1 to 1½ feet

Partial shade

Rich, well-drained, evenly moist soil

Native wildflower bearing clusters of bell-shaped sky blue flowers in late spring and early summer

Zones 2 to 8

P. 406

Polygonatum odoratum var. thunbergii 'Variegatum'
Variegated Fragrant Solomon's Seal

SIZE: 2½ to 3 feet

Partial to full shade; tolerates full sun in the North

Rich, moist, well-drained soil

Bears pendent white flowers from late spring to early summer and handsome white-striped leaves

Zones 4 to 8

P. 407

Polystichum acrostichoides
Christmas Fern
S I Z E : 1½ feet
Partial shade
Evenly moist, rich soil
Native fern forming clumps of once-cut, ever-
green fronds with stocking-shaped leaflets
Zones 3 to 9
P. 408

Potentilla atrosanguinea
'Gibson's Scarlet'
Himalayan Cinquefoil
S I Z E : 1 to 1½ feet
Full sun or light shade
Poor to moderately rich, well-drained soil
Bears gray-green leaves and branched clusters
of yellow, orange, and red flowers from
early summer to fall
Zones 5 to 8
P. 409

▲*Potentilla neumaniana*

SIZE: 4 inches
Full sun or light shade
Poor to moderately rich, well-drained soil
Creeping, mat-forming plant bearing loose
    clusters of yellow flowers from late spring
    into summer
Zones 4 to 8
P. 409

▼*Primula denticulata*
Drumstick Primrose

SIZE: 8 to 12 inches
Partial shade
Rich, evenly moist, well-drained soil
Bears round clusters of lavender purple or
    white flowers on erect stalks in early spring
Zones 3 to 8
P. 411

Primula elatior
Oxlip Primrose

SIZE: 10 to 12 inches

Partial shade

Rich, evenly moist, well-drained soil

Forms rosettes of puckered leaves topped in
early to midspring by clusters of yellow
flowers

Zones 3 or 4 to 8

P. 411

Primula japonica
Japanese Primrose

SIZE: 1½ to 2 feet

Partial to full shade

Rich, moist to wet soil

Bears erect stalks of tiered flowers in midspring
in red, white, and shades of pink

Zones 5 to 8

P. 411

▲*Primula* Polyanthus Group
Polyanthus Primroses
SIZE: 6 inches
Partial shade
Rich, evenly moist, well-drained soil
Bears clusters of showy flowers in midspring in
a wide range of colors
Zones 3 or 4 to 8
P. 412

▼*Primula veris*
Cowslip Primrose
SIZE: 5 to 6 inches
Partial shade
Rich, evenly moist, well-drained soil
Bears clusters of fragrant, nodding yellow flow-
ers in early to midspring
Zones 4 to 8
P. 412

Primula vulgaris
English Primrose, Common Primrose
SIZE: 9 to 10 inches
Partial shade
Rich, evenly moist, well-drained soil
Bears clusters of single or double flowers in early spring in many colors
Zones 4 to 8
P. 412

Prunella grandiflora
Large Selfheal
SIZE: 6 inches
Full sun or partial shade
Average, evenly moist soil
Vigorous perennial bearing upright spikes of purple, lavender purple, pink, and white blooms
Zones 5 to 8
P. 413

Pulmonaria hybrid 'Roy Davidson'

Hybrid Lungwort

SIZE: 9 to 14 inches

Partial to full shade

Rich, evenly moist soil

Bears green leaves evenly blotched with silver and sky blue flowers in early spring

Zones 5 to 8

P. 414

Pulmonaria longifolia

Longleaf Lungwort

SIZE: 9 to 12 inches

Partial to full shade

Rich, evenly moist soil

Forms mounds of long, lance-shaped silver-spotted leaves and bears purple-blue flowers in early spring

Zones 4 to 8

P. 414

▲*Pulmonaria saccharata*
'Mrs. Moon'

Bethlehem Sage

SIZE: 8 to 12 inches

Partial to full shade

Rich, evenly moist soil

Forms mounds of silver-spotted leaves and bears pink flower buds that open to bluish lilac flowers in early spring

Zones 3 to 8

P. 414

▼*Pulsatilla vulgaris*

Pasqueflower

SIZE: 6 to 10 inches

Full sun

Rich, very well-drained soil

Bears feathery silvery-hairy leaves and early spring flowers in shades of rosy purple, blue-violet, and white

Zones 5 to 8

P. 415

Ranunculus acris
Tall Buttercup, Meadow Buttercup
SIZE: 1 to 3 feet
Full sun or partial to full shade
Rich, moist, well-drained soil
Bears golden yellow flowers from early to mid-summer
Zones 3 or 4 to 8
P. 416

Ranunculus repens 'Pleniflorus'
Creeping Buttercup
SIZE: 1 to 2 feet
Full sun or partial to full shade
Rich, moist, well-drained soil
Fast-spreading, stoloniferous plant bearing clusters of double yellow flowers from late spring to midsummer
Zones 3 to 8
P. 416

▲*Ratibida columnifera*
Prairie Coneflower

SIZE: 3 feet

Full sun

Average, well-drained soil

Native wildflower bearing yellow, daisylike
flower heads with conelike centers from
early summer to fall

Zones 3 to 10

P. 417

▼*Rheum palmatum* 'Atrosanguineum'
Chinese Rhubarb

SIZE: 3 to 8 feet

Full sun or partial shade

Deeply prepared, rich, evenly moist soil

Produces mounds of very large leaves topped by
plumes of tiny creamy green to red flowers
in early summer

Zones 5 to 9

P. 418

Rodgersia pinnata 'Superba'
Fingerleaf Rodgersia

SIZE: 2 to 4 feet

Light to full shade

Rich, evenly moist to constantly wet soil

Bears handsome leaves, bronze-purple when young, and rose pink flowers in mid- to late summer

Zones 5 to 8

P. 419

Rodgersia podophylla
Bronze-leaved Rodgersia

SIZE: 4 to 5 feet

Light to full shade

Rich, evenly moist to constantly wet soil

Produces mounds of bold leaves, bronze-red in fall, and panicles of creamy flowers in mid- to late summer

Zones 5 to 8

P. 419

Rudbeckia fulgida var. *sullivantii* 'Goldsturm'

Orange Coneflower

SIZE: 2 feet

Full sun to light shade

Average to rich, evenly moist to somewhat dry soil

Cultivar of a native wildflower with orange-yellow daisy flowers with chocolate brown centers from midsummer to early fall

Zones 3 to 9

P. 420

Rudbeckia hirta 'Indian Summer'

Black-eyed Susan

SIZE: 1 to 3 feet

Full sun to light shade

Average to rich, evenly moist to somewhat dry soil

Cultivar of a native wildflower bearing large, showy yellow flowers from summer to early fall

Zones 3 to 9

P. 420

Rudbeckia laciniata

Ragged Coneflower, Green-headed
Coneflower, Cut-leaved Coneflower

SIZE: 3 to 6 feet

Full sun to light shade

Average to rich, evenly moist to somewhat dry
soil

Native wildflower bearing daisylike flower
heads with yellow petals and green centers
from midsummer to fall

Zones 3 to 9

P. 421

Rudbeckia maxima

Giant Coneflower

SIZE: 5 to 9 feet

Full sun to light shade

Average to rich, evenly moist to somewhat dry
soil

Native wildflower bearing handsome gray-
green leaves and orange-yellow daisylike
flower heads in late summer

Zones 3 to 9

P. 421

Ruta graveolens
Common Rue

SIZE : 1½ to feet

Full sun or partial shade; tolerates heat and drought

Average, moist, very well drained soil

Shrubby perennial with handsome blue-green fernlike leaves and clusters of yellow flowers in summer

Zones 4 to 9

P. 422

Salvia officinalis 'Tricolor'
Common Sage, Garden Sage

SIZE : 2 to 2½ feet

Full sun to light shade

Average to rich, well-drained soil

Shrubby, evergreen herb with woolly variegated leaves marked with green, purple, pink, and cream

Zones 5 to 9

P. 423

Salvia × sylvestris 'May Night'

Hybrid Sage

SIZE: 2 to 3 feet

Full sun to light shade

Average to rich, well-drained soil

Bears dense racemes of indigo blue flowers on
 compact plants from early to midsummer

Zones 4 to 9

P. 423

Sanguinaria canadensis 'Flore Pleno'

Double Bloodroot, Red Puccoon

SIZE: 4 to 6 inches

Partial to full shade

Rich, evenly moist, well-drained soil

Cultivar of a native wildflower with scalloped
 leaves and double white flowers in spring

Zones 3 to 9

P. 424

Sanguisorba canadensis
Canadian Burnet

SIZE: 6 feet

Full sun or partial shade

Well-drained, fairly rich, evenly moist soil

Native wildflower bearing fluffy spikes of white
    flowers from midsummer to fall

Zones 3 to 8

P. 424

Santolina chamaecyparissus
Lavender Cotton

SIZE: 1 to 2 feet

Full sun

Poor to average, very well drained soil

Mounding shrub with finely cut gray-white
    leaves and buttonlike yellow flowers from
    mid- to late summer

Zones 6 to 9

P. 425

▲*Saponaria × lempergii* 'Max Frei'

Soapwort

SIZE: ½ to 1 foot

Full sun

Average, well-drained soil

Sprawling hybrid bearing clusters of hot pink
flowers from midsummer to fall

Zones 5 to 8

P. 426

▼*Saponaria ocymoides*

Rock Soapwort

SIZE: 3 to 6 inches

Full sun

Average, well-drained soil

Low, spreading species that bears loose clusters
of pink flowers in summer

Zones 4 to 8

P. 426

Satureja montana
Summer Savory
SIZE: 16 inches

Full sun

Loose, average to rich soil

Shrubby perennial with lance-shaped leaves
and spikes of tiny lavender-pink flowers in
summer

Zones 5 to 8

P. 427

Saxifraga stolonifera
Strawberry Geranium, Mother of Thousands
SIZE: 2 to 4 inches

Partial to full shade

Well-drained, rich, moist soil

Stoloniferous species with kidney-shaped leaves
and loose panicles of small white flowers in
summer

Zones 6 to 9

P. 428

Scabiosa caucasica
Pincushion Flower, Scabious

SIZE: 2 feet

Full sun

Average, well-drained soil

Bears rounded clusters of lavender, white, yellow, and rose-purple flowers from summer to early fall

Zones 4 to 9

P. 429

Sedum hybrid 'Autumn Joy'
Hybrid Sedum

SIZE: 2 feet

Full sun

Well-drained, average to rich soil; also poor, dry soil

Bears rounded heads of densely packed flowers in early fall that open dark pink and turn to red-brown

Zones 3 to 9

P. 430

▲*Sedum kamtschaticum*

SIZE: 4 inches

Full sun

Well-drained, average to rich soil; also poor, dry soil

Slow-spreading, rhizomatous species bearing clusters of golden yellow flowers in late summer

Zones 4 to 9

P. 431

▼*Sedum spurium* 'Dragon's Blood'

Two-row Sedum

SIZE: 4 inches

Full sun

Well-drained, average to rich soil; also poor, dry soil

Fast-spreading cultivar with fleshy, evergreen purple-tinted leaves and dark pink flowers

Zones 4 to 9

P. 431

Sempervivum tectorum
Hen and Chicks, Roof Houseleek

SIZE: 2 to 4 inches

Full sun or light shade

Poor to average, well-drained soil

Produces rosettes of fleshy leaves sometimes
flushed purple or maroon and clusters of
small red-purple flowers in summer

Zones 4 to 8

P. 432

Sidalcea malviflora 'Party Girl'
Checkerbloom

SIZE: 2 to 4 feet

Full sun to light shade; afternoon shade in hot-
summer areas

Average to somewhat rich, moist, well-drained
soil

Bears gray-green leaves and erect racemes of
pink flowers from early to midsummer

Zones 5 to 8

P. 433

▲*Silene schafta*

Schafta Campion, Shafta Pink

SIZE: 3 to 6 inches

Full sun or partial shade

Average, well-drained soil

Bears clusters of showy magenta-pink flowers from late summer to fall

Zones 5 to 7

P. 434

▼*Silene virginica*

Fire Pink

SIZE: 2 to 3 feet

Full sun or partial shade

Average, well-drained soil

Native wildflower bearing clusters of brilliant red flowers in spring and early summer

Zones 4 to 7

P. 435

Silphium perfoliatum
Cup Plant
SIZE: 5 to 8 feet

Full sun or light shade

Average, deeply prepared, evenly moist soil

Native wildflower bearing clusters of yellow
flowers with darker yellow centers from
midsummer to fall

Zones 5 to 9

P. 435

Sisyrinchium graminoides
Blue-eyed Grass
SIZE: ½ to 1½ feet

Full sun

Poor to average, well-drained soil

Native wildflower with grassy leaves and starry
purple-blue flowers over a long period in
summer

Zones 3 to 9

P. 436

▲*Smilacina racemosa*
Solomon's Plume, False Solomon's Seal

SIZE: 1½ to 3 feet

Partial to full shade

Rich, moist, well-drained soil

Native wildflower with arching stems ending in plumes of tiny creamy white flowers in spring

Zones 4 to 9

P. 437

▼*Solidago rugosa* 'Fireworks'
Rough-leaved Goldenrod, Rough-stemmed Goldenrod

SIZE: 3 to 4 feet

Full sun

Poor to average, moist, well-drained soil

Cultivar of a native wildflower bearing arching, plumelike panicles of golden yellow flowers in fall

Zones 4 to 9

P. 438

Solidago sphacelata
'Golden Fleece'

Dwarf Goldenrod

SIZE: 1½ feet

Full sun

Poor to average, moist, well-drained soil; grows in poor, even sandy soil

Cultivar of a native wildflower bearing an abundance of flowers in arching, branched panicles in fall

Zones 4 to 9

P. 438

× *Solidaster luteus*

SIZE: 2 to 3 feet

Full sun

Average to rich, well-drained soil

Hybrid bearing branched clusters of daisylike flower heads with pale yellow ray florets from midsummer to fall

Zones 5 to 8

P. 439

Spigelia marilandica
Indian Pink, Maryland Pinkroot

SIZE: 2 feet

Partial shade

Rich, moist, well-drained soil

Native wildflower bearing clusters of erect red flowers from spring to summer

Zones 6 to 9

P. 440

Stachys byzantina
'Countess Helene von Stein'
Lamb's Ears, Woolly Betony

SIZE: ½ to 1 foot

Full sun or partial shade

Very well drained, average soil

Mounding perennial with white woolly leaves and woolly, erect spikes of purple-pink flowers from early summer to fall

Zones 4 to 8

P. 440

Stachys macrantha
Betony

SIZE: 1 to 2 feet

Full sun or partial shade

Very well drained, average soil

Bears hairy green leaves and showy, dense
 spikes of pinkish purple flowers from early
 summer to fall

Zones 3 to 8

P. 441

Stokesia laevis
Stokes' Aster

SIZE: 1 to 2 feet

Full sun or light shade

Rich, evenly moist, well-drained soil

Native wildflower bearing daisylike flower
 heads with fringed petals from midsummer
 to fall in shades of violet, pink, and white

Zones 5 to 9

P. 441

▲ *Stylophorum diphyllum*
Celandine Poppy

SIZE: 1 to 1½ feet

Partial to full shade

Average to rich, moist soil

Native wildflower with deeply lobed leaves and
clusters of golden yellow flowers from
spring to summer

Zones 4 to 8

P. 442

▼*Symphytum officinale*
Common Comfrey

SIZE: 3 to 4 feet

Full sun or partial shade

Average to rich, moist soil

Vigorous species bearing branched clusters of
flowers from late spring to summer in
shades of violet purple, pink, and creamy
yellow

Zones 3 to 9

P. 443

▲*Symphytum × uplandicum* 'Variegatum'

Variegated Russian Comfrey

SIZE: 3 feet

Full sun or partial shade

Average to rich, moist soil

Bears white-edged gray-green leaves and clusters of purple-blue flowers from late spring to late summer

Zones 3 to 9

P. 443

▼*Tanacetum coccineum*

Painted Daisy, Pyrethrum

SIZE: 1½ to 2½ feet

Full sun

Average, well-drained soil

Bears deeply cut leaves and daisylike flowers in early summer with ray florets in shades of pink, red, yellow, and white

Zones 3 to 7

P. 444

Tanacetum parthenium
Feverfew

SIZE: 1½ to 2 feet

Full sun

Average, well-drained soil

Bears aromatic, feathery leaves and small white
daisylike flowers with yellow centers in
summer

Zones 4 to 9

P. 444

Teucrium chamaedrys
Germander, Wall Germander

SIZE: 1 to 2 feet

Full sun

Poor to average, well-drained soil

Subshrub with dark green leaves and loose
racemes of pale pink to purple flowers from
summer to early fall

Zones 5 to 9

P. 445

Thalictrum aquilegifolium
Columbine Meadow Rue
SIZE: 2 to 3 feet
Partial shade
Rich, moist soil
Bears mounds of handsome leaves topped by
clusters of fluffy flowers with showy purple
or white stamens in early summer
Zones 4 to 8
P. 446

Thalictrum flavum
ssp. glaucum
Yellow Meadow Rue
SIZE: 1 to 3 feet
Partial shade
Rich, moist soil
Vigorous species that spreads by rhizomes and
bears panicles of yellow flowers in summer
Zones 5 to 9
P. 446

Thalictrum rochebruneanum
Lavender Mist

SIZE: 3 to 5 feet

Partial shade

Rich, moist soil

Produces mounds of attractive leaves topped in summer by loose panicles of lilac-pink or white flowers

Zones 4 to 7

P. 446

Thermopsis villosa
Carolina Lupine

SIZE: 3 to 5 feet

Full sun or very light shade

Average, well-drained, evenly moist

Native wildflower bearing dense, erect racemes of yellow flowers in late spring and early summer

Zones 3 to 9

P. 447

▲ *Thymus × citriodorus* 'Argenteus'

Lemon Thyme

SIZE: 10 to 12 inches

Full sun or very light shade

Poor to rich, well-drained soil

Shrub that forms mounds of lemon-scented silver-edged leaves topped by clusters of pale lilac flowers in summer

Zones 5 to 9

P. 448

▼ *Thymus serpyllum*

Wild Thyme, Creeping Thyme

SIZE: 1 to 10 inches

Full sun or very light shade

Poor to rich, well-drained soil

Ground-hugging subshrub with aromatic leaves and purple flowers in summer

Zones 4 to 9

P. 448

Tiarella cordifolia
Allegheny Foamflower
SIZE: 6 to 10 inches

Partial to full shade

Rich, evenly moist, well-drained soil

Native wildflower bearing fluffy, spikelike
   racemes of white flowers in spring above
   mounds of maplelike leaves

Zones 3 to 8

P. 449

Tiarella wherryi
Wherry's Foamflower
SIZE: 6 to 10 inches

Partial to full shade

Rich, evenly moist, well-drained soil

Native wildflower bearing fluffy, spikelike
   racemes of white or pink-tinged flowers in
   spring and mounds of maplelike leaves

Zones 3 to 8

P. 450

Tradescantia
Andersoniana Group

Spiderwort

SIZE: 1½ to 2 feet

Light to full shade

Rich, moist, well-drained soil

Mounding perennial with clusters of saucer-
shaped flowers in shades of violet, lavender-
blue, pink, rose-red, and white

Zones 3 or 4 to 9

P. 450

Tricyrtis hirta

Toad Lily

SIZE: 2 to 3 feet

Light to full shade

Rich, moist, well-drained soil

Bears clusters of white, purple-spotted flowers
in late summer and fall in the leaf axils
along the stems

Zones 4 to 9

P. 451

Trillium grandiflorum

Great White Trillium, Wood Lily,
Wake-robin

S I Z E : 1 to 1½ feet

Partial to full shade

Rich, moist, well-drained soil

Native wildflower that bears showy, short-
stalked white flowers in spring that fade to
pink

Zones 4 to 8

P. 452

Trollius × *cultorum*
'Golden Queen'

Hybrid Globeflower

S I Z E : 2 to 3 feet

Full sun or partial shade

Very rich, constantly moist or wet soil

Bears buttercup-like flowers from spring to
midsummer in shades of orange and yellow

Zones 3 to 6

P. 453

▲ *Uvularia grandiflora*
Large Merrybells, Great Merrybells

SIZE: 1 to 1½ feet
Partial to full shade
Rich, moist, well-drained soil
Native wildflower bearing pendent, yellow to
orange-yellow flowers in mid- to late spring
Zones 3 to 9
P. 454

▼ *Vancouveria hexandra*
Vancouveria, American Barrenwort

SIZE: 10 to 14 inches
Partial shade
Rich, evenly moist, well-drained soil
Native woodland wildflower forming mounds
of fine-textured leaves and bearing white
flowers in spring
Zones 5 to 7
P. 455

Veratrum viride
Indian Poke
SIZE: 2 to 6 feet

Partial shade

Deep, very rich, moist but well-drained soil

Native wildflower bearing bold, pleated leaves and panicles of starry flowers from early to midsummer

Zones 3 to 8

P. 456

Verbascum chaixii f. *album*
Nettle-leaved Mullein
SIZE: 3 feet

Full sun

Poor to average, well-drained soil

Forms a low rosette of gray-green leaves topped by branched panicles of densely packed white flowers from mid- to late summer

Zones 4 to 8

P. 456

Verbascum olympicum
Olympic Mullein

SIZE: 6 feet

Full sun

Poor to average, well-drained soil

Bears silvery white woolly leaves and candelabra-like bloom stalks with golden yellow blooms from early to late summer

Zones 6 to 8

P. 456

Verbena hastata
Blue Vervain

SIZE: 3 to 5 feet

Full sun to light shade

Poor to average, well-drained soil

Native wildflower bearing branched clusters of flowers from early summer to early fall in violet, purple, or white

Zones 3 to 7

P. 457

Vernonia noveboracensis
Ironweed

SIZE: 3 to 7 feet

Full sun

Average, evenly moist, well-drained soil

Native wildflower bearing branched flower
   clusters consisting of many small red-
   purple flower heads

Zones 5 to 9

P. 458

Veronica austriaca
ssp. *teucrium*
Hungarian Speedwell

SIZE: ½ to 2 feet

Full sun or partial shade

Average to rich, moist, well-drained soil

Bears spikes of rich, deep blue flowers from late
   spring to early summer

Zones 3 to 8

P. 459

▲ *Veronica longifolia*
Long-leaved Speedwell

S I Z E : 2 to 4 feet

Full sun or partial shade

Average to rich, moist, well-drained soil

Bears dense clusters of small flowers in late summer and early fall in pale to deep blue, pink, and white

Zones 3 to 8

P. 459

▼ *Veronicastrum virginicum*
Culver's Root, Culver's Physic

S I Z E : 4 to 6 feet

Full sun to partial shade

Average to rich, moist soil

Native wildflower producing fluffy, bottle-brush-like racemes of white, pinkish, or pale bluish purple flowers from midsummer to early fall

Zones 3 to 8

P. 461

Vinca minor 'Bowles' Variety'

Common Myrtle, Lesser Periwinkle, Common Periwinkle

SIZE: 4 to 6 inches

Full sun or partial shade

Average to rich, well-drained soil

Mat-forming subshrub bearing oval leaves and lavender-blue flowers in spring

Zones 4 to 9

P. 461

Viola cornuta 'Alba'

Horned Violet

SIZE: 4 to 12 inches

Partial to full shade

Rich, moist, well-drained soil

Bears rounded, toothed leaves and small white flowers from spring to summer

Zones 6 to 9

P. 462

▲ *Waldsteinia ternata*
Barren Strawberry

SIZE: 4 to 10 inches

Partial to full shade

Average to rich, moist soil; tolerates drought

Native wildflower bearing three-parted leaves and clusters of saucer-shaped golden yellow flowers in spring and summer

Zones 3 to 8

P. 464

▼ *Yucca filamentosa* 'Golden Sword'
Adam's Needle

SIZE: 1½ to 6 feet

Full sun or very light shade

Poor to rich, well-drained soil

Cultivar of a native species forming clumps of stiff yellow-edged leaves and tall panicles of white flowers in summer

Zones 4 to 10

P. 465

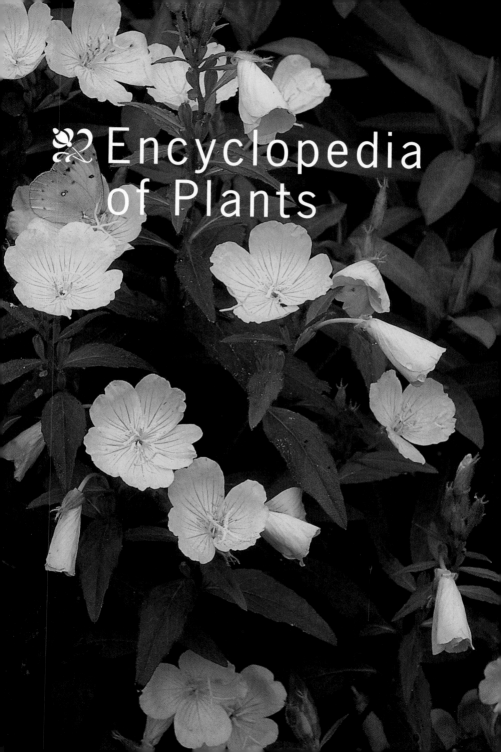

Encyclopedia
of Plants

❦ Encyclopedia of Plants

❦ *Acanthus*

ah-CAN-thuss. Acanthus family, Acanthaceae.

Commonly called bear's breeches, *Acanthus* species are perennials that produce clumps of handsome foliage and erect spikes of densely packed, two-lipped, hooded flowers. Showy, spiny, petal-like bracts and sepals, often in a contrasting color, decorate each 1½- to 2-inch-long flower. The variously toothed, lobed, and/or spiny leaves can reach 3 feet in length, and established plants form huge, bold clumps. About 30 species belong to the genus. Plants are often evergreen in mild climates.

HOW TO GROW

Bear's breeches grow in full sun or light shade, but bloom best in full sun. Deeply prepared, evenly moist, well-drained soil is ideal, but plants are relatively drought tolerant once established. They will not tolerate wet, poorly drained soil, especially in winter. Plants spread by fleshy, creeping roots to form large shrub-sized clumps ranging from 2 to 3 feet or more in width, so give them plenty of space at planting time. Cut tattered foliage to the ground in late winter. Propagate by division in spring or fall (dig with care, as plants have deep roots) or take root cuttings in spring or late fall. Or sow seeds. Near the northern limit of hardiness, protect plants with evergreen boughs or salt hay over winter.

A. mollis   P. 28

a. MOL-liss. Common Bear's Breech. Produces 2½-foot-tall clumps of shiny, lobed, spiny-toothed leaves topped by erect spikes of white flowers with purple bracts in late summer. To 5 feet tall in bloom. Zones 7 to 10.

A. spinosus

P. 28

a. spy-NO-sis. Spiny Bear's Breech. Forms handsome 2½-foot-tall mounds of deeply cut, spiny-margined leaves topped by racemes of white flowers with spiny purple bracts from late spring to midsummer. To 5 feet tall in bloom. Zones 5 to 10.

❧Achillea

ah-KILL-ee-ah. Aster family, Asteraceae.

Long-blooming achilleas, also called yarrows, bear dense, flat-topped or slightly rounded clusters of tiny daisylike flower heads. Some 85 species belong to the genus, most flowering from late spring into midsummer. Many also bloom intermittently into fall. The flowers come in yellows, pinks, reds, and white and are borne above mounds of aromatic, feathery leaves that may be green, blue-gray, or gray-green. The botanical name commemorates the Greek god Achilles, who was believed to have used these plants to heal wounds — they have a long history of herbal use.

HOW TO GROW

Give plants full sun and average to poor, well-drained soil. They thrive in dry or sandy conditions but also grow in moist, rich soil provided it is well drained. Too-rich soil encourages lush, rank growth. A site with good air circulation is best. Give yarrows plenty of room to spread at planting time — all the species listed here form clumps 2 feet or more across. Divide clumps in spring or early fall every 3 to 5 years to keep them vigorous. Stake tall cultivars. Remove spent flowers to encourage reblooming. Propagate plants by dividing, by taking cuttings from the base of the plant as shoots emerge in early spring or in summer, or by sowing seeds.

A. filipendulina

a. fil-ih-pen-due-LEE-nuh. Bears gray-green leaves and flat-topped 5-inch-wide clusters of golden yellow flowers on 4-foot-tall stems from early summer to fall. 'Gold Plate' bears 6-inch-wide flowers. Zones 3 to 9.

A. hybrids

P. 29

Many popular yarrows are the result of complex crosses. 'Coronation Gold' bears 4- to 5-inch-wide mustard yellow flowers on 3- to 3½-foot stems all summer long. Hardy in Zones 3 to 9, it tolerates hot, humid summers. 'Moonshine' has gray-green foliage and sulphur yellow blooms all summer on 1- to 2-foot stems and is best in Zones 3 to 8. Galaxy hybrid cultivars, hardy in Zones 4 to 8, bear 2- to 4-inch-wide flower clusters all summer on compact 2- to 3-foot-tall plants. Galaxy cultivars include lilac-pink 'Appleblossom' ('Apfelblüte'), red-flowered 'Fanal', and dark red 'Summerwine'.

A. millefolium

P. 29

a. mil-leh-FOE-lee-um. Vigorous to invasive North American native with flat-topped flower clusters atop 2-foot-tall plants from early to late summer. Blooms come in pink, red, and pastel shades. Cultivars, which have showier flowers and spread less quickly than the species, include orange-red 'Paprika', magenta 'Cerise Queen', red 'Fire King', and 'Summer Pastels'. Zones 3 to 9.

A. ptarmica

P. 30

a. TAR-mih-kuh. Sneezewort. A weedy 1- to 3-foot-tall species with narrow, lance-shaped leaves and loose sprays of white flowers from early to late summer. Double-flowered cultivars such as 'The Pearl', which bears buttonlike ¾-inch blooms are the best choices for the garden. Zones 2 to 9.

A. tomentosa

P. 30

a. toe-men-TOE-suh. Woolly Yarrow. Low-growing mounds of woolly gray-green leaves and 3-inch-wide clusters of yellow flowers on 1-foot-tall stems. Blooms early summer to fall. Plants require perfect drainage, do not tolerate heat and humidity, and are best for rock gardens or other very well drained sites. Zones 3 to 7.

Aconitum

ack-oh-NYE-tum. Buttercup family, Ranunculaceae.

The genus *Aconitum* contains 100 species of perennials and biennials commonly called monkshoods or aconites. They are grown for their erect racemes or panicles of showy hooded flowers that bring rich blues and purples to the garden from summer to fall. There also are yellow-flowered monkshoods. The showy portion of the flowers actually is made up of five petal-like sepals, including one that forms the hood-shaped topmost "petal" for which the plants are named. The true petals have been reduced to spurlike nectaries. The flowers are borne above clumps of handsome leaves, which usually are deeply cut or lobed in a palmate (handlike) fashion. Another common name, wolfsbane, refers to a more sinister characteristic of these plants: the leaves, roots, flowers, and seeds are all quite poisonous.

HOW TO GROW

Give monkshoods a site in partial or dappled shade and rich, evenly moist but well-drained soil. Plants will grow in full sun, but in southern zones a site with afternoon shade helps plants cope with the heat. Monkshoods won't grow well in areas where night temperatures do not drop below 70°F. A protected site helps prevent the brittle stems from breaking in wind and rain. Plants resent transplanting and can be left in place for many years, so space them generously at planting time — the species listed here form 2- to 3-foot-wide clumps. Handle the plants carefully: the large fleshy, tuberlike roots break easily. Since monkshoods emerge late in spring, mark the location of the clumps to avoid digging into them accidentally. Water deeply during dry spells. Feed in spring with a mix of well-rotted manure and compost. Taller monkshoods require staking. Divide plants in spring or fall if necessary or for propagation. Wear rubber gloves when handling the roots (rubbing the plant's sap on skin causes tingling and numbness), and keep hands away from your face, especially your eyes and mouth.

A. × cammarum

a. × cam-MAR-um. Bicolor Monkshood. Formerly *A. × bicolor*. A 3- to 4-foot-tall hybrid with violet-blue, bluish purple, or blue-and-white flowers from mid- to late summer. 'Bicolor' bears loose clusters of blue-and-white flowers. 'Bressingham Spire' bears violet-blue flowers on 3-foot plants and doesn't need staking. Zones 3 to 7.

A. carmichaelii   P. 31

a. car-mih-KELL-ee-eye. Azure Monkshood. A 3- to 6-foot-tall species with rich violet-blue blooms from late summer through fall. 'Arendsii' bears violet-blue flowers in early to midfall on 3- to 4-foot plants. Zones 3 to 7.

A. lycoctonum

a. lie-COCK-ton-um. Wolfsbane. Bears yellow or sometimes purple flowers from midsummer to early fall on 2- to 6-foot plants. *A. lycoctonum* ssp. *vulparia* (formerly *A. vulparia*) bears pale yellow flowers. Zones 4 to 8.

A. napellus

P. 31

a. NAP-ell-us. Common Monkshood. Old-fashioned 3- to 4-foot-tall species with dense, showy clusters of dark blue-violet flowers in mid- to late summer. Zones 3 to 8.

ꙮ Acorus

ah-CORE-us. Arum family, Araceae.

Despite the common name sweet flag, *Acorus* species are more closely related to jack-in-the-pulpits (*Asarum* species) than flags or irises (*Iris* species). Two species belong here, both wetland perennials grown for their attractive clumps of strap-shaped or grasslike foliage. They bear insignificant rounded or club-shaped flowers in brownish green or white that jut out just below the tops of leaflike flower stalks. The plants spread by fleshy, aromatic rhizomes. Sweet flags have a long history of herbal uses. The rhizomes can be dried and ground for use as a fixative in potpourri. The leaves, which have a slightly sweet, spicy fragrance, have been used as a strewing herb.

HOW TO GROW

Select a site in full sun or partial shade with constantly moist or wet soil rich in organic matter. Plants also grow in standing water. Sites in bogs, wet borders, and along natural ponds are ideal: the plants spread steadily but generally aren't invasive. Divide them every 3 or 4 years to keep the clumps vigorous and contain their spread. Propagate by division in spring.

A. calamus

P. 32

a. KAL-ah-mus. Sweet Flag, Sweet Calamus. A deciduous species forming 2-foot-wide clumps of strap-shaped ¾-inch-wide 3- to 4-foot-long leaves. 'Variegata' bears leaves striped lengthwise with cream and white. Plants grow with up to 6 inches of standing water over the rhizomes. Zones 4 to 11.

A. gramineus

P. 32

a. gra-MIN-ee-us. Grassy-leaved Sweet Flag. An evergreen to semievergreen species with glossy, linear, grasslike leaves that form arching clumps to about 12 inches in height and width. Plants grow with 1 to 2 inches of standing water over the rhizomes. Variegated and dwarf cultivars are available. Zones 5 to 11.

᭗ *Actaea*

ack-TEE-uh. Buttercup family, Ranunculaceae.

Members of this genus of eight species of woodland perennials are grown for their foliage and showy fruit rather than their flowers. Commonly known as baneberries because the attractive berries and the roots are extremely toxic if ingested, *Actaea* species bear fluffy racemes of small white flowers in late spring and early summer. The flowers are followed by clusters of round berries that add color to the shade garden in late summer and fall. The plants form handsome 2- to 3-foot-wide clumps of leaves that are divided in a featherlike fashion and have toothed leaflets.

H O W T O G R O W
Select a site in partial shade with average to rich, evenly moist soil. Amend the soil with compost or humus at planting time, and water deeply in dry weather. Abundant soil moisture is essential to success in areas with hot summers. To propagate, divide plants in spring or sow seeds as soon as they are ripe in fall.

A. alba   P. 33
a. AL-buh. Doll's Eyes, White Baneberry. Formerly *A. pachypoda*. Native 2- to 4-foot-tall wildflower bearing fluffy, rounded 2- to 4-inch-long racemes of white flowers well above the foliage. The flower stalks (pedicels) turn red as the ⅜-inch-wide berries ripen to white. Zones 3 to 7.

A. rubra   P. 33
a. RUE-brah. Red Baneberry, Snakeberry. Native 2- to 4-foot-tall wildflower that bears fluffy, rounded 1¼- to 2-inch-long racemes of flowers followed by clusters of round red ¼-inch-wide berries. Zones 3 to 7.

᭗ *Adenophora*

ah-den-OFF-or-uh. Bellflower family, Campanulaceae.

The nodding flowers of *Adenophora* species, commonly called ladybells, reveal a close kinship with bellflowers (*Campanula* species). *Adenophora* contains 40 species, all perennials with bell- or funnel-shaped flowers that feature a swollen disk surrounding the style, just above the ovary, which distinguishes them from the true bellflowers. Flowers are carried in erect, showy terminal racemes or panicles and come in shades from pale lavender or white to violet-blue. Most species produce clumps of rounded basal leaves and bear smaller leaves along the flowering stems.

HOW TO GROW

Give ladybells a site in full sun to partial shade with rich, deeply dug, evenly moist, well-drained soil. Plants are deep rooted and resent being disturbed, so prepare the soil thoroughly at planting time. Because of the deep, fleshy roots, the plants seldom tolerate division and are best propagated by cuttings taken from shoots that arise near the base of the plant in late spring. Or propagate by seeds.

A. confusa

P. 34

a. con-FEW-suh. Common Ladybells. An erect 2- to 2½-foot-tall perennial forming 2-foot-wide clumps of toothed, scalloped leaves. Bears loose panicles of ¾-inch-wide bell-shaped purple-blue flowers for three to four weeks in early summer. Zones 3 to 8.

❧ Adiantum

ah-dee-AN-tum. Brake Fern family, Pteridaceae.

Better known as maidenhair ferns, Adiantum species are moisture-loving perennials with branched, delicate-looking fronds with shiny black stems that are divided into three to five featherlike (pinnate) leaflets. Fiddleheads and new leaves often are pink in color. Between 200 and 250 species, both hardy and tropical, belong to this genus. The plants spread via creeping rhizomes and in the right site form large lacy-textured mounds of foliage.

HOW TO GROW

Give maidenhairs a site in partial shade with evenly moist, well-drained, slightly acid soil. They will tolerate some sun if soil moisture is plentiful and reliable, but unlike many ferns do not grow well in deep shade. Propagate by dividing the plants in early spring.

A. pedatum

P. 34

a. peh-DAY-tum. Northern Maidenhair Fern. A 1- to 1½-foot-tall native North American fern with lacy, flat fronds that are branched in a horseshoelike manner. Western maidenhair (A. aleuticum, formerly A. pedatum var. aleuticum), native to western North America and eastern Asia, is a similar species. Both are hardy in Zones 2 to 8.

❦ *Aegopodium*

ee-goe-POE-dee-um. Carrot family, Apiaceae.

Five species of fast-spreading perennials belong to the genus *Aegopodium*. The common names of these plants — bishop's weed and goutweed — suggest the garden management problems they create when poorly used. Plants have compound leaves with three leaflets and umbels of white flowers in summer.

HOW TO GROW

Select a site in partial to full shade. Although bishop's weed will thrive in any soil, a spot with poor, dry soil where little else will grow is best, and therein lies the benefit of this invasive spreader. Plants easily compete with tree roots. However, established plants root very deeply and are difficult to eradicate. Unchecked clumps easily smother less-vigorous plants. Consider a site surrounded by mown lawn on all sides, either alone or under shrubs. Remove the flowers as they fade to prevent self-sown seedlings. The variegated form of *A. podagraria* isn't quite as aggressive as the species but still spreads quickly. If variegated plants revert to green or mostly green, promptly dig up reverted portions of the clump and discard them. Otherwise the green portions will overwhelm the remaining variegated ones. Cut plants to the ground in summer if their foliage looks tattered. Propagate plants by division in spring or fall.

A. podagraria   P. 35

a. poe-duh-GRAIR-ee-uh. Bishop's Weed. Invasive 1- to 1½-foot-tall species with deep, wide-spreading rhizomes. 'Variegata' bears attractive three-part leaves with irregular creamy white margins and is more commonly grown than the species. Zones 4 to 9.

❦ *Agastache*

a. ag-ah-STAH-chee. Mint family, Lamiaceae.

Closely related to mints, *Agastache* species bear square stems, ovate aromatic leaves, and erect clusters of small two-lipped flowers. Approximately 20 or so species belong to this genus of plants commonly called giant or Mexican hyssops. All are perennials, but only a few are hardy as far north as Zones 4 and 5. Tender species can be grown as annuals or tender perennials.

Giant hyssops need little more than full sun or very light shade and rich, well-drained soil to thrive. They spread to form 2- to 3-foot-wide clumps. Propagate by taking cuttings in spring or summer or dividing plants in spring. Plants may self-sow and can be started easily from seeds, but cultivars may not come true from seeds.

A. barberi

a. BAR-ber-eye. Giant Hummingbird Mint. Bushy 2-foot-tall plants with fragrant leaves. Bears loose 1-foot-long spikes of red-purple flowers from midsummer to fall. Zones 6 to 10.

A. cana

P. 35

a. CAY-nuh. Wild Hyssop, Hummingbird Mint, Mosquito Plant. Well-branched 2- to 3-foot-tall plant with aromatic leaves and loose 1-foot-long spikes of pink or rose-purple flowers from late summer to fall. Zones 5 to 10.

A. foeniculum

P. 36

a. foe-NICK-you-lum. Anise Hyssop. A 3- to 5-foot-tall species with anise-scented leaves. Bears spikes of blue flowers with violet bracts from midsummer to fall. Zones 6 to 10.

❦ Ajania

ah-JAY-nee-uh. Aster family, Asteraceae.

A genus of 30 species of perennials, subshrubs, and shrubs that once were classified in the genus *Chrysanthemum*. All bear attractive clusters of yellow buttonlike flower heads and leaves that are shallowly to deeply lobed and often covered with white woolly or silky hairs.

Select a site in full sun and poor to average, well-drained soil. Wet soil in winter is fatal. Propagate divisions in spring, by cuttings taken either from shoots at the base of the plant in spring or from shoots in summer, or by seeds.

A. pacifica

P. 36

a. pah-SIFF-ih-kuh. Gold-and-silver Chrysanthemum. Formerly *Chrysanthemum pacificum*. Shrubby to mounding 1-foot-tall species spreading by runners to form 3-foot-wide mounds of handsome silver-edged leaves. Bears branched clusters of golden buttonlike flower heads in fall. In the North, plants may not bloom but are still grown for their attractive foliage. Zones 5 to 9.

❦ *Ajuga*

ah-JEW-guh. Mint family, Lamiaceae.

Ajuga species, also called bugleweeds or just plain bugle, are vigorous perennials grown for their showy foliage as well as their short showy spikes of tiny, densely packed, two-lipped flowers. Flowers appear in spring and early summer and range from cobalt blue to bluish purple, as well as pink and white. Most ajugas — there are about 40 species in the genus — have green spoon-shaped, somewhat spinachlike leaves that are evergreen or semievergreen and borne in dense rosettes. Many cultivars have been selected for their handsome variegated leaves, and gardeners treasure these ground-hugging plants more for their foliage and carpeting habit than for their flowers.

HOW TO GROW

While ajugas grow in full sun to full shade, a site with light to partial shade is best. Well-drained, evenly moist, average to rich soil is fine. Be sure to consider the speed at which the plants spread when selecting a site. *A. reptans* spreads via fast-growing stolons, making it a terrific ground cover in the right site or an invasive weed in the wrong one. To keep spreading species in check, install an edging strip between the lawn and the garden. Trimming off wayward stolons also helps. Propagate by dividing the clumps any time from spring to fall or by potting up individual rosettes of leaves. Or, take root cuttings from the stolons (cut just below a node). Ajugas are seldom grown from seed because the cultivars must be propagated by cuttings or division.

A. genevensis

P. 37

a. jen-eh-VEN-sis. Blue Bugleweed, Geneva Bugleweed. A 6- to 12-inch-tall species that spreads gradually by rhizomes to form 1½-foot-wide clumps. Bears 2- to 4-inch-long spikes of indigo blue flowers in spring. 'Pink Beauty' bears pink flowers; 'Alba', white ones. Zones 4 to 8.

A. pyramidalis

P. 37

a. peer-ah-mih-DAL-iss. Pyramid Bugleweed, Upright Bugleweed. Compact 6- to 10-inch-tall species that forms 1½- to 2-foot-wide mounds of dark green leaves. Plants produce stolons but are fairly restrained spreaders because the stolons appear only at the end of the season. Bears dense 4- to 6-inch-tall spikes of purple-blue flowers in spring and early summer. 'Metallica Crispa', a 4- to 6-inch cultivar, has handsome, crinkled, dark green leaves flushed with metallic bronze-purple. Zones 3 to 8.

A. reptans

P. 38

a. REP-tanz. Common Bugleweed, Carpet Bugleweed. Fast-spreading species with ground-hugging rosettes of spoon-shaped leaves that quickly spreads to 3 feet or more. Bears 4- to 6-inch-tall spikes of violet-blue flowers in late spring. 'Catlin's Giant' and 'Jungle Beauty' are large-leaved, vigorous spreaders ideal for covering large areas. Variegated cultivars spread, but are less vigorous than green-leaved selections. These include 'Burgundy Glow' with white, pink, and green leaves, as well as 'Silver Beauty', with gray-green leaves edged in white. Zones 3 to 9.

❧ Alchemilla

al-kah-MILL-uh. Rose family, Rosaceae.

Grown as much for their handsome foliage as for their flowers, *Alchemilla* species are commonly called lady's mantles. About 250 species belong to the genus, most of which produce woody rhizomes and lobed, rounded, or kidney-shaped leaves that often are softly hairy. The individual greenish to yellow-green flowers are tiny (from ¹⁄₁₆ to ⅛ inch across), but they are borne in large branched clusters that have a frothy appearance.

HOW TO GROW

Select a site in partial shade with rich, evenly moist, well-drained soil. A spot with morning sun and afternoon shade is ideal. In the North, plants can be grown in full sun but will need constantly moist soil for best growth. Heat is a problem in the South (Zones 7 and 8), so give them partial to full shade and make sure the soil remains moist. Water during dry weather, although established plants are fairly drought tolerant. Cut tattered foliage to the ground in midsummer if necessary and water deeply: fresh new leaves will appear in fall. Plants self-sow, and since seeds are produced without pollination, the seedlings are identical to the parent plants. Propagate divisions in spring or fall or by seeds.

A. alpina

P. 38

a. al-PIE-nuh. Alpine Lady's Mantle. Ground-hugging 6- to 8-inch-tall species forming 1- to 2-foot-wide mounds of deeply lobed leaves edged with silver hairs. Bears loose sprays of yellow-green flowers in summer. Zones 3 to 7.

A. erythropoda

a. air-ith-row-POE-duh. Clump-forming 8- to 12-inch-tall species with 1-foot-wide mounds of lobed, sharp-toothed, blue-green leaves. Bears clusters of yellow-green flowers from late spring to summer. Zones 3 to 7.

A. mollis

P. 39

a. MOL-iss. Common Lady's Mantle. A 1- to 2-foot-tall perennial forming 2-foot-wide mounds of handsome, pleated, lobed leaves covered with tiny soft hairs. Bears frothy, somewhat sprawling clusters of tiny chartreuse flowers from late spring to early summer. Zones 4 to 7.

❦ Amsonia

am-SO-nee-uh. Dogbane family, Apocynaceae.

Commonly known as blue stars as well as dogbanes, *Amsonia* species are perennials or subshrubs bearing clusters of flowers that have funnel-shaped bases and flared, starry faces. The stems contain milky sap, and leaves are lance shaped to ovate or rounded. Some of the roughly 20 species in the genus feature brilliant yellow fall foliage.

HOW TO GROW

Select a site in sun or partial shade that has average, moist, well-drained soil. Established plants tolerate some drought. To keep plants growing in shade neat looking, cut them back after flowering. Propagate by dividing plants in spring or fall, taking stem cuttings in early summer, or sowing seeds.

A. ciliata

a. sil-ee-AH-tuh. Downy Blue Star. A 1- to 3-foot-tall species native to the southeastern United States forming 1-foot-wide clumps. Bears threadlike leaves that turn yellow in fall and clusters of pale blue ½-inch-wide flowers in summer. Zones 5 to 9.

A. hubrectii
P. 39

a. hu-BRECK-tee-eye. A 2- to 3-foot-tall species native to the United States forming handsome 3- to 4-foot-wide clumps of very narrow leaves that turn golden yellow in fall. Bears clusters of very pale blue 2- to 3-inch-wide flowers in summer. Zones 5 to 9.

A. tabernaemontana
P. 40

a. tah-ber-nay-mon-TAN-uh. Willow Blue Star. A 1- to 3-foot-tall species native to the eastern United States forming 2- to 3-foot-wide clumps. Bears lance-shaped leaves that turn yellow in fall and rounded clusters of ½-inch-wide star-shaped flowers in spring and early summer. Zones 3 to 9.

❦ Anaphalis

ah-NAFF-ah-liss. Aster family, Asteraceae.

Woolly gray-green leaves and rounded clusters of small buttonlike flower heads characterize *Anaphalis* species, commonly known as pearly everlastings. The flowers, which are excellent for drying, consist of yellow daisylike centers surrounded by white petal-like bracts that have a dry, papery texture. The leaves, which are linear to lance shaped, are covered with woolly hairs that give the foliage their silvery appearance.

HOW TO GROW

Select a site in full sun to partial shade with average to rich, evenly moist soil that is fairly well drained. Unlike many other silver-leaved perennials, pearly everlastings thrive in moist soil: in dry soil, the plants drop their lower leaves and generally look unattractive. To keep these clump-forming plants vigorous, dig and divide the clumps every 3 to 4 years in spring. In addition to division, propagate by cuttings taken from shoots at the base of the plant in spring, from stem cuttings taken in spring or early summer, or by seeds.

A. margaritacea
P. 40

a. mar-gar-ih-TAY-see-uh. Pearly Everlasting. A 2- to 3-foot-tall, 2-foot-wide species with lance-shaped leaves that are gray-green above and white and woolly beneath. The edges of the leaves roll upward, giving them a silver-edged appearance. Bears rounded 6-inch-wide clusters of flowers from midsummer to fall. Zones 4 to 8.

A. triplinervis

a. trip-lih-NERV-iss. Three-veined Everlasting. A 1- to 2-foot-tall species that spreads from 1½ to 2 feet and bears gray-green rounded to spoon-shaped leaves with woolly white hairs. Produces rounded 1½- to 2-inch-wide clusters of flowers with white bracts from mid- to late summer. Zones 3 to 8.

❦ *Anchusa*

an-KOO-suh. Borage family, Boraginaceae.

This genus contains about 35 species of annuals, biennials, and perennials commonly called anchusas, alkanets, or bugloss. They are grown for their clusters of five-lobed flowers with tubular bases in shades of blue, rich violet, or purple-blue. Leaves are linear to lance-shaped, and some species have leaves and stems covered with bristly hairs.

HOW TO GROW

Give anchusas a site in full sun to light shade with rich, well-drained, evenly moist soil. They do not tolerate drought. Water deeply during dry weather. To maintain the rich soil these plants require, top-dress annually with a balanced fertilizer in spring and again in summer. Cut plants back after the first flush of bloom to encourage a second flush of flowers. Tall cultivars require staking. Anchusas tend to be short-lived; divide clumps every 2 to 3 years to keep them vigorous. Plants self-sow, often freely, but the best cultivars do not come true from seeds: propagate these by root cuttings taken in early spring or late summer or by division in spring.

A. azurea   P. 41

a. ah-ZUR-ee-uh. Italian Alkanet, Italian Bugloss. Erect 2- to 5-foot-tall short-lived perennial forming 2-foot-wide clumps and bearing bristly leaves and stems. Produces showy, loose clusters of ¾-inch-wide flowers in early summer. 'Dropmore' bears deep purple-blue flowers on 4-foot plants. 'Loddon Royalist' reaches 3 feet and rarely needs staking. 'Little John' is a fairly long-lived 1½-foot cultivar. Zones 3 to 8.

❦ *Anemone*

ah-NEM-oh-nee. Buttercup family, Ranunculaceae.

The genus *Anemone* is a diverse genus of about 120 species that bear saucer- to cup-shaped flowers with a boss, or tuft, of showy yellow stamens in the center. The flowers have petal-like sepals instead of true petals and come in shades of pink, rose-red, scarlet, white, and lavender- and violet-blue. Blooms are borne one per stem or in branched clusters and may be single, semidouble, or double. Also called windflowers (the botanical name is from the Greek word *anemos,* wind), anemones have attractive, deeply cut, fernlike leaves. Most produce a cluster of leaves at the base of the plant, but some species also have leaves along the wiry flower stems. There are anemones that bloom from spring into early summer; others bloom in late summer and fall. Root systems are diverse, too: while many species grow from rhizomes or fleshy or fibrous roots, others produce woody tubers and are planted and treated like bulbs.

HOW TO GROW

For best results, select planting sites according to when plants bloom. Give spring-blooming species — *A. canadensis* and *A. sylvestris* — a site in partial shade and light, rich, evenly moist soil. Most spring-blooming species also grow in full sun provided the soil remains moist. Spring-blooming anemones usually go dormant after flowering, and once dormant they tolerate drier conditions. Combine them with other low-growing perennials to fill the space they leave. Divide clumps immediately after the foliage has turned yellow in late spring or early summer to control plants that have spread too far, to relieve overcrowding, or for propagation.

Fall-blooming anemones, often collectively referred to as Japanese anemones, thrive in full sun or partial shade with rich, evenly moist, well-drained soil. These species — *A. hupehensis, A.* × *hybrida, A. tomentosa,* and *A. vitifolia* — benefit from a spot with afternoon shade, especially in areas with hot summers. When planting, select the location carefully and dig the soil deeply: plants will thrive for years in one spot. Keep newly planted clumps well watered the first season or they can succumb to heat and drought. Propagate by dividing the clumps in spring or immediately after they flower in fall or by root cuttings dug in winter or early spring. All anemones grow slowly from seeds.

A. canadensis   P. 41

a. can-ah-DEN-sis. Meadow Anemone. Vigorous 6- to 8-inch-tall native North American wildflower spreading by rhizomes to 2 feet or more. Bears single 2-inch-wide white flowers from late spring to early summer. Zones 3 to 7.

A. hupehensis

a. hue-peh-HEN-sis. Chinese Anemone. Handsome 2- to 3-foot-tall species producing 2-foot-wide clumps of three-parted leaves. Bears long-stalked 2- to 2½-inch-wide flowers in pink or white borne in umbels of about 12 from midsummer to fall. 'Hadspen Abundance' bears dark reddish pink blooms. *A. hupehensis* var. *japonica*, commonly called Japanese anemone, bears creamy pink flowers on 2- to 4-foot plants. 'Bressingham Glow', 'Pink Shell' ('Rosenschale'), and 'September Charm' are among the many excellent cultivars. Zones 4 to 8.

A. × hybrida   P. 42

a. × HI-brih-duh. Japanese Anemone, Hybrid Anemone. Vigorous 2½- to 5-foot-tall species spreading by rhizomes to form clumps exceeding 3 feet in width. Bears long-stalked 3- to 3½-inch-wide flowers in 12- to 18-flowered umbels in shades of pink and white from summer to midfall. 'Honorine Jobert' bears single 2- to 3-inch-wide white flowers on 3- to 4-foot plants. 'Whirlwind' carries 4-inch-wide semidouble white blooms on 4- to 5-foot plants. 'Queen Charlotte' ('Königin Charlotte') produces semidouble 4-inch-wide pink blooms. 'Margarete' bears semidouble to double deep pink ones. Zones 4 to 8.

A. sylvestris   P. 42

a. sil-VES-tris. Snowdrop Anemone. Vigorous 1- to 1½-foot-tall species that has fibrous roots with a woody base and spreads via root suckers to about 2 feet. Bears single white 2-inch-wide flowers in spring. Zones 3 to 8.

A. tomentosa   P. 43

a. toe-men-TOE-suh. Grape-leaved Anemone. A 3-foot-tall species spreading by underground shoots to form clumps 3 feet wide or more. Bears 1½- to 3½-inch-wide flowers in loose umbels of five to seven blooms from late summer to fall. 'Robustissima', also listed as *A. vitifolia* 'Robustissima', is an especially hardy selection that can be grown in Zones 4 to 8. Zones 5 to 8.

❦ *Angelica*

an-JEL-ih-kuh. Carrot family, Apiaceae.

Statuesque short-lived perennials or biennials native to the Northern Hemisphere, *Angelica* species bear pinnately compound leaves ranging from 1 to 3 feet in length. The leaves are divided into large, roughly diamond-shaped leaflets arranged in a pinnate (featherlike) fashion. Flat-topped or rounded umbels of yellow-green or purple flowers are carried above the foliage in summer. There are 30 species in the genus, most native to rich, damp woodlands, meadows, or streambanks. *Angelica,* derived from the Latin for angel, *angelus,* is a reference to the healing properties of the best-known species in the genus, *A. archangelica.*

HOW TO GROW

Give these plants a spot in partial shade with rich, deep, moist soil, which yields the largest plants, although they will tolerate drier conditions. Plants grow in full shade but don't bloom as well. Angelicas are taprooted and resent transplanting. The species listed here are monocarpic, meaning they die after setting seeds. Some gardeners simply grow new plants from seeds annually to ensure a continuing supply of plants. (Transplant seedlings when they are still small to minimize damage to the taproot.) Others remove the flower heads as they fade to encourage plants to perform more as perennials. Plants treated this way generally bloom for 2 to 3 years. Plants self-sow.

A. archangelica
P. 43

a. ark-an-JEL-ih-kuh. Archangel, Wild Parsnip. Statuesque 6-foot-tall perennial producing 4-foot-wide mounds of pinnate 2-foot-long leaves. Bears rounded 10-inch-wide umbels of tiny greenish yellow flowers on thick, upright stalks from early to midsummer. Zones 4 to 9.

A. gigas
P. 44

a. JEE-gas. Clump-forming 3- to 6-foot-tall biennial or short-lived perennial that spreads to 4 feet and bears 5-inch-wide umbels of tiny purple flowers on purplish red stems in late summer and early fall. Zones 4 to 9.

❦ Antennaria

an-ten-NAR-ee-uh. Aster family, Asteraceae.

Commonly known as pussytoes, *Antennaria* species produce dense, ground-hugging mats of woolly silvery-gray leaves that are evergreen or semievergreen. Their flower heads, which are borne on short stalks above the foliage, are not particularly showy: they consist of small disk florets, which produce the seeds, surrounded by rows of papery bracts. Unlike many aster family plants, they lack petal-like ray florets. Gardeners value pussytoes for their tough constitution: they are valuable carpeting plants for hot, dry sites, between paving stones, and in the rock garden.

HOW TO GROW
Plant pussytoes in full sun to very light shade and average, well-drained soil. They tolerate poor soil and hot or dry locations, and also stand some foot traffic. Propagate by dividing the plants in spring or by seeds.

A. dioica   P. 44
a. die-OH-ih-kuh. Pussytoes. Mat-forming 2- to 4-inch-tall species spreading to about 1 to 1½ feet. Bears gray-green spoon-shaped leaves and fluffy clusters of white or pale pink flowers in early summer. 'Rosea' bears rose pink flowers. Spread: 6 to 8 inches. Zones 4 to 8.

❦ Anthemis

an-THE-mus. Aster family, Asteraceae.

Commonly called dog fennels — or, more poetically, golden marguerites — members of this genus bear cheerful daisylike flowers and aromatic stems and leaves. *Anthemis* contains about 100 species of mound-forming annuals and shrubby perennials that hail from the Mediterranean, northern Africa, and the Middle East. Although hardy, the two most popular species are short-lived perennials often grown as annuals.

HOW TO GROW
Full sun and very well drained poor to average soil are fine for golden marguerites, which also thrive in sandy or gravelly soil. The plants tolerate dry soil and are best in neutral to slightly alkaline conditions. Cut plants back hard after their first flush of bloom. Plants may need staking.

Propagate by dividing clumps in spring, taking cuttings from shoots at the base of the plants in spring or late summer, or by seeds, although named cultivars do not come true.

A. punctata ssp. *cupania*

a. punk-TAH-tuh. Formerly *A. cupania*. Low-growing 1-foot-tall species spreading to about 3 feet. Bears handsome, fernlike, silver-gray leaves and 2½-inch-wide white daisy flowers in early summer. Zones 6 to 9.

A. sancti-johannis

P. 45

a. SANK-tee joe-HAN-iss. Golden Marguerite. Clump-forming 2- to 3-foot-tall species spreading to 2 feet. Bears finely cut, fernlike, gray-green leaves and 1¼- to 2-inch-wide buttonlike orange daisies with rounded centers and short petals all summer. Zones 4 to 9.

A. tinctoria

P. 45

a. tink-TOR-ee-uh. Golden Marguerite. Clump-forming 1½- to 2½-foot-tall species spreading from 2 to 3 feet. Bears pinnate leaves that are gray-hairy underneath and yellow to cream-colored 1- to 1½-inch-wide daisy flowers from summer to fall. Many cultivars are available, including 'Sauce Hollandaise', with pale cream flowers, and 'Moonlight', with light yellow blooms. Zones 3 to 7.

❦ *Anthriscus*

an-THRIS-kus. Carrot family, Apiaceae.

The best-known member of this genus of 12 species is the annual herb chervil *(Anthriscus cerefolium)*. Several biennials and perennials belong here as well. All bear lacy clusters of tiny white flowers and deeply cut pinnate (featherlike) leaves.

HOW TO GROW
Select a site in full sun or partial shade with average to rich well-drained soil. Plants can self-sow with abandon, so deadhead as the flowers fade if you don't want seedlings. Propagate by seeds.

A. sylvestris

P. 46

a. syl-VES-tris. Cow Parsley. Short-lived perennial or biennial forming 2- to 3-foot-wide clumps of lacy, pinnate leaves. Plants are topped by rounded, lacy clusters of tiny white flowers in late spring and early summer and can reach 2½ to 3 feet in bloom. 'Ravenswing' features handsome purple-black leaves. Zones 6 to 10.

🌿 *Aquilegia*

ack-will-EE-juh. Buttercup family, Ranunculaceae.

Commonly known as columbines, *Aquilegia* species are perennials grown for their graceful flowers borne on wiry stems above mounds of attractive, lacy foliage. Both botanical and common names refer to the uniquely shaped flowers. *Aquilegia* is from the Latin *aquila,* eagle, a refence to the spurred petals, while the name columbine is from the Latin *columbinus,* meaning like a dove, or *columba,* dove. When looked at from above, the petals of short-spurred types resemble doves with their tails in the air, hence two lesser-known common names, doves-in-a-ring and doves-round-a-dish. Approximately 70 species belong here, all perennials producing mounds of compound, lobed leaves that range from rich green to silver-, gray-, or blue-green. The blooms, borne singly or in loose racemes, come in a wide range of colors, including true blue and violet as well as white, yellow, maroon, pink, lavender, and red. Many selections have bicolor flowers, and there are double-flowered columbines as well. While 1½ to 3 feet is the average height, taller columbines can reach 4 feet, and dwarf selections as small as 6 inches also are available.

HOW TO GROW

Columbines thrive in full sun or partial shade with rich, average to light, evenly moist, well-drained soil. Plants in full sun bloom more and are more compact than those grown in shade, but in hot climates dappled shade or afternoon shade provides essential heat protection. Plants form clumps that are about 1 foot in width. Columbines grow from long carrotlike taproots that make them drought tolerant but difficult to move once established. Plants self-sow, and self-sown seedlings are easy to transplant when they are small. Open-pollinated flowers may not resemble their parents, since columbines cross-pollinate with one another; pull up unattractive seedlings as they appear. Pinching off spent flowers helps prolong bloom and also reduces self-sowing. If plants have been plagued by leafminers or other pests, cut the foliage back in midsummer, and new leaves will appear once cool temperatures arrive. In general, columbines are not long-lived plants — 2 to 4 years is about average, although they can last considerably longer in good conditions. Start new ones from seeds (columbine cultivars do come true from purchased seed because pollination is controlled) or buy new plants every few years.

A. alpina

a. al-PIE-nuh. Alpine Columbine. Formerly *A. montana.* A 1- to 2-foot-tall, blue-green-leaved species with two- to three-flowered clusters of nodding, 1-inch-long blue-violet blooms from late spring through midsummer. Zones 3 to 8.

A. caerulea

P. 46

a. see-RUE-lee-uh. Rocky Mountain Columbine. Native North American wildflower ranging from 1½ to 3 feet tall. Bears green leaves and 2-inch-long, blue-and-white flowers from late spring to midsummer. Zones 3 to 8.

A. canadensis

P. 47

a. can-ah-DEN-sis. Wild Columbine. A 1- to 3-foot-tall native North American species producing mounds of green leaves topped by racemes of nodding, red-and-yellow, ½- to ¾-inch-long flowers from midspring to midsummer. The cultivar 'Corbett' bears pale yellow flowers on 1- to 2-foot plants. Zones 3 to 8.

A. chrysantha

P. 47

a. crih-SAN-tha. Golden Columbine, Yellow Columbine. A 3- to 4-foot-tall species native to the southwestern United States and northern Mexico. Bears pale to golden yellow 1½- to 3-inch-long flowers from late spring to late summer. Plants tolerate heat as well as shade. 'Texas Gold' is an especially heat-tolerant selection. Zones 3 to 9.

A. flabellata

P. 48

a. flah-bel-LAY-tuh. Fan Columbine. Compact, mounding, 1½-foot-tall species with fan-shaped blue-green leaves and long-spurred lilac- to purple-blue flowers with white tips in early summer. *A. flabellata* f. *pumila,* also listed as *A. flabellata* var. *nana,* reaches 6 to 8 inches in height. *A. flabellata* f. *pumila* 'Alba', also listed as *A. flabellata* 'Nana Alba', bears white flowers on 6- to 8-inch plants. Zones 3 to 9.

A. hybrids

P. 48

Of the wide variety of hybrids available, the long-spurred types are most popular. These bear flowers up to 3 inches wide and 4 inches long from late spring to midsummer and come in mixes of solid colors and bicolors; some are sold in separate colors. Most hybrids range from 2 to 2½ feet tall, but there also are dwarf types ranging from 15 inches to as little as 4 inches. There are also double-flowered, sometimes called carnation-flowered, hybrids. Standard-size hybrids include large-flowered McKana Hybrids in a range of colors. Song Bird Series plants, also called Dynasty Series, are 2 to 3 feet tall and come in a range of vivid colors; individual color selections in this series have names such as 'Dove', 'Blue Jay', and 'Cardinal'. Musik Series plants also come in a range of colors. Dwarf Fantasy Series plants are 4 inches tall. Zones 3 to 9.

A. longissima
a. lon-JISS-ih-muh. Long-spurred Columbine. Short-lived southwestern native species reaching 2 to 3 feet. Bears showy yellow flowers with 6-inch-long spurs in early summer. 'Maxistar' bears clear yellow flowers. Zones 4 to 9.

A. vulgaris   P. 49
a. vul-GAIR-iss. European Columbine. A 1½- to 3-foot-tall species with short-spurred violet-blue flowers in late spring and early summer. 'Nivea' is white flowered with gray-green leaves. 'Nora Barlow' bears double flowers. Zones 3 to 8.

❦ Arabis

AIR-ah-biss. Cabbage family, Brassicaceae.

Commonly known as rock cresses, *Arabis* species are annuals and perennials that range from erect to mat- or cushion-forming. About 120 species belong to the genus. All bear rosettes of basal leaves — perennial species are evergreen — topped in spring and early summer by clusters of tiny four-petaled flowers in shades of pink, purple, and white.

HOW TO GROW
Grow rock cresses in full sun or light shade and average, well-drained soil. They tolerate heat and drought as well as poor, dry soil. Plants do best in areas with cool summers and low humidity; give them a spot with afternoon shade in areas with warm summers. Shear plants after they flower to keep them neat looking. Divide plants every 2 to 4 years in spring after flowering to keep them vigorous. Propagate by cuttings in spring, division, or seeds.

A. blepharophylla

a. blay-fair-oh-FILL-uh. Fringed Rock Cress. A 4- to 8-inch-tall species with 1-foot-wide mounds of evergreen leaves and clusters of ½-inch-wide, fragrant, rosy purple flowers in late spring and early summer. 'Spring Charm' ('Frühlingszauber') bears rose-pink flowers. Zones 5 to 8.

A. caucasica

P. 49

a. caw-CASS-ih-kuh. Wall Rock Cress. Vigorous 6- to 10-inch-tall species that spreads to 2 feet or more. Bears gray-green leaves and racemes of fragrant ½-inch-wide white flowers in spring. Zones 4 to 8.

A. procurrens

a. pro-CUR-rens. Mat-forming 2- to 3-inch-tall species with glossy evergreen or semievergreen leaves and clusters of white ½-inch-wide flowers from spring to early summer. 'Variegata', also listed as *A. ferdinandi-coburgi* 'Variegata', bears attractive leaves edged with white. Zones 4 to 7.

❦ Armeria

are-MEER-ee-uh. Plumbago family, Plumbaginaceae.

Dense rosettes of linear or strap-shaped leaves topped by round clusters of tiny flowers characterize the 80 or so species of *Armeria*. Commonly known as sea pinks, thrifts, or simply armerias, they are low-growing evergreen perennials or subshrubs that form attractive mounds or tufts of basal foliage. The globular flower heads come in shades from pink to magenta-purple, purplish red, and white. They are carried above the foliage on thin, leafless, erect stems.

HOW TO GROW

Give armerias a spot in full sun with poor to average soil that is well drained and not too rich. Sandy soil is ideal. These perennials thrive by the ocean and prefer areas with cool summers: in areas with hot summers, give them shade during the afternoon. Propagate by division in early spring, by taking cuttings from shoots that appear at the base of the plants in summer, or by seeds.

A. juniperifolia

a. jew-nip-er-ih-FOE-lee-uh. Formerly *A. caespitosa*. Compact 2- to 3-inch-tall species forming 6-inch-wide mounds of gray-green ¾-inch-long leaves. In late spring and early summer, bears purplish pink ½-inch-wide flower clusters that are held about ¾ to 1 inch above the foliage. 'Alba' bears white flowers. 'Bevan's Variety' bears nearly stemless pink flowers on 2-inch-tall plants. Zones 4 to 8.

A. maritima   P. 50

a. mah-RIT-ih-muh. Sea Pink, Common Thrift. A variable species with rosettes of 1½- to 5-inch-long leaves that form 1-foot-wide mounds. Bears 1-inch-wide flower clusters in early summer in shades from pink to reddish purple or white on erect 6- to 8-inch-tall stems. 'Alba' bears white flowers. 'Dusseldorf Pride' bears deep rose pink flowers. 'Vindictive' bears rosy red blooms. 'Rubrifolia' has red-purple foliage and rosy pink flowers. All are hardy in Zones 3 to 8. 'Bees Ruby' produces hot pink 1¼- to 1½-inch-wide flowers on 12-inch-tall stems and is hardy to Zone 6.

❦ Artemisia

are-teh-MEE-see-uh. Aster family, Asteraceae.

Grown for their foliage rather than their flowers, artemisias are perennials, annuals, or shrubs usually native to dry or arid habitats in the Northern Hemisphere. About 300 species belong to the genus, and plants may be evergreen or deciduous. Most have aromatic foliage and many feature silver or gray-green leaves that may be smooth edged, toothed, or deeply cut and feathery. Artemisias produce tiny insignificant flower heads, usually carried in panicles or racemes but sometimes singly. The flower heads, which usually appear from mid- to late summer, are yellowish or grayish and lack ray florets. In addition to a variety of ornamental perennials, the genus also includes herbs, most notably tarragon (Artemisia dracunculus). The genus also includes some vigorous weeds, including mugwort (A. vulgaris).

HOW TO GROW

A site in full sun with average, well-drained soil will satisfy most artemisias. A. lactiflora is an exception: give it full sun and well-drained soil that remains evenly moist. Artemisias tolerate poor, dry conditions, sandy soils, and seaside conditions — most are quite drought tolerant — but heavy, wet soils are usually fatal. A. stelleriana is especially tolerant of saline soil and seaside conditions. Some species do not tolerate heat and humidity. Cut plants back hard in late fall or early spring annually, and cut species that tend to flop over during the growing season back hard again in early to midsummer to keep them compact and erect. Divide fast-spreading species, especially *A. lactiflora* and *A. ludoviciana* and their cultivars, every 2 to 3 years to keep them in check. Propagate by division in spring or fall, by stem or heel cuttings taken in early summer, or by mallet cuttings in late summer.

A. abrotanum

A. ah-broe-TAY-num. Southernwood, Lad's Love. Shrubby 3- to 4-foot-tall species that spreads as far to form feathery textured mounds of thread-like, aromatic, pale green to gray-green leaves. Zones 5 to 8.

A. absinthium

P. 50

a. ab-SIN-thee-um. Wormwood. Vigorous, shrubby, 2- to 3-foot-tall perennial that spreads as far. Forms mounds of aromatic, deeply divided, silky-hairy leaves. 'Lambrook Silver' produces silver-gray foliage on 2½-foot plants. Zones 3 to 9.

A. lactiflora

a. lack-tih-FLOR-uh. White Sage, White Mugwort. A 4- to 6-foot-tall species that spreads to about 4 feet. Bears deeply cut, dark green leaves and handsome creamy white panicles of flowers from late summer to fall that add airy texture to plantings. Zones 4 to 9.

A. ludoviciana

P. 51

a. loo-doe-vish-ee-AH-nuh. White Sage, Western Mugwort. Fast-spreading 2- to 4-foot-tall species that forms 2-foot-wide clumps of lance-shaped, silver-white, felted leaves that become greener with age. Plants spread vigorously by rhizomes and can be quite invasive if not divided regularly. 'Silver King' has white leaves. 'Silver Queen', another fast spreader, has larger leaves than the species and reaches about 2½ feet in height. 'Valerie Finnis' is a 1½-foot-tall selection that is not invasive, but is less tolerant of summer heat and rain than the species. Zones 3 to 9.

A. 'Powis Castle'

P. 51

Shrubby 2- to 3-foot perennial forming handsome, billowing 2- to 3-foot-wide clumps of feathery, aromatic, silver-gray foliage. Zones 5 to 8.

A. schmidtiana

P. 52

a. shmid-ee-AH-nuh. Silvermound Artemisia. Mound-forming 1- to 2-foot-tall perennial with 1½-foot-wide clumps of feathery, finely cut silver-gray leaves. The clumps often flop open in the center in areas with hot, humid summers. 'Nana' (also sold as 'Silver Mound'), a compact selection, is more common in cultivation than the species. Zones 3 to 7.

A. stelleriana

a. steh-LAIR-ee-AH-nah. Beach Wormwood, Old Woman, Perennial Dusty Miller. Compact 6- to 12-inch-tall species that spreads by rhizomes to about 2½ feet. Bears deeply lobed, felted white leaves. Zones 3 to 8.

❦ Aruncus

ah-RUN-kus. Rose Family, Rosaceae.

Aruncus species, or goat's beards, as they are also called, are handsome perennials grown for their clusters of creamy white flowers. While the individual flowers are tiny, they are borne abundantly in branched, airy clusters. Two or three species belong to the genus, all generally bearing male and female flowers on separate plants. (Botanically speaking, *Aruncus* species actually are polygamo-dioecious, rather than dioecious, since plants produce some perfect, or bisexual, flowers as well.) The flowers are carried above attractive mounds of leaves cut in a pinnate, or featherlike, fashion.

HOW TO GROW

Give goat's beards a site with partial or dappled shade and rich, evenly moist soil. In areas with cool summers they tolerate full sun provided they receive constant soil moisture. In most cases, a site that receives shade during the hottest part of the day is best, and constant soil moisture is essential for success in the South. Plants thrive along streams and ponds: in this case, plant them with the crown a foot or so above the water table. Leaves that develop crispy brown edges indicate the soil is too dry. Plants spread by rhizomes to form large handsome clumps. To propagate, divide clumps in spring or early fall, although established plants have deep, woody roots and are quite difficult to dig. Or sow seeds.

A. aethusifolius   P. 52

a. ee-thew-sih-FOE-lee-us. Dwarf Goat's Beard. Clump-forming 8- to 12-inch-tall species forming 1- to 1½-foot-wide mounds topped by creamy white flowers from early to midsummer. Zones 4 to 8.

A. dioicus

P. 53

a. die-OH-ee-kus. Goat's Beard. Shrub-sized native North American species ranging from 3 to 6 feet in height and spreading to 4 feet. Bears plumy 1- to 2-foot-long clusters of creamy white flowers from early to midsummer. Zones 3 to 7.

❦ *Arundo*

ah-RUN-doe. Grass family, Poaceae.

Arundo contains two or three species of grasses, one of which is grown for its distinctive, bamboolike foliage and giant stature. The plants have jointed, reedlike stems with long broadly linear leaves. They are evergreen in warm climates. Where seasons are long enough, the plants produce fluffy panicles of flowers in fall.

HOW TO GROW

Select a site in full sun and average, moist but well-drained soil. Plants tolerate heat and seaside conditions. In warm climates, they can become very invasive (especially in moist soil) and difficult to control, but they are rarely a problem at the northern limits of their hardiness. Cut the plants to the ground in late winter or very early spring, even in areas where they are evergreen. Divide as necessary to keep the clumps a manageable size. Propagate in spring either by division or by cuttings taken from stems at the base of the plant.

A. donax

P. 53

a. DOE-nax. Giant Reed. Enormous 10- to 25-foot-tall ornamental grass that forms clumps of thick reedlike stems and spreads by rhizomes to form clumps that exceed 5 feet. *A. donax* var. *versicolor*, commonly sold as 'Variegata', is 6 to 12 feet tall and has white-striped leaves that usually fade to green as they age. Zones 6 to 10.

❦ *Asarum*

ah-SAIR-um. Birthwort family, Aristolochiaceae.

Grown for their handsome, often glossy, evergreen or deciduous leaves, *Asarum* species are rhizomatous perennials prized by shade gardeners. The genus contains some 70 species, all low-growing plants with broadly heart- to kidney-shaped leaves. Asarums also are called wild gingers, a name that refers to the fact that when cut or crushed the fleshy rhizomes smell something like commercial ginger, a product derived from unrelated *Zingiber officinalis*. The small, somewhat fleshy flowers are jug- or bottle-shaped. For gardeners, these are plants usually grown for foliage rather than flowers: not only are the blooms brownish green, brownish purple, or red-brown in color, they also are borne under the leaves, next to the soil.

HOW TO GROW

Give asarums a site in partial to full shade with rich, evenly moist soil. Most species are best in acid soil, although *A. canadense* tolerates alkaline conditions. *A. canadense* and *A. europaeum* are especially easy to grow and will form large dense mounds. Clumps thrive for years without requiring division. For propagation, divide clumps in spring or early fall, or take cuttings of the rhizomes in spring (make cuttings 1 to 1½ inches long with at least one pair of leaves), or sow seeds. Plants self-sow.

A. canadense

a. can-ah-DEN-see. Canada Wild Ginger. Deciduous 6- to 12-inch-tall North American native wildflower that spreads to form broad drifts with time. Bears 5- to- 6-inch-wide leaves and brown-purple ¾-inch flowers in spring. Zones 3 to 8.

A. europaeum P. 54

a. your-oh-PEE-um. European Wild Ginger. Evergreen 6- to 8-inch-tall species forming 1-foot-wide mounds of glossy 2- to 3-inch-wide leaves. Bears insignificant red-brown flowers in late spring. Zones 4 to 8.

A. shuttleworthii P. 54

A. shut-ul-WORTH-ee-eye. Mottled Wild Ginger. North American native wildflower reaching 3 to 9 inches tall and spreading to 1 foot. Bears dark green 2- to 4-inch-long evergreen leaves that are often mottled with silver, and purple-brown flowers in early summer. 'Callaway' is a vigorous selection with very mottled leaves. Zones 5 to 9.

❦ *Asclepias*

as-KLEE-pee-uhs. Milkweed family, Asclepiadaceae.

Tough and easy to grow, *Asclepias* species are perennials, subshrubs, and shrubs native to North, Central, and South America as well as South Africa. There are about 110 species in the genus, most commonly called milkweeds, a name derived from the fact that most species have milky sap in their stems and leaves. Butterfly weed *(A. tuberosa)*, the best-known garden perennial that belongs here, lacks obvious milky sap, however. It is an important food source for monarch butterfly larvae (caterpillars), and milkweed flowers of all species are popular with adult monarchs, other species of butterflies, and bees. Milkweeds bear lance-shaped leaves and rounded clusters of small flowers with reflexed petals and five hoodlike lobes. The flowers are followed by seedpods filled with flat seeds, each attached to a tuft of silky hair. The pods open when ripe, allowing the silky parachutes to carry the seeds far and wide.

HOW TO GROW

All *Asclepias* species thrive in full sun, and most need average, well-drained soil. *A. tuberosa* thrives in poor, dry, even sandy or gravelly soil, while *A. incarnata* prefers rich, evenly moist to wet conditions, although it will grow in well-drained soils. All have deep, fleshy, brittle taproots, which make them quite drought tolerant once established but very difficult to dig successfully. Select a permanent spot when planting. Propagate by cuttings taken from shoots at the base of the plant in late spring or early summer, by root cuttings taken in fall, or by seeds.

A. incarnata   P. 55

a. in-car-NAH-tuh. Swamp Milkweed. Rhizomatous 3- to 5-foot-tall native North American species that spreads slowly to form 2-foot-wide clumps. Bears flat-topped 2- to 4-inch-wide clusters of pale to deep rose pink flowers in early midsummer. 'Ice Ballet' has white flowers. Zones 3 to 8.

A. tuberosa   P. 55

a. too-ber-OH-suh. Butterfly Weed. Shrubby 2- to 3-foot-tall native North American wildflower forming 2-foot-wide clumps. Bears rounded clusters of bright orange or orange-red flowers in midsummer. 'Gay Butterflies' has orange, yellow, and red flowers. Zones 3 to 9.

᭡ *Aster*

AS-ter. Aster family, Asteraceae.

The colorful blooms of asters are a familiar sight in fall, but this large genus contains a range of perennials that can provide a parade of daisy-like flowers beginning in early summer. Some 250 species of annuals, biennials, perennials, and subshrubs belong here, many native to North America. The individual blooms are starry — *aster* is the Latin word for star — and like daisies they consist of ray florets, commonly called petals, surrounding dense buttonlike centers of disk florets, which are generally yellow. Flowers usually range from 1 to 2 inches wide and may be single, semidouble, or double. They come in shades of purple, violet, lavender, blue, pink, ruby red, and white. A few species bear solitary flowers (one per stem), but most produce their blooms in loose, showy clusters. Leaves generally are lance shaped. Depending on the species or cultivar, the plants range from under a foot in height to 8 feet or more. Asters grow from creeping rhizomes and form spreading clumps.

HOW TO GROW

Most asters thrive in full sun and rich, well-drained, evenly moist soil. However, there are species suitable for other sites. *A. cordifolius, A. divaricatus,* and *A. macrophyllus* all grow in partial shade, while *A. ericoides* and *A. lateriflorus* thrive in full sun with very poor soil. *A. alpinus* is best in areas with cool summers. For all species, a site with good air circulation is best, since asters are subject to powdery mildew. Give plants plenty of room to ensure good air circulation; as a general rule, space plants at about half their height. Feed plants in spring with a topdressing of compost, well-rotted manure, or a balanced organic fertilizer. Mulch New England and New York asters to help hold moisture in the soil. To keep plants compact and encourage branching, in spring and again in early summer pinch out the stem tips or cut plants back by one-third to one-half with hedge shears. Do not pinch fall-blooming asters after June 15 from about Zone 6 north, or you may remove the flower buds. In the South, asters can be pinched as late as July 1. Pinch *A. × frikartii* only once in spring, and do not pinch *A. alpinus*. Stake taller-growing species in spring or very early summer. Remove flowers after they fade to curtail self-sowing: hybrid asters do not come true from seeds, and seedlings will compete with them. (You may decide to leave self-sown seedlings of species asters, especially in a wild garden.) Most asters need to be divided every 2 to 3 years to keep them vigorous. Propagate by division in spring or from cuttings taken in spring or early summer. Species can be started from seeds.

A. alpinus

P. 56

a. al-PIE-nus. Alpine Aster. A 6- to 12-inch-tall species, spreading to 1½ feet. Bears solitary flower heads from early to midsummer in violet purple to lavender, pink, and white. Zones 2 to 7.

A. amellus

a. ah-MELL-us. Italian Aster. A 1- to 2-foot-tall species, spreading to 1½ feet. Bears loose clusters of 1¼- to 2-inch-wide flower heads in shades from violet, violet-blue, and lilac to pink from late summer to frost. Thrives in alkaline soil. Cultivars include 'Sonia', pink; 'Nocturne', lilac; and 'Violet Queen' ('Veilchenkönigin'), violet. Zones 5 to 8.

A. carolinianus

a. kare-oh-lin-ee-AH-nus. Climbing Aster. Native North American subshrub with long arching branches that reach 5 to 10 feet or more and can be tied to trellises or trained through shrubs. Bears an abundance of solitary 1-inch-wide pale pink or purple flower heads in fall. In the North, it can be overwintered as a tender perennial by cuttings taken in late summer. Zones 6 to 9.

A. cordifolius

a. core-dih-FOE-lee-us. Blue Wood Aster, Heart-leaved Aster. Native North American species forming 2- to 5-foot-tall, 2-foot-wide clumps. Bears clusters of ¾-inch-wide pale lavender or white flower heads from late summer to fall. Zones 4 to 8.

A. divaricatus

a. dih-vair-ih-KAH-tus. White Wood Aster. Native North American species that reaches 1 to 2 feet and spreads as far. Produces loose clusters of starry white ¾-inch-wide flower heads in abundance from midsummer through fall. Zones 4 to 8.

A. ericoides

a. air-ih-KOY-deez. Heath Aster. Native North American species ranging from 1 to 3 feet tall and spreading to 2 feet. Bears needlelike leaves and loose clusters of white ¾-inch-wide flower heads in abundance from late summer to fall. Zones 3 to 8.

A. × frikartii P. 56

a. × frih-CAR-tee-eye. Frikart's Aster. A 2- to 3-foot-tall hybrid bearing loose sprays of lavender-blue 2- to 3-inch-wide flowers from midsummer through fall on 1½-foot-wide plants. 'Monch' and 'Wonder of Staffa', both lavender-blue, are the most popular cultivars. Zones 5 to 8.

A. lateriflorus P. 57

a. lah-ter-ih-FLOR-us. Calico Aster, Starved Aster. North American native reaching 2 to 4 feet and spreading from 2 to 3 feet. Bears clouds of starry ½-inch-wide flower heads in white to pale lavender from midsummmer to fall. Zones 3 to 8.

A. macrophyllus

a. mack-row-FILL-us. Large-leaved Aster, Bigleaf Aster. Native North American aster reaching 1 to 2½ feet in height and spreading as far. Bears flat clusters of 1-inch-wide white to pale lavender flower heads from late summer to fall. Zones 4 to 8.

A. novae-angliae P. 57

a. NO-vay ANG-lee-eye. New England Aster, Michaelmas Daisy. Much-hybridized native North American species that grows to 1½ feet and spreads from 2 to 4 feet. Bears showy clusters of violet, purple, lavender, rose-red, pink, or white flowers in fall. Individual flower heads are 1½ to 2 inches wide and leaves are lance shaped with lobes that clasp the hairy stem at the base. Cultivars include 'Alma Potschke' (rose pink), 'Hella Lacy' (royal purple), and 'Harrington's Pink' (light pink). 'Purple Dome' produces mounds of deep purple flowers on compact 1½-foot plants that do not need staking or pinching. Zones 3 to 8.

A. novae-belgii P. 58

a. NO-vay BELL-jee-eye. New York Aster, Michaelmas Daisy. Much-hybridized native North American species ranging from 1 to 4 feet and spreading from 2 to 3 feet. Bears showy clusters of lavender-blue, white, ruby red, pink, or purple flower heads in fall. Individual flower heads are 1 to 1½ inches wide and leaves are much narrower than those of A. novae-angliae. 'Fellowship' bears deep pink 3-inch blooms. 'Eventide' has semidouble purple blooms. Low-growing selections, including 14-inch lavender-blue 'Professor Anton Kippenburg' and 6- to 10-inch white-flowered 'Niobe', do not need staking. Zones 3 to 8.

A. tataricus
P. 58

a. tah-TAR-ih-kus. Tartarian Aster. Roubust, strong-stemmed 5- to 8-foot-tall species spreading to 3 feet or more. Bears large clusters of lavender-blue 1- to 1¼-inch-wide flower heads from mid- to late fall. 'Jindai' is a comparative dwarf, reaching only 4 to 5 feet. Zones 2 to 8.

❦ Astilbe

uh-STILL-bee. Saxifrage family, Saxifragaceae.

Astilbes are clump-forming, rhizomatous perennials that form 1- to 3-foot-tall mounds of handsome, fernlike foliage topped by feathery, plumelike flower clusters that rise several inches above the foliage in late spring and summer. Flowers come in white, shades of pink, ruby red to crimson, and rosy purple. The individual flowers are quite tiny but are borne in abundance in densely packed, branched panicles that may be roughly pyramidal in shape, weeping, or stiffly upright. About 12 species belong to the genus, all native to moist, generally shaded sites in eastern Asia and North America.

HOW TO GROW

Rich, constantly moist, well-drained soil is essential to success with astilbes. Partial shade is best — a site with sun in the morning and shade in the afternoon is ideal. In the North, where summers remain relatively cool, astilbes grow in full sun provided the soil remains moist. In the South, give them partial to full shade. Curled leaves with crispy brown edges signal that plants receive too little moisture and too much sun. Provided they are planted above the water line, astilbes are good choices for sites along streams and ponds. *A. chinensis* var. *davidii* and *A. chinensis* var. *taquetii* tolerate drier soil and more sun than most astilbes. Work plenty of compost or other organic matter into the soil at planting time and feed annually in spring by top-dressing with compost or a balanced organic fertilizer. If the woody crowns grow above the soil surface, either top-dress the plants with loose soil to cover them or divide and replant. Water regularly in dry weather, and mulch with chopped leaves or compost to hold in soil moisture. To keep plants vigorous or to propagate them, dig and divide them every 3 to 4 years in spring or early fall.

A. chinensis
P. 59

a. chi-NEN-sis. Chinese Astilbe. Vigorous species that reaches 2 feet tall and spreads as far. It bears pinkish white flowers in late summer. *A. chinensis* var. *pumila* is a dwarf form with foliage that reaches about 6 inches and erect 10- to 12-inch-tall purplish pink plumes in midsummer to early fall. In shade with abundant moisture plants reach 2 feet or more. *A. chinensis* var. *davidii* (formerly *A. davidii*) has purple-pink blooms, bronze-tinted leaves, and reaches 4 to 6 feet. *A. chinensis* var. *taquetii* (sometimes listed as *A. taquetii*) and its cultivars 'Superba' and 'Purple Lance' ('Purpurlanze') bear plumes in shades of red-purple from midsummer to fall on 4-foot-tall plants. Zones 4 to 8.

A. hybrids

PP. 59–60

Astilbes have been heavily hybridized (the species are seldom grown), and many cultivars are available. Hybrids range from 2 to 3 feet in height and spread to about 2 feet. Many feature showy red to bronze foliage in spring. Early to midseason cultivars bloom in late spring and early summer and include white-flowered 'Deutschland'; pink 'Europa', 'Rhineand', and 'Peach Blossom'; and crimson-rose 'Bremen'. Midseason bloomers include blood red 'Fanal', white 'Bridal Veil' and 'Snowdrift', and carmine-rose 'Federsee'. Late-season cultivars include scarlet 'Red Sentinel' and rose pink 'Cattleya'. All are cultivars of either *Astilbe* × *arendsii* or *A. japonica*. Zones 4 to 8, to Zone 3 with winter protection.

A. simplicifolia

a. sim-plih-sih-FOE-lee-uh. Star Astilbe. Dwarf 1- to 1½-foot-tall plants with glossy leaves and loose plumes of flowers in mid- to late summer. 'Sprite' bears pale pink flowers and bronzy foliage. Pale pink–flowered 'Gnom' reaches only about 6 inches. Zones 4 to 8.

A. thunbergii

a. thun-BER-jee-eye. Vigorous 3- to 4-foot-tall moisture-loving species that spreads to 3 feet. Its cultivar 'Ostrich Plume' ('Straussenfeder'), with coral pink flowers in mid- to late summer, is most often grown. Zones 4 to 9.

❦ *Astrantia*

ah-STRAN-tee-uh. Carrot family, Apiaceae.

Commonly known as masterworts, *Astrantia* species are clump-forming perennials that make attractive additions to the shade garden. About 10 species belong to the genus, all native to cool, alpine woods and meadows in Europe and Asia. At first glance, the buttonlike flowers do not seem to suggest a relationship to carrots or dill, two other well-known carrot family plants. However, close inspection reveals that each bloom consists of an umbel of small, tightly packed, five-petaled flowers. The umbels are surrounded by a showy ruff of papery, petal-like bracts. The flowers are borne on branched stems above loose mounds of leaves that are cut or lobed in a palmate, or fingerlike, fashion.

HOW TO GROW

Plant in partial or dappled shade and rich, evenly moist soil. Plants tolerate full sun provided the soil is very rich and remains evenly moist. Try them along ponds or streams, with the crowns planted above the water table, or in open, moist woodlands. They require cool night temperatures for best performance. Propagate by division in spring or by seeds. Plants self-sow.

A. major   P. 60

a. MAY-jor. Masterwort. Clump-forming 1- to 3-foot-tall perennial producing 1½-foot-wide mounds of attractive leaves with five to seven toothed lobes. The ¾- to 1¼-inch-wide umbels of flowers come in green, pink, or sometimes purplish red and have a ruff of green-veined white bracts beneath them. Blooms early to midsummer. 'Hadspen Blood' bears maroon bracts and flowers. 'Sunningdale Variegated' bears pink flowers and leaves edged in creamy yellow that fades to green. Zones 4 to 7.

❦ *Athyrium*

ah-THY-ree-um. Wood Fern family, Dryopteridaceae.

Athyrium species, commonly called lady ferns, are terrestrial, deciduous perennials with handsome fronds that are once-, twice-, or thrice-cut or divided in a pinnate (featherlike) fashion. The plants grow from rhizomes that either spread slowly to form compact, mounding clumps or grow erect to form crowns. There are 180 species in the genus, two of which are commonly grown in gardens.

HOW TO GROW

Select a site in partial to full shade with evenly moist, well-drained soil rich in organic matter. A spot with bright, indirect light or dappled shade under the high branches of oaks or other deep-rooted trees is ideal, as is one with morning sun and afternoon shade. Plants have somewhat brittle fronds that break easily, so keep them away from high-traffic or windy sites. Work plenty of organic matter such as compost or chopped leaves into the soil at planting time. Water deeply during dry weather. *A. filix-femina* has erect rhizomes that gradually grow too far out of the soil. Dig and divide the clumps every few years, and replant the divisions with the crowns at soil level to keep them vigorous. To propagate, divide the clumps in spring.

A. filix-femina   P. 61
a. FEE-lix FEM-in-uh. Lady Fern, European Lady Fern. Vigorous 2- to 3-foot-tall species that spreads as far and forms mounds of thrice-cut fronds that taper slightly at the base. Many forms of this fern are available, featuring branched, crested, or plumy fronds. Zones 4 to 8.

A. niponicum   P. 61
a. nih-PON-ih-kum. Japanese Painted Fern. Formerly *A. goeringianum*. Rhizomatous 1- to 1½-foot-tall Japanese native spreading vigorously to form drifts to 2 or more feet wide. Bears twice-cut fronds variously marked with silver or gray and maroon-purple midribs. *A. niponicum* var. *pictum* (also sold as 'Pictum') is more commonly sold than the species and has leaves splashed with burgundy and silver. Zones 4 to 9.

❦ *Aubrieta*

aw-BREE-sha. Cabbage family, Brassicaceae.

Commonly called rock cresses or simply aubrietas, *Aubrieta* species bear small clusters of four-petaled, cross-shaped flowers in spring. Blooms are carried atop dense mounds or mats of small, hairy, evergreen leaves that range from oval to oblong and may be toothed. About 12 species of perennials belong to the genus, but gardeners most often grow hybrids, collectively referred to as *A. × cultorum*.

HOW TO GROW
Give aubrietas full sun and average, well-drained soil. Neutral to alkaline pH is best, and plants grow well in sandy soil. Clayey soil that is poorly aerated and remains wet for long periods is fatal. Aubrietas do not tolerate heat well and are short-lived in the South, although a site with light shade during the afternoon can help them cope. Shear plants after the flowers fade to keep them compact. Especially in hot-summer areas,

propagate new plants every 2 to 3 years to keep them vigorous. Propagate by taking cuttings in spring after the flowers fade or by carefully dividing the clumps in spring or fall. Aubrietas are easy to grow from seeds, but most cultivated forms do not come true.

A. × cultorum

P. 62

a. × cul-TOR-um. Aubrieta, Rock Cress. Hybrids are sometimes listed as *A. deltoidea*, one of the parent species. These low-growing, mat-forming perennials reach 2 inches in height and spread to 2 feet or more. Hybrids bear single or double ½-inch-wide flowers in shades of pink, purple, mauve, violet purple, magenta, and red in spring. Variegated forms with leaves edged in white or yellow are available. Zones 4 to 7.

❧ *Aurinia*

aw-RIH-nee-uh. Cabbage family, Brassicaceae.

Clump-forming, evergreen biennials or perennials, *Aurinia* species are natives of rocky, mountainous areas from southern Europe east to Russia and Turkey. Plants produce low, tufted rosettes of hairy, lance- to spoon-shaped evergreen leaves. The clumps are topped in late spring and early summer by showy, rounded clusters of tiny four-petaled flowers in yellow or white. One of the seven species in the genus is commonly grown in gardens.

HOW TO GROW

Select a site in full sun with average soil that is well drained and not too rich. Cut the plants back hard after they flower to keep them neat looking and compact. To propagate, take cuttings in early summer of shoots that have not flowered or divide plants in spring. The plants are easy from seeds, but many cultivars do not come true.

A. saxatilis

P. 62

a. sax-ah-TILL-iss. Basket-of-gold, Cloth-of-gold, Gold Dust. Formerly *Alyssum saxatile*. Vigorous, mound-forming species with gray-green hairy leaves on 8-inch-tall plants that spread to 1 foot or more. Bears dense, rounded clusters of small brilliant yellow flowers. 'Citrina' bears lemon yellow flowers. Zones 4 to 8.

❦ Baptisia

bap-TEES-ee-uh. Pea family, Fabaceae.

Baptisias are long-lived shrub-sized perennials that bear erect, lupinelike racemes of pea-shaped flowers and have attractive, three-leaflet leaves. There are 20 or so species in the genus, all native to North America. Both the botanical name and the common name, false indigo, refer to the fact that members of the genus have been used as dye plants — *bapto* is from the Greek, to dye — most notably as a substitute for indigo. All are good cut flowers, and the inflated pods that follow the flowers are effective in dried arrangements.

HOW TO GROW

Select a site in full sun and give blue false indigo *(B. australis)* rich, evenly moist, well-drained soil. The other species are suitable for spots with poor, sandy, or dry soil. All are drought tolerant and difficult to move once established because of their deep taproots. Baptisias also grow in partial shade, but plants bloom less and are more likely to require staking. Select a site with care, since the plants establish slowly and thrive for years without being divided, eventually spreading via rhizomes to form broad 3- to 4-foot-wide clumps. Plants may need staking. Divide them in spring or fall if they outgrow their site or become overcrowded, or for propagation. Or sow fresh seeds.

B. alba
P. 63

b. AL-buh. White Wild Indigo. A 2- to 3-foot-tall species from the southeastern United States with racemes of white ¾-inch-wide flowers in early summer. 'Purple Smoke' is a pale blue–flowered hybrid with this species and *B. australis*. Prairie Wild Indigo *(B. lactea, formerly B. leucantha)*, another native species, is similar to *B. alba* but bears white flowers on 3- to 5-foot plants. Zones 4 to 9.

B. australis
P. 63

b. aw-STRAL-iss. Blue False Indigo, Plains False Indigo. Robust, showy, 3- to 5-foot-tall species with blue-green leaves and erect clusters of dark blue 1¼-inch-wide flowers in early summer followed by spikes of inflated blue-black seedpods. Zones 3 to 9.

B. bracteata

b. BRACK-tee-ah-tuh. Plains Wild Indigo, Buffalo Pea. Formerly *B. leucophaea*. Spreading 1- to 2-foot-tall plant with drooping clusters of creamy white to pale yellow 1- to 1½-inch-wide flowers. Blooms mid- to late spring. Zones 3 to 9.

B. pendula

b. PEN-due-luh. A 2- to 3½-foot-tall species with blue-gray leaves and erect racemes of 1-inch-wide white flowers in late spring to early summer followed by arching clusters of blue-black seedpods. Zones 5 to 9.

B. perfoliata

b. per-foe-lee-AH-tuh. Georgia Wild Indigo. Relatively low-growing 1- to 2-foot-tall species, native to the Southeast, that spreads to about 4 feet. Bears solitary ½-inch-wide yellow flowers in the leaf axils in early summer. The leaves are round and perfoliate, meaning the stem runs through the center of the leaf. Zones 5 to 9.

❦ Begonia

bih-GOAN-yah. Begonia family, Begoniaceae.

The vast *Begonia* clan contains some 1,300 species — annuals, perennials, shrubs, climbers, succulents, and epiphytes — native to tropical and subtropical regions worldwide. Begonias have fleshy leaves and stems and grow from rhizomes, fibrous roots, or tubers. Male and female flowers are borne separately, usually on the same plant. (Female flowers have a swollen winged seed capsule directly behind the petals; males don't.) The fleshy leaves vary in shape, size, and color. Rounded and wing-shaped foliage is common. One species — *B. grandis,* commonly known as hardy begonia — is an excellent hardy perennial for the shade garden.

HOW TO GROW

Plant hardy begonias in partial to full shade in rich, evenly moist, well-drained soil. To propagate, collect the tiny tubers that appear in the leaf axils in late summer or fall and plant them outdoors where they are to grow, or plant them indoors in late winter in pots. Either way, barely cover them with loose soil. Or start from seeds. Plants also self-sow.

B. grandis ssp. evansiana

P. 64

b. GRAN-diss ssp. e-van-see-AH-nuh. Hardy Begonia. Handsome 2- to 2½-foot perennial that grows from a small tuber and spreads to 1 foot. Bears arching clusters of pink flowers in summer above wing-shaped 4-inch-long leaves that are olive green above and usually red beneath. The variety *alba* bears white flowers. Zones 6 to 10; to Zone 5 with winter protection.

❦ *Belamcanda*

beh-lam-CAN-duh. Iris family, Iridaceae.

Commonly called blackberry lilies, *Belamcanda* species have irislike fans of sword-shaped leaves that grow from thick, fleshy rhizomes. The plants produce branched clusters of small flowers that have six petals, more properly called tepals. The flowers are followed by showy clusters of shiny blackberry-like fruit.

HOW TO GROW

Select a site in full sun with average to somewhat rich, well-drained, evenly moist soil. Plants grow well in sandy soil. Water during dry weather. Iris borers and the bacterial crown rot that they introduce to bearded irises can also attack blackberry lilies. Prevent them by removing dead or dying leaves and other litter that cover the rhizomes. This will also help control borers and rot on susceptible irises. Propagate by dividing the clumps in spring or early fall or by seeds. Plants self-sow.

B. chinensis   P. 64

b. chi-NEN-sis. Blackberry Lily, Leopard Flower. Produces clumps of erect, sword-shaped, 2-foot-tall leaves topped in summer by branched stems of flowers that reach 2 to 4 feet. Flowers are 1 to 2 inches wide and are bright orange or yellow with maroon spots. Beige seed capsules follow the flowers and open to reveal clusters of large shiny black seeds. Zones 5 to 9.

❦ *Bergenia*

ber-JIN-ee-uh. Saxifrage family, Saxifragaceae.

Grown more for their foliage than their flowers, bergenias produce clumps of leathery, rounded, cabbagelike leaves ranging from 8 to 12 inches long and up to 8 inches wide. The leaves turn from green to bronze-purple or reddish in fall. Most species are evergreen, but the leaves are damaged by harsh winter weather and often are not very ornamental by spring. Dense 5- to 6-inch-wide clusters of small funnel- to bell-shaped flowers appear above the leaves in spring in shades of pink, rose-red, or white. There are from six to eight species in the genus, all of which grow from thick, branching rhizomes that slowly spread into handsome clumps about 1 foot in width. Plants are about a foot tall when not in bloom, up to 1½ to 2 feet when they are.

HOW TO GROW

Give bergenias a site in partial to dappled shade with well-drained, humus-rich, evenly moist soil. Plants can take full sun in the North, provided the soil remains moist. In the South, shade is best, especially in the afternoon. A location sheltered from strong winds helps protect the foliage. Bergenias are ideal for growing along ponds or streams, but plant them above the water table so the soil is not constantly wet. Water during dry weather. Mulch in fall where snow cover is uncertain, and remove damaged foliage in spring. Clumps that have died out in the center need dividing. To propagate, divide plants in spring or fall or take cuttings (a piece of new rhizome that has a rosette of foliage attached) in spring. Or start from seeds, although hybrids will not come true.

B. ciliata

b. sill-ee-AH-tuh. Winter Bergenia. Deciduous species with oval or rounded 14-inch-long leaves and pink or white flowers in early spring. Zones 5 to 9.

B. cordifolia

P. 65

b. core-dih-FOE-lee-uh. Heart-leaved Bergenia. Clumping species with leathery, rounded to heart-shaped 10-inch-long leaves and rose pink to rose-red flowers in late winter and early spring. *B. crassifolia,* Siberian tea, is a similar species with slightly smaller leaves that are 4 to 7 inches long and have toothed margins. Zones 3 to 8.

B. hybrids

Hybrids, selected for either their spring flowers or fall foliage color, have been derived from heart-leaved bergenia, purple-leaved bergenia *(B. purpurascens),* and other species. 'Bressingham White' bears white flowers. 'Bressingham Ruby' has maroon-red flowers and leaves that turn maroon in fall. 'Sunningdale' has lilac-magenta flowers and copper red fall to winter foliage. 'Baby Doll' has 4-inch-long bronze-tinted leaves and pink flowers. Zones 3 to 8.

❦ *Boltonia*

bol-TOE-nee-uh. Aster family, Asteraceae.

Native North American wildflowers, boltonias are large shrub-sized perennials with lance-shaped leaves that bear clouds of tiny daisylike flowers with yellow centers in showy panicles that bloom from late summer to fall. About eight species belong to the genus, one of which is commonly grown in gardens.

HOW TO GROW

Give boltonias the same conditions you would asters: full sun and rich, well-drained, evenly moist soil. They also tolerate drought. The plants are stiff stemmed and generally stand without staking. Divide clumps every 2 to 3 years, and care for and propagate the plants as you would asters —see *Aster* on page 258.

B. asteroides   P. 65

b. as-ter-OY-deez. Boltonia. Robust, shrubby 4- to 6-foot-tall perennial with narrow blue-green leaves. Bears masses of ¾-inch-wide daisies in 4- to 6-inch-wide panicles from late summer to early fall. Flowers have yellow centers and white, pink, or pinkish purple ray florets. 'Snowbank', more often grown than the species, is a 5-foot plant with pure white ray florets. 'Pink Beauty' bears pale pink ray florets. Zones 3 to 9.

❦ *Brunnera*

BRUN-er-uh. Borage family, Boraginaceae.

Brunneras are rhizomatous perennials with dainty panicles of tiny purplish blue flowers in spring borne above mounds of handsome, rounded leaves. Of the three species in the genus, only one is commonly grown in gardens.

HOW TO GROW

Select a site in partial to full shade with rich, evenly moist soil. While plants tolerate drier conditions, moisture yields the largest, most eye-catching leaves. Plants go dormant during drought but reappear the following year. If the clumps die out in the center, dig and divide them. Propagate by division in spring, taking root cuttings in late winter or early spring, or by seeds. Variegated cultivars can be propagated only by division. Plants self-sow.

B. macrophylla

P. 66

b. mack-roe-FILL-uh. Siberian Bugloss. Formerly *Anchusa myosotidiflora*. A 1- to 1½-foot-tall species forming 1½- to 2-foot-wide mounds of 6- to 8-inch-long heart-shaped, coarsely hairy leaves. Bears clusters of ¼-inch-wide blue flowers in mid- to late spring. Variegated cultivars include 'Dawson's White', with creamy leaf edges, and 'Langtrees', with silver-spotted leaves. Zones 3 to 8.

❦ Calamagrostis

cal-ah-mah-GROSS-tiss. Grass family, Poaceae.

There are some 250 species of *Calamagrostis*, all perennial grasses with linear leaves that bear their tiny flowers in fluffy, airy-textured branched panicles. One species is popular as an ornamental.

HOW TO GROW

Give *Calamagrostis* full sun to light shade and average to rich soil that is well drained and evenly moist. Plants also tolerate a wide range of soils, including heavy clay. Cut the plants to the ground in late winter or very early spring, before new growth appears. Popular *C. × acutiflora* is a sterile hybrid and does not produce seeds, so plants do not self-sow. To propagate, divide the clumps in spring.

C × acutiflora

P. 66

c. × ah-cue-tih-FLOR-uh. Feather Reed Grass. Clump-forming hybrid producing arching mounds of 1½- to 3-foot-long leaves and spreading from 2 to 4 feet. Plants are deciduous to semievergreen in the North, evergreen in the South. Clumps are topped by erect 2- to 6-foot-tall panicles of fluffy, silvery brown to purplish flowers in mid- to late summer that fade to buff and last through winter. 'Karl Foerster' bears pinkish bronze panicles that fade to buff. 'Overdam', which has leaves striped with pale yellow or cream, is less vigorous and does not do well in hot, humid climates. Zones 5 to 9.

❦ Calamintha

cal-ah-MIN-tha. Mint family, Lamiaceae.

Aromatic leaves and clusters of small, tubular, two-lipped flowers characterize the members of this genus, which contains about eight species of perennials and subshrubs. Commonly called calamints, they bear small ovate to oblong leaves that usually are toothed. The flowers come in shades of lilac-blue as well as pink and white. The name *Calamintha* is from the Greek *kalos*, beautiful, and *minthe*, mint.

HOW TO GROW

Plant calamints in full sun or partial shade and average, moist, well-drained soil. They tolerate poorer soils. In areas with humid, wet summers, plant them in raised beds to ensure excellent drainage. Plants spread by rhizomes and form rounded mounds that spread from 1½ to 2½ feet. Cut them back after flowering to keep them neat. Cut plants back hard if they become woody. To propagate, divide plants in early spring, take cuttings in summer, or sow seeds.

C. grandiflora   P. 67

c. gran-dih-FLOR-uh. Large-flowered Calamint. Bushy 1½-foot-tall perennial bearing loose clusters of ½- to 1-inch-long pink flowers in summer. Zones 5 to 9.

C. nepeta

c. NEP-eh-tuh. Lesser Calamint. Lacy-textured 1- to 1½-foot-tall perennial with very aromatic, hairy leaves. Bears branched clusters of ¼-inch-long lilac to mauve flowers in summer. 'Alba' bears white flowers. Zones 5 to 9.

❧ *Caltha*

CAL-tha. Buttercup family, Ranunculaceae.

Commonly known as marsh marigolds, *Caltha* species are moisture-loving perennials bearing loose clusters of showy golden yellow or white flowers in spring. The usually cup-shaped flowers, which appear before the heart- or kidney-shaped leaves emerge, actually lack true petals. Instead they have petal-like sepals. *Caltha* contains about 10 species, all rhizomatous perennials.

HOW TO GROW

Select a site in full sun with rich, constantly moist to boggy soil. A spot in the wet soil at the edge of a stream or pond is ideal. *C. palustris* will grow in standing water up to a depth of about 9 inches, although plants do better in shallow water, boggy soil, or even containers in a water garden.

For propagation, divide plants in late summer or very early spring or sow seeds. Plants self-sow.

C. palustris

P. 67

c. pah-LUS-tris. Marsh Marigold. A 1- to 1½-foot-tall species native to North America, Europe, and Asia that spreads to 1 foot. Bears toothed, kidney-shaped leaves and clusters of waxy, golden yellow, 1½-inch-wide flowers on 1- to 1½-foot-tall stems in spring. 'Flore Pleno' bears double flowers on 10-inch plants. Zones 3 to 7.

☙ Campanula

cam-PAN-you-luh. Bellflower family, Campanulaceae.

Commonly known as bellflowers, *Campanula* species bring flowers in shades of blue, lavender, purple, and white to the garden. The genus contains about 300 species — annuals, biennials, and perennials — that vary in size and shape from mat-forming spreaders to stately, upright perennials for beds and borders. They have mounds or rosettes of entire or toothed leaves that are often heart shaped, as well as smaller leaves along the flowering stems. Flowers are borne in panicles, racemes, or clustered heads, although some species bear solitary blooms. Although *Campanula* means "little bell" in Latin, not all bellflowers have bell-shaped flowers. There are species with narrow, tubular blooms as well as ones with star-shaped or broader, cup- or saucer-shaped ones. The flowers are nodding, outward-facing, or upright.

HOW TO GROW

In general, give bellflowers full sun to partial shade and average to rich soil that is moist but well drained. Species requiring gritty, well-drained soil that remains cool and evenly moist are suitable for raised beds, rock walls, or rock gardens. These include *C. carpatica, C. cochleariifolia, C. garganica, C. portenschlagiana, C. poscharskyana,* and *C. rotundifolia. C. glomerata* tolerates wet soil. Most bellflowers do not tolerate heat well and grow best in areas where temperatures routinely dip below 70°F at night in summer. They languish and are usually short-lived where daytime temperatures rise above about 90°F. In the South — especially in Zone 8, but also in the hotter portions of Zone 7 — give them a site with partial shade during the hottest part of the day. Water deeply during dry spells, remove spent flowers regularly to extend bloom (deadheading or cutting back some bellflowers encourages repeat bloom), and mulch plants to keep the soil cool. Taller species need staking. Divide plants every 3 or 4 years to keep them vigorous. Fast-spreading species may need division every 2 or 3 years. Propagate by division in early spring or early fall, by cuttings taken in spring from shoots at the base of the plant before buds or flowers appear, or by seeds. Plants self-sow.

C. carpatica   P. 68

c. car-PAH-tih-kuh. Carpathian Harebell. Clump-forming 8- to 12-inch-tall perennial that spreads from 1 to 2 feet. Bears masses of upward-facing, cup-shaped flowers in blue, violet, and white over a long season from late spring through summer. Reblooms without deadheading. 'Blue Clips' and 'White Clips' are compact cultivars that come true from seeds. Zones 3 to 8.

C. cochleariifolia   P. 68

c. cock-lee-uh-ree-ih-FOE-lee-uh. Spiral Bellflower, Fairies' Thimbles. Creeping, mat-forming 3- to 6-inch-tall plants spreading to 1 foot. Produces nodding lilac-blue to white flowers in summer, borne one per stem. Zones 5 to 7.

C. garganica

c. gar-GAH-nih-kuh. Gargano Bellflower. A 5- to 6-inch-tall species that spreads quickly to 1 foot or more. Bears racemes of abundant ½-inch-wide starry lilac-blue flowers in summer. Zones 4 to 7.

C. glomerata   P. 69

c. glom-er-AH-tuh. Clustered Bellflower. Vigorous 1- to 2-foot-tall perennial that spreads by underground rhizomes to form broad clumps reaching 2 feet or more. Bears rounded clusters of ½- to 1½-inch-long flowers on erect stems from early to midsummer in shades of violet, lavender-blue, and white. 'Joan Elliott' bears abundant violet purple blooms. Violet purple–flowered 'Superba' is especially heat tolerant. 'Superba Alba' and 'Crown of Snow' ('Schneekrone') have white blooms. Zones 3 to 8.

C. lactiflora   P. 69

c. lack-tih-FLOR-uh. Milky Bellflower. Erect 3- to 5-foot-tall species forming 2-foot-wide clumps. Bears large branched clusters of white or lavender-blue 1-inch-long bell-shaped flowers from early to late summer. Established plants do not transplant well; best propagated by seeds sown where the plants are to grow. Self-sows. Zones 3 to 7.

C. latifolia
P. 70

c. lat-ih-FOE-lee-uh. Great Bellflower. Vigorous 4- to 5-foot-tall species that spreads rapidly by rhizomes to 3 feet or more. Bears narrow 2- to 3-inch-long bell-shaped flowers in summer in pale lilac-blue to violet or white. Blooms are carried in pairs or threes along leafy, erect, spikelike racemes. Zones 3 to 7.

C. latiloba

c. lat-ih-LOW-buh. Also listed as *C. persicifolia* ssp. *sessiliflora.* Clump-forming 3-foot-tall species producing 1½-foot-wide mounds. Bears racemes of cup-shaped 1¼- to 2-inch-wide lavender-blue flowers from mid- to late summer that are attached directly to the stalk. Zones 4 to 7.

C. persicifolia
P. 70

c. per-sis-ih-FOE-lee-uh. Peach-leaved Bellflower. A 1- to 3-foot-tall species forming 1- to 2-foot-wide clumps. Bears lance-shaped leaves topped by racemes of outward-pointing 2-inch-wide bell- to saucer-shaped blooms in pale blue, violet-blue, and white from early to midsummer. Zones 3 to 7.

C. portenschlagiana
P. 71

c. por-ten-schlag-ee-AH-nuh. Dalmatian Bellflower. Mound-forming 4- to 6-inch-tall perennial that spreads rapidly by underground stems to 2 feet or more. Bears evergreen to semievergreen leaves and panicles of bell-shaped 1-inch-wide violet purple flowers from late spring to early summer. A fairly heat-tolerant species. Zones 4 to 8.

C. poscharskyana
P. 71

c. pah-shar-skee-AH-nuh. Serbian Bellflower. Vigorous to invasive 6- to 12-inch-tall perennial that spreads by underground runners to form mounds 2 feet or more across. Bears loose, trailing panicles of starry 1-inch-wide pale blue flowers in early summer. 'Stella' has violet flowers and is somewhat less invasive. Zones 3 to 7.

C. rapunculoides

c. rah-pun-cue-LOY-deez. Creeping Bellflower. Extremely invasive 2- to 4-foot-tall species that spreads quickly and widely by underground stolons and by self-sowing. Bears one-sided racemes of 1-inch-long violet-purple bells in summer. Zones 3 to 7.

C. rotundifolia
P. 72

c. ro-tun-dih-FOE-lee-uh. Bluebell, Harebell. Dainty 5- to 12-inch-tall species that spreads as far and is native to North America as well as other parts of the Northern Hemisphere. Bears round basal leaves that die back early in the season and nodding, bell-shaped flowers on slender stems in summer in pale to violet-blue or white. Zones 2 to 7.

ꥲ *Cardamine*

car-dah-MIN-ee. Cabbage family, Brassicaceae.

Cardamines, or bittercresses, as they are also called, are annuals, biennials, or perennials bearing clusters of four-petaled flowers in white, pink, lilac, yellow, and red-violet. The leaves are simple, pinnate (featherlike), or palmate (handlike). The genus contains about 150 species, some persistent weeds, as well as a few worthy garden plants.

HOW TO GROW

Give cardamines partial to full shade and very rich, evenly moist soil. They are best in cool conditions; shade during the hottest part of the day is essential in warm-climate areas. Propagate by division in spring after they flower or sow seeds. *C. pratensis* also can be propagated by leaf cuttings in midsummer or by separating the bulblets or plantlets that appear in the leaf axils.

C. pratensis
P. 72

c. pray-TEN-sis. Lady's Smock, Cuckoo Flower. A 1 to 1½-foot-tall perennial that spreads by short rhizomes to form 1-foot-wide clumps. Bears rosettes of gray-green to dark green pinnate leaves and panicles of lilac, purple, or white ½- to 1-inch-wide flowers in late spring. 'Flore Pleno' produces double flowers on 8-inch-tall plants. Zones 5 to 8.

ꥲ *Carex*

CARE-ex. Sedge family, Cyperaceae.

Carex is a vast genus of grasslike perennials containing 1,500 or more species, most native to boggy areas and moist woodlands. Most are grown for their colorful, often handsomely variegated foliage, which can be deciduous or evergreen. Sedges differ from grasses in that they have solid, triangular stems, and the sheaths of the leaves, which are borne in threes, completely encircle the stems. The small green flowers also are quite different. Sedges bear separate male and female flowers that lack sepals and petals. The flowers usually are carried in dense heads or spikes arising from axils of leaves or bracts. Most plants are monoecious, meaning they bear both sexes of flowers on the same plant, sometimes even in different parts of the same inflorescence. Sedges are rhizomatous or clump forming.

HOW TO GROW

Give sedges full sun or partial shade and rich, moist, well-drained soil. *C. elata, C. muskingumensis,* and *C. siderosticha* also grow in wet soil. Cut deciduous sedges to the ground in spring. Evergreen and semievergreen species don't require an annual haircut: cut them back every few years as necessary in late spring to remove old or winterburned foliage. For propagation, divide the clumps from midspring to early summer.

C. conica

c. CON-ih-kuh. A 6-inch-tall sedge that forms dense 10- to 12-inch-wide clumps. Bears low, arching ⅛- to ⅜-inch-wide evergreen to semievergreen leaves. Variegated cultivars are most commonly grown, including white-edged 'Marginata' and 'Snowline'. Zones 5 to 9.

C. elata

P. 73

c. eh-LAY-tuh. Deciduous species forming dense 1½-foot-wide clumps of arching 1½- to 2-foot-long leaves that are ⅛ to ½ inch wide. 'Aurea', commonly called Bowles' golden sedge, has golden yellow leaves and is most often grown. This species requires shade and constant moisture in areas with warm summers, although yellow foliage is most pronounced in full sun. Zones 5 to 9.

C. morrowii

P. 73

c. more-ROE-ee-eye. Evergreen 16- to 20-inch-tall species forming 1-foot-wide clumps of stiff, shiny ½-inch-wide leaves. Variegated cultivars, including 'Gold Band', with leaves edged in creamy white, are most often grown. Zones 5 to 9.

C. muskingumensis

c. mus-king-um-EN-sis. Palm Branch Sedge. Deciduous native North American species with erect stems and leaves that spread out horizontally from the stems. Plants reach 2 feet, and clumps spread by rhizomes to 1½ feet. The species has green leaves, but variegated cultivars, including 'Oehme' and 'Silberstreif', also are available. Zones 4 to 9.

C. oshimensis

c. oh-she-MEN-sis. Deciduous, clumping 16-inch-tall species that forms dense 14-inch-wide mounds of glossy ⁵⁄₁₆-inch-wide leaves. The variegated cultivar 'Evergold' (sometimes listed as a cultivar of *C. hachijoensis*), which has leaves with dark green edges and creamy white centers, is most often grown. Zones 6 to 9.

C. siderosticha   P. 74

c. sid-er-oh-STY-kah. Deciduous species with strap-shaped 1¼-inch-wide leaves. Clumps reach 8 to 12 inches and slowly creep by rhizomes to form 1½-foot-wide clumps. 'Variegata', with white-margined leaves, is more often grown than the species. Zones 6 to 9.

❦ *Caryopteris*

care-ee-OP-ter-iss. Verbena family, Verbenaceae.

Six species belong to the genus *Caryopteris*, one of which is a small shrub usually treated as a perennial. *C. × clandonensis* is grown for its frothy, rounded flower clusters that appear in midsummer. The flowers are set against handsome gray-green, fine-textured foliage that emits a pleasant eucalyptus-like fragrance when rubbed.

HOW TO GROW

Select a site in full sun or very light shade with loose, well-drained soil that is not too rich in organic matter. Established plants tolerate dry conditions but benefit if watered during droughts. Bluebeard *(C. × clandonensis)* is root hardy to Zone 4, but the shoots are routinely killed to the ground in winter from Zone 6 north, and occasionally in Zone 7. In the North, cut plants to the ground in spring. From Zone 7 south, cut the stems back hard in spring — to within a few inches of the ground — to encourage dense growth and more flowers. After the main flush of bloom, trim off stem tips with spent flower clusters to encourage new shoots and flowers to form. For propagation, dig clumps in spring or fall or root softwood cuttings taken in late spring.

C. × clandonensis

P. 74

c. × clan-do-NEN-sis. Bluebeard, Blue-mist Shrub, Blue Spirea. Mounding shrub or woody-based perennial reaching 2 to 3 feet in height and spreading as far. Bears aromatic, broadly lance-shaped leaves and dense, many-flowered clusters of ½-inch-long flowers both in the leaf axils and on stem tips. Flowers appear from late summer and early fall. 'Blue Mist' bears pale blue flowers. 'Dark Knight' has silvery leaves and violet-blue flowers. 'Worcester Gold' has purple-blue flowers and golden foliage. Zones 4 to 9.

❦ Catanache

cat-ah-NAH-chee. Aster family, Asteraceae.

Commonly called Cupid's darts, *Catanache* species are annuals and perennials native to the Mediterranean region. About five species belong to the genus, one of which — *C. caerulea* — is an old-fashioned summer-blooming perennial. Cupid's darts produce tufts or mounds of grayish green linear to inversely lance-shaped leaves. Their solitary flower clusters have strap-shaped ray florets, or "petals," and usually come in lavender-blue as well as white or yellow. The blooms somewhat resemble cornflowers (*Centaurea* spp.) or chicory (*Chicorium intybus*) and have a collar of papery, silvery bracts beneath the flowers.

HOW TO GROW

A site in full sun or very light shade with average, well-drained soil suffices for these easy-to-please perennials. *C. caerulea* is best in sandy or dry soils and is short-lived in heavy, clayey conditions. Dividing clumps annually or every two years in early spring or fall keeps them very vigorous. Grow plants from seeds sown indoors in late winter for bloom the first year. Or sow outdoors where plants are to grow in midspring. In addition to division, propagate plants by root cuttings taken in winter.

C. caerulea

P. 75

c. see-ROO-lee-uh. Cupid's Dart. A 1½- to 2-foot-tall perennial that spreads to 1 foot and has grassy 1-foot-long leaves. Plants produce solitary 1- to 2-inch-wide lilac-blue flower heads atop wiry stems from midsummer to fall. 'Blue Giant' bears dark lilac-blue flowers on 2-foot plants. Zones 3 to 8.

❦ Centaurea

sen-TOR-ee-uh. Aster family, Asteraceae.

Better known as cornflowers, knapweeds, or just centaureas, *Centaurea* species bear rounded, thistlelike flower heads with conelike bases made up of scaly, fringed, toothed, or spiny bracts. Each flower head consists of a cluster of small, deeply lobed florets that give the blooms a ragged appearance. Blooms come in colors ranging from deep rich blue to mauve, hot pink, white, pale pink, and yellow. The leaves may be undivided and entire to cut or lobed in a featherlike (pinnate) fashion. About 450 species of annuals, perennials, and subshrubs belong to this genus, most native to dry soils in Europe and the Mediterranean. A few species are found in North America, Asia, and Australia.

HOW TO GROW

Plant cornflowers in full sun and average to rich, well-drained soil that is evenly moist. *C. montana* also grows in partial shade. Although cornflowers tolerate dry conditions, they perform best if watered during dry weather. Plants may or may not need staking, but in areas with warm summers they usually do and also tend to be short-lived. Regular deadheading encourages new flowers to form. Or cut the plants to within several inches of the ground to eliminate their unsightly, flopping stems and encourage repeat bloom in fall. Plants self-sow. Divide *C. montana* every 2 to 3 years in spring or fall to keep plants contained and vigorous. Other perennial species generally need dividing every 3 to 4 years. Propagate by division or seeds.

C. dealbata P. 75

c. deal-BAH-tuh. Persian Centaurea. A 2- to 3-foot-tall species that spreads to 2 feet. Bears pink 1½-inch-wide flower heads with white centers in summer. Zones 3 or 4 to 8.

C. hypoleuca

c. hy-poe-LOO-kuh. Clump-forming 2-foot-tall plant that spreads to 1½ feet. Produces fragrant 2½-inch-wide pale to dark pink flower heads in summer. 'John Coutts' bears bright rose-pink blooms. Zones 4 to 8.

C. macrocephala P. 76

c. mack-roe-SEFF-ah-luh. Globe Centaurea, Giant Knapweed. Vigorous 3- to 5-foot-tall perennial that spreads to 2 feet. Produces showy 1½- to 2-inch-wide blooms with yellow florets and prominent brown conelike bases. Blooms mid- to late summer. Zones 3 to 7.

C. montana

P. 76

c. mon-TAN-uh. Mountain Bluet. Vigorous, even weedy, clump-forming perennial that reaches 1½ to 2 feet and spreads by rhizomes to about 2 feet. Plants produce rich blue 2-inch-wide flower heads in early summer. It prefers cool temperatures and spreads less vigorously in the South than in the North. Zones 3 to 8.

☙ Centranthus

cen-TRAN-thus. Valerian family, Valerianaceae.

Native to dry, sunny slopes, often on alkaline soil, *Centranthus* species hail primarily from the Mediterranean region and southern Europe. The genus contains some 8 to 12 species of annuals as well as herbaceous and subshrubby perennials. They bear rounded clusters of small, spurred, funnel-shaped flowers at the stem tips and in leaf axils. *Centranthus* is from the Greek *kentron,* spur, and *anthos,* flower, a reference to the spurred flowers.

HOW TO GROW

Give these plants a spot in full sun with poor to average, well-drained soil. They thrive in poor soils, with pH ranging from slightly acid to alkaline, and also are excellent for planting in walls. Deadhead regularly, and cut plants back by half after flowering if they become floppy. The plants are not long-lived, so plan on replacing them every 3 to 5 years. Established specimens are difficult to move and divide because of their deep roots. Propagate by division in early spring (dig deeply and handle plants very carefully) or seeds. They also self-sow, and seedlings are easy to move.

C. ruber

P. 77

c. ROO-ber. Valerian, Jupiter's Beard. Clumping, woody-based perennial that ranges from 1 to 3 feet tall and spreads as far. Bears blue-green lance-shaped leaves and dense, rounded clusters of fragrant ½-inch-long flowers from late spring through late summer. Blooms are pinkish red, crimson, or white. 'Albus' has white flowers; 'Coccineus', carmine red ones; and 'Roseus' rose pink blooms. Zones 4 to 8.

❦ *Cerastium*

seh-RAS-tee-um. Pink family, Caryophyllaceae.

Cerastium is a genus of mostly annuals and perennials that form mats or low mounds of simple, often gray-green or silvery leaves and tiny white, usually five-petaled, flowers. The petals have notched tips and most often are carried in small clusters. Between 60 and 100 species belong here, including a few valuable garden plants grown for their starry flowers as well as some troublesome weeds. Mouse-ear chickweed *(C. vulgatum)* is a common lawn weed.

HOW TO GROW

Select a site in full sun with poor to average, very well drained soil. Plants tend to "melt out" in summer in areas with hot weather, so give them light shade, especially during the hottest part of the day in the South. They are quite drought tolerant and grow in almost pure sand, in dry-laid stone walls, and on dry slopes. Shear the plants after the flowers fade. Mow clumps in early spring if overwintered plants look unkempt. Dig and divide them if clumps spread too far. In addition to division, propagate by stem tip cuttings taken in summer or sow seeds.

C. tomentosum   P. 77

c. toe-men-TOE-sum. Snow-in-summer. Vigorous to invasive, mat-forming 6- to 10-inch-tall perennial that spreads rapidly and widely, especially in areas with cool, wet summers. Bears woolly silver-gray 1-inch-long leaves and clusters of 1-inch-wide white flowers in late spring and early summer. 'Yo-Yo' is a compact 6-inch-tall cultivar that does not spread as quickly. *C. alpinum*, alpine chickweed, is a mat-forming 2- to 6-inch-tall species with small woolly leaves topped by few-flowered clusters of very small white flowers in late spring and early summer. It is less rampant than *C. tomentosum*. *C. biebersteinii* is another similar species with 1- to 1½-inch-long silver-gray leaves. Zones 2 to 7.

❦ *Ceratostigma*

sir-rat-oh-STIG-muh. Plumbago family, Plumbaginaceae.

Grown for their flat-faced blue flowers, *Ceratostigma* species are herbaceous perennials, shrubs, and subshrubs that are closely related to, and sometimes called, plumbagos *(Plumbago* spp.). About eight species belong to the genus, native from tropical Africa to China and India. One species — *C. plumbaginoides* — is a vigorous perennial most often used as a ground cover.

HOW TO GROW

Select a site in full sun with rich, evenly moist but well-drained soil. *C. plumbaginoides* also tolerates partial shade. Established plants tolerate dry soil. Mark the locations of the clumps because plants emerge late in spring. Propagate by division in spring.

C. plumbaginoides P. 78

c. plum-bah-gin-oh-EYE-deez. Plumbago, Leadwort. Semiwoody 6- to 12-inch-tall rhizomatous species that spreads quickly to several feet. Features reddish stems, showy clusters of brilliant blue ¾-inch-wide flowers from summer to fall, and rounded leaves that turn glowing orange or red in fall. Zones 5 to 9.

❦ *Chamaemelum*

cam-eh-MEL-um. Aster family, Asteraceae.

Chamaemelum species bear finely cut, fernlike leaves and daisylike flower heads with yellow centers and white ray florets, or "petals." One of the four species that belong to this genus of aromatic annuals and perennials is the popular herb chamomile.

HOW TO GROW

Select a site in full sun with light, well-drained soil. Sandy soil is ideal. Propagate by dividing plants in spring or by seeds. Use division for cultivars, which do not come true from seeds.

C. nobile P. 78

c. no-BIL-ee. Roman Chamomile. Formerly *Anthemis nobilis.* Mat-forming 6- to 12-inch-tall plants that spread to 1½ feet. Bears threadlike, apple-scented leaves and ¼- to ½-inch-wide daisies in summer on long stalks above the foliage. 'Flore Pleno' bears double white buttonlike blooms on 6-inch plants. 'Treneague' is a compact 4-inch-tall nonflowering cultivar with especially aromatic leaves. Zones 6 to 9.

❦ *Chasmanthium*

chas-MAN-thee-um. Grass family, Poaceae.

Chasmanthium contains about six species of perennial grasses native to North and Central America that are commonly called wild oats or wood oats. They bear linear to narrowly lance-shaped leaves and oatlike panicles of flowers. One species is grown as an ornamental grass.

HOW TO GROW

A site in partial shade with rich, moist, well-drained soil is ideal. Plants also will grow in full sun and tolerate dry soil — including dry shade. Cut the plants to the ground in late winter to very early spring. Or, since they self-sow with enthusiasm, cut them back in fall before the seed heads shatter to curtail this tendency. For propagation, divide clumps in spring or early summer, sow seeds, or pot up self-sown seedlings.

C. latifolium   P. 79

c. lat-ih-FOE-lee-um. Northern Sea Oats. Formerly *Uniola latifolia.* Native North American warm-season grass forming 2- to 3-foot-tall, 2-foot-wide clumps. Has bamboolike leaves and showy, drooping green seed heads in midsummer that ripen to light brown. Zones 5 to 9.

❦ *Chelidonium*

kel-ih-DOH-nee-um. Poppy family, Papaveraceae.

Chelidonium contains a single species, a biennial or short-lived perennial native to Europe and western Asia that has naturalized throughout North America. Plants bear leaves that are deeply cut in a pinnate (featherlike) fashion and yellow poppylike flowers in summer. They have orange-yellow sap that can cause skin irritation.

HOW TO GROW

Greater celandine grows in sun or shade and almost any soil, although it is happiest in partial shade in rich, well-drained conditions. The plants do not transplant well, but grow easily from seeds sown where they are to grow. They self-sow with enthusiasm.

C. majus   P. 79

c. MAY-jus. Greater Celandine. Clump-forming 1½- to 2-foot-tall species with brittle stems and loose umbels of ¾- to 1-inch-wide bright yellow flowers in summer. 'Flore Pleno' bears double flowers. Zones 5 to 8.

❦ *Chelone*

chee-LOW-nee. Figwort family, Scrophulariaceae.

Both the common and botanical names of these native North American perennials refer to the unusual shape of their tubular, two-lipped flowers. They are commonly called turtleheads, and *Chelone* is the Greek word for tortoise. Six species belong to the genus, all stiff-stemmed plants with simple, toothed leaves. They bear terminal racemes of pink, purple, or white flowers from late summer to fall. The flowers have a beard on the lower lip.

HOW TO GROW

Plant turtleheads in partial shade or full sun in a site that has deep, rich, moist soil. In the South, constant soil moisture is essential for plants grown in full sun. They grow in heavy clay and also are ideal for the wet conditions of a bog garden. Plants usually stand without staking and spread to form 1½- to 2-foot-wide clumps. Propagate by dividing the clumps in spring or late fall, taking stem-tip cuttings in late spring or early summer, or sowing seeds.

C. glabra

c. GLAY-bruh. White Turtlehead, Snakeshead Turtlehead. A 3- to 5-foot species with square stems, lance-shaped leaves, and 1-inch-long flowers that are white or white blushed with pink. Zones 3 to 8.

C. lyonii   P. 80

c. lie-OH-nee-eye. Pink Turtlehead. A 1- to 3-foot-tall species with square stems; ovate, toothed leaves; and purple-pink 1-inch-long flowers that have yellow beards. Zones 3 to 8.

C. obliqua   P. 80

c. oh-BLEE-kwah. Rose Turtlehead. A 1½- to 2-foot-tall species with somewhat rounded stems, broadly lance-shaped toothed or cut leaves, and ¾-inch-long dark pink or purple-pink flowers with sparse yellow beards. Zones 5 to 9.

❦ *Chrysanthemum*

kris-AN-theh-mum. Aster family, Asteraceae.

Chrysanthemums bear single, semidouble, or double flower heads made up of dense clusters of tiny flowers, usually called florets. The genus contains about 20 species of annuals and perennials. Botanists reclassified many species once included in *Chrysanthemum,* including popular garden flowers such as Shasta, painted, and oxeye daisies. See species list below to find them. Until recently, fall mums were classified in the genus *Dendranthema,* but they have been restored to *Chrysanthemum* and are covered here. Whatever they're called, all make rewarding, easily cultivated garden plants.

HOW TO GROW

Give chrysanthemums full sun and average to rich, well-drained soil. Mums *(C. × morifolium)* are commonly treated as annuals for temporary, late-season color. That's because fall-planted specimens often aren't well enough established to overwinter successfully in cold climates. To grow them as perennials, start in spring with rooted cuttings or small unbloomed plants of hardy cultivars, available from mail-order specialists. Add compost or other organic matter to the soil at planting time and water regularly throughout summer. To encourage branching and lots of flowers, pinch plants about 2 weeks after planting and again each time the shoots and branches are about 6 inches long. Stop pinching in early July in the North, and in mid-July in the South to give plants plenty of time to form flower buds. Taller cultivars require staking. After flowering, cut plants back hard — to 3 to 6 inches. Once the soil has frozen solid, mulch with straw, hay, or evergreen branches. Dig and divide plants annually or every other year in spring as soon as growth appears. Mums also are easy to root from cuttings taken in early spring, and cuttings will produce good-size blooming plants by fall.

C. coccineum. See *Tanacetum coccineum*

C. maximum. See *Leucanthemum × superbum*

C × morifolium   P. 81

c. × more-ih-FOE-lee-um. Mum, Hardy Fall Mum, Garden Mum. Formerly *Dendranthema × grandiflora.* Clump-forming 1- to 5-foot-tall perennials that spread to 2 feet or more and have lobed, often hairy leaves. They bear late-summer to fall flowers in shades of bronze, purple, yellow, mauve, red, and white. Flower form varies widely and includes single daisies, 1-inch-wide buttons, and enormous doubles that exceed 12 inches in width. All mums start forming flower buds when days begin to shorten in mid- to late July, but cultivars take different amounts of time to come into bloom. Mail-order specialists offer early-, midseason-, and late-blooming cultivars. Early-blooming ones generally bloom in September and are the best choice in areas with very short seasons. Midseason types typically bloom in late September through October; late cultivars after mid-October. Florist mums usually take longer to come into bloom than cultivars grown for garden use and generally don't make good garden plants. Hardiness varies greatly, and depending on the cultivar, fall mums are hardy in Zones 4 or 5 to 9.

C. nipponicum. See *Nipponanthemum nipponicum*

C. pacificum. See *Ajania pacifica*

C. parthenium. See *Tanacetum parthenium*

C. × superbum. See *Leucanthemum × superbum*

C. vulgare. See *Leucanthemum vulgare*

C. weyrichii. See *Dendranthema weyrichii*

❦ *Chrysogonum*

cry-SOG-oh-num. Aster family, Asteraceae.

A single native perennial wildflower that belongs to the genus *Chrysogonum*. Found in rich woodlands from Pennsylvania and Ohio south to Florida, it bears starry yellow flowers consisting of five ray florets with yellow "eyes" made up of disk florets. Plants spread moderately by rhizomes and runners, making them excellent ground covers.

HOW TO GROW

Select a site in full sun or partial shade with rich, moist, well-drained soil. Plants also tolerate nearly full shade, although they bloom less. Propagate by dividing clumps in spring or fall, by separating and potting up the runners, or by seeds.

C. virginianum
P. 81

c. ver-jin-ee-AH-num. Green-and-gold, Goldenstar. Creeping 6- to 8-inch-tall perennial with hairy, heart-shaped leaves that spreads to 2 feet. Bears solitary, star-shaped 1½-inch-wide yellow flower heads on branched stems from spring to early summer. Zones 5 to 8.

Chrysopsis. See *Heterotheca*

☙ *Cimicifuga*

sim-ih-sih-FEW-guh. Buttercup family, Ranunculaceae.

Commonly known as snakeroots, bugbanes, or black cohosh, *Cimicifuga* species are large perennials native to moist, shady areas in North America, Europe, and Asia. They produce large handsome mounds of compound leaves that are divided two or three times. The tiny flowers lack petals, but are borne in graceful, dense, bottlebrush-like wands from midsummer onward. Eighteen species belong to the genus.

HOW TO GROW

Give snakeroots a spot in partial to dappled shade with rich, evenly moist soil. In the North, they will grow in full sun with rich, moist soil, but in southern climates, a spot with consistent soil moisture and shade during the hottest part of the day is essential. Plants are slow to establish and are best left undisturbed once planted. To propagate, divide clumps in fall or in spring. Plants self-sow in a good site.

C. americana

c. ah-mer-ih-CAH-nuh. American Bugbane. An East Coast native that ranges from 2 to 8 feet in height when in bloom and spreads from 2 to 3 feet. Bears 2-foot-long racemes of creamy white ¼- to ½-inch-long flowers from late summer (midsummer in the South) to fall. Zones 3 to 8.

C. racemosa
P. 82

c. ray-ceh-MO-suh. Black Snakeroot, Black Cohosh. A clump-forming, native North American wildflower ranging from 4 to 7 feet tall when in bloom (foliage mounds are about half that height) and spreading from 2 to 4 feet. Bears fluffy, branched racemes of tiny white ¼- to ½-inch-long flowers, which have an unpleasant odor, high above the foliage in midsummer. Zones 3 to 8.

C. simplex

c. SIM-plex. Kamchatka Bugbane, Autumn Snakeroot. A clump-forming perennial that reaches 3 to 4 feet in height and spreads between 2 and 3 feet. Bears arching 3- to 12-inch-long racemes of fragrant ¾-inch-long flowers in fall that are usually unbranched. 'Brunette' features brown-purple foliage, purple stems, and 8-inch-long racemes of white flowers with a purple cast. 'White Pearl' bears white flowers on 2- to 3-foot plants. 'Atropurpurea' bears leaves with a purplish cast. Zones 4 to 8.

❦ Clematis

KLEM-ah-tiss/klem-AT-iss. Buttercup family, Ranunculaceae.

While the best-known *Clematis* species are woody or semiwoody vines, this genus of more than 200 species also contains a few herbaceous perennials that deserve wider cultivation. All clematis bear flowers that lack true petals — the showy "petals" actually are petal-like sepals — and blooms are carried singly or in panicles or cymes. The flowers are followed by feathery, silvery seed heads that often are quite ornamental in their own right. Leaves are either undivided or divided in a featherlike (pinnate) fashion.

HOW TO GROW

Select a site in full sun to partial shade, but since the plants prefer cool soil conditions (they struggle if soil temperatures exceed about 80°F in summer) look for a spot on the north side of low-growing perennials, a low wall, or other structure where the roots will be shaded. Mulch also helps keep the roots cool. A site with dappled to partial shade, particularly during the hottest part of the day, is ideal. Rich, well-drained soil with a slightly acid to alkaline pH is fine, but clematis also grow in heavy clay soil, provided it has been worked deeply and amended with plenty of organic matter. Use twiggy brush or pea stakes to help keep herbaceous species upright. Cut their stems back to the ground in early spring. Propagate herbaceous species by division in spring, by cuttings taken from shoots at the base of the plant in spring, or by semiripe cuttings in early summer. Or sow seeds.

C. heracleifolia

c. her-ah-klee-ih-FOE-lee-uh. Tube Clematis. Sprawling, woody-based perennial or subshrub with toothed, deeply lobed leaves that reaches 2 to 3 feet and spreads to about 3 feet. Bears clusters of tubular 1¼-inch-long pale blue flowers in summer. *C. heracleifolia* var. *davidiana* bears fragrant violet-blue flowers and is more upright than the species. Zones 3 to 8.

C. integrifolia   P. 82
c. in-teg-rih-FOE-lee-uh. Mounding 2-foot-tall perennial that spreads as far. Bears simple, bell-shaped 2-inch-long blue-violet flowers over a long period in summer. Zones 3 to 7.

C. recta
c. RECK-tuh. Ground Clematis. Clump-forming perennial with compound gray-green leaves. Plants can reach 3 to 6 feet if supported but also can be allowed to sprawl. Bears dense clusters of fragrant, starry ¾-inch-wide white flowers in summer. The young foliage of 'Purpurea' is reddish purple. Zones 3 to 7.

❦ *Convallaria*
con-vah-LAIR-ee-uh. Lily family, Liliaceae.

Commonly known as lilies-of-the-valley, these lily family plants bear arching racemes of small, sweetly scented, nodding, bell-shaped flowers. Plants have leaves ranging from ovate-lance-shaped to rounded, and they spread by freely branching rhizomes to form dense mats. Experts differ on whether *Convallaria* contains three species or a single, variable one.

HOW TO GROW
A site in partial shade with evenly moist, rich soil is ideal, although plants grow in full sun (with adequate moisture) to full shade. Established clumps tolerate dry shade, but will not survive in wet, poorly drained sites. In the South, where plants struggle with the heat, a site in partial to full shade is best. In cooler zones, plants spread vigorously, so keep them away from other perennials or divide clumps frequently to keep them in check. Plant lily-of-the-valley pips — bare-root pieces of the fleshy rhizome that have both growing buds and roots — in fall, late winter, or early spring, ideally before the leaves emerge. Divide them in summer or fall if they encroach on other plantings, if flowering is reduced because of overcrowding, or for propagation.

C. majalis   P. 83
mah-JAH-liss. Lily-of-the-valley. Vigorous ground-covering perennial that reaches 6 to 9 inches in height and spreads to several feet. Bears one-sided

racemes of waxy white ¼-inch-wide bells in spring followed by round, glossy red berries. 'Fortin's Giant' is a vigorous selection with ½-inch-wide flowers on 1-foot-tall plants. *C. majalis* var. *rosea* bears very pale mauve pink flowers. Zones 2 to 8.

❧ *Coreopsis*

core-ee-OP-sis. Aster family, Asteraceae.

Also called tickseeds, coreopsis are long-blooming annuals and perennials that bear daisylike, single or double flowers. From 80 to 100 species belong here, most bearing gold to yellow-orange blooms, but there also are species with pale yellow or pink flowers. The flowers are borne on leafless stems and consist of ray florets (the "petals") surrounding a dense cluster of disk florets (the "eye"). Coreopsis are native to North and Central America and usually have upright stems. The leaves either are simple or are cut in a pinnate (featherlike) or palmate (handlike) fashion. Both the botanical name *Coreopsis* and the common name tickseed refer to the black seeds that follow the flowers. *Coreopsis* is from the Greek *koris*, bug, and *opsis*, resemblance.

HOW TO GROW

Give coreopsis full sun and average to rich, well-drained soil. These heat-loving plants also are happy with some morning shade and afternoon sun. *C. auriculata* and *C. rosea* also grow in partial shade. The plants prefer evenly moist conditions, but once established withstand considerable drought. Too-rich soil causes them to flop. Deadhead to lengthen the flowering season by cutting off individual blooms or cutting the plants back by about one-third. Allow some flowers to form seeds if you want plants to self-sow. Divide perennials every 2 to 3 years in early spring or early fall to keep them vigorous. Propagate by division, taking cuttings in spring from shoots at the base of the plant or in summer from stem tips, or by seeds.

C. auriculata   P. 83

c. aw-rick-you-LAH-tuh. Mouse-ear Coreopsis. Mounding 1- to 2-foot-tall perennial that spreads to about 1 foot by stolons. Bears ovate or lobed leaves and solitary yellow-orange 2-inch-wide flowers from late spring to summer. 'Nana' is an 8-inch-tall dwarf cultivar. Zones 4 to 9.

C. grandiflora

c. gran-dih-FLOR-uh. Large-flowered Coreopsis. Short-lived 1½- to 3-foot-tall perennial that spreads to about 1½ feet. Bears lance-shaped or palmately lobed leaves and yellow to yellow-orange 1- to 2½-inch flowers from spring to late summer with regular deadheading. There are single-, semidouble-, and double-flowered cultivars that can be grown from seeds. (Many cultivars are hybrids between this species and *C. lanceolata.*) 'Early Sunrise' blooms the first year from seeds sown indoors in mid-winter. Zones 3 or 4 to 9.

C. lanceolata   P. 84

c. lan-see-oh-LAH-tuh. Lance-leaved Coreopsis. A 1- to 2-foot-tall species that spreads to 1½ feet and tends to be longer-lived than *C. grandiflora.* Bears lance-shaped leaves and solitary 1½- to 2½-inch-wide flowers from late spring to midsummer. There are single-, semidouble-, and double-flowered cultivars. 'Goldfink' bears 2- to 3-inch-wide flowers on 9-inch plants. Zones 3 or 4 to 9.

C. rosea   P. 84

c. RO-see-uh. Pink Coreopsis. Mounding 1- to 2-foot-tall plants spreading to 2 feet or more and especially vigorous in fertile, moist soil. Bears needlelike leaves and small rosy pink 1-inch-wide flowers with yellow centers from summer to early fall. Zones 4 to 8.

C. tripteris

c. TRIP-ter-iss. Tall Tickseed, Atlantic Coreopsis. Native wildflower from the East Coast ranging from 3 to 9 feet in height and spreading to 2 feet or more. Bears palmately divided, anise-scented leaves and clusters of pale yellow 2-inch-wide flowers from summer to fall. Zones 3 to 8.

C. verticillata   P. 85

c. ver-tih-sill-LAH-tuh. Thread-leaved Coreopsis. A 1- to 2-foot-tall species spreading slowly via rhizomes to form shrubby 2- to 3-foot-wide clumps. Bears pinnate leaves with threadlike leaflets and pale to golden yellow 1- to 2-inch-wide daisies in summer. 'Moonbeam' bears pale yellow flowers, reblooms without deadheading, and will flower from early summer to fall. 'Zagreb' bears deep yellow flowers on 1-foot plants. Zones 3 to 9.

✿ *Corydalis*

cor-IH-dah-liss. Poppy family, Papaveraceae.

Corydalis species produce handsome mounds of delicate-looking, ferny foliage and racemes of tubular, spurred flowers in spring. About 300 species, both biennials and perennials, belong to the genus, which was once classified in the fumitory family, Fumariaceae. *Corydalis* resemble bleeding hearts (*Dicentra* species), but while bleeding hearts have two spurs per flower, *Corydalis* blooms have only one. The perennials grow from rhizomes or tubers.

HOW TO GROW

Give most corydalis full sun to partial shade with rich, well-drained soil. *C. lutea* also grows well in average, well-drained soil as well as the conditions that *C. flexuosa* requires: partial shade and rich, well-drained soil that remains evenly moist. *C. flexuosa* is best in areas with cool summers. Most resent being transplanted, but they can be dug and divided for propagation in early spring or early fall. Plants self-sow.

C. cheilanthifolia

c. key-lanth-ih-FOE-lee-uh. Ferny Corydalis. Produces 10- to 12-inch-tall mounds of very lacy, pinnate leaves that spread as far. Bears dense racemes of ½-inch-long bright yellow flowers from spring to summer. Zones 3 to 7.

C. flexuosa   P. 85

c. flex-you-OH-suh. Blue Corydalis. Bears 12-inch-tall mounds of glaucous leaves and racemes of bright blue 1-inch-long flowers from late spring to summer. Plants go dormant after flowering. 'Blue Panda' bears sky blue flowers. Zones 6 to 8.

C. lutea   P. 86

c. LOO-tee-uh. Yellow Corydalis. Forms handsome mounds of ferny bluish green leaves that are 1½ feet tall and wide. Foliage remains attractive from early spring through late fall, and even into winter in milder climates. Bears racemes of abundant ½- to ¾-inch-long golden yellow flowers over a long season from midspring to early fall. Zones 5 to 8.

C. ochroleuca
P. 86

c. oh-crow-LEW-cuh. Bears 1-foot-tall mounds of ferny leaves that spread as far and are topped by racemes of ½-inch-long white flowers with yellow throats from spring to summer. Zones 6 to 8.

❦ Crambe

CRAM-bee. Cabbage family, Brassicaceae.

Crambes, or sea kales, as they also are called, are grown for their abundant clusters of small, cross-shaped, four-petaled flowers. They produce large cabbagelike mounds of bold, usually pinnately lobed leaves. About 20 species of annuals and perennials belong to the genus, native primarily from central Europe, tropical Africa, and central Asia. The young shoots of one species, *C. maritima,* are sometimes eaten as a vegetable.

HOW TO GROW
A site with full sun and deep, rich, well-drained soil is ideal, although crambes also tolerate poor soil and partial shade. Neutral to alkaline pH is best. Plants die back after flowering, so combine them with annuals to fill the gap in mid- to late summer. They do not tolerate heat and humidity well. The plants are deep rooted and resent transplanting, but they can be divided for propagation if necessary in early spring. Or take root cuttings in late fall or winter or sow seeds.

C. cordifolia
P. 87

c. core-dih-FOE-lee-uh. Giant Kale, Colewort. A giant perennial with heart-shaped, toothed 2-foot-wide leaves forming mounds of leaves that reach about 2 feet and can spread to 5 feet. Bears airy 6- to 8-foot-tall panicles of tiny white flowers from late spring to early summer. Zones 6 to 9.

C. maritima
P. 87

c. mah-RIT-ih-muh. Sea Kale. A mounding perennial that reaches 2½ feet and spreads to 2 feet. Bears rounded, lobed, blue-green leaves and dense 2-foot-wide racemes of tiny white flowers in early summer. Zones 6 to 9.

❦ *Cynara*

sin-AH-ruh. Aster family, Asteraceae.

Commonly called cardoons or artichokes, thistlelike *Cynara* species are perennials native to the Mediterranean, northern Africa, and the Canary Islands. They bear clumps of handsome, often gray-green leaves that are cut in a featherlike (pinnatifid) fashion and rounded flower heads that resemble thistles. The flower heads, which have a conelike base consisting of spiny bracts surrounding a dense tuft of soft disk florets, are carried singly or in clusters on stalks above the foliage. About 10 species belong to the genus, one of which is grown primarily for its foliage as a perennial, tender perennial, or annual.

HOW TO GROW

Give cardoons full sun and well-drained, average to rich soil. For best foliage effect, remove flower stalks as they appear. Mulch plants over winter with salt hay or weed-free straw where they are marginally hardy. Propagate by seeds, divide clumps in spring, or take root cuttings in late fall or winter.

C. cardunculus   P. 88

c. car-DUN-cue-lus. Cardoon. A large perennial that forms 4-foot-wide clumps of 2-foot-long deeply cut leaves that are gray-green above and silvery beneath. Bears 1½- to 3-inch-wide flower heads on stalks up to 5 feet tall from early summer to fall. Zones 6 or 7 to 9.

❦ *Darmera*

dar-MEER-uh. Saxifrage family, Saxifragaceae.

Darmera contains a single species primarily grown for its enormous foliage. The rounded leaves are peltate, meaning the stem is attached in the center of the leaf, much like an umbrella. Plants bear small clusters of dainty flowers that appear before the leaves emerge and grow from thick mats of fleshy rhizomes.

HOW TO GROW

Select a site in full sun or partial shade with rich, constantly moist to boggy soil. A site along a pond or stream or in a bog garden is ideal. Plants tolerate drier conditions but produce smaller foliage and will not be as vigorous. To propagate, divide the clumps in spring or sow seeds.

D. peltata

P. 88

d. pel-TAH-tuh. Umbrella Plant. Formerly *Peltiphyllum peltatum*. A bold perennial native to the Pacific Northwest that reaches 4 feet tall and 3 to 4 feet wide. Leaves reach 2 feet across and turn brilliant red in fall. Rounded clusters of five-petaled ½-inch-wide flowers appear in late spring. Zones 5 to 9.

❧ Delosperma

del-oh-SPER-muh. Carpetweed family, Aizoaceae.

Fleshy triangular to cylindrical leaves and daisylike flowers characterize members of this genus of about 150 species native to Africa. Commonly called ice plants, *Delosperma* species are evergreen or semievergreen shrubs or mat-forming perennials. Although the flowers resemble those of daisies and other aster family plants, they actually are single blooms rather than flower heads consisting of many small florets. Blooms are borne singly or in clusters.

HOW TO GROW

Select a site in full sun with very well drained soil. Plants tolerate heat and poor, dry soil. Propagate by cuttings in late spring or summer or sow seeds.

D. nubigerum

P. 89

d. new-bih-JER-um. Ice Plant. A creeping 2- to 3-inch-tall species that forms mats several feet across. Bears narrow, fleshy, 1½-inch-long leaves with warty-looking bumps and orange-red, ¾-inch-wide flowers in summer. Zones 6 to 9.

❧ Delphinium

del-FIN-ee-um. Buttercup family, Ranunculaceae.

Delphiniums are prized by gardeners for their stately flower spikes that come in shades from true sky blue to dark royal blue as well as violet, lavender, pink, mauve, and white. The bloom stalks tower above mounds of maplelike leaves borne from a fleshy crown. About 250 species of annuals, biennials, and perennials belong here, most native to mountainous regions worldwide. They bear flowers in spikes, racemes, or panicles, and the individual blooms consist of five petal-like sepals, one of which forms a spur at the back of the flower, and usually four petals. The most popular delphiniums in gardens are hybrids.

HOW TO GROW

Grow delphiniums in full sun to partial shade in very rich, deeply prepared, well-drained soil. Neutral to alkaline pH is ideal, but plants also grow in slightly acid soil. They thrive in areas with cool summers; where hot summer weather prevails, a site with morning sun and partial or dappled shade during the hottest part of the day is best. Constantly wet soil leads to crown rot and death. A spot with good air circulation helps prevent disease problems, but do protect plants from strong winds. Belladonna Group Hybrids tend to be more tolerant of hot summer weather than Elatum Group plants, and they usually are longer-lived as well. At best, most delphiniums are short-lived perennials. Dig in compost, well-rotted manure, or other organic matter at planting time, and grade the soil surface so water will not collect on the crowns. Handle the plants with care, as the brittle roots are easy to break. Stake stems when they are about 1 foot tall, water weekly throughout the season, and feed plants in spring and again when the first blooms appear. Remove the flower stalks as they fade, and new spikes may emerge and bloom in late summer or fall. Propagate by sowing seeds or taking cuttings from shoots at the base of the plant in early spring. (Each cutting should have a sliver of the crown attached at the base.)

Belladonna Group Hybrids

Also called *D. × belladonna* hybrids. Upright 3- to 4-foot-tall plants forming 1½-foot-wide mounds of leaves. Produces loosely branched stalks of flowers on wiry stems in early and late summer. Individual blooms are single, ¾ inch wide, with prominent spurs. 'Bellamosum' bears deep blue flowers. The Connecticut Yankee Series cultivar 'Blue Fountains' is more heat tolerant than most and can be grown in Zone 8. Zones 3 to 7.

Elatum Group Hybrids   P. 89

Also called *Delphinium × elatum* hybrids. These are 4- to 6-foot-tall plants that spread from 2 to 3 feet and produce dense spikes of single, semidouble, or double 2½-inch-wide flowers. They bloom in early and midsummer. Many cultivars are available, including 'Butterball', with creamy white flowers; 'Blue Dawn', with pale blue semidouble blooms; and 'Emily Hawkens', with semidouble lavender blooms. The popular Pacific Hybrids, also sold as Pacific Giants, resemble Elatum Group delphiniums, but are shorter-lived and best grown as annuals or biennials.

Pacific Hybrids cultivars usually have Arthurian names, including 'King Arthur', 'Guinevere', and 'Galahad'. Zones 3 to 7.

❧ *Dendranthema*

den-DRAN-theh-muh. Aster family, Asteraceae.

About 20 species belong to this genus, all of which were once classified as chrysanthemums (*Chrysanthemum* spp.). They bear aromatic, somewhat fleshy leaves that are lobed in a palmate (handlike) fashion. Daisylike flower heads have white, yellow, or pink ray florets ("petals") and are borne singly or in loose clusters.

HOW TO GROW
Select a site in full sun with rich, moist, well-drained soil. Sandy soil is ideal, and plants tend to be short-lived in heavy clay. Propagate by dividing plants in spring or after they flower in fall, or by sowing seeds.

D. × grandiflorum. See *Chrysanthemum × morifolium*

D. weyrichii   P. 90

d. way-RICH-ee-eye. Formerly *Chrysanthemum weyrichii*. A 1-foot-tall species that forms 1½-foot-wide mounds of five-lobed leaves topped with 2-inch-wide daisies in late summer and fall with white or pink ray florets and yellow centers. 'White Bomb' has pink-tinged ray florets. 'Pink Bomb' bears pink flowers. Zones 3 to 8.

❧ *Deschampsia*

des-CHAMP-see-uh. Grass family, Poaceae.

Commonly known as hair grass, *Deschampsia* species are clump-forming grasses with threadlike or linear leaves topped by airy panicles of flowers. About 50 species belong to the genus. Most are perennials, although there are some annuals in the genus.

HOW TO GROW
Plant hair grasses in full sun or partial shade and average garden soil. They thrive in moist, even heavy soils as well as in boggy conditions. *D.*

flexuosa tolerates dry soils and also grows in dry shade. Neutral to acid pH is best. Hair grasses are cool-season grasses, meaning they grow in late summer or fall when daytime temperatures are between about 60° and 75°F, stop growing over winter, and resume growing in early spring once the weather warms up but before hot summer temperatures arrive. Cut the plants to the ground in late winter or early spring before new growth begins. Propagate by dividing the clumps in spring or early fall or sow seeds. Plants self-sow.

D. cespitosa

P. 90

d. ses-pih-TOE-suh. Tufted Hair Grass. Ornamental grass that forms dense 2-foot-tall clumps of foliage that reach 4 to 5 feet wide. Foliage is evergreen from about Zone 8 south. Bears cloudlike 1½-foot-long spikelets of flowers from early to late summer. Plants can be 4 feet tall in bloom. Zones 4 to 9.

D. flexuosa

d. flex-you-OH-suh. Crinkled Hair Grass. Compact species forming 1-foot-tall, 1-foot-wide clumps of evergreen or semievergreen foliage. Bears airy 5-inch-long panicles of flowers in early and midsummer. Plants are 2 feet tall in bloom. Zones 4 to 9.

❦ Dianthus

die-AN-thuss. Pink family, Caryophyllaceae.

Dianthus contains a wealth of charming, old-fashioned garden plants bearing dainty, often spicy-scented flowers over a long season. Blooms come in all shades of pink plus white, maroon, and ruby red. There also are many bicolor pinks. Flowers, which appear from late spring into summer, may be single, semidouble, or fully double. The plants are generally low growing and mound shaped and feature attractive blue- or gray-green lance-shaped to grasslike leaves that are often evergreen. The genus contains more than 300 species of annuals, biennials, perennials, and subshrubs along with thousands of cultivars. The name *Dianthus* is from the Greek *dios*, god, and *anthos*, flower, or "flower of the gods." The common name "pinks" refers not to the color of the flowers, but to the fringed or ragged edges of the petals, which look as if they were trimmed with pinking shears.

HOW TO GROW

Give pinks full sun and well-drained, dry to evenly moist soil that is slightly acid to alkaline. They prefer cool conditions, and a site with partial shade during the hottest part of the day provides essential heat protection and helps keep the plants vigorous. Pinks require well-drained conditions, especially in winter. Don't mulch them with organic mulches such as shredded bark, because they tend to keep the soil too damp; stone chips are a better option. Use loose soil mixed with compost to cover the shallow feeder roots if they become exposed. Divide clumps every 2 to 3 years in spring to keep them vigorous. Deadheading helps prolong bloom. Many pinks self-sow if conditions are right, but seed-grown plants often do not resemble their parents. Propagate by division in spring or take cuttings in summer from nonflowering shoot tips.

D. alpinus
P. 91

d. al-PIE-nus. Alpine Pinks. Mound-forming 3- to 6-inch-tall plants that spread as far. Bears single 1½-inch-wide flowers in late spring or early summer. Zones 3 to 8.

D. deltoides
P. 91

d. del-TOY-deez. Maiden Pinks. Mat-forming 6- to 12-inch-tall species that spreads to 1 or 2 feet. Bears single ¾-inch blooms from early to midsummer. 'Zing Rose' bears rose-red flowers. 'Microchip' bears flowers in the full range of dianthus colors. Zones 3 to 9.

D. gratianopolitanus
P. 92

d. grah-tee-AH-no-pol-ih-TAY-nus. Cheddar Pinks. Dense, mat-forming 4- to 12-inch-tall plants that spread to 1½ feet. Bears fragrant 1-inch-wide flowers in late spring that can be single or double. Heat tolerant. 'Tiny Rubies' bears double ½-inch-wide rose-pink flowers on 4-inch plants. Zones 3 to 9.

D. hybrids
P. 92

Thousands of hybrid cultivars are available, the result of crosses made by countless hybridizers. It's not always easy to guess their parentage, and sources vary on which cultivars are attributed to which species. Heights range from about 8 to 18 inches, and they bloom in spring and summer. Allwood pinks (frequently listed as D. × allwoodii) are the result of crosses between D. plumarius and florist's carnations (D. caryophyllus) and are hardy from Zones 4 or 5 to 8. They bear 2-inch-wide flowers, but many are not very fragrant. 'Doris' is an Allwood pink with fragrant salmon pink flowers with darker eyes. Other outstanding *Dianthus* cultivars include 'Bath's Pink' (Zones 3 to 9), which bears soft pink 1-inch-wide blooms with fringed petals that bloom from spring to summer; 'Essex Witch' (Zones 5 to 9) has rose pink flowers with fringed petals; 'Gran's Favorite' (Zones 5 to 10) bears white flowers with mauve petal edges that have a spicy scent; 'Little Jock' (Zones 5 to 9) has pink flowers with mauve pink eyes and fringed petals; 'Mrs. Sinkins' (Zones 5 to 9) bears exceptionally fragrant white flowers; and 'Pikes Pink' (Zones 5 to 9) bears spicy-scented double flowers on 6-inch plants.

D. plumarius

P. 93

d. plu-MAIR-ee-us. Cottage Pinks, Border Pinks, Grass Pinks. Mound-forming 1- to 2-foot-tall plants that spread to 2 feet. Bears fragrant 1-inch-wide single, semidouble, or double flowers carried two to five per stem from spring to early summer. Zones 3 to 9.

❦ Dicentra

die-SEN-truh. Fumitory family, Fumariaceae.

Commonly called bleeding hearts, *Dicentra* species are primarily plants native to lightly shaded woodlands in North America and eastern Asia. About 20 species belong to the genus, both annuals and perennials. They feature deeply cut, fernlike leaves and pendent flowers that have more or less heart-shaped corollas. The flowers have two petals that are modified into pouches or spurs (*Dicentra* is from the Greek *dis*, twice, and *kentron*, spur) and come in pink, red-pink, white, yellow, and purple.

HOW TO GROW

Give bleeding hearts a site in light to full shade with moist, rich, well-drained soil. Wet, poorly drained soil, especially in winter, leads to root rot and death. A spot with morning sun and afternoon shade helps encourage summer-long bloom for *D. eximia* and *D. formosa* and also provides essential heat protection in the South. Handle plants carefully to avoid breaking the brittle roots or rhizomes. Keep the soil evenly moist. Remove bloom spikes of *D. eximia* and *D. formosa* as they fade to encourage new flowers to form. Cut *D. spectabilis* plants to the ground when the leaves turn yellow. Be sure to mark their location to keep from digging into the crowns accidentally later in the season. Once planted, bleeding hearts are best left undisturbed, but can be divided in early spring if they outgrow their site, if the clumps become woody and die out in the center, if blooming decreases, or for propagation.

D. eximia

P. 94

d. ex-EEM-ee-uh. Fringed Bleeding Heart. A native North American wildflower forming mounds of delicate-looking blue-green fernlike leaves that are 1½ feet tall and wide. Bears racemes of pendent, heart-shaped ½- to 1½-inch-long pink flowers above the foliage from spring to fall, provided the soil is kept evenly moist. A number of hybrid cultivars between this species and D. formosa are available, including 'Bountiful' with rose-red flowers, 'Luxuriant' with cherry red blooms and blue-green leaves, and 'Snowdrift' with white flowers. 'Langtrees' bears white flowers on rhizomatous 12-inch plants with lacy blue-green leaves. Zones 3 to 9.

D. formosa

d. for-MOE-suh. Western Bleeding Heart. A native North American wildflower reaching 1½ feet and spreading widely by rhizomes to 2 or 3 feet. Bears ferny leaves and racemes of pink ½- to 1-inch-long heart-shaped flowers from late spring to early summer. Zones 3 to 9.

D. scandens

d. SCAN-denz. Climbing Bleeding Heart. A climbing species that reaches 3 feet and spreads as far. Bears deeply lobed green leaves and climbs by tendrils. Racemes of ¾- to 1-inch-long yellow flowers appear in summer. Zones 6 to 9.

D. spectabilis

P. 94

d. spec-TAB-ah-liss. Common Bleeding Heart. Bushy 1½- to 2½-foot-tall species with brittle, fleshy stems and divided leaves with wedge-shaped leaflets. Clumps spread to 2 feet or more. Bears arching racemes of dangling, heart-shaped flowers in rosy pink, rose-red, or white for a few weeks in spring. Plants go dormant after blooming. 'Pantaloons' bears white flowers and is more vigorous than 'Alba', also white. Zones 2 to 9.

❦ Dictamnus

dick-TAM-nus

Dictamnus contains a single species commonly called gas plant, dittany, or fraxinella. A sturdy, dependable, long-lived perennial, it produces handsome clumps of glossy, dark green, pinnately compound leaves that are lemon scented when bruised. The small sweetly fragrant flowers are borne in racemes. Two other common names — burning bush and candle plant — allude to the fact that the leaves, flowers, and unripe fruit give off a volatile oil that in still, sultry weather *sometimes* can be ignited for a split second with a match. The oils in the foliage also can cause a blistering, poison ivy–like rash in some gardeners, especially in hot weather.

HOW TO GROW

Select a site in full sun or light shade with rich, well-drained soil. Poor drainage leads to root rot. Select a site with care, since the plants establish slowly — they take 3 to 4 years to begin blooming well — and do not transplant well. Disturbing the roots can be fatal. If absolutely necessary, divide clumps in spring or fall. Fresh seeds sown in individual pots offer the best propagation method. To collect them, place a nylon stocking over the ripening flower stalks — otherwise the spring-loaded capsules scatter seeds everywhere when they ripen — and sow immediately.

D. albus

P. 95

d. AL-bus. Gas Plant. Robust 1½- to 3-foot-tall plant that forms 2-foot-wide clumps with time. Bears racemes of ¾- to 1-inch-long flowers from late spring to early summer. White or pinkish white blooms have five showy petals and long curled stamens. *D. albus* var. *purpureus* bears purple-pink flowers with darker veins. Zones 3 to 8.

Digitalis

dih-jih-TAL-iss. Figwort family, Scrophulariaceae.

Digitalis contains about 22 species, including biennials and short-lived perennials native from Europe and northwestern Africa to central Asia. All commonly referred to as foxgloves, they bear erect racemes of tubular to funnel-shaped flowers above a rosette of large broadly lance-shaped leaves that spreads to about 1½ or 2 feet. Flowers come in shades of pink as well as white and creamy yellow. The botanical name *Digitalis* is from the Latin word for finger, *digitus,* and refers to the fingerlike shape of the flowers. All parts of these plants are poisonous.

HOW TO GROW

Give foxgloves full sun or partial shade and rich, evenly moist, well-drained soil. In areas with hot summers (Zone 7 south), a spot with afternoon shade is best. Water deeply during dry weather. Cut the flower stalks to just above the foliage after the flowers fade unless you want self-sown seedlings. Propagate by dividing the clumps in early spring or fall or by starting seeds.

D. ferruginea

d. fer-rue-JIN-ee-uh. Rusty Foxglove. A 3- to 4-foot-tall biennial or perennial bearing racemes of 1½-inch-long flowers in midsummer that are golden brown with red veins on the inside. Zones 4 to 7.

D. grandiflora   P. 95

d. gran-dih-FLOOR-uh. Yellow Foxglove. A 3- to 4-foot-tall biennial or perennial bearing racemes of 1½- to 2-inch-long flowers in midsummer that are pale yellow with brown veins on the inside. Zones 3 to 8.

D. lutea   P. 96

d. LOO-tee-uh. A 3- to 4-foot-tall biennial or perennial bearing glossy leaves and then racemes of pale yellow ½- to 1-inch-long flowers from early to midsummer. Zones 3 to 8.

D. × mertonensis   P. 96

d. × mer-ton-EN-sis. Strawberry Foxglove. A 3-foot-tall perennial that produces racemes of 2½-inch-long flowers in shades from pinkish to rose pink and white in late spring and early summer. Comes true from seeds. Zones 3 to 8.

D. purpurea   P. 97

d. pur-PUR-ee-uh. Common Foxglove. A 2- to 6-foot-tall biennial or short-lived perennial with showy racemes of 2- to 2½-inch-long flowers in rose-purple, white, pink, and creamy yellow. Blooms commonly are spotted with purple inside. 'Excelsior Hybrids' reach 5 feet and come in a range of pastel shades. Blooms in early summer. Zones 4 to 8.

❦ *Disporum*

die-SPOR-um. Lily family, Liliaceae.

Commonly called fairy bells, *Disporum* species are rhizomatous perennials native to moist woodlands in North America and eastern Asia. Between 10 and 20 species belong to the genus. They bear ovate to lance-shaped leaves and small clusters of flowers that are usually pendent and range in shape from tubular or trumpet shaped to cup shaped. Flower colors include white, greenish yellow, and purplish or brownish red. The flowers are followed by fleshy red, orange, or black berries. Fairy bells are closely related to bellworts (*Uvularia* spp.) and toad lilies (*Tricyrtis* spp.).

HOW TO GROW

Select a site in partial shade with rich, moist, well-drained soil. Plants prefer cool conditions, so a site with afternoon shade is best. Mulch with chopped leaves or other organic matter to keep the soil cool, retain moisture, and add beneficial organic matter. Water during dry weather. To propagate, divide plants in early spring or start from seeds.

D. flavens

P. 97

d. FLAY-vuns. Fairy Bells. A clumping 2½-foot-tall species spreading to 1 foot or more with clusters of one to three tubular, pendent, 2-inch-long pale yellow flowers in early spring. Black berries follow the flowers in fall. Zones 4 to 9.

D. sessile

d. SES-sil-ee. Fairy Bells. A 1- to 2-foot-tall species that slowly forms 2-foot-wide clumps. Bears nearly stalkless leaves and clusters of one to three pendent, tubular 1-inch-long flowers in late spring and early summer. Flowers are creamy white, very pale yellow, or greenish and are followed by black berries in fall. Zones 4 to 9.

❦ *Dodecatheon*

doe-dee-KATH-ee-on. Primrose family, Primulaceae.

Grown for their spring clusters of cyclamen- or shuttlecock-shaped flowers, *Dodecatheon* species are perennials primarily native to North America. About 14 species belong here, found in moist grasslands, alpine meadows, and sometimes woodlands. Commonly known as shooting stars (another common name is American cowslip), they produce a low basal rosette of lance-shaped, spoon-shaped, or rounded leaves topped in spring by umbels of flowers held on leafless stalks high above the foliage. The small pendent flowers have reflexed (backward pointing) petals and stamens united to form a beaklike projection. Plants go dormant shortly after they finish blooming.

HOW TO GROW

Select a site in full sun or partial shade with rich, moist, well-drained soil. In areas with warm summers, a spot with afternoon shade is best, since plants prefer cool conditions. Mulching helps keep the soil moist and cool. Since the plants go dormant and disappear completely in summer, mark their locations and combine them with other perennials that are not too vigorous or with annuals to fill the sites they leave. Propagate by division in spring or by seeds.

D. meadia
P. 98

d. MEE-dee-uh. Common Shooting Star. A native clump-forming wildflower that forms a low 1-foot-wide rosette of leaves. Bears clusters of 12 to 15 magenta-pink ½- to ¾-inch-long flowers on 1½-foot-tall stalks in mid- and late spring. *D. meadia* forma *album* bears white flowers. Zones 4 to 8.

❦ Dryopteris

dry-OP-ter-iss. Wood Fern family, Dryopteridaceae.

Dryopteris species are known by a variety of common names, including shield ferns, wood ferns, male ferns, and buckler ferns. The genus contains about 225 species, most native to moist woodlands and boggy sites in the Northern Hemisphere. Plants bear scaly rhizomes that either creep to form small clumps or are erect and form crowns. The pinnate (featherlike) fronds have dense brown, gold, black, or tan scales at the base and usually form vase-shaped clumps.

HOW TO GROW

Select a site in partial shade with moist, well-drained soil rich in organic matter. Plants also thrive in evenly moist to wet soil. *D. affinis* and *D. filix-mas* tolerate considerable sun, provided soil moisture is consistent. Divide clumps in spring or fall for propagation, to keep the size of the clumps manageable and to preserve the handsome vaselike shape of the clumps.

D. affinis

d. aff-IN-iss. Golden-scaled Male Fern. A semievergreen to evergreen species bearing 2- to 3-foot-tall fronds with golden brown scales in vase-shaped clumps that spread to 3 feet. Many forms with crested fronds are available (these come true from spores). 'Cristata', sometimes sold as 'The King', is a popular selection that has 2- to 4-foot fronds with crests at the top of the frond as well as at the tips of the pinnae (leaflets). Zones 4 to 8.

D. erythrosora

d. ee-rith-ro-SOR-uh. Autumn Fern. An evergreen to deciduous species with 1½- to 2-foot-tall fronds that are bronze- to copper red when they emerge in spring and slowly turn to green by summer. Plants spread slowly to form 1½-foot-wide clumps. Zones 5 to 8.

D. filix-mas

P. 98

d. FEE-lix-MAS. Male Fern. A deciduous species native to North America as well as Europe and Asia that reaches 3 feet in height and spreads as far. Many forms with crested fronds are available, including 'Cristata' and 'Grandiceps', both with crested pinnae (leaflet) tips. Zones 4 to 8.

❦ Echinacea

eck-in-AY-see-uh. Aster family, Asteraceae.

Echinacea species are stalwart, sun-loving native North American wildflowers best known as purple coneflowers. About nine species belong to the genus, all with daisylike flower heads with raised, cone- or pincushion-like centers consisting of spiny yellow-brown or orange disk florets. The ray florets, or "petals," are purple, purple-pink, or white and generally drooping. Flowers appear from early to midsummer atop stiff-stemmed clumps of bristly leaves that range from linear to lance shaped or ovate. The botanical name *Echinacea* refers to the spiny cones: it is from the Greek *echinos*, meaning hedgehog.

HOW TO GROW

Give coneflowers full sun and well-drained, average soil. They tolerate drought and heat and also bloom in light shade. Plants in shade tend to get leggy, but pinching in spring helps keep them compact. Dig and divide the plants in spring or fall if they die out in the center or outgrow their space. Division offers a fairly easy propagation method, although the plants have deep taproots and are happier if left undisturbed. Or take basal cuttings (cuttings of shoots from the base of the plant) in spring, root cuttings in fall, or start from seeds. Plants self-sow.

E. angustifolia

e. an-gus-tih-FOE-lee-uh. Narrow-leaved Coneflower. Clump-forming 1- to 2-foot plant spreading to 1½ feet. Bears 2-inch-wide flowers in early summer with 1-inch-long rose pink ray florets. Zones 3 to 8.

E. pallida

e. PAL-lih-duh. Pale Coneflower. Clump-forming 3- to 4-foot-tall species that spreads to about 2 feet. In summer, bears 4- to 6-inch-wide flower heads with drooping 1½- to 3½-inch-long pale pink ray florets. Zones 4 to 8.

E. purpurea   P. 99

e. pur-PUR-ee-ah. Purple Coneflower. Shrubby 2- to 4-foot-tall species that occasionally reaches 6 feet and spreads from 1½ to 2 feet. Bears 1½- to 3-inch-wide flower heads with drooping 1½- to 2½-inch-long ray florets from midsummer to fall. Several cultivars are more compact than the species and bear wider blooms with more horizontal petals than the species. 'Bravado' bears 4-inch-wide flowers on 2-foot plants. 'Magnus' bears 7-inch-wide blooms. 'Leuchtstern' (also sold as 'Bright Star') has purple-red ray florets and reaches about 2½ feet. 'White Swan' bears white blooms on 1- to 2-foot plants, while 'White Lustre' reaches 3 feet. Zones 3 to 9.

❧ Echinops

ECH-in-ops. Aster family, Asteraceae.

As their common name suggests, globe thistles are spiny-leaved plants with round, spiny flower heads. Blooms are silvery to metallic blue in color. Like *Echinacea*, *Echinops* takes its name from the Greek for hedgehog, in this case *echinos*, hedgehog, and *opsis*, appearance. About 120 species belong to the genus — annuals, biennials, and perennials that have deep taproots and are found growing naturally in hot, dry areas such as gravelly slopes and grasslands mostly from central and southern Europe to central Asia.

HOW TO GROW

Select a site in full sun with poor to average, well-drained soil. Good drainage is especially important in winter. Established plants are very drought tolerant. Prepare the soil deeply at planting time to ensure good drainage, and space plants generously because they resent transplanting and can be left undisturbed for many years. Deadhead to encourage reblooming and curtail self-seeding. Propagate by washing away some soil from around the base of the plant and slicing off the small side plants that have arisen there, or take root cuttings in spring or fall. Or start from seeds, although cultivars don't come true.

E. bannaticus

e. ban-NAT-ih-kus. A 1½- to 4-foot-tall species forming clumps that spread to about 2 feet. Bears 1- to 2-inch-wide violet-blue to blue-gray flower heads from mid- to late summer. 'Blue Globe' bears dark violet-blue 2½-inch-wide flower heads on 3-foot plants and reblooms if plants are cut back hard after the first flush of flowers. 'Taplow Blue' bears 2-inch-wide metallic blue flower heads. Zones 3 to 9.

E. ritro

P. 99

e. REE-tro. Small Globe Thistle. Compact 2-foot-tall species spreading to 1½ feet. Bears 1- to 1¾-inch-wide flower heads in mid- to late summer. 'Veitch's Blue' has dark metallic blue flowers on sturdy plants and is an especially good rebloomer. Zones 3 to 9.

E. sphaerocephalus

e. sphare-oh-SEFF-ah-lus. Large clump-forming species that reaches 6 feet and spreads to about 3 feet. Bears silver-gray 1¼- to 2½-inch-wide flower heads on gray stems in mid- and late summer. Zones 3 to 9.

Epimedium

eh-pih-MEE-dee-um. Barberry family, Berberidaceae.

Epimedium species are grown for their delicate sprays of spring flowers, their handsome foliage, and their tough, no-nonsense constitution. Also commonly called barrenworts and bishop's caps (the latter a reference to the flower shape), they bear loose, airy racemes or panicles of ½- to 1-inch flowers on wiry stems in spring. Blooms have eight sepals, four of which are petal-like, and four true petals that are hooded or spurlike and serve as nectaries. Flowers are white, rose, red, yellow, or bicolored. The wiry-stemmed leaves emerge with or slightly after the flowers. Each leaf consists of several heart-shaped or somewhat triangular leaflets (from three to nine or more) that have either spiny or smooth edges. New leaves are bright green, sometimes marked with bronze or maroon, and they turn darker green and become more leathery as they mature. The leaves are attractive from early spring into late fall and even early winter and often exhibit good fall color. Plants described as evergreen or semievergreen generally exhibit this characteristic in areas with mild winters. From about Zone 6 north, the foliage turns brown and curls over winter. The genus contains between 30 and 40 species native to the Mediterranean and eastern Asia.

HOW TO GROW

Give epimediums partial to full shade and rich, evenly moist soil. They also grow in sun, provided the soil is rich and consistently moist. Established plants tolerate dry shade and can compete with the roots of established trees. Epimediums are rhizomatous, and most species spread steadily, but slowly, to form broad 1- to 2-foot-wide mounds. In late winter cut back the old foliage so it will not hide the spring flowers. Propagate by dividing the clumps in spring. Another option is to root individual sections of rhizomes.

E. alpinum

e. al-PIE-num. Alpine Epimedium. A 6- to 9-inch-tall species with deciduous leaves and red, nearly spurless flowers in spring. Zones 3 to 8.

E. grandiflorum   P. 100

e. gran-dih-FLOR-um. Long-spurred Epimedium. Deciduous 8- to 12-inch-tall species with large 1- to 1½-inch-wide flowers in white, yellow, pink, or purple, which bloom in spring. 'Crimson Beauty' has coppery red flowers. 'Rose Queen' bears bronzy young leaves and rose pink blooms. 'White Queen' bears white flowers. Zones 4 to 8.

E. × perralchicum

e. × per-RAL-chee-cum. Vigorous 12- to 16-inch-tall hybrid that spreads to 2 feet or more. Bears evergreen or semievergreen leaves and bright yellow ¾-inch-wide flowers in spring. 'Frohnleiten' bears showy, 1-inch-wide blooms. Zones 5 to 8.

E. perralderianum

e. per-ral-der-ee-AY-num. A 10- to 12-inch-tall species that spreads to 2 feet or more. Bears evergreen to semievergreen leaves and ¾-inch-wide short-spurred yellow flowers in spring. Zones 5 to 8.

E. pinnatum

e. pin-NAH-tum. An 8- to 12-inch-tall species that bears evergreen to semievergreen leaves and ¾-inch-wide yellow flowers with brown-purple spurs in spring. Zones 4 to 8.

E. × rubrum

P. 100

e. × ROO-brum. Red-flowered Epimedium. An 8- to 12-inch-tall species with deciduous leaves and ¾-inch-wide flowers in spring that are red and pale yellow. Zones 4 to 8.

E. × versicolor

P. 101

e. × vers-ih-COL-er. Bicolor Epimedium. Vigorous 12-inch-tall species with evergreen to semievergreen leaves and ¼- to ¾-inch-wide flowers in spring that are pinkish red and yellow with red spurs. 'Neosulfureum' bears pale yellow flowers. 'Sulfureum' bears flowers that are darker yellow and have longer spurs than those of 'Neosulfureum'. Zones 4 to 8.

E. × warleyense

e. × war-lee-EN-see. Warley Epimedium. Vigorous 8- to 12-inch-tall species that bears evergreen to semievergreen leaves and ½-inch-wide brick to orange-red flowers. Zones 4 to 8.

E. × youngianum

e. × young-ee-AH-num. Young's Epimedium. Compact 6- to 8-inch-tall species that spreads to 1 foot or less and bears deciduous, delicate-looking fernlike leaves and ½- to ¾-inch-wide white or rose pink flowers in spring. 'Niveum' bears white flowers. 'Roseum', sometimes called 'Lilacinum', bears pale mauve pink to lilac flowers. Zones 4 to 8.

❧ Erigeron

ee-RIDG-er-on. Aster family, Asteraceae.

Commonly called erigerons or fleabanes, *Erigeron* species are annuals, biennials, and perennials with daisylike flowers. There are about 200 species in the genus native to mountainous regions and dry grasslands, especially in North America. Erigerons usually produce a rosette of simple, lance- to spoon-shaped or oval leaves, although some species also bear leaves along the stems. Their daisylike blooms are single or double and consist of many very narrow ray florets (the "petals") in yellow, purple, white, pink, orange, or violet-blue. The ray florets surround dense, usually yellow, buttonlike centers of disk florets, which produce the seeds. Flowers are borne singly or in small clusters and usually appear in summer.

HOW TO GROW

Give commonly cultivated erigerons, including the species listed here, full sun or light shade and rich soil that is well drained yet remains evenly moist. (Alpine or rock garden species require extremely well drained soil and are especially intolerant of wet soil in winter.) A spot with shade during the hottest part of the day is beneficial, especially in Zones 7 and 8, to help the plants cope with heat. Taller species and cultivars require staking. Deadhead to encourage repeat bloom. Divide plants every 2 to 3 years in spring or fall to keep them vigorous. Propagate by division, cuttings taken from shoots at the base of the plants in spring, or seeds.

E. hybrids
P. 101

Most hybrids range from 1½ to 2 feet in height, spread to about 1½ feet, and bloom from early to midsummer. 'Charity' bears semidouble pink flowers. 'Darkest of All' ('Dunkelste Aller') bears semidouble flowers with violet ray florets. 'Prosperity' bears lavender-blue flowers. 'Gaiety' and 'Pink Jewel' bear pink flowers. 'Summer Snow' ('Sommerneuschnee') bears white flowers. 'Foersters Liebling' bears semidouble, deep reddish pink blooms with yellow centers from early to midsummer. Hardiness varies among the cultivars, but most are hardy from Zones 4 or 5 to 8.

E. pulchellus

e. pul-CHELL-lus. Poor Robin's Plantain. A 2-foot-tall species that spreads by stolons to about 1½ feet. Bears 1-inch-wide yellow-centered flowers in summer, either singly or in small clusters, with about 60 lavender ray florets. Zones 4 to 8.

E. speciosus

e. spee-see-OH-sus. A 2-foot-tall species that spreads as far and bears 1- to 2-inch-wide flower heads in summer with more than 100 lavender-blue ray florets. Zones 2 to 9.

❦ *Eryngium*

eh-RIN-jee-um. Carrot family, Apiaceae.

Commonly called sea hollies, the 230 species of *Eryngium* are annuals, biennials, and perennials native to dry, sandy, or rocky soils primarily in the Mediterranean, although there also are native North American species. Unlikely-looking relatives of carrots and Queen Anne's lace (*Daucus carota*), they bear leathery, oval-, heart-, or sword-shaped leaves that often are deeply divided and thistlelike with spiny margins. Their tiny flowers are borne in dense, rounded conelike umbels with a ruff of showy, stiff, spiny bracts at the base. Foliage comes in shades of steely blue-gray, gray-green, or silver-green, while flowers are metallic purple-blue or blue-gray.

HOW TO GROW

Most sea hollies thrive in full sun and average, well-drained soil. They tolerate heat, drought, and poor soil, although some species, including *E. agavifolium* and *E. yuccifolium*, thrive in rich, evenly moist, well-drained soil. For all, good soil drainage is essential, especially in winter. Sea hollies have deep taproots and generally resent being disturbed, so select a permanent spot at planting time. Most spread to form 1½- to 2-foot-wide clumps. Propagate by separating small plantlets from the base of the clump. Plants also self-sow, and seedlings are easily moved.

E. agavifolium

e. ah-gav-ih-FOE-lee-um. Evergreen species with rosettes of sword-shaped, sharp-toothed leaves and branched 3- to 5-foot-tall stalks of round 2-inch-long greenish white flower heads with spiny bracts in late summer. Zones 6 to 9.

E. alpinum

e. al-PIE-num. Alpine Sea Holly. A 2-foot-tall species with rosettes of spiny, heart-shaped leaves. From midsummer to fall it bears branched stalks of round 1½-inch-long flower heads that are metallic blue-gray with spiny, lacy-looking bracts. Zones 5 to 8.

E. amethystinum   P. 102

e. am-eh-thuh-STY-num. Amethyst Sea Holly. A 2-foot-tall species forming clumps of rounded, pinnately cut (featherlike), spiny leaves. Bears round metallic blue ¾- to 1-inch-long flower heads with spiny silver-gray bracts from mid- to late summer. Zones 3 to 8.

E. bourgatii
P. 102
e. bour-GAH-tee-eye. Mediterranean Sea Holly. A 1- to 2-foot-tall plant with spiny, pinnate (featherlike) leaves with silver veins. From mid- to late summer it bears branched stems of rounded gray-green ½- to 1-inch-long flower heads with a starlike ruff of lance-shaped bracts. Zones 5 to 9.

E. planum
e. PLAY-num. Flat Sea Holly. Evergreen 3-foot-tall species with rounded, toothed, and lobed leaves. From midsummer to fall it bears branched stems of rounded ½- to ¾-inch-long flower heads that are pale steely blue surrounded by narrow blue-green bracts. Zones 5 to 9.

E. yuccifolium
P. 103
e. yuck-ih-FOE-lee-um. Rattlesnake Master. Native North American species forming 2-foot-tall rosettes of semievergreen, sword-shaped blue-gray leaves with spiny margins. From midsummer to fall it bears branched 4-foot-tall stalks of round ¾- to 1-inch-long flower heads that are whitish green with very small gray-green bracts. Zones 4 to 8.

✺ Eupatorium
you-pah-TORE-ee-um. Aster family, Asteraceae.

Commonly known as bonesets or Joe-Pye weeds, *Eupatorium* species are annuals, perennials, subshrubs, and shrubs. There are about 40 species in the genus, and the ones most often grown in gardens are native North American wildflowers. Commonly cultivated species usually have whorls of lance-shaped to wedge-shaped or rounded leaves and bear showy, rounded clusters of small fuzzy flowers in summer and fall.

HOW TO GROW
Select a site in full sun or partial shade with average to rich soil. Evenly moist to wet conditions are ideal and yield the tallest plants, although plants also grow in rich, well-drained conditions. *E. rugosum* is best in partial shade; both it and *E. purpureum* grow well in alkaline soils. Dig plants in spring or fall if they outgrow their space: *E. coelestinum* benefits from being divided every 3 to 4 years, while the other species can thrive for years untouched. Established plants spread to form 3- to 4-foot-wide clumps. Propagate by division in spring or by cuttings taken in early summer. Most species will self-sow or can be grown from seeds, but cultivars should be propagated by cuttings or division.

E. coelestinum

P. 103

e. so-les-TEE-num. Hardy Ageratum, Mistflower. Native North American wildflower ranging from 2 to 3 feet tall. Bears slightly hairy leaves and fluffy, flat-topped 2- to 4-inch-wide clusters of lilac-blue flowers from late summer to fall. Zones 5 to 9.

E. fistulosum

P. 104

e. fis-tew-LO-sum. Hollow Joe-Pye Weed. A 5- to 10-foot-tall native species with hollow wine-purple stems and rounded 6- to 10-inch-wide clusters of mauve pink flowers in midsummer. 'Gateway' bears pink flowers on 5-foot black-stemmed plants. Zones 3 to 8.

E. maculatum

e. mack-you-LAH-tum. Spotted Joe-Pye Weed. A 4- to 7-foot-tall native species with stems spotted in purple. Bears flat-topped 4- to 6-inch-wide clusters of pale to dark purple flowers from midsummer to fall. 'Bartered Bride' has white flowers. Zones 3 to 7.

E. purpureum

e. pur-PUR-ee-um. Joe-Pye Weed. Native 3- to 6-foot-tall wildflower with rounded 4- to 6-inch-wide clusters of pale rose pink or purplish flowers from midsummer to fall. Zones 3 to 8.

E. rugosum

e. roo-GO-sum. White Snakeroot. A native 5- to 6-foot-tall species with brown stems and 2½-inch-wide clusters of white flowers from midsummer to fall. 'Chocolate' bears purple-brown leaves. Zones 3 to 7.

❧ Euphorbia

you-FOR-bee-uh. Spurge family, Euphorbiaceae.

An enormous and varied genus, Euphorbia contains some 2,000 species of annuals, biennials, perennials, subshrubs, and trees, as well as exotic-looking succulents. Poinsettias (Euphorbia pulcherrima) and crown-of-thorns (E. milii) are well-known houseplants that belong here; several species are easy-to-grow, hardy perennials valued for their spring to summer flowers, their handsome foliage color, or their evergreen leaves. All euphorbias have very small flowers clustered together in an arrangement called a cyathium, in which a single female flower is surrounded by several male flowers. The showy "flowers" of these plants are actually colorful petal-like bracts (modified leaves) borne beneath the true flowers. The stems contain milky sap that flows when stems or leaves are cut or damaged and may irritate skin.

HOW TO GROW
For most perennial euphorbias, select a site in full sun to partial or light shade with loose, poor to average, well-drained soil; exceptions are noted in the species descriptions below. A site with sun in the morning and dappled shade in the afternoon is suitable for many species. Most euphorbias are very drought tolerant once established. Cut off the flowering shoots at the base of the plant after they have bloomed. Divide plants in spring to control their spread. Propagate by division, by cuttings of shoots that appear at the base of the plants in spring or early summer, by tip cuttings taken in summer, or by seeds. Plants self-sow.

E. amygdaloides var. *robbiae*   P. 104
e. ah-mig-dal-OY-deez var. ROW-bee-eye. Wood Spurge, Robb's Spurge. Forms 1½- to 2-foot-tall mounds of shiny, handsome evergreen leaves topped by greenish yellow flowers from midspring to early summer. Grows in evenly moist, rich soil in partial to full shade and also tolerates dry shade. Spreads vigorously by rhizomes to 2 feet or more and can become invasive. Zones 6 to 9.

E. characias   P. 105
e. kah-RAH-key-iss. Evergreen 3- to 4-foot-tall species with gray-green foliage that spreads to 4 feet. Bears rounded 4- to 10-inch-long clusters of chartreuse flowers from spring to summer. *E. characias* ssp. *wulfenii* bears showy yellow-green flower heads. Zones 7 to 10.

E. dulcis   P. 105
e. DUL-sis. Rhizomatous 1-foot-tall species that forms 1-foot-wide mounds of dark green or bronze-green leaves. Produces small 2- to 5-inch-wide clusters of greenish yellow flowers in early summer. Grows in evenly moist, rich soil in light shade, but also tolerates dry shade. 'Chameleon' has colorful purple-maroon foliage and yellow-green flowers. Zones 4 to 9.

E. griffithii   P. 106
e. grih-FITH-ee-eye. Griffith's Spurge. Mounding, shrublike 2- to 3-foot species that spreads to 2 feet and bears dark green lance-shaped leaves

that turn red in fall. Produces 4- to 6-inch-long clusters of orange-red flowers in early summer. Needs evenly moist, rich soil in light shade. Tolerates full sun in northern zones, but does not tolerate drought. 'Fireglow' bears showy scarlet-orange flowers. Zones 4 to 8.

E. myrsinites

e. mir-sin-EYE-tees. Myrtle Euphorbia. Evergreen species with blue-gray foliage and trailing, prostrate stems that reach 6 to 10 inches tall and spread to about 1 foot. Bears 2- to 3-inch-wide clusters of yellow flowers in spring. Zones 5 to 9.

E. polychroma

P. 106

e. poly-CROW-muh. Cushion Spurge. Formerly *E. epithymoides*. Compact 1- to 2-foot-tall mounding species that spreads to 2 feet. Bears green leaves and bright yellow-green flowers beginning in early spring and lasting to late spring if cool weather prevails. A spot with afternoon shade is best because it protects the plants from heat. Zones 4 to 9.

❦ Ferns

A variety of hardy, perennial ferns are covered in the individual entries of this encyclopedia. See *Adiantum, Athyrium, Dryopteris, Matteuccia, Onoclea, Osmunda, Polystichum.*

❦ Festuca

fess-TOO-kuh. Grass family, Poaceae.

The genus *Festuca* contains from 300 to 400 species of deciduous or evergreen perennial grasses commonly called fescues. Apart from the fine-textured lawn grasses, the species most often seen in gardens are clump-forming plants grown for their dense mounds of linear gray-green or silvery blue leaves.

HOW TO GROW

Select a site in full sun to partial shade with moist, well-drained soil. Good soil drainage is crucial in areas with wet summers. These plants do not grow well where summers are hot and humid, but a site with afternoon shade helps them cope. Cut the plants back to a height of 3 or 4 inches annually in early spring or fall to keep them neat looking. Many gardeners clip off the seed heads when they appear to focus attention on the foliage. Divide the clumps every 3 years or so to keep them vigorous. Propagate by division. Plants self-sow and can be grown from seeds, but cultivars do not come true and should be propagated by division.

F. glauca

P. 107

f. GLAW-cuh. Blue Fescue. Formerly *F. cinerea* and *F. ovina* 'Glauca'. Clump-forming 6- to 12-inch-tall cool-season grass forming evergreen mounds of blue- or silver-green leaves. 'Elijah Blue' has pale blue leaves on 1-foot-tall plants. 'Sea Urchin' ('Seeigel') forms tight 6-inch-tall mounds of silver-blue leaves. Zones 4 to 9.

☙ Filipendula

fill-ih-PEN-joo-luh. Rose family, Rosaceae.

These rose family members are vigorous perennials bearing plumy flower clusters that resemble astilbes (*Astilbe* spp.) more than they do roses. The individual flowers are tiny and five petaled and come in various shades of pink as well as white. The showy clusters of flowers are borne above mounds of large, handsome, pinately divided (featherlike), lobed leaves. There are about 10 species in the genus, commonly called meadowsweets and queen-of-the-prairie; goat's beards (*Aruncus* spp.) and spireas (*Spiraea* spp.) are both close relatives.

HOW TO GROW

Plant meadowsweets in full sun or light shade with average to rich soil that is moist but well drained. *F. rubra* and *F. ulmaria* will grow in boggy soil. Give *F. vulgaris* a spot in full sun or partial shade, preferably with dry, alkaline soil. Cut plants to the ground if the leaves become tattered looking in summer, then keep the soil moist until new leaves emerge. Divide clumps in spring or fall, as necessary, if they become crowded, begin to flower less, or spread too far. In addition to division, propagate by taking root cuttings in late winter or early spring, or sow seeds.

F. palmata

f. pal-MAY-tuh. Siberian Meadowsweet. A 3- to 4-foot-tall species that spreads to about 2 feet. Bears frothy 8-inch-wide clusters of pink flowers in midsummer. 'Nana' bears fernlike leaves and rose pink flowers on 2-foot-tall plants. 'Rubra' bears reddish pink blooms. Zones 3 to 8.

F. purpurea

f. pur-PUR-ee-uh. Japanese Meadowsweet. Mounding 3- to 4-foot-tall species that spreads to 2 feet and has large 10-inch-wide leaves. Bears dense 2-inch-wide clusters of hot pink flowers in mid- and late summer. Zones 4 to 9.

F. rubra

P. 107

f. ROO-bruh. Queen-of-the-prairie. A native North American wildflower ranging from 6 to 8 feet tall and spreading to 4 feet. Bears mounds of large 8-inch-wide leaves and fluffy 5- to 6-inch-wide clusters of fragrant pink flowers from early to midsummer. 'Venusta' (also sold as 'Venusta Magnifica' and 'Magnifica') bears rose pink flowers. Zones 3 to 9.

F. ulmaria

P. 108

f. ul-MAIR-ee-uh. Meadowsweet, Queen-of-the-meadow. A 3- to 6-foot-tall species forming 2-foot-wide mounds of 8-inch-long leaves. Bears 4- to 6-inch-wide clusters of white flowers in summer. 'Aurea' is grown for its leaves rather than its insignificant flowers, which should be removed. Leaves emerge yellow, then turn to creamy yellow, and finally pale green. Zones 3 to 9.

F. vulgaris

f. vul-GAIR-iss. Dropwort. Compact 2-foot-tall species with 1½-foot-wide rosettes of fernlike leaves. Bears loose 4- to 6-inch-wide clusters of creamy white flowers in early and midsummer. 'Multiplex' (also sold as 'Flore Pleno' and 'Plena') bears bronze buds and creamy white double flowers. Zones 4 to 9.

❦ Foeniculum

feh-NICK-you-lum. Carrot family, Apiaceae.

Foeniculum contains a single species, *F. vulgare*, better known as fennel. This biennial or perennial is grown for its feathery-textured, aromatic leaves and flat-topped umbels of tiny yellow flowers. The flowers are followed by aromatic seeds.

HOW TO GROW

Give fennel a spot in full sun and average to rich soil that is moist yet well drained. Plants have deep taproots and resent being moved once established. To propagate, sow seeds into pots or where the plants are to grow in early spring or fall. Plants self-sow, often with abandon. Remove the flowers as they fade to restrict seed formation.

F. vulgare
P. 108

f. vul-GAR-ee. Fennel. Stately 5- to 6-foot-tall perennial forming 1½- to 2-foot-wide clumps of threadlike, airy-textured leaves. Bears 4- to 5-inch-wide clusters of bright yellow flowers from mid- to late summer. Purple-leaved cultivars such as 'Rubrum' and 'Purpureum', commonly called bronze fennel, are especially attractive in perennial plantings and come true from seeds. Zones 4 to 9.

❧ Fragaria

fray-GAIR-ee-uh. Rose family, Rosaceae.

Better known as strawberries, *Fragaria* species are perennials that bear five-petaled, usually white flowers followed by fleshy fruits. One species, alpine strawberry *(F. vesca)*, is grown in perennial gardens as an edging plant or ground cover.

HOW TO GROW

Give alpine strawberries full sun or light shade and rich, moist, well-drained soil. Plants tolerate acid conditions, but prefer neutral to alkaline pH. Propagate by separating and potting up the plants that form on the ends of the stolons or by sowing seeds.

F. vesca
P. 109

f. VES-kuh. Alpine Strawberry, Fraise de Bois. A 6- to 12-inch-tall species with evergreen to semievergreen, three-leaflet leaves. Bears white ¾-inch-wide flowers from late spring into summer followed by edible red ½-inch-long fruit. 'Albicarpa' bears white fruit. Zones 5 to 9.

❧ Gaillardia

gah-LAIR-dee-uh. Aster family, Asteraceae.

Commonly called blanket flowers or simply gaillardias, the 30 species in this genus of aster family plants are annuals, biennials, and perennials primarily native to North America. They bear rosettes of hairy leaves topped by single or double, daisylike flowers in shades of red, red-orange, maroon, and yellow over a long season in summer.

HOW TO GROW

Gaillardias thrive in full sun and average to rich, well-drained soil. They also tolerate poor, dry soil and sandy conditions and are drought and salt tolerant enough for seaside gardens. Too-rich soil yields floppy plants, and heavy clay spells certain death due to root and crown rots, especially in winter. Deadheading encourages repeat bloom and keeps the plants neat looking. Divide plants every 2 to 3 years in early spring to keep them vigorous. Propagate by division, by stem cuttings taken in early summer, or by root cuttings taken in winter. Seed-grown plants are somewhat variable, and vegetative methods are best for producing plants with uniform characteristics.

G. aristata

g. air-is-TAH-tuh. Blanket Flower. Native North American wildflower ranging from 2 to 2½ feet tall and spreading to about 2 feet. From summer to fall, bears 4-inch-wide flowers with red-orange centers and yellow petals with lobes at the tips, giving the flowers a ragged appearance. Zones 3 to 8.

G. × grandiflora

P. 109

g. × gran-dih-FLOOR-uh. Blanket Flower. A short-lived perennial created by crossing perennial *G. aristata* and annual *G. pulchella*, both native North American species. Plants range from 2 to 3 feet tall and spread to about 1½ feet. From early summer to fall they bear showy 3- to 5½-inch-wide flower heads, most often in brilliant combinations of reds, maroons, oranges, and yellows. Dwarf cultivars are especially popular, including 8-inch 'Baby Cole', 12-inch 'Kobold' (also sold as 'Goblin'), and 14- to 16-inch-tall 'Dazzler'. Zones 3 to 8.

❦ Galium

GAL-ee-um. Madder family, Rubiaceae.

About 400 species of annuals and perennials belong to the genus *Galium*. Most are weak-stemmed plants with linear leaves arranged in whorls. They bear small tubular flowers that have four or five petal lobes. Although sometimes borne singly, the white, pinkish, or yellow blooms usually are arranged in clusters. One species, *G. odoratum,* commonly known as sweet woodruff, is used as a ground cover in shade.

HOW TO GROW

Give sweet woodruff a spot in partial to deep shade with rich, well-drained soil. Plants also tolerate sandy soil or heavy clay. They spread at a moderate speed: divide them as necessary in spring or fall to keep them in bounds or for propagation.

G. odoratum

P. 110

g. oh-dor-AH-tum. Sweet Woodruff. Creeping 6- to 8-inch-tall perennial with whorls of narrow leaves and dainty clusters of starry, fragrant ⅛- to ¼-inch-wide white flowers from late spring to summer. Zones 4 to 8.

❦ Gaultheria

gaul-THEER-ee-uh. Heath family, Ericaceae.

Gaultheria species are evergreen shrubs grown for their glossy leaves, bell- to urn-shaped blooms, and fleshy berries. One species, wintergreen *(G. procumbens)*, is a shrublet, native to eastern North America, grown in shade gardens as a perennial ground cover. About 170 species belong to the genus.

HOW TO GROW

Give wintergreen partial shade and moist, acid to neutral soil. Mulch plants with chopped leaves to retain soil moisture and add essential organic matter. Water during dry weather. Propagate by dividing plants in spring or sowing seeds.

G. procumbens

P. 110

g. pro-CUM-benz. Wintergreen, Checkerberry. Evergreen 4- to 6-inch-tall shrublet with aromatic leaves that spreads slowly but steadily to form 2- to 3-foot-wide patches. Bears white or pale pink ½- to 1-inch-long flowers in summer followed by showy red ½-inch berries. Zones 3 to 8.

❦ Gaura

GAU-ruh. Evening Primrose family, Onagraceae.

Gaura species are annuals, biennials, perennials, and subshrubs primarily native to North America. Of the some 20 species in the genus, one is commonly grown in gardens — *G. lindheimeri*. The plants mostly bear basal leaves — usually lance shaped to elliptic or spoon shaped — and small, somewhat star-shaped pink or white flowers carried in spikes or racemes.

HOW TO GROW

Select a site in full sun with moist, well-drained soil. Good soil drainage is essential to success. Plants form deep taproots and are quite drought tolerant (and difficult to dig) once established. They also tolerate heat and humidity as well as light shade. To propagate, take cuttings from shoots that arise at the base of the plant in spring or from stem tips in spring or early summer. Plants also can be divided in spring, but are best left undisturbed. Or sow seeds.

G. lindheimeri

P. 111

g. lind-HEIM-er-eye. White Gaura. A shrubby 3- to 4-foot-tall native wildflower with airy, erect panicles of 1-inch-wide white flowers that fade to pink from early summer to fall. 'Whirling Butterflies' bears an abundance of white flowers on 2½-foot-tall plants. 'Corrie's Gold' has leaves edged in gold. 'Siskiyou Pink' bears bright pink flowers. Zones 5 to 9.

❦ Gentiana

jen-shee-AH-nuh. Gentian family, Gentianaceae.

Treasured by gardeners for the rich shades of true blue they bring to the beds and borders, gentians also come in shades of violet as well as yellow, white, and red. The plants have simple, often lance-shaped leaves and carry their trumpet- or bell-shaped flowers singly or in clusters. Depending on the species, blooms appear anywhere from spring to fall. The genus contains about 400 species of hardy annuals, biennials, and perennials, which may be deciduous, semievergreen, or evergreen. Most gentians are native to alpine habitats and are suitable only for areas that have cool summers, such as the Pacific Northwest. A few species can be grown successfully over a wider area.

HOW TO GROW

Ideally, gentians prefer a site in full sun with well-drained soil that remains evenly moist. In areas with summers that are warm to hot and dry, however, give them a spot that receives shade during the hottest part of the day. The plants resent disturbance and thrive for years without needing to be divided, so try to select a permanent site. Propagate by carefully dividing the clumps in spring, by lifting and separating offsets in spring, or by sowing seeds.

G. andrewsii P. 111

g. an-DREW-see-eye. Bottle Gentian, Closed Gentian. A 1- to 2-foot-tall native North American wildflower that spreads from 1 to 2 feet. In late summer it bears clusters of tubular to urn-shaped 1½-inch-long flowers at the stem tips that never open completely and are dark blue with white on the petal lobes. Zones 3 to 7.

G. asclepiadea

g. ah-sklee-pee-ah-DEE-uh. Willow Gentian. A 2- to 3-foot-tall perennial forming 1½-foot-wide clumps. Bears narrow, willowlike leaves and 2-inch-long, trumpet-shaped, pale to dark blue flowers in late summer and fall. Zones 5 to 7.

G. septemfida P. 112

g. sep-tem-FIH-duh. Crested Gentian. A low-growing 6- to 8-inch-tall species spreading to 1 foot. In late summer it bears clusters of 1½-inch-long trumpets that are narrowly bell-shaped and blue to purple-blue with white throats. Zones 3 to 8.

Geranium

jer-AY-nee-um. Geranium family, Geraniaceae.

Commonly called hardy geraniums or cranesbills, *Geranium* species are versatile, long-lived perennials producing mounds of handsome foliage and loose clusters of five-petaled cup- or saucer-shaped flowers. The leaves are lobed in a palmate (handlike) fashion and often have toothed or lobed margins. Some species have very lacy-textured foliage. The genus contains about 300 species, including annuals, biennials, and perennials. Perennial species can be hardy or tender and are either herbaceous or, in areas with mild winters, semievergreen to evergreen. Blooms come in shades of pink and magenta as well as white, purple, and violet-blue. The main flush of bloom occurs from late spring into early summer, and some geraniums rebloom into fall, especially if the plants are cut back. Some species also feature colorful fall foliage. Too often hardy geraniums are confused with zonal or ivy geraniums (*Pelargonium* spp.), which are popular tender perennials grown as annuals. Hardy geraniums are sometimes dubbed "true" geraniums to distinguish them from their better-known cousins.

HOW TO GROW

Most hardy geraniums thrive in full sun or partial shade with rich, evenly moist, well-drained soil. In most parts of the country, especially the South, shade during the hottest part of the day is best. Taller species tend to flop: either stake them with peabrush or let the plants sprawl. After most of the flowers fade, cut plants to within 1 inch of the ground and a fresh new mound of leaves will arise in a few weeks. Many hardy geraniums need to be divided regularly to look their best, especiallly *G. endressii, G. himalayense, G. sanguineum,* and *G. sylvaticum,* which should be divided every 2 to 3 years. Hardy geraniums can be grown from seeds, and plants may self-sow, but most cultivars are best propagated vegetatively — by dividing the clumps in spring or fall, by root cuttings taken in fall, or by cuttings taken in spring from shoots at the base of the plant.

G. × cantabrigiense

g. × can-tah-brih-gee-EN-see. Cambridge Geranium. Mounding 1-foot-tall hybrid with glossy, aromatic leaves that spreads slowly to form dense clumps 2 feet or more in width. Bears clusters of 1-inch-wide purple-pink or white flowers from early to midsummer. 'Biokovo' has white flowers tinged pink and spreads to 3 feet via long runners. Zones 5 to 8.

G. cinereum

g. sih-NEER-ee-um. Grayleaf Cranesbill. A 6- to 12-inch species that spreads to 1 foot. Bears gray-green leaves, evergreen in mild climates, and 1-inch-wide purplish pink flowers from late spring to early summer. Requires gritty, very well drained soil. 'Ballerina' produces purplish red flowers with dark eyes all summer long on 4- to 6-inch-tall plants. Zones 5 to 8.

G. clarkei

P. 112

g. CLARK-ee-eye. Clark's Geranium. Mounding 1½-foot-tall species that spreads quickly by rhizomes to 3 feet or more. Produces deeply cut leaves and abundant ¾-inch-wide violet-purple or white flowers with lilac veins from late spring into early summer. 'Kashmir Purple' has purple-blue flowers with red veins and comes true from seeds. 'Kashmir White' has white flowers with lilac-pink veins and can be grown from seeds, though some seedlings will be purple flowered. Zones 4 to 8.

G. dalmaticum

g. dal-MAT-ih-cum. Dalmatian Cranesbill. Mounding to trailing 4- to 6-inch-tall species that spreads by rhizomes to about 2 feet. Bears soft pink 1-inch-wide flowers in late spring and early summer and has good red-orange fall foliage color that is evergreen in mild-climate areas. Grows well in shade. Zones 4 to 8.

G. endressii
P. 113

g. en-DRESS-ee-eye. Endres Cranesbill. Mounding to sprawling 1½-foot-tall species, evergreen in mild climates, that spreads to about 2 feet. Bears pale pink 1-inch flowers in spring, but blooms all summer (and grows best) in areas with cool temperatures. Tolerates drought. Zones 4 to 8.

G. himalayense

g. him-ah-lay-EN-see. Lilac Cranesbill. Clump-forming species with sprawling 1- to 1½-foot-long stems that spread to about 2 feet. Bears violet-blue 2-inch-wide flowers in early summer. Foliage turns orange-red in fall. Zones 4 to 8.

G. hybrids
PP. 113–14

Many outstanding hybrids are available. 'Johnson's Blue', a cross between *G. himalayense* and *G. pratense*, bears lavender-blue 1½- to 2-inch-wide flowers in early summer on mounding 1½-foot-tall plants that spread via rhizomes to form 2½-foot-wide clumps. It is hardy in Zones 4 to 8. 'Ann Folkard', a cross between *G. procurrens* and *G. psilostemon*, bears 1½-inch-wide magenta flowers with dark centers from midsummer to fall. It features yellow-green leaves and trailing stems that reach about 2 feet in height and scramble and spread to 3 feet or more. Zones 5 to 9.

G. ibericum

g. eye-BER-ih-kum. Caucasus Geranium. Clump-forming 1½-foot-tall, 2-foot-wide species that bears violet 2-inch-wide flowers with dark veins in early summer. Zones 3 to 8.

G. macrorrhizum
P. 114

g. mack-row-RISE-um. Bigroot Geranium. Mounding 1½-foot-tall species that spreads vigorously via fleshy, deep roots to 2 feet or more. Bears aromatic leaves and pink to purplish pink 1-inch-wide flowers in spring. Evergreen in mild climates. 'Ingwersen's Variety' has soft pink flowers. Tolerates drought and grows well in shade. Zones 3 to 8.

G. maculatum

g. mack-you-LAH-tum. Wild Cranesbill, Spotted Geranium. Native North American wildflower that reaches 1 to 2 feet in height and spreads to about 1½ feet. Bears pink 1¼-inch-wide flowers from late spring to mid-summer. Does best in partial shade in moist, well-drained soil. Zones 4 to 8.

G. × magnificum

P. 115

g. × mag-NIFF-ih-cum. Showy Geranium. Clump-forming 2-foot-tall, 2-foot-wide hybrid *(G. ibericum × G. platypetalum)* with deeply lobed and toothed leaves. Bears 1½- to 2-inch-wide violet flowers with darker veins in midsummer and features good fall foliage color. Zones 4 to 8.

G. × oxonianum

P. 115

g. × ox-oh-ee-AH-num. Vigorous 1½- to 3-foot-tall hybrid *(G. endressii × G. versicolor)* that spreads from 2 to 3 feet or more. Bears pink 1½-inch-wide flowers from spring to fall. 'Claridge Druce' is a very vigorous selection with grayish green leaves and rose pink flowers. 'Wargrave Pink', also vigorous, bears salmon pink flowers. Zones 4 to 8.

G. phaeum

g. FAY-um. Dusky Cranesbill, Mourning Widow. Clump-forming 1½- to 2½-foot-tall species that spreads as far and bears black-purple, maroon, violet, or white 1-inch-wide flowers with reflexed petals from late spring to early summer. Grows best in partial shade in moist, well-drained soil, but will tolerate dry soil. Zones 5 to 7.

G. platypetalum

g. plah-tee-PET-ah-lum. Broad-petaled Geranium. Clump-forming 1- to 1½-foot-tall species that spreads about as far. Bears 1¼- to 1¾-inch-wide violet-blue flowers from early to midsummer. Zones 3 to 8.

G. pratense

g. pray-TEN-see. Meadow Cranesbill. Vigorous, clump-forming 2- to 3-foot-tall species forming 2-foot-wide mounds of deeply lobed leaves. Bears blue-violet 1½-inch-wide flowers in late spring and early summer. Zones 2 or 3 to 8.

G. psilostemon

g. sigh-LAH-steh-mon. Armenian Cranesbill. Shrublike 2- to 4-foot-tall species that forms 3-foot-wide clumps. Bears 2-inch-wide magenta flowers with black eyes from early to late summer. Good fall foliage color and evergreen to semievergreen leaves. Zones 5 to 8.

G. sanguineum
P. 116

g. san-GWIN-ee-um. Bloody Cranesbill. An 8- to 12-inch-tall species that forms 1-foot-wide mounds of lacy leaves topped by bright pink 1- to 1½-inch flowers from spring into summer. Leaves turn red in fall. Tolerates drought and does well in shade. 'Shepherd's Warning' is compact — from 4 to 6 inches tall, and *G. sanguineum* var. *striatum* (also listed as *G. sanguineum* var. *lancastriense*) bears pale pink flowers on 4- to 6-inch plants. 'New Hampshire Purple' bears rose-purple flowers. 'Album' bears white flowers. 'Elsbeth' bears pink flowers with dark veins all summer. Zones 3 to 8.

G. sylvaticum
P. 116

g. sil-VAT-ih-cum. Wood Cranesbill. Bushy, clump-forming 2½- to 3-foot-tall species with deeply cut leaves and violet-blue 1-inch-wide flowers in early to midspring. Best in partial shade and evenly moist soil. Zones 3 to 8.

❦ Geum

JEE-um. Rose family, Rosaceae.

Geums, sometimes called avens, are rose family plants with pinnate (featherlike) leaves and small saucer- to bowl-shaped flowers that normally have five petals. Blooms are borne in shades of orange, red, and yellow as well as cream and pink. They are carried singly or in small clusters and appear from late spring to early summer.

HOW TO GROW

Select a site in full sun with average to rich, evenly moist, well-drained soil. South of Zone 6, a site with afternoon shade is best. Good soil drainage is especially important in winter. *G. rivale* prefers moist or even boggy conditions, however. Plants can be short lived: divide them every 2 to 3 years to keep them vigorous. Water during dry weather. Propagate named cultivars by division in spring or fall. Seed-grown plants aren't identical to asexually propagated ones, but 'Lady Stratheden' and 'Mrs. J. Bradshaw' can be grown from seeds.

G. chiloense
P. 117

g. chil-oh-EN-see. Geum, Avens. Formerly *G. quellyon.* Clump-forming 1½- to 2-foot-tall species that spreads to about 2 feet. Bears deeply lobed, toothed leaves and clusters of saucer-shaped 1½-inch-wide red flowers in summer. 'Fire Opal' bears semidouble red-orange blooms. 'Lady Stratheden' bears semidouble golden yellow blooms. 'Mrs. J. Bradshaw' bears 1¾-inch-wide scarlet blooms. Zones 4 to 7 or 8.

G. coccineum

g. cock-SIN-ee-um. Geum, Avens. Formerly *G. × borisii*. A clump-forming 1- to nearly 2-foot-tall species with saucer-shaped 1½-inch-wide orange-yellow flowers from late spring to midsummer. Zones 4 to 7 or 8.

G. rivale

P. 117

g. rih-VAL-ee. Water Avens, Indian Chocolate. A ½- to 2-foot-tall species spreading from 1 to 2 feet. Bears pendent, bell-shaped ¾-inch-wide flowers from late spring to midsummer that have purple-pink petals and red-brown sepals. Zones 3 to 8.

G. triflorum

P. 118

g. tri-FLOR-um. Prairie Smoke, Purple Avens. Native North American wildflower that creeps to form 1½-foot-tall, 1-foot-wide mounds of ferny gray-green leaves. In summer, bears 1½-inch-wide flowers with creamy petals and long purple bracts followed by plumy, silvery pink seedpods that have a fuzzy, smokelike appearance. Zones 1 to 7.

❦ Gillenia

gih-LEN-ee-uh. Rose family, Rosaceae.

Two species of native North American woodland perennials belong to this rose family genus. Both are shrubby, spring-blooming perennials with palmate (handlike), three-leaflet leaves with toothed margins. The leaves have stipules (leaflike appendages) at the base of the leaf stalks, which offer the easiest way to distinguish the two species. The white or pale pink flowers are borne in loose panicles and have five lance-shaped to linear petals.

HOW TO GROW

Select a site in partial shade with rich, moist, well-drained soil that has a slightly acid to neutral pH. Established plants tolerate drought. *Gillenia* species will grow in full sun if the soil is consistently moist or if they have shade during the hottest part of the day. They spread slowly by rhizomes, but seldom need dividing. To propagate, divide plants in spring or fall, or sow seeds.

G. stipulata

g. stip-you-LAH-tuh. American Ipecac, Indian Physic. Also listed as *Porteranthus stipulatus*. A 1- to 3-foot-tall species that spreads to about 2 feet. Bears broadly ovate, toothed stipules that are leaflike and remain on the plant. Flowers, borne in spring to early summer, are white to pale pink with 1-inch-wide flowers. Zones 5 to 8.

G. trifoliata

P. 118

g. tri-foe-lee-AH-tuh. Bowman's Root, Indian Physic. Also listed as *Porteranthus trifoliata*. A 2- to 4-foot-tall species forming 2-foot-wide clumps of bronzy green leaves bearing small awl-shaped stipules that drop off the plant. Bears starry 1- to 1½-inch-wide flowers with pinkish calyces from late spring to early summer. Zones 4 to 8.

Gypsophila

jip-SOF-ih-luh. Pink family, Caryophyllaceae.

Best known as baby's breaths, *Gypsophila* species are annuals and perennials native from the Mediterranean to central Asia. Most of the 100 species in the genus are found on dry, rocky, or sandy soil that is alkaline in pH. Plants bear lance-shaped to linear gray-green leaves and clouds of tiny five-petaled white or pink flowers that are star- or trumpet-shaped. The name *Gypsophila* is from the Greek *gypsos,* chalk, and *philos,* loving, and refers to the preference some species have for alkaline soils rich in chalk, a soft form of limestone rich in calcium carbonate.

HOW TO GROW

Give baby's breaths full sun or very light shade and rich, evenly moist, very well drained soil. Deeply prepared soil is best, because the perennial species have deep, wide-ranging roots and deep digging improves soil drainage. Wet soil in fall and winter leads to crown rot, and plants in poorly drained conditions tend to be short-lived. *G. paniculata* tolerates slightly acid soil (only to pH 6.5), but plants tend to be short-lived in such conditions and are best in neutral to alkaline soil, pH 7.0 to 7.5. *G. repens* grows well in acid or alkaline soils. Cutting bloom stalks to the ground as the flowers fade — or shearing *G. repens* — encourages rebloom. Plants have deep root systems and are best left undisturbed once planted. Propagate *G. paniculata* cultivars by cuttings in early summer. *G. repens* can be divided in early spring or in midsummer, after flowering. Or sow seeds.

G. paniculata
P. 119

g. pan-ick-you-LAH-tuh. Baby's Breath. A shrubby perennial forming 2- to 4-foot-wide clumps that range from 2 to 4 feet tall when in bloom. Bears cloudlike panicles of tiny white or pink flowers from mid- to late summer. Full-size plants need staking, but dwarf cultivars, which are about 2 feet tall, do not. Dwarf types include 18-inch 'Pink Fairy' and 15-inch-tall 'Viette's Dwarf'. 'Perfecta' is a robust 3- to 4-foot double-flowered cultivar. 'Snowflake', another double, reaches 3 feet. Zones 3 to 9.

G. repens
P. 119

g. REE-penz. Creeping Baby's Breath. A 4- to 8-inch-tall perennial spreading to form 1-foot-wide mats of bluish to gray-green semievergreen leaves. Bears loose, broad clusters of ½-inch-wide pink or white flowers from early to midsummer. Zones 4 to 8.

❧ Hakonechloa

hah-co-neh-KLO-uh. Grass family, Poaceae.

A handsome ornamental grass native to Japan is the only species in this genus. Commonly known as hakone grass, it produces handsome mounds of arching, bamboolike foliage and small panicles of flowers borne among the leaves in mid- to late summer. The botanical name combines the Greek *chloa*, grass, with *hakone* for Mount Hakone, one of the mountains on Japan's main island, where the grass is found.

HOW TO GROW

Select a site in partial shade with rich, evenly moist, well-drained soil. Although this is a warm-season grass, the plants grow best in cool, moist conditions. In areas with cool summers, plants thrive in full sun, but where summers are hot, partial shade is best. Variegated cultivars usually are most colorful in partial shade. The plants spread gradually, but not invasively, by rhizomes. Cut the foliage back in spring. To propagate, divide plants in spring. The species can be grown from seeds, but variegated cultivars do not come true.

H. macra
P. 120

h. MACK-ruh. Hakone Grass. Handsome 1½- to 2-foot-tall grass forming 2-foot-wide mounds of arching, linear, bamboolike leaves. 'Aureola' bears stunning green-and-yellow striped leaves. Zones 5 to 9.

❦ *Helenium*

hel-EE-nee-um. Aster family, Asteraceae.

The genus *Helenium* contains about 40 species of annuals, biennials, and clump-forming perennials that grow naturally in areas with moist soils and along woodland edges. The perennials in the genus are prized for their late-season daisylike flower heads in shades of yellow, orange, bronze, and red. The flower heads consist of ray florets, commonly called petals, surrounding dense, buttonlike centers of disk florets. Leaves usually are ovate to inversely lance shaped. Commonly called sneezeweeds, the plants do not cause sneezing, but contact with the foliage can cause an allergic skin reaction, and all parts of the plants are poisonous if eaten. Although the botanical name *Helenium* honors Helen of Troy, these plants are native to North and Central America.

HOW TO GROW

Give sneezeweeds full sun and rich, evenly moist, well-drained soil. *H. autumnale* also grows in constantly moist to wet conditions, while *H. hoopesii* tolerates dry soil. Feed plants in spring with a balanced organic fertilizer or a topdressing of compost or well-rotted manure. Water during dry weather. Taller-growing cultivars require staking. Pinching in midsummer reduces the ultimate height of the plants and keeps them compact. Sneezeweeds perform best when divided frequently: dig them every 3 to 4 years in spring. Propagate named cultivars by division in early spring or by cuttings taken from shoots at the base of the plant in spring or early summer. The species also are easy to propagate from seeds.

H. autumnale   PP. 120–21

h. aw-tum-NAL-ee. Common Sneezeweed. Native North American perennial ranging from 2 to 5 feet tall and forming 2- to 3-foot-wide clumps. From late summer to fall, it bears 2- to 3-inch-wide yellow flowers with brown centers and wedge-shaped petals that are toothed at the ends. Cultivars are more often grown than the species. Cultivars that stay under 3 feet include yellow-flowered 'Butterpat', bronze-red 'Crimson Beauty', and early-blooming, coppery red 'Moerheim Beauty', which blooms from early to late summer. 'Zimbelstern', which bears yellow-brown flowers on 4-foot plants, also blooms early — from mid- to late summer. 'Kugelsonne' is a strong-stemmed 5-foot cultivar with yellow flowers. 'Brilliant', also a 4- to 5-foot cultivar, bears bronze-red flowers in late summer. Zones 3 to 8.

H. hoopesii

h. HOOPS-ee-eye. Orange Sneezeweed. A 2- to 3-foot-tall North American native forming 2-foot-wide clumps. Bears yellow to orange 3-inch-wide flowers in early to midsummer. Zones 3 to 7.

❦ Helianthus

hee-lee-AN-thuss. Aster family, Asteraceae.

Known by gardeners and nongardeners alike as sunflowers, *Helianthus* species are annuals and perennials native to North, Central, and South America. The genus contains about 70 to 80 species of usually tall, often coarse plants with showy, daisylike flowers in shades of yellow and gold. The flowers, borne from summer to fall, consist of ray florets ("petals") surrounding dense centers of disk florets, which produce the seeds. Sunflowers have large coarse oval, lance-, or heart-shaped leaves. Both the common and botanical names celebrate the fact that these are plants for full sun: *Helianthus* is from the Greek *helios,* sun, and *anthos,* flower.

HOW TO GROW

Full sun and average, moist but well-drained soil are all these plants require. A few species — *H. angustifolius, H. decapetalus, H. divaricatus,* and *H. strumosus* — thrive in sites that receive shade for part of the day or high, dappled shade (but good light) all day. *H. angustifolius, H. decaptalus,* and *H. maximiliani* also grow in wet soil. Pinch stem tips once in early summer or midsummer — or both times — if you want to curtail height and encourage branching. Plants growing in shady or windy spots may need staking. Deadheading extends the flowering season. Divide plants every 3 to 4 years in early spring or fall to keep them looking their best and prevent them from overtaking the garden — the species listed below easily spread into 3- to 4-foot-wide clumps. Propagate plants (especially cultivars) by division, or take cuttings from stems at the base of the plant in spring. Some sunflowers also produce small plantlets along the outside of the clumps, which can be dug without disturbing the rest of the clump. Or sow seeds.

H. angustifolius

P. 121

h. an-gus-tih-FOE-lee-us. Swamp Sunflower. A 4- to 8-foot-tall North American native species with lance-shaped leaves and branched clusters of yellow 3-inch-wide flower heads with purple to brown centers from early to midfall. Zones 6 to 9.

H. decapetalus

h. deck-ah-PET-ah-lus. Thin-leaved Sunflower. Rhizomatous 4- to 5-foot-tall North American native bearing yellow 2- to 3-inch-wide flower heads with yellow centers from late summer to midfall. Zones 4 to 8.

H. divaricatus
P. 122

h. dih-vair-ih-KAH-tus. Woodland Sunflower. A 2- to 6-foot-tall North American native with yellow 2-inch-wide flower heads with yellow centers from midsummer to midfall. Zones 3 to 8.

H. maximiliani
P. 122

h. max-ih-mil-lee-AN-ee. Maximillian Sunflower. A 4- to 10-foot-tall North American native with clusters of 2- to 3-inch-wide yellow flowers with brown centers from late summer to fall. Will grow in wet soil. Zones 3 to 8.

H. × multiflorus

h. × mul-tih-FLOR-us. Many-flowered Sunflower. A 3- to 5-foot-tall hybrid (annual sunflower, *H. annuus*, × thin-leaved sunflower, *H. decapetalus*). Bears golden yellow flowers, to 5 inches across, from late summer to midfall. Double-flowered cultivars, including 'Loddon Gold' and 'Flore Pleno', are available. Zones 5 to 9.

H. salicifolius
P. 123

h. sah-lih-sih-FO-lee-us. Willow-leaved Sunflower. A 3- to 7-foot-tall North American native with clusters of golden yellow 2- to 3-inch-wide flowers from early to midfall. Zones 3 or 4 to 8.

H. strumosus

h. strew-MOE-sus. Pale-leaved Wood Sunflower. A 3- to 6-foot-tall North American native bearing yellow 4½-inch-wide flowers with yellow centers from midsummer to early fall. Zones 4 to 9.

H. tuberosus

h. too-ber-OH-sus. Jerusalem Artichoke. Extremely vigorous to invasive, rhizomatous 5- to 10-foot-tall North American native producing edible, potatolike tubers. Bears 4-inch-wide flower heads in fall with yellow petals and centers. Zones 4 to 9.

❦ *Helictotrichon*

hel-ick-toe-TRY-kon. Grass family, Poaceae.

Of the 50 species of clump-forming grasses in this genus, one species, commonly known as blue oat grass, is grown as an ornamental. *Helictotrichon* species bear linear green or gray-blue leaves and erect panicles of flattened flower spikelets.

HOW TO GROW

Select a site in full sun to light shade with poor to average, well-drained soil. Plants may succumb to root rot in heavy clay and do not grow well in areas with hot, humid summers. Cut back plants in early spring. For propagation, divide clumps in spring or sow seeds.

H. sempervirens   P. 123

h. sem-per-VIE-rens. Blue Oat Grass. Clump-forming, cool-season grass with 2-foot-tall, 2-foot-wide clumps of erect, evergreen to semievergreen leaves that are gray-blue. Bears 3- to 4-foot-tall spikes of yellow oatlike seed heads in early summer. Zones 4 to 9.

❦ *Heliopsis*

he-lee-OP-sis. Aster family, Asteraceae.

Commonly called oxeyes, false sunflowers, and sunflower heliopsis, *Heliopsis* species are native North American wildflowers that bear sunflower-like flower heads with golden yellow ray florets (the "petals") and centers (or "eyes") with darker yellow disk florets. About 12 or 13 species belong to the genus, all perennials native to dry prairies and woodlands. The plants are coarsely branched and bear ovate to lance-shaped leaves with toothed margins. Oxeyes differ from true sunflowers (*Helianthus* spp.) in that their ray florets are fertile rather than sterile. *Heliopsis* is from the Greek *helios,* sun, and *opsis,* resembling.

HOW TO GROW

Select a site in full sun or partial shade with average to rich soil. Evenly moist, well-drained soil is best, but plants tolerate dry conditions. Pinch and deadhead oxeyes just as you would sunflowers. Plants growing in rich, moist soil may need dividing frequently, about every 2 to 3 years. Propagate by dividing the clumps in spring or fall or by sowing seeds.

H. helianthoides

P. 124

h. he-lee-an-thee-OY-deez. Oxeye. A 3- to 6-foot-tall North American native wildflower spreading from 2 to 4 feet. It bears yellow 1½- to 3-inch-wide flower heads from midsummer to early fall. *H. helianthoides* ssp. *scabra* is more compact than the species — to about 3 feet — and a better garden plant. Its cultivars 'Gold Greenheart' (also sold as 'Goldgrünherz') with lemon yellow flowers, bright yellow 'Light of Loddon', and golden yellow 'Sommersonne' (also sold as 'Summer Sun') are all good choices with semidouble or double flowers. Zones 4 to 9.

❦ *Helleborus*

hell-eh-BORE-us. Buttercup family, Ranunculaceae.

Long-lived, shade-loving hellebores are treasured by gardeners not only for their early-season bloom, but also for their handsome evergreen or semievergreen foliage. About 15 species belong to the genus, all perennials — several with shrubby habits. They have leathery, usually dark green leaves divided into lobes or leaflets that often are toothed. The flowers are borne singly or in small clusters in winter and early spring and come in subtle shades of cream, purple, dusty mauve, cream-pink, and green. The showy parts of the flowers are not true petals, but petal-like sepals, which remain attractive for 2 to even 4 months as seed capsules form. All parts of the plants are poisonous if ingested, and the sap from bruised leaves can cause a skin rash in some individuals.

HOW TO GROW

Plant hellebores in light to full shade with rich, evenly moist, well-drained soil. Neutral to slightly alkaline pH is best, although *H.* × *hybridus* tolerates slightly acid soil. A sheltered site protected from winter winds helps keep the evergreen foliage at its best. On shrubby species, which have biennial stems (they produce foliage the first year, flowers the second), cut back the stems that have already bloomed to make room for new growth. Leave some stems if you want seedlings. Once planted, hellebores are best left undisturbed and thrive for years without needing division. Established clumps spread from about 1 to 1½ feet. If you must move them, or want to divide the clumps, dig them in spring after flowering. Handle the plants carefully. Do not divide *H. argutifolius* or *H. foetidus:* the rhizomes of these shrubby species are very short, and division is nearly always fatal. The easiest way to propagate hellebores is to dig self-sown seedlings in spring or summer and replant them.

H. argutifolius

h. are-goo-tih-FOE-lee-us. Corsican Hellebore. Shrubby species that ranges from 1½ to 2 feet in height and bears clusters of nodding, pale green, bowl-shaped 1- to 2-inch-wide flowers from late winter to early spring. Zones 6 or 7 to 9.

H. atrorubens

h. ah-trow-ROO-benz. A 1-foot-tall perennial bearing purple-blushed leaves and small clusters of purple saucer-shaped 1½- to 2-inch-wide flowers from late winter into spring. Zones 5 to 9.

H. foetidus

P. 124

h. FEH-tid-us. Stinking Hellebore. Shrubby species, ranging from 1½ to 2 feet tall and bearing handsome, deeply cut leaves with narrow leaflets. Leaves have an unpleasant scent when crushed. Produces large showy clusters of nodding, bell-shaped ½- to 1-inch green flowers from midwinter to early spring. Zones 6 to 9; to Zone 5 with protection.

H. × hybridus

P. 125

h. × HY-brih-dus. Lenten Rose. Often listed as *H. orientalis*. A 1- to 1½-foot-tall perennial with leathery leaves and loose, showy clusters of outward-facing, saucer-shaped 2- to 3-inch-wide flowers. Blooms come from late winter to early spring in shades of cream, greenish white, white, purple, and mauve. Zones 4 to 9.

H. niger

h. NYE-jer. Christmas Rose. A low-growing 12- to 15-inch-tall species with saucer-shaped 2- to 3-inch-wide flowers that are white or white flushed with pink. Blooms are borne one per stem or occasionally in clusters of two or three. Plants can bloom beginning in early winter but generally flower in early spring. Zones 4 to 8.

H. purpurascens

h. pur-pur-AS-scens. A 4- to 12-inch perennial with loose clusters of cup-shaped 1½- to 3-inch flowers from midwinter to early spring in shades of purple or pinkish purple flushed with green. Zones 5 to 8.

❦ Hemerocallis

hem-er-oh-CAL-iss. Lily family, Liliaceae.

Hemerocallis species, better known as daylilies, are versatile, long-lived perennials grown for their colorful, trumpet-shaped flowers carried on erect stalks, called scapes. Blooms are borne from 1 to as many as 7 feet above low clumps of long, arching, sword-shaped or grassy leaves that are arranged in fans. The flowers have six petals (more correctly called tepals because three are true petals and three are petal-like sepals) and last for only a day. The botanical name *Hemerocallis* commemorates the fleeting nature of the blooms; it's from the Greek *hemera,* day, and *kallos,* beauty. While only about 15 species belong to the genus — all native to China, Japan, and Korea — thousands of cultivars are available. Better selections produce a wealth of buds and bloom over a period of three to four weeks in summer. The plants have thick, fibrous roots with fleshy, tuberlike swellings on them. Well-formed clumps of standard-size plants spread 2 to 4 feet, with the foliage ranging from about 1 to 2 feet in height. Small daylily cultivars spread from 1 to 2 feet.

HOW TO GROW

Select a site in full sun or light shade and average to rich soil that is well drained and evenly moist. Modern hybrids bloom best with 8 hours of full sun. Daylilies tolerate poor soil and drought but do not bloom as abundantly. Too-rich soil leads to foliage production at the expense of flowers. Plants bloom best when the soil remains evenly moist, so water during dry weather. Remove faded blooms regularly to keep plants attractive and prevent the limp, old flowers from interfering with new ones that are opening. (Tetraploid daylilies are especially notorious for needing regular deadheading.) Pick off any seedpods that begin to form — cultivars do not come true from seed. Remove bloom stalks after the last flowers fade. Divide plants in early spring or early fall when the clumps become crowded, begin to bloom less, or outgrow their space, or for propagation.

H. citrina

h. sih-TREE-nuh. Citron Daylily. Vigorous, heavy blooming, herbaceous species reaching about 4 feet in bloom. Produces fragrant, pale lemon yellow 3½- to 5-inch-wide trumpets in summer. Zones 5 to 9.

H. fulva

h. FUL-vuh. Tawny Daylily. A 3-foot-tall nonnative roadside flower originally from eastern Asia with semievergreen leaves and rusty orange 2½- to 4-inch-wide flowers in summer. 'Flore Pleno' bears double flowers. Zones 2 to 9.

H. hybrids   PP. 125–26

Hybrid daylilies are far more commonly grown than the species and come in many colors, shapes, and sizes. Colors include peach, apricot, yellow-orange, maroon, orange-red, buffy orange, pinkish lavender, plum, and pale yellow or pink blooms that are nearly white. 'Gentle Shepherd' is a midseason cultivar with handsome near-white to ivory blooms. Blooms may be a solid color or feature contrasting colors. Shapes include classic trumpets and recurved blooms with petals curving back to form an almost flat face, as well as spider- and star-shaped blooms with narrow, widely spaced petals. Some are fragrant. Diploid daylilies have two sets of chromosomes; tetraploids, four — twice the normal number. Tetraploids, which often have ruffled or frilled petal edges, usually are larger plants than diploids, with bigger, more brightly colored flowers. So-called miniature daylilies bear flowers under 3 inches across, often on full-size plants. The term "dwarf" is sometimes used to indicate small plants. 'Peach Fairy' bears 2½-inch flowers on 26-inch plants, while 'Mini Pearl' bears 3-inch flowers on 16-inch plants. Both are miniatures. Daylilies also are classified by bloom season, and selecting a mix of early, midseason, and late cultivars extends bloom season. Reblooming daylilies produce a main flush of bloom, followed by additional spikes later in the season. 'Happy Returns', 'Pardon Me', 'Little Grapette', and 'Eenie Weenie' are rebloomers. Everbloomers, such as 'Stella de Oro', flower continuously through the season after a first main flush of bloom. Hybrids may be deciduous (also called dormant), semievergreen, or evergreen. The leaves of evergreen types remain green all winter in the South; protect them with a layer of mulch in winter in Zone 6 and the northern part of Zone 7. Semievergreens are deciduous in the North, semievergreen in the South. Deciduous types go dormant in fall and return in spring wherever they are grown. Hardiness and heat tolerance vary, so buy from a local grower or mail-order supplier in a climate similar to your own. Cultivars that have received the Stout Medal from the American Hemerocallis Society include 'Fairy Tale Pink' (ruffled pink), 'Mary Todd' (ruffled yellow), 'Ruffled Apricot' (ruffled apricot), 'Barbara Mitchell' (ruffled orchid pink), and 'Ed Murray' (deep red). Zones 3 to 10.

H. lilioasphodelus

h. LIL-ee-oh-ass-foe-DEL-us. Lemon Lily. Formerly *H. flava*. Vigorous, semievergreen 3-foot-tall species bearing fragrant lemon yellow 3½-inch-wide flowers in late spring or early summer. Zones 3 to 9.

H. middendorfii

h. mid-den-DOR-fee-eye. Middendorff Daylily. A 3-foot-tall semievergreen species with red-brown buds and star-shaped yellow-orange 2½- to 3-inch-wide flowers in early summer. Zones 3 to 9.

❦ *Heuchera*

YOU-ker-uh. Saxifrage family, Saxifragaceae.

Heuchera species are native North American plants once grown solely for their airy sprays of tiny colorful flowers. Today, heucheras are just as like-ly to be planted for their ornamental foliage. About 55 species of ever-green or semievergreen perennials belong to the genus, all forming mounds of rounded to heart-shaped leaves and delicate-looking panicles or racemes of tiny, sometimes petalless flowers on erect stems above the foliage. Some heucheras have colorful bell- or funnel-shaped flowers, in which case the showy part of the flower is a five-lobed calyx. Others have inconspicuous blooms. Common names reflect this distinction: heu-cheras grown for their flowers are commonly called coral bells, while those grown for their foliage are typically referred to as alumroots or sim-ply heucheras. Hybrid heucheras have all but replaced the species in cul-tivation.

HOW TO GROW

Select a site with rich, evenly moist, well-drained soil. Although plants will grow in full sun to full shade, a site with morning sun and afternoon shade is often the best choice. Heucheras take a season or two to settle in after planting. Water regularly during dry weather, and mulch plants with chopped leaves to keep the soil moist and rich. Deadhead coral bells (*H. sanguinea* and *H.* × *brizoides)* to encourage new flowers to form. Some gardeners remove the flowers of foliage heucheras when they appear. Heucheras have shallow, woody roots and are frequently heaved out of the soil in winter by cycles of freezing and thawing. Check plants during mild spells in winter and reset them if necessary or cover the crowns with mulch. All can be grown into Zone 3 with a protective winter mulch of evergreen boughs or salt hay. Divide plants in spring about every 4 or 5 years, especially clumps that have congested, woody crowns that have risen above the soil surface. Propagate plants by division or by cutting off and planting individual "branches" or sections of the woody roots in spring or early summer. Most heuchera cultivars don't come true from seeds, but some self-sow, and self-sown seedlings may or may not be attractive. Remove the flowers if you want to discourage this or rogue out unattractive seedlings.

H. americana

h. ah-mair-ih-KAN-uh. American Alumroot. Native perennial grown for its low, 6- to 12-inch-tall and 1-foot-wide mounds of handsome rounded leaves that are marbled and veined with purple-brown when young. Bears 1½-foot-tall panicles of brown-green flowers in early summer. Zones 4 to 8.

H. × brizoides

P. 126

h. × briz-OY-deez. Hybrid Coral Bells. Low-growing hybrids (crosses between *H. sanguinea, H. americana,* and *H. micrantha*) with 6-inch-tall, 1- to 1½-foot-wide mounds of lobed and scalloped evergreen leaves. Plants bear airy 1½- to 2½-foot-tall clusters of tiny ⅜- to ½-inch-long flowers from late spring into early summer in shades of pink, coral, red, rose-red, and white. *H. × brizoides* cultivars tend to be more heat tolerant than *H. sanguinea* cultivars, making them better choices for southern gardens. Cultivars include 'Chatterbox' (rose pink), 'Firefly' (vermilion red), 'Firebird' (scarlet), 'June Bride' (white), 'Mt. St. Helens' (brick red), 'Raspberry Regal' (raspberry red with marbled leaves), and 'Rosamundi' (coral pink). Zones 4 to 8.

H. hybrids

P. 127

Heuchera hybrids form 1-foot-tall, 1½-foot-wide mounds of showy lobed and/or ruffled leaves that are 3 to 6 inches long. Leaves can be green with gray and silver overtones and veins, purple-brown with metallic mottling, rose-burgundy with silver overtones and purple veins, and green with purple-red mottling. New leaves are most colorful and are produced all season long, although the color may fade during the hottest part of the summer. Clusters of tiny white, greenish white, or pinkish flowers appear in early summer above the foliage on 1- to 2-foot-tall stalks. Cultivars include 'Chocolate Veil', 'Chocolate Ruffles', 'Dale's Strain', 'Garnet', 'Persian Carpet', 'Pewter Veil', 'Ruby Ruffles', and `Velvet Knight'. Zones 4 to 8.

H. micrantha

P. 127

h. mih-CRAN-tha. Mound-forming native North American species with 1-foot-tall, 1½-foot-wide mounds of silver-gray marbled, ovate to heart-shaped leaves. Bears loose 2- to 3-foot-tall panicles of tiny white to pink-flushed flowers in early summer. *H. micrantha* var. *diversifolia* `Palace Purple' has shiny, metallic bronze-red leaves and greenish white flowers. Zones 4 to 8.

H. sanguinea

h. san-GWIN-ee-uh. Coral Bells. Native wildflower with low 6-inch-tall, 10- to 12-inch-wide mounds of kidney-shaped leaves. Bears loose 1- to 2-foot-tall panicles of tiny red, pink, or white flowers in summer. Many cultivars are now listed under *H. × brizoides* to reflect their hybrid origin. Cultivars include 'Cherry Splash' (rose-red), 'Coral Cloud' (coral red), 'Pluie de Feu' (red), 'Splendens' (scarlet red), and 'White Cloud' (white). Zones 4 to 8.

❦× *Heucherella*

× you-ker-ELL-uh. Saxifrage family, Saxifragaceae.

Plants in this hybrid genus are commonly called foamy bells, a name derived from the parent species used to create it: coral bells *(Heuchera)* and foamflower *(Tiarella)*. Foamy bells produce mounds of evergreen, heart-shaped or broadly ovate leaves topped by loose panicles of tiny pink or white flowers from spring to fall.

HOW TO GROW

Select a site in sun or partial shade with light, rich soil that is moist but well drained. Neutral to slightly acid pH is best. Plants also grow in full shade, but do not tolerate heat and humidity and are not long-lived in southern gardens. To propagate, divide plants in spring or fall or sever and pot up runners that appear. They do not set seeds.

× *H. alba*   P. 128

× h. AL-buh. Foamy Bells. Clump-forming perennial that develops low 12-inch-wide mounds topped by airy 16-inch-tall panicles of ⅛- to ¼-inch-long white flowers from late spring to fall. 'Bridget Bloom' bears white flowers. 'Pink Frost' bears pink flowers on 2-foot stalks. Zones 5 to 8.

× *H. tiarelloides*

× h. tee-ah-rell-OY-deez. Foamy Bells. Hybrid spreading by stolons to form 1½-foot-wide clumps topped by 1½-foot-tall panicles of ⅛-inch-long flowers in spring and early summer. Plants may rebloom in fall. Zones 5 to 8.

❦ *Hibiscus*

hy-BISS-kus. Mallow family, Malvaceae.

More than 200 species of annuals, perennials, shrubs, and trees — both hardy and tender — belong to the genus *Hibiscus.* They bear showy, funnel-shaped flowers, each with a prominent central column consisting of the stamens and pistil. The flowers have five petals and are borne either singly or in clusters. The leaves are entire (unlobed) to palmately lobed (like a hand).

HOW TO GROW

Select a site in full sun or very light shade with rich, well-drained soil. Evenly moist conditions are best for both species listed here, and *H. coccineus* thrives in wet to boggy soil. The plants tend to be late to emerge in spring, so mark the locations of the clumps. Propagate plants by dividing the woody clumps in spring, by taking cuttings in summer, or by sowing seeds.

H. coccineus
P. 128

h. cock-SIN-ee-us. Scarlet Rose Mallow, Swamp Rose Mallow. North American native perennial with a woody base that reaches 5 to 10 feet in height and forms 4-foot-wide clumps. Bears lacy, palmately lobed (handlike) leaves with linear leaflets and deep red 6-inch-wide flowers from summer to fall. Zones 6 to 11.

H. moscheutos
P. 129

h. moe-SHOO-tos. Common Rose Mallow, Common Mallow. Vigorous North American native perennial ranging from 4 to 8 feet in height and forming 3-foot-wide clumps. Bears ovate to lance-shaped, shallowly lobed leaves and funnel-shaped 8- to 10-inch-wide flowers in summer in red, pink, and white. Compact 2- to 2½-foot-tall Disco Belle Series plants bear 9-inch-wide flowers. Pink-flowered 'Lady Baltimore' and scarlet-flowered 'Lord Baltimore' bear 10-inch-wide flowers on 4-foot plants. Both Disco Belle and Baltimore cultivars come true from seeds. Zones 5 to 10.

❧ *Hosta*

HOSS-tuh. Lily family, Liliaceae.

Hostas, or plantain lilies, as they are sometimes called, are tough, shade-loving perennials that produce lush mounds of handsome, often variegated leaves and racemes of trumpet-shaped flowers. There are about 70 species in the genus and hundreds of cultivars. Leaves can be heart shaped, nearly round, or lance shaped, and from 1 inch long to as many as 12 inches or more. Foliage color is quite variable: leaves can be solid dark to mid-green, chartreuse, blue-green, blue-gray, or variegated. Leaf texture varies from smooth or ribbed to deeply corrugated. The 1- to 2-inch-long flowers, which are borne on erect spikes that rise above the mounds of leaves, come in white, pale lavender, and deep purple. Flowering time is variable — from late spring to fall — and depends on the parentage of the particular cultivar. Funkia, another common name, is a former botanical name.

HOW TO GROW

Ideally, select a site in light to full shade with rich, evenly moist soil. A site with a few hours of morning sun and shade for the rest of the day is fine. In the South, shade during the hottest part of the day is essential for success. Blue-leaved cultivars generally retain their color best in cool, shady spots that receive good light but no direct sun, while a spot in bright, dappled shade brings out the best color in variegated cultivars. Golden-leaved cultivars tolerate considerable sun but still benefit from shade during the hottest part of the day. Plants are fairly drought tolerant but grow best (and largest) with even moisture. They grow in heavy clay as well as constantly moist conditions, and they can be planted along streambanks, bogs, and ponds, provided the crowns are set above the water line. Hostas can emerge late in spring, so mark the location of the clumps at planting time. They take from two to four seasons to become established and reach their full size after planting. Cut the bloom stalks back to below the foliage as the flowers fade. Plants grow well for years without needing to be divided. Dig plants in spring before the leaves unfurl or in early fall for propagation or to move a clump. Another propagation option is to dig a plant or two from the edge of an existing clump by severing it with a sharp spade. Hosta cultivars do not come true from seeds, but will self-sow (remove flower stalks to prevent this).

H. fortunei

h. for-TOO-nee-eye. Sometimes listed as H. 'Fortunei'. A 1½- to 2-foot-tall species spreading from 2 to 3 feet. Bears clumps of 8- to 12-inch-long leaves topped with mauve flowers on 2½-foot-tall stalks in summer. 'Aureomarginata' has dark green leaves with yellow margins. 'Albomarginata' has white margins. Zones 3 to 8.

H. hybrids
PP. 129-31

Hosta hybrids range from 2 inches to more than 3 feet in height and form dense clumps that spread one and a half to two times as far as they are tall. Unless otherwise noted, plants have pale lavender flowers in mid-summer. All are hardy in Zones 3 to 8.

LARGE CULTIVARS. These form 2½- to 3-foot-tall clumps and spread from 3 to 4 feet or more. 'Black Hills' has corrugated dark green leaves and pale lavender flowers in late spring to early summer. 'Blue Angel' has blue-gray heart-shaped leaves and white flowers in midsummer. 'Blue Umbrellas' has heart-shaped blue to blue-green leaves that turn green by midsummer and pale lavender flowers in early summer. 'Krossa Regal' has vase-shaped clumps of ribbed blue-gray leaves and lavender flowers in mid- to late summer. 'Regal Splendor' has vase-shaped clumps of ribbed blue-gray to gray-green leaves variegated with creamy white and yellow. 'Sagae' (formerly *H. fluctuans* 'Variegata') has blue-gray creamy-edged leaves and white flowers in mid- to late summer. 'Sum and Substance' has heart-shaped yellow-green leaves and pale lilac flowers in mid- to late summer.

MEDIUM CULTIVARS. These range from 1 to 2 feet in height and spread from 1½ to about 3 feet. 'Abba Dabba Do' has green leaves edged in yellow. 'Birchwood Parky's Gold' has green-gold heart-shaped leaves. 'Blue Cadet' has heart-shaped blue-green foliage. 'Blue Wedgwood' has blue-gray-green wedge-shaped leaves. 'Brim Cup' bears puckered, cupped dark green leaves with white margins. 'Francee' has dark green heart-shaped leaves that have white margins and also bears handsome lavender flowers in summer. 'Golden Tiara' bears small round to heart-shaped green leaves with irregular golden margins. 'Gold Standard' has golden, green-edged leaves. 'Great Expectations' has yellow leaves that have blue-green edges and gold centers turning to creamy white by midsummer and white flowers in early summer. 'Halcyon' has rounded blue leaves. 'Wide Brim' has green leaves that have wide creamy white margins. 'Zounds' has puckered golden yellow leaves and white flowers in early summer. 'Undulata', often listed as *H. undulata,* bears rounded lance-shaped leaves that have very wavy margins and are splashed and striped with pale yellow and/or white and bears pale lilac purple flowers in early and midsummer.

SMALL CULTIVARS. All of these are under 1 foot in height and spread from 1½ to 3 feet. 'Chartreuse Wiggles' has lance-shaped yellow-green wavy-margined leaves and lavender late-summer flowers. 'Ginkgo Craig' bears lance-shaped dark green leaves edged in white and lavender flowers in late summer. 'Gold Edger' has heart-shaped chartreuse leaves. 'Kabitan' has lance-shaped yellow leaves with dark green margins. 'Little Aurora' bears round gold leaves. And 2-inch-tall 'Tiny Tears' has dense clumps of green heart-shaped leaves.

H. montana

h. mon-TAN-uh. A 2- to 2½-foot-tall species with deeply ribbed leaves that forms 3-foot-wide mounds. Bears white flowers in early summer on 3-foot-tall scapes. 'Aureomarginata' has dark green leaves with irregular yellow margins. 'Mountain Snow' has white-margined leaves. 'On Stage' bears green leaves with gold to white centers. Zones 3 to 8.

H. plantaginea   P. 131

h. plan-tuh-JIH-nee-uh. August Lily. A 2- to 2½-foot-tall species producing 3-foot-wide clumps of heart-shaped green leaves and showy racemes of large very fragrant white flowers on erect stalks high above the foliage in late summer. 'Aphrodite' bears double flowers. Zones 3 to 8.

H. sieboldiana

h. see-bol-dee-AH-nuh. Vigorous 2- to 2½-foot-tall species forming 4-foot-wide mounds of heart-shaped, puckered, gray-green leaves. Bears dense racemes of pale lilac-white flowers just above the foliage in early summer. *H. sieboldiana* var. *elegans,* also sold as 'Elegans', has very puckered blue-gray leaves. 'Frances Williams' produces 2-foot-tall clumps of blue-green leaves with irregular greenish yellow edges. Zones 3 to 8.

H. tokudama   P. 131

h. tow-koo-DAH-muh. A 1½-foot-tall species forming 3-foot-wide clumps of heart-shaped, heavily puckered leaves. Bears white flowers in summer. 'Aureonebulosa' has yellow-green leaves with irregular blotches and margins of blue-green. 'Flavocircinalis' has blue-green leaves with irregular yellow-green margins. Zones 3 to 8.

H. venusta

h. veh-NEW-stuh. A dwarf species with 4-inch-tall clumps of heart-shaped leaves that spread to about 10 inches. Bears pretty lavender flowers on 1- to 1½-foot-tall stalks in midsummer. Zones 3 to 8.

H. ventricosa

h. ven-trih-KO-suh. A 1½- to 2-foot-tall species forming 3-foot-wide clumps of dark, glossy green leaves and handsome dark purple flowers in late summer. 'Aureomarginata' has leaves variegated with yellow and cream. 'Aureomaculata' bears leaves with green edges and a central yellow blotch; its leaves fade to yellow-green in summer. Zones 3 to 8.

❧ *Houttuynia*

hoo-TIH-nee-uh. Lizard's Tail Family, Saururaceae.

Houttuynia contains a single species native to eastern Asia grown primarily for its heart-shaped leaves. *H. cordata* bears dense spikes of tiny green flowers in summer, each of which has four small petal-like white bracts at the base. All parts of the plant are foul smelling when crushed. The species spreads quite rapidly via rhizomes.

HOW TO GROW

Select a site in full sun or partial shade with average to rich soil. Plants prefer evenly moist conditions and will grow in boggy soil as well as shallow standing water, but in such sites they are especially invasive. Keep them in containers sunk to the rim in the soil (or set in a water garden) to control their spread. They are slightly less invasive in average, somewhat drier soil. The variegated form tends to revert to green, especially in too much shade: rogue out reverted plants regularly. Propagate by division in spring or by cuttings taken in late spring or early summer.

H. cordata

P. 132

h. cor-DAH-tuh. A vigorous ½- to 1-foot-tall perennial that easily spreads to 3 feet or more. 'Chameleon', also sold as 'Tricolor' and 'Variegata', bears leaves variegated with red, pink, green, and pale yellow. Zones 3 to 9.

❧ *Iberis*

eye-BEER-iss. Cabbage family, Brassicaceae.

Better known as candytufts, *Iberis* species are annuals, perennials, and subshrubs grown for their rounded clusters of flowers. They bear linear to ovate leaves, and their showy flower clusters, which are sometimes fragrant, are made up of tiny four-petaled flowers. The genus contains about 40 species that thrive in alkaline, fast-draining soils and are found from Spain and southern Europe through North Africa to Turkey and Iran.

HOW TO GROW

Plant candytufts in a site with full sun or very light shade and average, well-drained soil. Wet soil, especially in winter, leads to root rot and death. Immediately after they've flowered, cut plants back by one-third to remove spent blooms and encourage branching. Every 2 to 3 years, cut plants back hard — by about two-thirds — to keep growth compact and dense. Plants seldom need dividing, but dig them in spring immediately after they flower to propagate them or if they outgrow their space. Another propagation option is to sever and pot up pieces of stem, which often root where they touch the ground. Or take tip cuttings in late spring or early summer. Candytufts can be grown from seeds, but most cultivars are propagated asexually, and seed-grown plants will be variable.

I. saxatilis

i. sax-ah-TILL-iss. Rock Candytuft, Perennial Candytuft. Woody-based 3- to 6-inch-tall subshrub spreading to about 1 foot. Bears evergreen, needlelike leaves and flat-topped 1¼- to 1½-inch-wide clusters of white flowers in midspring. Zones 2 to 7.

I. sempervirens

P. 132

i. sem-per-VYE-rens. Perennial Candytuft, Common Candytuft. Woody-based 6- to 12-inch-tall evergreen subshrub spreading to 1½ feet. Bears very dark green 1- to 1½-inch-long leaves and 1½- to 2-inch-wide clusters of tiny white flowers in midspring. 'Little Gem' is a dwarf 5- to 8-inch cultivar. 'Autumn Beauty' and 'Autumn Snow' both bloom in spring and again in fall. Zones 3 to 9.

🌿 Inula

IN-you-luh. Aster family, Asteraceae.

The genus *Inula* contains about 100 species that bear showy, daisylike flower heads in shades of orange-yellow to yellow. The blooms are borne singly or in clusters and consist of a central "eye" of closely packed disk florets surrounding numerous, narrow ray florets, or "petals," that in some species are nearly threadlike.

HOW TO GROW

Select a site in full sun with rich, moist soil that is well drained. *I. helenium* and *I. hookeri* grow in partial shade. *I. magnifica* grows in wet and even boggy conditions and also tolerates partial shade. Taller species generally need staking. To propagate, divide the clumps in spring or fall or sow seeds.

I. ensifolia

P. 133

i. en-sih-FOE-lee-uh. Sword-leaved Inula. A 1- to 2-foot-tall species that spreads to about 1 foot. Bears narrow, lance-shaped leaves and small clusters of 1- to 2-inch-wide golden yellow flowers in mid- to late summer. Zones 4 to 9.

I. helenium

P. 133

i. heh-LEE-nee-um. Elecampane. Robust 3- to 6-foot-tall herb (the dried roots were once used as an expectorant) forming low 3-foot-wide clumps of ovate, toothed 32-inch-long leaves. Bears 3-inch-wide yellow flowers, either singly or in small clusters, in mid- to late summer. Zones 5 to 8.

I. hookeri

i. HOOK-er-eye. A 2- to 2½-foot-tall species with lance-shaped leaves and pale yellow 1½- to 3-inch-wide flowers borne singly or in small clusters in late summer and fall. Zones 4 to 8.

I. magnifica

i. mag-NIFF-ih-kuh. Vigorous 5- to 6-foot-tall species with 3-foot-wide clumps of rounded 10-inch-long leaves. Bears clusters of 6-inch-wide daisies in late summer. Zones 5 to 8.

❧ *Iris*

EYE-riss. Iris family, Iridaceae.

Named in honor of the mythological Greek goddess Iris who rode to earth on a rainbow, *Iris* is a vast genus containing about 300 species — both perennials and bulbs — along with thousands of cultivars. All bear flowers with six petals, three of which point up or out and are called standards, and three of which point out or down and are called falls. Generally the flowers are borne in small clusters and the buds open in succession, a characteristic that lengthens the display from each flower stalk. The foliage is sword shaped, strap shaped, or grassy. While some rhizomatous species spread widely, others form dense, grasslike clumps.

HOW TO GROW

The ideal site for iris varies according to species. Plant bearded irises in full sun and average to rich, well-drained soil from midsummer to early fall, setting the tops of the fleshy rhizomes just above the soil surface. Rhizomes planted too deeply or covered with mulch are susceptible to rot. Tall bearded cultivars may need staking. Cut back and destroy old foliage and rake up debris around the plants in fall to help control iris borers. Dig and divide bearded irises every 3 years in midsummer or early fall to keep them healthy and vigorous, as well as for propagation. (Discard spongy, old portions along with any rhizomes infested with fat, fleshy iris borer larvae or any that smell or are slimy, both signs of bacterial soft rot.) Cut the leaves back by two-thirds, then replant. Water deeply to settle the plants in the soil, and every 10 days to 2 weeks for the rest of the growing season if the weather is dry. Established plants are quite drought tolerant. See the individual descriptions below for recommended care for other species.

I. bearded hybrids   P. 134

Sometimes listed as *I. germanica,* these hybrids bloom in late spring or early summer with flowers that have fuzzy beards at the top of each fall. They come in various heights and flower sizes, although tall bearded irises, with 4- to 8-inch-wide blooms atop 27-inch-tall plants, are by far the best known. Other size classes can be as small as 8 inches in height and bloom at slightly different times. Hundreds of cultivars are available in colors from white and pale yellow through peach, pink, raspberry, bronze-red, lilac, purple, and violet-blue to chocolate brown and red-black. The falls and standards may be the same color, contrasting solid colors, or have margins or mottling in contrasting colors. Many are fragrant. Winners of the American Iris Society's Dykes Medal are all good cultivars, including 'Beverly Sills' (pink), 'Bride's Halo' (white and lemon yellow), 'Dusky Challenger' (purple and violet), 'Edith Wolford' (yellow and blue-violet), 'Honky Tonk Blues' (blue and white), 'Jessy's Song' (white with red-violet, and lemon yellow beards), 'Silverado' (silvery lavender-blue), 'Victoria Falls' (blue and white), and 'Hello Darkness' (violet-black). Zones 3 to 9.

I. cristata   P. 134

i. cris-TAH-tuh. Crested Iris. Clump-forming 4- to 8-inch-tall native North American wildflower that spreads via fleshy rhizomes to form 1½- to 2-foot-wide mats. In late spring it bears pale lavender-blue or white 1½- to 2-inch-wide flowers with yellow or orange crests on each fall. Grows in partial to full shade and rich, evenly moist, well-drained soil with a slightly acid pH. Divide the clumps in early spring as necessary or for propagation. Zones 3 to 9.

I. ensata

P. 135

i. en-SAH-tuh. Japanese Iris. Formerly *I. kaempferi.* Sturdy perennial form-ing 2½- to 3-foot-tall clumps of grasslike leaves that spread to 2 feet via short rhizomes. Bears beardless, flat 4- to 8-inch-wide flowers in early to midsummer in shades of violet-blue, purple, lavender-blue, white, rose pink, and wine red. Blooms are single or double and have large falls with standards that point downward. Select a site in full sun to partial shade with very rich acid soil — pH 5.5 to 6.5. It requires constantly moist to even boggy soil in spring and summer but needs drier conditions in win-ter. Divide clumps in early spring or early fall every 3 to 4 years. Zones 4 to 9.

I. foetidissima

i. feh-tih-DISS-ih-muh. Stinking Iris. Unusual 1- to 3-foot-tall species that spreads to 1½ feet. Bears dull purple flowers in early summer followed by showy scarlet seeds in fall. Plant in partial to full shade in evenly moist, well-drained soil that is rich in organic matter. Zones 7 to 9; to Zone 6 with protection.

I, Louisiana hybrids

P. 135

Louisiana Irises. Hybrid irises derived from several native species ranging in height from 1½ or 2 feet to 5 feet and spreading to 3 feet or more via wide-spreading rhizomes. They bear flowers in shades of purple to blue-black, sky blue, vermilion red, and violet from midspring to early sum-mer. Plant in full sun to partial shade and very rich, constantly moist to wet soil with an acid pH. They also grow in rich, well-drained soil that remains evenly moist. Zones 6 to 11, but hardiness varies depending on the cultivar, and some are hardy to Zone 4 with winter protection.

I. pseudacorus

P. 136

i. sue-DACK-or-us. Yellow Flag. Vigorous 3- to 4-foot-tall species that spreads as far. Produces clumps of sword-shaped leaves topped by bright yellow 2½-inch-wide flowers in early summer. Grows in full sun or light shade in a range of soils, from evenly moist, well-drained, to constantly wet or boggy, as well as with up to 10 inches of water over the crowns. Zones 4 to 9.

I. sibirica

P. 136

i. sigh-BEER-ih-kuh. Siberian Iris. A 1- to 3-foot-tall clump-forming species spreading to 2 feet. Produces clumps of handsome, grassy leaves and beardless 3-inch-wide flowers in early summer in shades from violet-blue, blue, and purple to white or yellow. Many cultivars are available, including ones with bicolor blooms. Plants grow in full sun to light shade and evenly moist, well-drained or constantly wet soil. They also grow with up to 2 inches of standing water over the crowns. 'Butter and Sugar' bears white-and-yellow blooms. 'White Swirl' bears white flowers that have yellow centers. 'Super Ego' bears pale blue flowers with darker violet-blue falls. 'Caesar' bears violet purple blooms. Plants take a season or two to become established and resent being disturbed. Divide them in early spring or early fall only when they become so very crowded that blooming is reduced or for propagation. Zones 2 to 9.

I. tectorum

i. teck-TOR-um. Roof Iris. A 10- to 16-inch-tall species spreading by fleshy rhizomes to form broad 1½-foot-wide clumps. Bears crested 2- to 5-inch-wide flowers in lavender or white in late spring or early summer. Select a site in full sun or partial shade with rich, evenly moist well-drained soil. Also tolerates dry soil in shade. Divide immediately after flowering every 3 to 5 years when clumps become overcrowded or for propagation. Set the rhizomes with the tops just above the soil surface. Zones 5 to 9.

I. versicolor   P. 137

i. ver-sih-CUH-lor. Blue Flag. A native North American wildflower ranging from 2 to 2½ feet in height and spreading to 2 or 3 feet. Bears blue-violet or purple 2- to 3-inch-wide flowers in early to midsummer. Zones 2 to 9. Southern blue flag (I. virginica) is a similar native species hardy in Zones 7 to 11. Both species grow in full sun in constantly moist soil or standing water.

🌀 Kirengeshoma

kih-ren-guh-SHOW-muh. Hydrangea family, Hydrangeaceae.

Two species of perennials native to Japan and Korea belong to the genus *Kirengeshoma*. They bear branched clusters of nodding, tubular to bell-shaped blooms above mounds of large maplelike leaves.

HOW TO GROW

Select a site in partial shade with rich, evenly moist soil with an acid pH. Clumps are best left undisturbed, so try to pick a permanent site and prepare the soil deeply at planting time by adding plenty of compost or other organic matter. To propagate, carefully dig and divide the plants in spring.

K. palmata
P. 137

k. pal-MAH-tuh. Yellow Wax Bells. A 3- to 4-foot-tall species that forms 2½- to 4-foot-wide clumps. Bears 5- to 8-inch-long palmately lobed leaves and pale yellow, waxy-textured, 1½-inch-long flowers in late summer and early fall. Zones 5 to 8.

❦ Knautia

NAW-tee-uh. Teasel family, Dipsacaceae.

Knautia contains 40 or more species of annuals and perennials sometimes grown for their pincushion-like flower heads that resemble scabiosas (*Scabiosa* spp.). The flowers are bluish lilac or red-purple and are carried in loose, branched clusters above rosettes of leaves that are simple or lobed in a featherlike (pinnate) manner.

HOW TO GROW
Select a site in full sun with average to rich, well-drained soil. Neutral to alkaline pH is best. Plants are short-lived, especially in areas with hot, humid summers. They tend to flop in midsummer in hot climates: cut them back in spring to keep them compact and prevent this. Propagate by taking cuttings from shoots that appear at the base of the plant in spring or by seeds.

K. macedonica
P. 138

k. mah-sih-DON-ih-kuh. Formerly *Scabiosa rumelica*. Clump-forming 2- to 2½-foot-tall perennial spreading to about 1½ feet. Bears purple- to maroon-red ½- to 1½-inch-wide flower heads from mid- to late summer. Zones 4 to 8.

❦ Kniphofia

nih-FOE-fee-uh. Lily family, Liliaceae.

Kniphofia species bear erect spikes of flowers aptly described by common names such as torch lilies, red-hot pokers, and poker plants. The blooms consist of densely packed, tubular flowers above clumps of grassy ever-green or deciduous leaves. They usually are pendent but sometimes are held erect and come in fiery oranges, reds, and yellows as well as pale yellows, cream, and shades of pink. About 70 species — all perennials — belong to the genus.

HOW TO GROW

Give torch lilies full sun and average to rich soil that is evenly moist but well drained. Good soil drainage is especially important in winter. Plants do well in sandy soil. Cut the flower stalks to the ground after the blooms fade; cut the foliage back by half in late summer if it becomes unkempt looking. Plants resent being disturbed and can be left for years without needing division. Divide them in spring if they become crowded, out-grow their space, or for propagation. To make divisions without disturb-ing the thick rhizomes and fleshy roots, try severing offsets from the out-side of the clumps in spring. Or sow seeds, although cultivars do not come true.

K. uvaria   P. 138

k. you-VAIR-ee-uh. Common Torch Lily. A clump-forming perennial with roughly 2-foot-tall, 2-foot-wide mounds of grassy evergreen leaves. Bears spikes of red-orange and yellow flowers from early to late summer. Plants are 2 to 4 feet tall in bloom. Many cultivars are available. 'Primrose Beau-ty' bears yellow blooms. 'Royal Standard' bears spikes of scarlet buds that open into yellow flowers. 'Little Maid' bears yellow blooms on 1½- to 2-foot plants. Zones 5 to 9.

Lamiastrum See *Lamium*

❦ *Lamium*

LAY-mee-um. Mint family, Lamiaceae.

Lamium contains a variety of garden-worthy perennials commonly known as deadnettles. There are about 50 species of perennials and sel-dom-cultivated annuals in the genus, with square stems and ovate to kid-ney-shaped leaves. They bear small two-lipped flowers either singly or in whorls on short, dense spikes. Most cultivated forms are valued for their handsome, variegated foliage.

HOW TO GROW

Select a site in partial to full shade with average to rich, moist, well-drained soil. They will grow in sun with constantly moist soil. Keep the species listed here away from less-vigorous perennials, because they spread quickly by rhizomes and/or stolons to form mounds to 3 feet or more across. Shear plants in midsummer if they become ragged looking. Divide plants as necessary to contain their spread. To propagate, divide the clumps in spring or fall or take cuttings of nonflowering shoots in early summer. Deadnettles are seldom grown from seeds since variegated forms do not come true. Plants often self-sow.

L. galeobdolon
P. 139

l. gah-lee-OB-doe-lon. Yellow Archangel. Formerly *Galeobdolon luteum, Lamiastrum galeobdolon.* Vigorous 2-foot-tall species that spreads quickly by rhizomes and stolons. Bears ovate to diamond-shaped, toothed leaves and spikelike whorls of yellow ¾-inch-long flowers in summer. 'Hermann's Pride' bears silver-streaked leaves and is somewhat less invasive than the species. Zones 4 to 8.

L. maculatum
P. 139

l. mack-you-LAH-tum. Spotted Deadnettle. An 8- to 10-inch-tall species bearing toothed leaves with heart-shaped bases and whorls of ¾-inch-long red-purple flowers in summer. 'Beacon Silver' has silver leaves with green margins and pink flowers. 'Beedham's White' bears chartreuse leaves and white flowers. 'White Nancy' has silver leaves with green edges and white flowers. Zones 3 to 8.

❦ *Lathyrus*

LATH-ur-us. Pea family, Fabaceae.

Lathyrus species are annuals and perennials with showy, butterfly-like flowers botanists describe as papilionaceous: they have a large upright petal, called a banner or standard, and two side, or wing, petals. The two lower petals are joined at the base to form a sheath, called a keel. Many of the 150 species in the genus climb by means of tendrils on the leaves, which are divided into leaflets in a pinnate (featherlike) fashion.

HOW TO GROW

Select a spot in full sun or light shade with rich, well-drained soil. Both *L. grandiflorus* and *L. latifolius* require a trellis or other support. Or, train them up shrubs or leave them to sprawl. Plants resent being disturbed, although they can be propagated by division in early spring. Or start from seeds.

L. grandiflorus

l. gran-dih-FLOR-us. Everlasting Pea, Perennial Pea, Two-flowered Pea. A climber reaching about 5 feet with support and spreading by suckers to form loose, sprawling clumps. In summer it bears unwinged stems and two- to sometimes four-flowered racemes of 1½-inch-wide blooms in pinkish purple to pinkish red. Zones 6 to 9.

L. latifolius   P. 140

l. lat-ih-FOE-lee-us. Everlasting Pea, Perennial Pea. A climber reaching 5 to 6 feet with support. Bears winged stems, blue-green leaves, and racemes of 5 to 15 flowers in summer to early fall. Blooms are pink to rose-purple and about 1¼ wide. Cultivars include white-flowered 'Albus' and 'White Pearl', and 'Blushing Bride', with white blooms flushed with pink. All come true from seeds. Zones 5 to 9.

L. vernus   P. 140

l. VER-nus. Spring Vetchling. Clump-forming 1- to 1½-foot-tall species that spreads as far. Bears racemes of 3 to 15 purple-blue ¾-inch-wide flowers in spring. 'Rose Fairy' bears 3-inch-wide magenta blooms. Zones 5 to 9.

❦ Lavandula

lah-VAN-due-luh. Mint family, Lamiaceae.

Although lavenders are actually shrubs and subshrubs rather than herbaceous perennials, most gardeners consider them classic components of sunny perennial beds and borders. All bear aromatic linear to oblong or needlelike leaves that may be simple, toothed, or pinnately lobed or cut. The tubular, two-lipped flowers are borne in dense spikes. About 25 species native to dry, sunny sites mostly in the Mediterranean belong to the genus.

HOW TO GROW

Plant lavender in full sun with poor to rich soil that is quite well drained. Plants also tolerate very light shade, although they are leggier and bloom less. Wet soil is fatal. A spot protected from winter winds is best in Zone 5 and colder parts of Zone 6. Established plants are quite drought tolerant and best left unmulched during the growing season. In the North, after the soil freezes in fall, mulch around the plants to protect the roots (use a loose, free-draining material), and consider covering plants with cut evergreen boughs in late fall. If desired, cut or shear off spent flower spikes after the main flush of bloom in summer. To keep plants bushy, prune annually (or at least every few years) in spring just as the new growth begins or in summer either as you cut flowers or immediately after the main flush of bloom. To propagate, take heel cuttings in mid- to late summer or try dividing in spring or fall, but established plants resent disturbance and it's best to leave them alone.

L. angustifolia

P. 141

l. an-gus-tih-FOE-lee-uh. Common Lavender, English Lavender. Evergreen 2- to 3-foot-tall shrub that forms 3- to 4-foot-wide mounds of aromatic, needlelike, gray-green to silvery leaves. Bears erect 2- to 3-inch-long spikes of tiny fragrant lavender purple flowers in summer. 'Hidcote' is a compact 1½- to 2-foot-tall selection with dark purple flowers. 'Munstead' reaches about 1½ feet. 'Jean Davis' bears pale pink flowers. 'Nana Alba' bears white flowers on 1-foot-tall plants. Zones 5 to 9.

❧ Lavatera

lah-vah-TAIR-uh. Mallow family, Malvaceae.

Some 25 species of annuals, biennials, perennials, subshrubs, and shrubs belong to this widely distributed genus. Most *Lavatera* species are plants of dry, rocky soils found from the Mediterranean to Russia, central Asia, Australia, and California. They are grown for their showy, five-petaled saucer- or funnel-shaped flowers that resemble small hibiscus and come in shades of pink and white. Leaves usually are lobed in a palmate (hand-like) fashion.

HOW TO GROW

Full sun and average, well-drained soil are ideal. Too-rich soil yields abundant foliage but few flowers. Plants may need staking. Propagate by taking cuttings from shoots that arise at the base of the plant in spring, by stem cuttings in early summer, or sowing seeds.

L. thuringiaca

P. 141

l. thur-in-jee-AH-kuh. Tree Mallow, Tree Lavatera. Shrubby 5- to 6-foot-tall perennial that forms 5- to 6-foot-wide clumps. Bears funnel-shaped 2- to

2½-inch-wide flowers in summer either singly or in loose clusters. 'Shorty' bears rose pink 2-inch-wide flowers on 3-foot plants. 'Barnsley' bears pink 3-inch-wide flowers on 6-foot plants. Zones 7 to 9; to Zone 6 with winter protection.

❦ *Lespedeza*

less-peh-DEEZ-uh. Pea family, Fabaceae.

Commonly known as bush clovers, *Lespedeza* species are perennials, subshrubs, shrubs, or annuals native to North America, Australia, and eastern Asia. They bear compound leaves with three leaflets and are grown for their racemes or heads of small pealike flowers in late summer and fall. About 40 species belong to the genus.

HOW TO GROW
Full sun and average well-drained soil suit bush clovers. Cut plants to the ground in late winter (in the North, they are killed to the ground) to keep them compact and bushy. Propagate by cuttings in early summer, by dividing the clumps in spring, or by seeds.

L. bicolor

l. BYE-cuh-lor. A 6-foot-tall shrub with arching branches that spread as far. Bears ½-inch-wide purplish pink flowers in slender 2- to 5-inch-long racemes from mid- to late summer. Zones 5 to 8.

L. thunbergii   P. 142

l. thun-BER-jee-eye. Bush Clover. A shrubby 6-foot-tall perennial or subshrub with arching branches that spread to 10 feet. Bears arching, pendent, 6-inch-long racemes of bright purplish pink ½-inch-wide flowers in late summer to fall. 'Gibraltar' bears rose pink flowers on 5-foot plants. 'White Fountain' bears white blooms on 6-foot plants that spread to 12 feet. Zones 4 to 8.

❦ *Leucanthemum*

leu-CAN-thuh-mum. Aster family, Asteraceae.

The genus *Leucanthemum* contains 26 species of annuals and perennials, many of which once belonged to the genus *Chrysanthemum*. They bear daisylike flower heads and entire to deeply lobed, toothed, or scalloped leaves. The flowers, which are solitary and borne at the stem tips, generally have white ray florets, or "petals," surrounding yellow centers consisting of densely packed disk florets.

HOW TO GROW

Select a site in full sun with average to rich, well-drained soil. Well-drained conditions are especially important in winter, since water collecting around the crowns causes rot. Plants may need staking. *L. × superbum* also grows in light shade and tolerates somewhat dry, sandy soil and seaside conditions, but tends to be short-lived, especially in hot climates. Regular deadheading lengthens bloom time. Cut *L. vulgare* to the ground after flowering to encourage repeat bloom and discourage abundant self-seeding. Divide plants in spring every 2 to 3 years, because the clumps tend to die out in the center. In addition to division, propagate by cuttings taken from shoots at the bottom of the plant in spring or by seeds.

L. × superbum
P. 142

l. × sue-PUR-bum. Shasta Daisy. Formerly *Chrysanthemum maximum, C. × superbum.* Clump-forming 1- to 4-foot-tall species that spreads to about 2 feet. Bears single, semidouble, or double 2- to 5-inch white daisies on stiff stems from early summer to early fall. Many cultivars are available. 'Little Miss Muffet' is 8 to 12 inches tall and does not need staking. 'Aglaia' produces semidouble flowers with fringed ray florets. 'Snow Lady' bears white flowers on 1- to 1½-foot-tall plants and blooms the first year from seeds. Zones 4 to 8; 'Alaska' is hardy to Zone 3.

L. vulgare
P. 143

l. vul-GAR-ee. Oxeye Daisy. Formerly *Chrysanthemum vulgare.* Weedy, vigorous 1- to 3-foot-tall species spreading by rhizomes to form 2- to 3-foot-wide clumps. Bears white 1- to 2-inch-wide daisies with yellow centers in late spring and early summer. Zones 3 to 8.

❦ *Lewisia*

lew-ISS-ee-uh. Portulaca family, Portulacaceae.

Native to western North America, *Lewisia* species are low-growing perennials forming rosettes or tufts of fleshy deciduous or evergreen leaves. They produce clusters of funnel-shaped pink, magenta, white, orange, or yellow flowers in spring or summer. About 20 species, all perennials, belong to the genus.

HOW TO GROW

Give evergreen species, including *L. cotyledon,* a site in light shade with fairly rich, very well drained soil that has an acid to neutral pH. Grow deciduous species and hybrid lewisias in full sun, also with perfect drainage. Constantly damp soil around the crowns and fleshy rootstocks of these plants is fatal, as is wet soil in winter. To help improve drainage, mulch around the crowns with granite chips or coarse grit. Lewisias are ideal for rock gardens, or along rock walls, gravel paths, or other spots with very well drained soil. Propagate by severing offsets that appear in summer or by seeds.

L. cotyledon P. 143

l. coh-teh-LEE-don. Evergreen perennial with a low, leafy rosette that can reach 10 inches wide. Bears 8- to 12-inch-tall clusters of 1-inch-wide funnel-shaped flowers from spring to summer in pink, white, cream, or yellow, often striped or marked with a second color. Zones 6 to 8.

Liatris

lee-AT-riss. Aster family, Asteraceae.

Commonly called gayfeathers or blazing stars, *Liatris* species are native North American perennials that produce erect feather- or wandlike spikes or racemes of flowers that open from the top of the stalk down. Each fuzzy-textured wand consists of many buttonlike flower heads arranged along the stalk. The individual flower heads are made up of all tubular disk florets (they lack ray florets, or "petals") and come in shades of pinkish purple, purple, and white. The plants produce clumps of linear to lance-shaped leaves at the base, with smaller leaves growing up the flower stalks. They grow from thick roots with swollen, flattened stems that are tuber- or cormlike. About 40 species belong to the genus.

HOW TO GROW

Select a site in full sun with average to rich, well-drained soil. Unlike other gayfeathers, which succumb to crown rot in damp soil, *L. spicata* also grows in evenly moist soil. *L. aspera* and *L. punctata* are suitable for sites with dry, well-drained soil. Too-rich soil leads to plants that require staking. Established plants of all species are quite drought tolerant and can remain undisturbed for years. Divide plants, which generally form 1½- to 2-foot-wide clumps, only if they outgrow their space or die out in the center. Propagate by dividing the clumps or separating the tubers in early spring or fall or by seeds. Several cultivars, including 'Kobold', come true from seeds.

L. aspera

l. ASS-per-uh. Rough Blazing Star, Rough Gayfeather. A 3- to 6-foot-tall species with tuberous roots. Bears 1½- to 3-foot-long spikes of ¾- to 1-inch-wide lavender purple flower heads in late summer and early fall. Zones 3 to 9.

L. punctata   P. 144

l. punk-TAH-tuh. Dotted Blazing Star. Compact 6- to 14-inch-tall species with tuberous roots. Bears dense 6- to 12-inch-long spikes of small ⅛-inch-wide rosy purple flower heads in late summer. Zones 2 to 8.

L. pycnostachya

l. pik-no-STAY-kee-uh. Kansas Gayfeather, Prairie Blazing Star. A 3- to 5-foot-tall species bearing 1- to 2½-foot-long spikes of densely packed ½-inch-wide mauve purple flower heads in midsummer. Zones 3 to 9.

L. scariosa

l. scare-ee-OH-suh. Tall Gayfeather. A 2½- to 3-foot-tall species with 1- to 1½-foot-long spikes of pale purple 1-inch-wide flower heads in late summer and early fall. Zones 4 to 9.

L. spicata   P. 144

l. spih-KAH-tuh. Spike Gayfeather. Handsome 2- to 5-foot-tall species with erect 1½- to 2-foot-long spikes of densely packed ½-inch-wide pinkish purple flower heads from mid- to late summer. Compact, mauve violet–flowered 2- to 2½-foot-tall 'Kobold' (also sold as 'Gnom') is the most widely available cultivar. 'Floristan White' has white flowers on 3-foot plants. Zones 3 to 9.

❦ Ligularia

lig-you-LAIR-ee-uh. Aster family, Asteraceae.

Ligularia species are bold, sometimes coarse-looking perennials native to central and eastern Asia. They produce 2- to 3-foot-tall mounds of large rounded to kidney-shaped or lobed leaves that are 1 foot long or more in length. The foliage is topped in summer by tall, erect spikes or rounded clusters of golden yellow to orange daisylike flowers. About 150 species belong to the genus.

HOW TO GROW

Select a site in light to partial shade with very rich soil that remains constantly moist. A spot with shade from midday to early afternoon is best, since plants wilt dramatically during the heat of the day if soil moisture is inadequate. A site protected from wind is best. Plants can be left undisturbed for years without needing to be divided. They form 3- to 5-foot-wide mounds of foliage. To propagate, divide clumps in spring or fall.

L. dentata

l. den-TAH-tuh. Big-leaved Ligularia, Golden Groundsel. Formerly *L. clivorum*, *Senecio clivorum*. Clumping species producing kidney- to heart-shaped leaves and flattened clusters of yellow-orange 4-inch-wide daisylike flowers from summer to early fall. Leaf and flower stalks are red, and plants are from 3 to 5 feet tall in bloom. 'Desdemona' bears orange flower heads and brown-green leaves that are purple-maroon underneath. 'Othello' has purple-green leaves that are purple-red underneath. Hybrid 'Gregynog Gold' has pyramidal clusters of orange-yellow flowers. Zones 4 to 8.

L. przewalskii

l. she-VALL-skee-eye. Formerly *Senecio przewalskii*. Clumping species with mounds of toothed leaves irregularly cut in a palmate (handlike) fashion. Bears erect, lacy-textured 6-foot-tall racemes of ¾-inch-wide flower heads from early to late summer. Zones 4 to 8.

L. stenocephala   P. 145

l. steh-no-SEFF-ah-luh. Clumping species bearing toothed, triangular leaves with heart-shaped bases and erect 5-foot-tall racemes of 1½-inch-wide yellow flower heads in late summer. 'The Rocket' reaches 6 feet and bears lemon yellow flowers. Zones 4 to 8.

❦ Limonium

lih-MOW-nee-um. Plumbago family, Plumbaginaceae.

Limonium species are commonly known as sea lavender or statice, a former botanical name for this genus of 150 species of perennials and subshrubs, along with some annuals and biennials. Most produce a rosette of leaves clustered at the base of the plant. Leaf shape ranges from simple and entire to deeply lobed and featherlike. Plants produce small spikes of small papery flowers in summer and fall that are arranged in larger panicles.

HOW TO GROW

Provide full sun or partial shade and average to rich, well-drained soil. Sea lavenders are good plants for sandy soils and seaside gardens. Perennial sea lavender (*L. latifolium*) grows from a woody crown and is deep rooted: plants are slow to establish and best left undisturbed once planted. Propagate by severing small new crowns that arise around the outside of the main plant in spring (be sure to get some roots) or by seeds.

L. latifolium   P. 145

l. lat-ih-FOE-lee-um. Sea Lavender. Bears low 1½-foot-wide rosettes of spoon-shaped leaves topped by airy, branched, 2- to 2½-foot-tall clusters of tiny ¼-inch-long pale lavender to bluish purple flowers in late summer. Zones 3 to 9.

❦ *Linaria*

lin-AR-ee-uh. Figwort family, Scrophulariaceae.

Sometimes called spurred snapdragons, *Linaria* species have two-lipped flowers with snapdragon-like jaws, but with a spur at the base. The genus contains about 100 species of annuals, biennials, and perennials with ovate, linear, to lance-shaped leaves and erect or trailing stems. Their flowers are carried in erect racemes from spring to fall and come in shades of yellow, orange, white, pink, purple, and red.

HOW TO GROW

Linarias thrive in full sun and average to rich soil that is light and well drained. Most are plants of dry, sandy or rocky soil; they don't tolerate wet feet. Cut plants back after the first flush of bloom to encourage new flowers to form. Propagate by dividing plants in spring, by taking cuttings of shoots that arise at the base of the plant in spring, or by seeds. Plants self-sow.

L. purpurea   P. 146

l. pur-PUR-ee-uh. Purple Toadflax. A 3-foot-tall perennial that spreads to about 1 foot. Bears airy racemes packed with tiny ½-inch-long purple flowers from early summer to fall. 'Canon J. Went' bears pink flowers and comes true from seeds if grown away from the species. Zones 5 to 8.

❦ *Linum*

LYE-num. Flax family, Linaceae.

This genus contains some 200 species of annuals, biennials, perennials, subshrubs, and shrubs that bear simple, generally narrow leaves and clusters of five-petaled, funnel- to saucer-shaped flowers. Individual flowers open for only a day, but they are borne in abundance and come in shades of blue, lavender, white, yellow, red, and pink. Common flax *(L. usitatissimum)*, the source of the fiber from which linen is made, belongs here.

HOW TO GROW

Full sun to partial shade and average to rich, light, well-drained soil are ideal. Excellent drainage is essential to success, and wet soil in winter is fatal. Perennial species tend to be short-lived, but they self-sow. Plants may need staking. Propagate by cuttings in early summer, by division in spring or fall, or by seeds.

L. flavum   P. 146

l. FLAY-vum. Golden Flax, Yellow Flax. Woody-based 1- to 1½-foot-tall perennial that spreads about as far. Bears clusters of 1-inch-wide funnel-shaped yellow flowers in summer. 'Compactum' produces a 6- to 9-inch mound of flowers. Zones 4 to 7.

L. narbonense

l. nar-boe-NEN-see. Narbonne Flax. Long-lived 1- to 2-foot-tall species forming 1½-foot-wide clumps. Bears small clusters of saucer-shaped 1½-inch-wide blue flowers with white eyes from early to midsummer. 'Heavenly Blue' produces rich blue flowers on 1½-foot plants and is less likely to flop than the species. Zones 6 to 9; to Zone 5 or even Zone 4 with winter protection.

L. perenne   P. 147

l. per-EN-ee. Perennial Flax. Wiry-stemmed, heat tolerant 1- to 1½-foot-tall species that spreads to about 1 foot. Bears panicles of rich blue ¾- to 1-inch-wide flowers, which lack white eyes, from early to midsummer. Zones 4 to 8.

Liriope

lih-RYE-oh-pee. Lily family, Liliaceae.

Commonly known as lilyturf, *Liriope* species are grassy-leaved perennials that often have tuberous roots and spread by rhizomes to form dense clumps or mats. Leaves are narrow and arching and either evergreen or semievergreen. The small flowers (¼ to ⅜ inch wide) are borne in dense spikes or racemes and are followed by round black berries. About five or six species belong to the genus, all native to Asia.

HOW TO GROW

Select a site in partial to full shade with rich, well-drained soil. Plants also grow in full sun. They tolerate heat, humidity, drought, competition from tree roots, and heavy shade, but are slower to spread in tough conditions. Cut plants to the ground in late winter to make room for the fresh new foliage. Propagate by division in spring. Plants self-sow and can be grown from seeds, but cultivars must be propagated by division.

L. muscari

P. 147

l. mus-CAR-ee. Big Blue Lilyturf. Tuberous-rooted 1- to 1½-foot-tall perennial that spreads slowly to about 1½ feet. Bears 1- to 1½-inch-wide evergreen leaves and spikes of tiny lilac purple or white flowers above the leaves in fall. 'John Burch' bears gold-edged leaves. 'Big Blue', from 8 to 10 inches, bears violet purple flowers and dark green leaves. 'Variegata' has leaves edged in creamy white and spreads relatively slowly. Zones 6 to 9.

L. spicata

l. spy-KAH-tuh. Semievergreen 1 to 1½-foot-tall species with ¼-inch-wide leaves that spreads fairly quickly by rhizomes to form 1½- to 2-foot-wide mats. Bears pale lavender or white flowers in late summer. Zones 5 to 10.

Lobelia

loe-BEE-lee-uh. Bellflower family, Campanulaceae.

While most of the 365 to 370 species in this diverse genus are annuals and perennials, *Lobelia* also contains shrubs, treelike plants, and even an aquatic species that grows partially submerged. Most are native to the Americas; the treelike species, which can reach 10 to 30 feet, are from east Africa. All produce simple leaves and tubular flowers that are slit almost to the base to form two lips; the top lip has two lobes, the bottom one, three. Flowers are borne singly or in erect racemes or panicles and come in shades of blue, lilac, violet, red, pink, white, and yellow.

HOW TO GROW
Plant the commonly grown perennial species — *L. cardinalis, L. siphilitica,* and related hybrids — in light to partial shade and rich, constantly moist soil. With consistent soil moisture they tolerate full sun in areas with cool summers. For best results, plant them in marshy spots or along streams or ponds. Plants are short-lived, but self-sow where happy. Clumps spread to about 1 foot. To keep them vigorous, dig clumps every 2 or 3 years in spring or early fall and replant the new rosettes of leaves that arise around the old rootstock. Or sow seeds.

L. cardinalis P. 148

l. car-dih-NAL-iss. Cardinal Flower. A 2- to 4-foot-tall native North American wildflower bearing erect racemes of scarlet 2-inch-long flowers in summer and early fall. 'Ruby Slippers' bears ruby red flowers. 'Rosea' bears rose pink blooms. Zones 2 to 9.

L. siphilitica P. 148

l. sih-fih-LIT-ih-kuh. Great Blue Lobelia. A 2- to 4-foot-tall native North American wildflower bearing dense racemes of blue 1- to 1½-inch-wide flowers from late summer to fall. *L. siphilitica* f. *albiflora,* also sold as 'Alba', bears white flowers. Zones 4 to 8.

L. × *speciosa*

l. × spee-see-OH-suh. Hybrid Cardinal Flowers. A catchall species for the many hybrid perennials available, which range from 2 to 4 feet tall and bloom from summer to fall. 'Bee's Flame' features red-purple leaves and crimson red flowers. 'Queen Victoria' bears bronze-red leaves and scarlet flowers. Zones 5 to 9.

❦ *Lupinus*

lu-PIE-nus. Lupine. Pea family, Fabaceae.

Lupines are annuals, perennials, subshrubs, and shrubs with palmate (handlike) leaves and showy clusters of pealike flowers. The flowers, which are borne in spikelike panicles or sometimes whorls, have an upright petal, called a standard; two side or wing petals; and two lower petals joined at the base to form a sheath, called a keel. About 200 species belong to the genus, most native to the Americas, the Mediterranean, and North Africa.

HOW TO GROW

Select a site with full sun and average to rich, well-drained soil. Most lupines need cool, moist conditions — they thrive in the Pacific Northwest and in coastal New England — and usually fail or are short-lived in hot, humid climates. They resent root disturbance, so select a permanent location at planting time. Propagate by seeds sown in individual pots and transplant with care or take cuttings from shoots at the base of the plant in spring. Plants self-sow.

L. hybrids

P. 149

These are 3- to 5-foot-tall plants with erect, densely packed spikes of flowers in early and midsummer. Blooms come in purple, violet, yellow, pink, red, and white. The popular Russell hybrids are 2½ to 3 feet tall and are hardy in Zones 3 or 4 to 8, but are best treated as annuals south of Zone 6 in eastern and central states.

L. perennis

l. per-EN-iss. Wild Lupine. A 2-foot-tall species native from Florida to Maine that forms 1½-foot-wide clumps. Bears 6- to 12-inch-long spikes of blue or sometimes pink or white ½-inch-long flowers in early summer. Zones 4 to 9.

L. polyphyllus

l. pol-ee-FILL-us. A 3- to 5-foot-tall species native to western North America that spreads to about 2½ feet. Bears 1- to 1½-foot-long spikes of lilac-blue ½-inch-long flowers in summer. Blooms are sometimes white or pink. Zones 3 to 7.

❦ Lychnis

LICK-niss. Pink Family, Caryophyllaceae.

Lychnis contains some 15 to 20 species of biennials and perennials bearing five-petaled flowers that have tube-shaped bases and flattened faces with petal lobes that are rounded, notched, or sometimes fringed at the tips. Flowers are carried singly on branched stems or in small rounded clusters. The plants have rounded, often hairy leaves. *Lychnis* species are quite similar to *Silene* species and share the common names campion and catchfly. It's no wonder they look so similar, since the two genera differ only in the number of styles (the narrow stalk that joins the stigma and ovary of a pistil, the female part of a blossom) in the flowers. *Lychnis* species have five, or sometimes four styles, while *Silene* species have three or sometimes four. *Saponaria,* another similar species commonly called soapwort, has flowers with two styles.

HOW TO GROW

Select a site in full sun or partial shade with light, average to rich, well-drained soil. In areas with hot summers, a spot that receives afternoon shade is best. *L. chalcedonica* and *L. viscaria* are best in rich, evenly moist soil, while *L. × haageana* requires constant moisture for best growth. Gray-leaved *L. coronaria* exhibits the best foliage color when grown in dry soil. Perennial catchflies tend to be short-lived, but they self-sow. Taller species require staking. Divide them every 2 to 3 years in spring to keep the clumps vigorous and for propagation. Or sow seeds.

L. × *arkwrightii*   P. 149

l. × ark-RY-tee-eye. Arkwright's Campion. A 1½- to 2-foot-tall species that spreads to about 1 foot. Bears brownish green leaves and clusters of starry, orange-red 1½-inch-wide flowers in early to midsummer. 'Vesuvius' bears scarlet-orange flowers and dark brown-green leaves. Zones 4 to 8.

L. *chalcedonica*   P. 150

l. chal-sih-DON-ih-kuh. Jerusalem Cross, Maltese Cross. A 3- to 4-foot-tall species that spreads to about 1 foot. Bears rounded clusters of star-shaped ½-inch-wide flowers with deeply notched petals in early to midsummer. Blooms are brilliant scarlet. 'Alba' has white flowers. 'Rosea' has pink blooms. Zones 4 to 8.

L. *coronaria*   P. 150

l. cor-oh-NAIR-ee-uh. Rose Campion, Mullein Pink, Dusty Miller. A 2½- to 3-foot-tall biennial or short-lived perennial that spreads to 1½ feet with rosettes of woolly silver-gray leaves. Carries branched clusters of 1- to 1¼-inch-wide flowers with rounded, notched petals in mid- to late summer in magenta-pink or white. 'Angel's Blush' bears white flowers with bright pink eyes. Zones 4 to 8.

L. × haageana

l. × hah-jee-AH-nuh. A 1½- to 2-foot-tall hybrid that spreads to about 1 foot. Bears loose clusters of brilliant red or orange-red flowers in summer. Zones 4 to 8.

L. viscaria

l. vis-CAR-ee-uh. German Catchfly. A 1- to 1½-foot-tall species that spreads as far. Bears loose, spiky clusters of purplish pink ¾-inch-wide flowers in early and midsummer. 'Alba' bears white flowers. 'Fire' (also sold as 'Feuer') bears red, sometimes double flowers. Zones 3 or 4 to 8.

❧ Lysimachia

lye-sih-MOCK-ee-uh. Primrose family, Primulaceae.

About 150 species of perennials and shrubs belong to the genus *Lysimachia*. The perennials range from erect, clump-forming plants to creeping species suitable for use as ground covers. They bear five-petaled flowers that usually are yellow or white and range from starry to cup or saucer shaped. Blooms are carried singly or in racemes or panicles. Leaves are simple. Commonly called loosestrifes, *Lysimachia* species are not to be confused with purple loosestrifes (*Lythrum* spp.), which are perennials that have become noxious weeds in many areas.

HOW TO GROW

Select a site in full sun or partial shade with rich, well-drained, evenly moist soil. They are excellent choices for bog gardens, along ponds or other water features, and in moist borders, since they tolerate constantly moist soil. Dry soil slows their growth, and they do not tolerate drought. Most spread vigorously by rhizomes and can become invasive. To propagate, or to control their spread, divide plants in spring or fall or root cuttings in spring or summer. Plants self-sow.

L. ciliata

l. sih-lee-AH-tuh. Fringed Loosestrife. A 1- to 3-foot-tall species that spreads by rhizomes to form clumps 2 feet or more in width. Bears star-shaped 1-

inch-wide yellow flowers that are solitary or paired in the leaf axils in midsummer. 'Purpurea' bears purple-black leaves. Zones 3 to 9.

L. clethroides
P. 151

l. cleth-ROY-deez. Gooseneck Loosestrife. Rhizomatous 3-foot-tall species that spreads vigorously and quickly to form broad clumps several feet across. Bears dense, curved racemes of ½-inch-wide white flowers from mid- to late summer. Zones 3 to 9.

L. nummularia
P. 151

l. num-you-LAH-ree-uh. Creeping Jenny. Mat-forming 2- to 4-inch-tall perennial that spreads quickly to several feet by stems that root as they touch the soil. Bears rounded, evergreen to semievergreen leaves and solitary yellow 1-inch-wide flowers in summer. 'Aurea' has yellow foliage and spreads somewhat more slowly than the species. Zones 3 to 8. *L. japonica* 'Minutissima' is another creeping, prostrate selection that stays under 2 inches and bears small cup-shaped yellow flowers in summer. Zones 4 to 9.

L. punctata
P. 152

l. punk-TAH-tuh. Whorled Loosestrife. Handsome 3-foot-tall species spreading to 2 feet or more by rhizomes. Bears erect stems with whorls of yellow 1-inch-wide flowers in early summer. Plants can become invasive and need to be divided regularly.. Zones 4 to 8.

❧ Lythrum

LITH-rum. Loosestrife family, Lythraceae.

This genus contains 38 species of annuals and perennials that bear spikes of small star-shaped flowers and lance-shaped to ovate leaves. The commonly grown perennials — *L. salicaria* and *L. virgatum* — spread rampantly in wetland areas, crowding out species that provide valuable food for wildlife, but offering little for them to eat in exchange. For this reason, their cultivation has been banned in many areas.

HOW TO GROW
These plants grow in full sun and moist soil. Never plant them where they could escape into natural wetland areas. (Responsible gardeners avoid them altogether!) Avoid sites along water such as streams and ponds,

because the seeds float and will be carried far and wide. Cut the plants back hard immediately after flowering to prevent them from self-sowing. Even cultivars that previously were thought to be sterile will set seeds and self-sow when cross-pollinated with species plants. Plants form 1½- to 2-foot-wide clumps. Propagate cultivars by dividing the clumps in spring or taking cuttings from shoots at the base of the plants in spring or early summer.

L. salicaria

l. sal-ih-CAR-ee-uh. Purple Loosestrife. A 3- to 5-foot-tall species with 1-foot-long spikes of ¾-inch-wide flowers in summer in shades of pink or rose-purple. 'Firecandle', also sold as 'Feuerkerze', bears rose-red flowers on 3-foot plants. 'Robert' bears pink flowers on 2- to 3-foot plants. Zones 4 to 9.

L. virgatum

P. 152

l. vir-GAH-tum. Wand Loosestrife. Clump-forming 2- to 3-foot-tall species that bears spikelike 1-foot-long racemes of ½-inch-wide purple-red flowers from early to late summer. 'The Rocket' bears dark pink blooms; 'Rose Queen', rose pink ones. Zones 3 to 8.

❦ Macleaya

mah-CLAY-uh. Poppy family, Papaveraceae.

Macleaya species, commonly known as plume poppies, are bold, vigorous perennials with handsome, heart-shaped, palmately lobed (handlike) leaves and large airy, plumy-textured panicles of tiny flowers. The individual flowers are ½ inch long and have two to four sepals surrounding a cluster of stamens. Stems and leaves exude yellow sap when cut. Three species belong to the genus, and all are large plants that easily reach 8 feet in height and spread vigorously by rhizomes to form clumps that are 4 feet across or more.

HOW TO GROW

Select a site in full sun with average soil that is moist but well drained. Plants also grow in partial shade and tolerate most soils, including drier ones, although this restricts their height. Give them plenty of room to spread, and plan on managing the amount of space they occupy by digging up plants and rhizomes that pop up where they are not wanted. Planting in a large container, either above ground or sunk in the soil, also offers a way to control their spread. Another option is a site bordered on two or more sides by a wall or other barrier. To propagate, divide the clumps in spring or fall, pot up plants that appear along rooted rhizomes, or take root cuttings in winter.

M. cordata

P. 153

m. core-DAH-tuh. Plume Poppy. Formerly *Bocconia cordata*. Rhizomatous perennial with lobed 10-inch-long gray- to olive-green leaves that are white beneath. Bears 1-foot-long plumes of creamy flowers that have 25 to 40 stamens from mid- to late summer. *M.* × *kewensis* is a hybrid between this species and *M. microcarpa*. *M.* × *kewensis* 'Flamingo' bears pink buds and pinkish tan flowers. All are hardy in Zones 4 to 9.

❦ *Malva*

MAL-vuh. Mallow family, Malvaceae.

Closely related to *Hibiscus, Malva* species are annuals, biennials, or perennials commonly known as mallows. About 30 species belong to the genus, all bearing five-petaled, cup- or saucer-shaped flowers with petals that are somewhat squared off at the ends. Blooms are borne singly, in clusters at the leaf axils, or in racemes. They come in shades of rose and pink as well as blue, purple, and white. Leaves are rounded or heart- to kidney-shaped and either entire or variously toothed and lobed.

HOW TO GROW

Select a site in full sun with average to moderately rich, well-drained soil. Mallows tolerate partial shade and perform better in cooler zones than they do in the warm, humid South. Stake the clumps to keep them erect. Plants tend to be short-lived, but they self-sow. Propagate by taking cuttings from shoots at the base of the plant in spring, taking tip cuttings in early summer, or sowing seeds.

M. alcea

P. 153

m. al-SEE-uh. Hollyhock Mallow. A 2- to 4-foot-tall species that forms 2-foot-wide clumps. Bears funnel-shaped 1½- to 2-inch flowers with notched petals from early summer to fall both in the leaf axils and in racemes. *M. alcea* var. *fastigiata* (also sold as 'Fastigiata'), more commonly grown than the species, bears rose pink 2-inch-wide flowers on erect 2½- to 3-foot-tall plants. Zones 4 to 9.

M. moschata

m. moe-SHA-tuh. Musk Mallow. A 3-foot-tall species that forms 2-foot-wide clumps. Bears clusters of pale pink or white 2- to 2½-inch-wide saucer-shaped flowers from early summer to fall. Zones 3 to 7.

M. sylvestris

P. 154

m. sil-VES-tris. Tree Mallow, Cheeses. Woody-based 3- to 4-foot-tall peren-nial sometimes grown as a biennial. Plants form 2-foot-wide clumps and bear clusters of funnel-shaped pinkish purple 2½-inch-wide flowers with notched petals from late spring or early summer to fall. *M. sylvestris* f. *alba* (also sold as 'Alba') bears white flowers. 'Primley Blue' bears pale blue flowers on 2-foot plants. 'Zebrina' bears white to pale pink flowers striped with dark pink on 2- to 3-foot plants. Zones 4 to 8.

❦ Matteuccia

mat-TOO-see-uh. Wood Fern family, Dryopteridaceae.

Ostrich fern *(Matteuccia struthiopteris)* is by far the best known of the three to four species that belong to this genus. All are terrestrial ferns growing from erect or creeping rhizomes that have featherlike fronds arranged in vase-shaped clumps. In addition to the sterile fronds, which form the main clumps, *Matteuccia* species bear spores on separate fertile fronds that appear in mid- to late summer.

HOW TO GROW

Plant ostrich ferns in partial shade and rich soil that is marshy or wet. Plants also grow well in evenly moist, well-drained conditions, but they bear the largest fronds in constantly moist soil. *Matteuccia* species do not tolerate hot southern summers well. To propagate plants — or contain their spread — dig clumps in spring to divide them. Or dig the new plants arising from the stolons.

M. struthiopteris

P. 154

m. stru-thee-OP-ter-iss. Ostrich Fern. Formerly *M. pennsylvanica*. A large fern native to North America as well as Europe and eastern Asia that forms vase-shaped 2- to 6-foot-tall clumps of twice-cut fronds. Brown fertile fronds appear at the center of the clumps in summer and remain erect over winter. While each clump has an erect rhizome, plants spread to 3 feet or more by underground stolons. Zones 2 to 6.

❧ *Mazus*

MAY-zus. Figwort family, Scrophulariaceae.

Of the 30 or so species of annuals and prostrate perennials that belong to this genus, one species — *Mazus repens* — is commonly grown in gardens as a mat-forming ground cover. Members of the genus bear linear, rounded, or spoon-shaped leaves and tubular flowers with large spreading lower lips that have three lobes.

HOW TO GROW

Select a site in full sun or partial shade with average to somewhat rich, moist, but well-drained soil. Plants do not tolerate constantly wet soil. In the South, a site with shade during the hottest part of the day is best. *M. repens* spreads widely by rhizomes that root where they touch the soil and will overwhelm less aggressive plants. To propagate, divide the clumps in spring or any time during the season, or take cuttings.

M. repens   P. 155

m. REE-pens. Mat-forming 2-inch-tall species that spreads to 1 foot or more. From late spring to summer it bears few-flowered racemes of purple ½- to ¾-inch-long flowers with yellow and white spots on their lower lips. 'Albus' bears white flowers. Zones 5 to 8.

❧ *Melissa*

meh-LISS-uh. Mint family, Lamiaceae.

Melissa species bear aromatic, ovate, toothed leaves and spikes of small tubular, two-lipped flowers in summer. Three species belong to this genus, one of which is a popular herb grown for its fragrant, lemon-scented foliage.

HOW TO GROW

Select a site in full sun with poor to average, well-drained soil. Plants tolerate partial shade but not heat: a site with shade during the hottest part of the day is best from Zone 7 south. For best foliage color on variegated forms, cut the plants back hard in early summer. Propagate by division in spring, by cuttings taken in spring or summer, or by seeds.

M. officinalis
P. 155

m. oh-fish-in-AL-iss. Lemon Balm. A 2- to 4-foot-tall species with lemon-scented leaves that forms 1½-foot-wide clumps. Bears spikes of small pale yellow to white flowers in summer. 'All Gold' bears yellow leaves. 'Aurea', also sold as 'Variegata', bears green leaves that are splashed with gold. Zones 4 to 10.

᭙ Mertensia

mer-TEN-see-uh. Borage family, Boraginaceae.

Some 50 species belong to the genus *Mertensia*, all perennials, about half of which are native North American wildflowers. They bear loose clusters of pendent, bell-shaped or tubular flowers and rounded to lance-shaped leaves. Blooms commonly come in shades of blue to purple, as well as white or sometimes pink.

HOW TO GROW

Select a site in sun or shade with rich, evenly moist, well-drained soil. *M. pulmonarioides* goes dormant and disappears after flowering in spring, so pick a spot where you will not dig into its stout, fleshy rootstocks by mistake. To propagate, dig the clumps in early summer before the leaves disappear completely. Plants self-sow, and seedlings are easy to move in spring.

M. pulmonarioides
P. 156

m. pul-moe-nair-ee-OY-deez. Virginia Bluebells, Virginia Cowslip. Formerly *M. virginica*. A 1- to 2-foot-tall wildflower native to the eastern half of North America that grows from fleshy white carrotlike roots and spreads to 1 foot. Produces mounds of bluish green leaves, and in spring bears nodding clusters of pink buds that open into pale lilac-blue to purple-blue ¾- to 1-inch-long bells. Zones 3 to 9.

❦ *Miscanthus*

mis-CAN-thus. Grass family, Poaceae.

Commonly called eulalia grass, Japanese silver grass, or simply miscanthus, *Miscanthus* species are deciduous or evergreen grasses native from Africa to eastern Asia. From 17 to 20 species belong to the genus, all of which have reedlike stems with linear or narrowly lance-shaped leaves. (The leaves often are sharp edged: although they don't cut deeply, long sleeves and gloves are advisable when working around these plants.) The plants are topped by dense, airy panicles of tiny flowers in summer and fall. Miscanthus are especially valued for their four-season interest: foliage and flowers ripen to shades of tan and brown and add texture and color to the winter landscape.

HOW TO GROW

Select a site in full sun with average soil that is moist but well drained. Give plants plenty of room at planting time, as mature clumps can be 6 feet or more across. Let the foliage stand over winter, then cut plants to the ground in late winter or early spring. Miscanthus are warm-season grasses, so they are late to start growth in the spring. Divide clumps in early spring (use an ax or mattock) for propagation or to control their size; overgrown clumps tend to flop over in summer and also to die out in the center. *M. sinensis* and its cultivars (as well as other species) can become invasive because of prolific self-sowing. Old-fasioned cultivars ('Gracillimus', 'Zebrinus', and 'Variegatus', for example) usually require a very long, hot summer to bloom at all, and for these self-sowing has not been much of a problem. New, early blooming selections, developed so gardeners in cool northern zones can enjoy the flowers, can self-sow with abandon in areas with warm, wet summers, including the Southeast and the Middle Atlantic states. There, they have escaped cultivation and naturalized both in and out of gardens.

M. sinensis   PP. 156–57

m. sy-NEN-sis. Eulalia, Japanese Silver Grass. Shrub-sized grass forming vase-shaped 3- to 5-foot-tall clumps of foliage that spread from 4 to 6 feet. Bears plumy purplish flowers from summer to fall that range from 6 to 10 feet tall. Flowers and foliage turn light tan and stand though winter. 'Gracillimus', commonly called maiden grass, forms rounded 4½- to 5-foot-tall mounds of fine-textured leaves and bears coppery red blooms in midfall. 'Morning Light' produces rounded mounds of fine-textured silvery leaves with white edges and reddish flowers, and does not flop over in summer. Variegated cultivars include white-striped 'Variegatus', which reaches 7 feet and needs staking to remain erect, and 'Zebrinus', commonly called zebra grass, a 6- to 9-foot cultivar with pale yellow bands across the leaves. 'Strictus', commonly called porcupine grass, is similar but less likely to flop in summer. *M. sinensis* var. *condensatus* 'Cabaret' is a 6- to 9-foot late-blooming selection with a broad band of creamy white in the center; it seldom needs staking. 'Purpurascens', also sold as *M. sinensis* var. *purpurascens*, is a 3- to 4-foot-hybrid (to 6 feet in bloom) grown for its late summer flowers and brilliant red fall foliage. Zones 4 to 9.

☙ *Mitchella*

mit-CHEL-luh. Madder family, Rubiaceae.

Two species, one native to North America and one to Japan, belong to this genus named in honor of Dr. John Mitchell, an early American botanist. Both are woodland species with trailing stems and evergreen, ovate to lance-shaped leaves. They bear pairs of small funnel-shaped flowers followed by red berries.

HOW TO GROW

Select a site in dappled or partial shade with rich, evenly moist, well-drained soil that is acid in pH. Since the species in cultivation — *Mitchella repens* — is a native perennial, make sure to buy nursery-propagated plants rather than ones dug from the wild. *M. repens* spreads steadily but slowly, by rooting at leaf nodes, and more aggressive ground covers will overwhelm it. To propagate, divide the clumps in spring or pot up rooted sections of the stems.

M. repens   P. 157

m. REE-penz. Partridge Berry, Twin Berry, Running Box. Prostrate, mat-forming 1- to 2-inch-tall perennial that spreads to 1 foot or more. Bears glossy, dark green leaves with white veins and ½-inch-long white flowers in early summer followed by round ½-inch-wide red berries. Zones 4 to 9.

❦ *Molinia*

moe-LIN-ee-uh. Grass family, Poaceae.

Of the two species that belong to the genus *Molinia,* one is grown as an ornamental grass for its handsome clumps of fine-textured leaves and showy flower panicles that are held well above the foliage. Both species are native to moist moors, heaths, and lake shores from Europe to western Russia, Turkey, China, and Japan.

HOW TO GROW
Select a site in full sun to partial shade with poor to average, moist, well-drained soil. *M. caerulea* is best in areas with cool, moist summers; plants don't flower well in hot, and especially dry weather. In areas where hot weather may be a problem, select a spot with shade during the hottest part of the day. Plants take a year or two to become established and bloom well. The flowers and foliage break off in late fall or early winter, so plants do not need to be cut back in spring. Propagate by dividing the clumps in spring or by seeds, although cultivars do not come true.

M. caerulea   P. 158
m. see-RUE-lee-uh. Purple Moor Grass. Clump-forming, warm-season grass producing 1- to 2-foot-tall and wide mounds of linear leaves topped by airy spikes of purplish flowers in early to midsummer that are 2 to 4 feet tall. Flowers fade to yellow-brown and are handsome through fall. *M. caerulea* ssp. *arundinacea* 'Karl Foerster' has 2½-foot-long leaves and reaches 5 to 7 feet in bloom. 'Variegata' forms 2-foot mounds of white-striped leaves. Zones 5 to 9, to Zone 4 with winter protection.

❦ *Monarda*

moe-NAR-duh. Mint family, Lamiaceae.

Also called bergamots and horsemints, bee balms feature fragrant foliage and showy, ragged-looking clusters of two-lipped, tube-shaped flowers. The flower clusters, which are popular with hummingbirds, often are surrounded by a collar of showy bracts. Blooms come in red and various shades of pink, as well as purple, violet, and white. Bee balms have lance-shaped to oval leaves that are usually toothed and square stems. They spread by fast-creeping rhizomes to form broad clumps. All of the 15 species in the genus are native North American wildflowers.

HOW TO GROW

Plant bee balms in full sun or light shade in a site with evenly moist, well-drained soil. *M. didyma* requires rich, evenly moist soil but good drainage. *M. fistulosa* and *M. punctata* tolerate average to rich soil as well as drier conditions. To help combat powdery mildew, select a site with good air circulation and select mildew-resistant cultivars. Deadhead flowers to encourage plants to rebloom. Divide the clumps in spring or early fall every 2 to 3 years to keep them vigorous and control their spread. (The plants are especially aggressive in rich, moist soil; all easily spread to 3 feet or more.) Propagate by division, taking cuttings in spring from stems that arise at the base of the plant, or by seeds, although most cultivars do not come true.

M. didyma   PP. 158–59

m. DID-ih-muh. Bee Balm, Bergamot, Oswego Tea. Rhizomatous 2- to 4-foot-tall perennial that bears aromatic leaves and whorls of scarlet or pink flowers from mid- to late summer. Mildew-resistant cultivars include red-flowered 'Jacob Cline', pink 'Marshall's Delight', and lilac purple 'Prairie Night' (also sold as 'Prärienacht'). 'Petite Delight' is mildew resistant and reaches only 12 to 15 inches in height. Popular 'Cambridge Scarlet' produces stunning red flowers but is not mildew resistant. 'Panorama Mix', which comes true from seeds, produces plants with red, pink, and salmon flowers. Zones 4 to 8.

M. fistulosa   P. 159

m. fiss-tue-LO-suh. Wild Bergamot. A 3- to 5-foot-tall species with leaves that are less susceptible to mildew and clusters of ¾-inch-long lavender-pink flowers in mid- to late summer. Zones 3 to 9.

M. punctata

m. punk-TAH-tuh. Spotted Bee Balm, Spotted Horsemint. A 1- to 3-foot-tall annual, biennial, or perennial with whorls of ½- to 1-inch-long yellow flowers with a collar of pink to purplish bracts from midsummer to early fall. Zones 4 to 9.

❧ *Myosotis*

my-oh-SO-tis. Borage family, Boraginaceae.

Myosotis species, commonly known as forget-me-nots, are erect or sprawling annuals, biennials, and perennials with hairy leaves and clusters of tiny flowers in shades of blue, violet, pink, and white. The trumpet- to funnel-shaped blooms have five "petals," or lobes, flat faces, and a contrasting yellow or white eye. Some 50 species belong to this widespread genus: plants are native from woods, meadows, and boggy spots mostly in Europe and New Zealand, but also Asia and North and South America.

HOW TO GROW

Select a site in full sun or light shade and any well-drained, moist soil. *M. scorpioides* requires constantly moist to wet soil for good performance, and it also will grow in standing water up to a depth of 4 inches. Shade during the hottest part of the day is best in hot climates. Propagate by sowing seeds where they are to grow or by dividing the plants in spring. Cut back *M. sylvatica* or pull plants up after flowering to prevent excessive self-sowing.

M. scorpioides

m. scor-pee-OY-deez. True Forget-me-not, Water Forget-me-not. Moisture-loving 6- to 12-inch-tall perennial that spreads to about 1 foot. Bears ovate leaves and clusters of ¼-inch-wide blue flowers with yellow eyes in early summer. 'Sapphire' bears brilliant blue flowers on compact plants. Zones 5 to 9.

M. sylvatica   P. 160

m. syl-VAT-ih-cuh. Forget-me-not, Woodland Forget-me-not. A 5- to 12-inch-tall biennial or short-lived perennial producing tufts of ovate or lance-shaped gray-green leaves. Bears clusters of tiny ⅜-inch-wide saucer-shaped flowers in shades of blue, pink, and white in spring and early summer. Many cultivars are available. Ball Series plants are compact and 6 inches tall; Victoria Series plants reach only 4 inches. 'Ultramarine' reaches 6 inches and bears indigo blue flowers. Zones 5 to 9.

❧ *Nepeta*

NEP-uh-tuh. Mint family, Lamiaceae.

Commonly called catmints, *Nepeta* species bear aromatic gray-green leaves, square stems, and showy spikes of small two-lipped flowers, primarily in shades of lavender, purple, violet, and white. About 250 species belong to the genus, and most are perennials, although there are a few annuals. Leaves are ovate to lance shaped and have entire, toothed, or scalloped edges; some species have hairy leaves. Catnip *(N. cataria)* is the member of the clan that has an intoxicating effect on cats. Commonly grown in herb gardens, it has a long history of herbal use but is not especially ornamental. Catmints, which are popular in flower gardens, have less effect on cats.

HOW TO GROW
Grow catmints in full sun or light shade with average, well-drained soil. They thrive in drier sites than many commonly grown perennials, and damp soil leads to crown rot and death. Catmints can be short-lived in the South and are best in a spot with shade during the hottest part of the day in hot-summer areas. *N. nervosa* is the most heat-tolerant selection. Taller-growing catmints may need staking, but also are attractive when simply allowed to flop. Shear plants back hard — by one- or two-thirds — after the main flush of flowers fades to encourage fresh new foliage and renewed flowering until frost. Divide clumps in spring or fall if they outgrow their site or begin to look less vigorous, or for propagation. Or, propagate by taking cuttings in summer. *N. cataria* can be grown from seeds and self-sows with abandon unless deadheaded, but none of the commonly grown ornamentals come true (*N.* × *faassenii* plants are sterile and thus produce no seeds).

N. cataria

n. cah-TAR-ee-uh. Catnip. Clumping 3-foot-tall perennial with aromatic gray-green woolly leaves that spreads to about 1½ feet. In summer and fall it bears spikes of small white flowers spotted with purple. Zones 3 to 7.

N. × *faassenii*   P. 160

n. × fahs-SEN-ee-eye. Nepeta, Catmint. Formerly *N. mussinii.* Clump-forming 1- to 2-foot-tall hybrid that forms 1½-foot-wide mounds of aromatic, hairy, silvery gray-green leaves. Bears spikes of lavender-blue ½-inch-long flowers from early summer to fall. 'Snowflake' and 'White Wonder' bear white flowers. 'Six Hills Giant', a popular cultivar of uncertain parentage, reaches 3 feet in height and bears showy spikes of violet purple flowers. 'Dropmore' bears larger leaves and flowers than the species and is a more erect, 2-foot-tall selection. Zones 4 to 8, to Zone 3 with winter protection.

N. govaniana

n. go-van-ee-AH-nuh. Yellow Catmint. Formerly *Dracocephalum govaniana-num*. A 3-foot-tall clump-forming species that spreads to about 2 feet. Bears large aromatic 4-inch-long leaves and loose racemes of pale yellow 1¼-inch-long flowers from midsummer to fall. Zones 5 to 9.

N. nervosa

n. ner-VO-suh. Veined Nepeta. Mounding 1½- to 2-foot-tall species that spreads to about 2 feet. Bears mildly aromatic gray-green leaves with prominent veins and dense racemes of purple-blue ½-inch-long flowers from midsummer to fall. Zones 5 to 9.

N. sibirica   P. 161

n. sigh-BEER-ih-kuh. Siberian Catnip. Formerly *Dracocephalum sibiricum*, *Nepeta macrantha*. A 3-foot-tall species with lance-shaped dark green leaves that spreads to 2 feet. Bears racemes of 1½-inch-long lavender-blue flowers in summer. Zones 3 to 9.

❦ *Nipponanthemum*

nip-oh-NAN-the-mum. Aster family, Asteraceae.

Nipponanthemum contains a single species once classified in the vast genus *Chrysanthemum*. A herbaceous perennial or subshrub native to sandy, coastal regions in Japan, it bears daisylike flowers and aromatic leaves.

HOW TO GROW

Select a site in full sun with average, very well drained soil. Plants thrive in sandy soils. Pinch stem tips in spring to encourage branching. In areas where plants are not killed to the ground over winter, in early spring cut them nearly to the ground to keep them from becoming leggy and falling open at the centers of the clumps later in the season. Propagate by dividing the clumps in spring or by seeds.

N. nipponicum

P. 161

n. nih-PON-ih-cum. Nippon Daisy. Formerly *Chrysanthemum nipponicum*. A somewhat shrubby 2-foot-tall perennial that spreads as far and bears toothed, spoon-shaped, dark green leaves and 2½-inch-wide daisylike flowers in fall that have white ray florets ("petals") surrounding yellow centers. Zones 5 to 9.

ꙮ *Oenothera*

ee-no-THAIR-uh. Evening primrose family, Onagraceae.

The 125 species in this genus are commonly called sundrops, evening primroses, golden eggs, or just oenotheras. They are annuals, biennials, and perennials mostly native to North America (a few species are from South America) that bear showy, sometimes fragrant flowers in brilliant yellow, white, and pink. Blooms are borne singly or in clusters, have four petals, and usually are saucer to cup shaped. They open either in the morning or the evening, depending on the species. Although individual flowers fade quickly, they are borne in abundance over a long season in summer.

HOW TO GROW

Select a site in full sun with poor to average, well-drained soil. Sundrops resent wet soil, especially in winter, but tolerate dry, rocky conditions. Too-rich soil yields lots of foliage but few flowers and also leads to short-lived plants. *O. fruticosa* and its cultivars tolerate richer soil than other species and are suitable for planting in beds and borders with well-drained, evenly moist soil. Some species, especially *O. speciosa,* can be invasive. Many oenotheras have taproots and resent being disturbed. Divide clumps in early spring or late summer only if they outgrow their space or begin to lose vigor, or for propagation. Or propagate by removing offsets from the outside of the clumps, by taking stem cuttings in spring or early summer from shoots at the base of the plant, by taking root cuttings in fall from roots that run along the soil surface, or by sowing seeds. Some species self-sow.

O. caespitosa

P. 162

o. see-pih-TOE-suh. Tufted Evening Primrose. A 4- to 8-inch-tall biennial or perennial that spreads as far. Bears richly fragrant 4-inch-wide white flowers in summer that open at sunset and fade to pink and die on the following morning. Zones 4 to 8.

O. fruticosa

P. 162

o. fru-tih-COE-suh. Common Sundrops. Clump-forming 1- to 3-foot-tall species that spreads to 1 foot. Bears racemes of deep yellow 1- to 3-inch-wide flowers from late spring through summer. Plants once sold as *O. tetragona* have been moved here and are currently listed as *O. fruticosa* ssp. *glauca*. Compact cultivars, which range from 1½ to 2 feet tall, make outstanding garden plants. These include 'Summer Solstice' ('Sonnen-wende'), which blooms from early summer to fall and features maroon fall foliage. 'Youngii' blooms from early to midsummer and has scarlet autumn leaves. Zones 4 to 8.

O. macrocarpa

P. 163

o. mack-ro-CAR-puh. Ozark Sundrops, Missouri Evening Primrose. Formerly *O. missouriensis*. A 6-inch-tall perennial with trailing stems that spread to 2 feet. Bears solitary 5-inch-wide yellow flowers from late spring to fall. Zones 5 to 8.

O. perennis

o. per-EN-iss. Sundrops, Nodding Sundrops. An 8-inch-tall perennial that spreads to about 1½ feet. Bears loose racemes of ¾-inch-wide funnel-shaped yellow flowers in summer. Zones 5 to 8.

O. speciosa

P. 163

o. spee-see-OH-suh. Showy Evening Primrose. Vigorous 1-foot-tall perennial that spreads rapidly by runners to form drifts that easily exceed 2 or 3 feet. Bears solitary, cup-shaped 1- to 2½-inch-wide flowers from early summer to fall. The species bears white flowers, but pink-flowered forms such as 'Rosea' are most often grown. 'Siskiyou Pink' bears 2-inch flowers on 10-inch plants. Zones 5 to 8.

❦ Omphalodes

om-fah-LO-deez. Borage family, Boraginaceae.

Grown for their forget-me-not–like flowers, the 28 species of *Omphalodes* are annuals, biennials, and perennials native to Europe, northern Africa, Asia, and Mexico. They bear simple, oblong to ovate leaves and blue or white flowers, which are usually carried in small terminal clusters. The flowers have five lobes, or "petals," flat faces, and a paler-colored eye in the center. Both the botanical name and the common names navelwort and navelseed refer to the seeds, which are actually nutlets that have a depressed spot on them: *Omphalodes* is from the Greek *omphalos,* navel, and *oides,* resembling.

HOW TO GROW

Select a site in partial shade with rich, moist, well-drained soil. *O. verna* tolerates dry soil, but performs better with even moisture. Established plants (especially of *O. cappadocica*) resent being disturbed but can be divided in early spring for purposes of propagation. Or sow seeds. Plants self-sow.

O. cappadocica

o. cah-pah-DOE-see-kuh. Navelwort. Rhizomatous 10-inch-tall perennial that forms 1½-foot-wide clumps. In early spring it bears loose 10-inch-long racemes of ¼-inch-wide blue flowers with white eyes. Zones 6 to 8.

O. verna

P. 164

o. VER-nuh. Blue-eyed Mary, Creeping Forget-me-not. Stoloniferous 8-inch-tall species that forms 1-foot-wide clumps. Bears racemes of bright blue ½-inch-wide flowers in spring. 'Alba' bears white flowers. Zones 6 to 9.

Onoclea

oh-no-CLAY-uh. Wood Fern family, Dryopteridaceae.

A single species belongs to this genus in the wood fern family — sensitive fern *(Onoclea sensibilis).* Native to eastern Asia as well as eastern North America, it produces spreading clumps of coarse-looking, roughly triangular fronds. The common name refers to the fact that the fronds turn yellow at the first fall frost.

HOW TO GROW

Sensitive fern grows in a wide range of conditions, from full sun, provided the soil remains moist, to shade. It thrives in constantly wet, even swampy soil as well as in dry conditions and also flourishes in the moist, well-drained soil of the average fern garden. The plants spread steadily by branched rhizomes to form dense, broad clumps. To propagate, as well as to keep clumps from spreading too far, divide them every 2 to 3 years.

O. sensibilis

P. 164

o. sen-sih-BIL-iss. Sensitive Fern. Vigorous 1- to 3-foot-tall native fern that easily spreads to 3 feet or more. Bears roughly triangular, featherlike (pinnate) fronds with wavy-edged leaflets or lobes sometimes cut all the way to the main stem and sometimes nearly to the main stem. Separate dark brown fertile fronds with beadlike leaflets hold the spores. Zones 2 to 10.

ꬅ Ophiopogon

oh-fee-oh-POE-gon. Lily family, Liliaceae.

Ophiopogon species are evergreen perennials commonly known as mondo grass. They also are sometimes called lily turf, a common name that indicates their close resemblance to another popular genus that goes by that name, *Liriope.* There are some 50 species of *Ophiopogon,* all native to eastern Asia. All produce clumps of grasslike leaves topped with racemes of tiny flowers in summer. The flowers, which are mostly hidden by the leaves, are followed by round, glossy, blue or black berries.

HOW TO GROW

Select a site in full sun or partial shade with rich, moist, well-drained soil. *O. japonicus* and *O. planiscapus* are both rhizomatous and spread steadily to form 1-foot-wide clumps. *O. japonicus* has fleshy, tuberous roots, and established plantings are quite drought tolerant. Propagate by digging and dividing the clumps in spring or by seeds.

O. japonicus

o. jah-PON-ih-kus. Mondo Grass. An 8- to 12-inch-tall species with tuberous roots that forms handsome clumps of grassy leaves. Bears 2- to 3-inch-long racemes of bell-shaped ¼-inch-wide flowers in summer followed by blue-black berries. 'Variegatus' bears white-striped leaves. 'Compactus' is only 2 inches tall. Zones 7 to 10.

O. planiscapus

P. 165

o. plan-ih-SCAPE-us. An 8-inch-tall species that bears grassy, dark green leaves and 1- to 3-inch-long racemes of bell-shaped ¼-inch-long purplish white flowers. Blooms in summer. 'Nigrescens' (also sold as 'Black Dragon' and 'Ebony Knight') is grown for its nearly black leaves. Zones 6 to 10.

❦ *Opuntia*

oh-PUN-tee-uh. Cactus family, Cactaceae.

Native to North, Central, and South America, *Opuntia* species are succulent, perennial cacti from a wide range of habitats. About 200 species belong here. All lack true leaves and instead bear fleshy branches that are either flat and padlike or rounded. Whatever their shape, the fleshy branches are well armed with barbed spines, which can be large or very small and hairlike. *Opuntia* species bear showy bowl-shaped flowers in summer that open during the day. The common name prickly pear refers to the spiny, rounded fruits that follow the flowers. The "pears" of some species, which also are called tunas and Indian-figs, are edible; in some cases they turn a handsome red when ripe.

HOW TO GROW

Select a site in full sun with sandy or gritty soil that is fairly rich in organic matter and very well drained. Wet soil, especially in winter, is fatal. When siting plants be sure to consider the spines, which will pierce and/or work their way through gloves: keep plants away from areas where unwary visitors may come in contact with the spines, and weed thoroughly before planting to avoid problems later. *O. compressa* is an excellent container plant and also a good choice for planting along the top of a rock wall where drainage is excellent. Propagate it by dividing the clumps in spring or rooting the individual flattened pads. Wrap the pads in folded pieces of newspaper to avoid contact with the spines.

O. compressa   P. 165

o. com-PRESS-uh. Hardy Cactus. Formerly *O. humifusa.* A 4- to 12-inch-tall species that forms 3-foot-wide clumps and is native from Montana and Massachusetts south to Florida and Texas. Plants bear fleshy, rounded, gray-green pads with brown spots, called areoles, that carry the tiny barbed spines. Some selections also bear larger white spines with black tips. Produces showy 2- to 2½-inch-wide yellow flowers, which may have red centers, from late spring to early summer. The 1½-inch-long "pears" ripen to red or purplish and are edible. The pads are limp during the winter. Zones 4 or 5 to 9.

ꙮ Oreganum

ore-eh-GAN-um. Mint family, Lamiaceae.

Best known as residents of the herb garden, members of this genus are commonly known as oregano or marjoram. About 20 species of perennials and subshrubs belong here, all of which bear pairs of simple, aromatic leaves and whorls of small flowers.

HOW TO GROW
Select a site in full sun with poor to somewhat fertile, well-drained soil. Alkaline pH is best. Plants tolerate drought. Wet soil, especially in winter, can be fatal. For foliage to use in cooking, look for *Origanum vulgare* ssp. *hirtum* (sometimes sold as *O. heracleoticum*) and taste a leaf before you buy, because flavor and fragrance vary. Seed-grown plants often have no flavor, so purchase only vegetatively propagated ones. Cut back plants after flowering to curtail self-sowing. Propagate by division in spring or early fall, or take cuttings of shoots that appear at the base of the plants in late spring.

O. vulgare   P. 166
o. vul-GAIR-ee. Oregano. Woody-based 1- to 3-foot-tall perennial that spreads steadily by rhizomes to form broad 2- to 3-foot-wide clumps. Bears oval gray-green leaves and sprays of tiny white or purplish pink flowers in summer. 'Aureum', commonly called golden oregano, bears golden yellow leaves. 'Compactum' is a dense 6-inch-tall selection. Zones 5 to 9.

ꙮ Osmunda

os-MUN-duh. Flowering Fern family, Osmundaceae.

Osmunda species are vigorous, stately ferns that have featherlike, once- or twice-cut fronds and grow from a thick mat of horsehairlike roots. The fiddleheads and leaf stalks are densely covered with hair. The common name flowering fern refers to the manner in which the spores are borne. They are produced either on separate, specialized, often cinnamon-colored or brown fronds or on separate leaflets (pinnae) on the main fronds. In either case, spore-bearing parts lack leafy tissue altogether. Plants range from 2 to 5 feet or more in height. About 12 species belong to the genus.

HOW TO GROW

Select a site in partial shade with rich soil that ranges from evenly moist and well drained to constantly moist or wet. Site them beside a pond or stream, or in a bog garden; *O. regalis* will grow in shallow standing water. Acid pH is best. Most species — especially *O. regalis* — grow well in full sun, provided water is plentiful. *O. claytonia* tolerates dry conditions as well as considerable sun or shade. To propagate, divide the clumps in spring or fall.

O. cinnamomea P. 166

o. sin-uh-MOE-mee-uh. Cinnamon Fern. A native North American fern that reaches 3 feet and spreads to form 2-foot-wide clumps. It has twice-cut fronds that taper somewhat at the base and have woolly tufts at the base of the leaflets. Plants produce tall fertile fronds in late spring that turn cinnamon brown after the spores are shed. Zones 2 to 10.

O. claytonia

o. clay-TOE-nee-uh. Interrupted Fern. A native North American species with 2- to 4-foot-tall fronds that resemble those of cinnamon fern. This species does not bear specialized fertile fronds; instead fronds have specialized brown, spore-bearing leaflets that "interrupt" the frond. Zones 2 to 8.

O. regalis P. 167

o. ree-GAL-iss. Royal Fern, Flowering Fern. A 5- to 6-foot-tall species that spreads as far and bears somewhat coarse-looking, twice-cut fronds with widely spaced oval leaflets. It produces fronds with tassel-like tips (about one quarter of the frond) that are covered with showy brown clusters of spores. Zones 2 to 10.

❧ *Pachysandra*

pack-uh-SAN-druh. Boxwood family, Buxaceae.

Pachysandra contains four species of perennials or subshrubs that bear erect branches with clusters of evergreen or deciduous leaves that are rounded and entire or coarsely toothed. Three are native to China and Japan, while one — *P. procumbens* — is an underappreciated wildflower native to the southeastern United States. They produce clusters of small petalless flowers in spring or early summer.

HOW TO GROW

Select a site in partial to full shade with average to rich, evenly moist soil. Plants do not tolerate dry soil well. All species spread by underground rhizomes — some spread quickly, others slowly — making them excellent ground covers. Propagate by dividing the clumps in spring or fall or by taking cuttings in early summer.

P. procumbens   P. 167

p. pro-CUM-benz. Allegheny Spurge. A native 1-foot-tall wildflower that slowly spreads to form broad 1- to 2-foot-wide clumps. Grown for its handsome semievergreen leaves that emerge green and often are marked with maroon-brown as the season progresses. Bears white flowers in spring. Zones 5 to 9.

P. terminalis   P. 168

p. ter-min-AH-liss. Japanese Spurge. A ½- to 1-foot-tall evergreen species that spreads relatively quickly to form broad 2- to 3-foot-wide clumps. Bears tiny creamy white flowers in early summer. Compact cultivar 'Green Carpet' is 6 to 8 inches tall. 'Variegata' has leaves marked in white and requires partial shade. Zones 4 to 9.

❦ Paeonia

pay-OH-nee-uh. Peony family, Paeoniaceae.

Grown for their showy, often fragrant flowers, peonies are herbaceous perennials, shrubs, or subshrubs. About 30 species belong to the genus, most native from Europe to eastern Asia. Flowers are cup, bowl, or saucer shaped. Single-flowered peonies have 5 to 10 petals surrounding a central boss, or cluster, of showy yellow or cream-colored stamens. Double-flowered forms either lack stamens altogether or have a few hidden among showy, sterile petal-like structures called staminodes. Plants bear handsome, deeply cut leaves. Herbaceous peonies, which die to the ground each year, are best known. They bloom from late spring to early summer, and their dark to bright green leaves remain attractive all season.

HOW TO GROW

Plant peonies in full sun with average to rich, well-drained soil. They do not tolerate poorly drained soil. Plants flower, although less abundantly, in light shade. In the South (Zone 7, and especially Zone 8), summer heat and humidity are a problem, so look for a cool site with afternoon shade.

Plants still may be short-lived or fail to bloom in the warmest parts of Zone 8. Select a site with care, because peonies are deep-rooted plants with thick, fleshy roots and almost woody crowns. They grow best if planted in a permanent location, and plants thrive for years without needing to be divided. Peonies are commonly sold as bare-root plants, with three- to five-eye, or bud, divisions for planting in mid- to late fall. Container-grown peonies can be planted in early spring. Peonies buried too deeply will not bloom: in northern zones, plant bare-root plants with the buds *no more than* 2 inches below the soil surface. In central portions of the country 1 inch deep is fine, while in the South, even shallower planting is best. When in doubt, plant more shallowly. Feed plants annually each spring with a topdressing of well-rotted manure, compost, or a balanced organic plant food. Most peonies need staking, but single-flowered cultivars, especially those described as "strong stemmed," often stand without staking. Divide in late summer or early fall, either for propagation or to separate large overcrowded clumps.

P. hybrids

PP. 168–69

Common Garden Peony. Most commonly cultivated peonies are hybrids that range from 1½ to about 3 feet in height and form handsome 3- to 4-foot-wide clumps. Hundreds of cultivars are available in colors from white to red, including pure white, ivory, cream, pale yellow, pale pink, rose pink, crimson, and maroon. Flowers may be single, semidouble, double, or Japanese type (with a ring or two of petals around a cluster of modified petal-like stamens and carpels). Peonies with a dense, rounded center are called "bombs" or "anemones." Early-, midseason-, and late-blooming cultivars are available. Early cultivars include 'America', single with red flowers and golden stamens; 'Bowl of Beauty', Japanese type with rose pink outer petals and creamy white centers; 'Festiva Maxima', double with very fragrant white flowers flecked with red; 'Krinkled White', single with white crepe paper–textured petals and showy yellow stamens; 'Miss America', semidouble with white petals and gold stamens; 'Monsieur Jules Elie', double with fragrant rose pink flowers; and 'Scarlett O'Hara', an early single with vibrant red flowers and yellow centers. Midseason cultivars include 'Bowl of Cream', double with white flowers; 'Do Tell', Japanese type with pale pink outer petals and cream, pink, and rose-red centers; 'Kansas', double with red flowers; 'Mrs. F. D. Roosevelt', double with fragrant shell pink blooms; 'Pink Lemonade', anemone or bomb with pink outer petals surrounding a dense cluster of pink, cream, and yellow petals; 'Raspberry Sundae', anemone or bomb with pale pink outer petals and a dense center of darker pink petals rimmed with creamy white petals; and 'Seashell', a midseason single with shell pink flowers. Late cultivars include 'Nippon Beauty', Japanese type with dark red blooms; and 'Sarah Bernhardt', a late double with fragrant shell pink blooms occasionally flecked with red. Zones 3 to 8.

P. lactiflora

p. lack-tih-FLOR-uh. Common Peony. A parent of hybrid herbaceous peonies that reaches about 2 feet in height and bears fragrant, single 3- to 4-inch-wide flowers in early summer. Blooms usually are white, but sometimes pink or red. Zones 2 to 8.

P. officinalis

p. oh-fish-in-AL-iss. Common Peony, Memorial Day Peony. A parent of today's hybrid herbaceous peonies that reaches 2 feet in height and bears red flowers in early summer. 'Rubra Plena' bears double red blooms; 'Rosea Superba', double pink ones. Zones 3 to 8.

P. tenuifolia   P. 169

p. ten-you-ih-FOE-lee-uh. Fernleaf Peony. A 2-foot-tall species with finely divided, fernlike leaves and single ruby red 3-inch-wide flowers from mid- to late spring. 'Rubra Plena' bears double flowers. Zones 3 to 8.

❧ Panicum

PAN-ih-kum. Grass family, Poaceae.

The genus *Panicum* contains some 470 species of annual and perennial grasses with narrowly lance-shaped or linear-ovate leaves and airy, branched panicles of flowers in late summer and fall.

HOW TO GROW

Select a site with full sun and rich, evenly moist, well-drained soil. *P. virgatum*, the species most often grown as an ornamental grass, tolerates dry, sandy conditions as well as boggy soil and also grows in light shade. Propagate by dividing the clumps in late spring or early summer or by sowing seeds.

P. virgatum   P. 170

p. vir-GAH-tum. Switch Grass. A 3-foot-tall warm-season native North American prairie grass forming 2½- to 3-foot-wide clumps of fine-textured leaves topped by silvery or pinkish 4- to 8-foot-tall flowers. In fall, flowers turn whitish or buff-brown and foliage turns yellow, then brown. 'Heavy Metal' has metallic blue-green leaves and good yellow fall color. 'Haense Herms' turns orange-red in fall. Zones 5 to 9.

❦ *Papaver*

PAH-pah-ver. Poppy family, Papaveraceae.

Although many plants are commonly called poppies, *Papaver* is the genus of the true poppies, which are grown for their showy, bowl- or cup-shaped flowers with silky, crepe paper–textured petals. Some 70 species of annuals, biennials, and perennials belong here. They bear simple to deeply cut, fernlike leaves, and their stems contain a milky latex when cut. Blooms come in hot colors — oranges, orange-reds, scarlet, hot pink, and yellow — as well as soft pink, pale yellow, and white. The flowers are followed by distinctive, rounded seed capsules.

HOW TO GROW

Give poppies full sun and average to rich, evenly moist, well-drained soil. Alpine poppies *(P. alpinum)* require excellent drainage and are good choices for rock gardens or along the tops of low walls where they get very good soil drainage. For all poppies, a site protected from wind is best, and in areas with hot summers, a spot with morning sun and afternoon shade provides beneficial heat protection. Both *P. alpinum* and *P. croceum* grow best in areas with cool nights and warm days and die out in midsummer in regions with hot, humid summers. Oriental poppies *(P. orientale)* go dormant in midsummer after they flower, so combine them with plants that cover the space they leave. Clumps of *P. orientale* have deep roots and are happiest if left undisturbed, but usually spread enough to need dividing every 5 years or so. Divide them in late summer to early fall, just as the new leaves are beginning to emerge from summer dormancy. Poppies self-sow, and self-sown seedlings are a good option for propagating short-lived perennials — *P. alpinum* and *P. croceum* — so let some seedpods ripen. Don't let cultivars of *P. orientale* self-sow, because the seedlings will most likely have the typical brilliant orange flowers of the species. Instead, propagate by division or by root cuttings taken in fall.

P. alpinum

p. al-PIE-num. Alpine Poppy. Short-lived 6- to 10-inch-tall perennial with a 4- to 6-inch-wide tuft of fernlike leaves. Bears cup-shaped 1½-inch-wide flowers in early to midsummer in white, yellows, oranges, and reds. Zones 4 to 7.

P. croceum
P. 170

p. CRO-see-um. Iceland Poppy, Arctic Poppy. Formerly *P. nudicaule*. A 1- to 2-foot-tall short-lived perennial often grown as a biennial or annual. Bears showy 3- to 5-inch-wide flowers in spring and early summer in the full range of poppy colors. Zones 2 to 8.

P. orientale
P. 171

p. or-ee-en-TAL-ee. Oriental Poppy. Clump-forming perennial producing 1-foot-tall mounds of deeply divided, coarse-looking foliage and spreading by rhizomes to form 2- to 3-foot-wide drifts. Bears brilliant red-orange flowers with purple-black centers on 2- to 4-foot-tall stems for a few weeks in early summer. Blooms usually are 4 to 6 inches wide, but improved cultivars bear flowers that can reach 8 inches or more across and come in a range of colors, including red, pale salmon, pink, white, and scarlet-orange. Cultivars include 'Helen Elizabeth' (salmon pink), 'Glowing Rose' (deep pink), 'Turkenlouis' (ruffled, orange-red), and 'Snow Queen' (white). Zones 3 to 7.

❧ Patrinia

pah-TRIN-ee-uh. Valerian family, Valerianaceae.

Some 15 species belong to the genus *Patrinia*, all clump-forming perennials native to Siberia and Japan. They produce low mounds of rounded leaves that usually are deeply cut in a pinnate (featherlike) or palmate (handlike) fashion. The mounds of foliage are topped in late summer by branched panicles of small cup-shaped yellow or white flowers that have five petal lobes.

HOW TO GROW
Select a site in full sun or partial shade with average to rich, moist but well-drained soil. Plants tolerate heat and humidity. Plants need staking to remain erect, or they can be allowed to sprawl. Clumps can grow for years without needing division but can be dug and divided in either spring or fall for purposes of propagation. They also self-sow: cut off faded blooms to reduce the number of self-sown seedlings.

P. scabiosaefolia

P. 172

p. scah-bee-oh-see-FOE-lee-uh. Clump-forming 1- to 2-foot-tall species forming 2-foot-wide mounds of leaves and branched 3- to 7-foot-tall clusters of yellow flowers in late summer and fall. Zones 4 to 8.

🌿 *Pennisetum*

pen-ih-SEE-tum. Grass family, Poaceae.

Pennisetums, also called fountain grasses, are grown for their feathery, bottlebrush or bushy, foxtail-like seed heads, which are produced over clumps of arching, linear leaves. The botanical name refers to the feathery flowers: it is from the Greek *penna,* feather, and *seta,* bristle. The genus contains about 120 species of annuals and hardy and tender perennials.

HOW TO GROW

Give pennisetums full sun and average to rich, well-drained soil. *P. alopecuroides* tolerates light shade. Cut back the foliage in late winter before growth resumes. Propagate by division in spring or early summer or by seeds. Perennial species self-sow prolifically and can easily become invasive. Cut off the seed heads before they begin to shatter in late fall and/or pull up seedlings regularly.

p. alopecuroides

P. 172

p. al-oh-peh-cure-OY-deez. Fountain Grass. Clump-forming, warm-season grass with rounded 2- to 3-foot-tall mounds of narrow ½-inch-wide leaves that spread as far. Bears bottlebrush-like pinkish to white flowers in midsummer, and clumps are 3 to 4 feet tall in bloom. Compact cultivars include 2- to 3-foot-tall 'Hameln', 8- to 10-inch-tall 'Little Bunny', and 1½-foot-tall 'Little Honey', which has silver variegated leaves. 'Moudry' bears black-purple flowers but reseeds especially prolifically. Zones 6 to 9, to Zone 5 with winter protection.

🌿 *Penstemon*

PEN-steh-mun. Figwort family, Scrophulariaceae.

Primarily native to North and Central America, *Penstemon* species are perennials and subshrubs with linear to lance-shaped leaves and panicles of tubular or bell-shaped, two-lipped flowers in shades of lavender, purple, purple-blue, lilac-blue, pink, red, yellow, and white. The 250 species in the genus are found in a wide range of habitats — cool, moist, western mountains; dry plains and deserts; and both dry and moist woodlands and prairies in the eastern half of the country.

HOW TO GROW
Give the penstemons listed here full sun to partial shade and rich, very drained, evenly moist soil. They grow best in areas with cool summers; in areas with hot summers, select a site with shade in the afternoon. *P. digitalis* tolerates heat and humidity well. Many penstemons are short-lived or will not grow well outside their native range, so for best results with these plants, match the requirements of the species to the existing site and soil conditions in your garden. Water during dry weather. Where plants are marginally hardy, in late fall cover them with a dry winter mulch such as evergreen boughs or weed-free straw. Divide plants every 5 to 6 years to keep them vigorous. Propagate by dividing plants in spring, taking cuttings in spring or summer, or by seeds.

P. barbatus   P. 173
p. bar-BAY-tus. Common Beardtongue, Beardlip Penstemon. A 1½- to 4-foot-tall species native to the western United States and Mexico. Produces low 2-foot-wide mounds of semievergreen leaves topped by panicles of pendent, tubular 1½-inch-long flowers from early summer to fall. Blooms are red with tinges of pink. 'Elfin Pink' bears pink flowers on 1-foot-tall plants. 'Albus', from 1½ to 4 feet in height, bears white flowers. 'Coccineus' bears red flowers on 1½-foot-tall plants. Zones 4 to 9.

P. digitalis   P. 173
p. dih-jih-TAL-iss. A 2- to 4-foot species native to the eastern and southeastern United States. Bears 1½-foot-wide rosettes of shiny, semievergreen leaves topped by panicles of tubular to bell-shaped 1-inch-long white flowers from early to late summer. 'Husker Red' has leaves that are maroon-red when young and white flowers tinged with pink. Zones 2 to 8.

P. hirsutus   P. 174
p. her-SUE-tus. A 1½- to 2½-foot-tall subshrub native to the Northeast that produces low 1- to 2-foot-wide mounds of evergreen leaves. In summer, it bears loose racemes of tubular- to funnel-shaped 1- to 2-inch-long flowers with white throats that are tinged with lavender or pale purple on the

outside. Dwarf *P. hirsutus* var. *pygmaeus* reaches 4 inches in height, spreads from 4 to 6 inches, and bears maroon-purple–tinged leaves. Zones 3 to 9.

P. hybrids
P. 174

A wide variety of hybrids with variable hardiness and adaptability are available. Most cultivars offered are hardy from Zone 7 south and best in gardens on the West Coast because of their preference for cool summers. Treat them as biennials or short-lived perennials in the East. Hybrids bear tubular, bell-shaped flowers in summer that are 1 to 2 inches long. Plants range from 1½ to 2 feet and spread about 1 to 1½ feet. 'Prairie Fire' bears bell-shaped crimson flowers. 'Prairie Dusk' bears purple blooms. 'Rose Elf' bears rose pink flowers. All three cultivars are hardy in Zones 3 to 8. 'Sour Grapes', hardy in Zones 6 to 8, bears purple-pink flowers with white throats.

P. pinifolius
P. 175

p. pin-ih-FOE-lee-us. An evergreen subshrub with needlelike leaves. Plants reach 1½ feet tall and spread about as far. Bears loose racemes of scarlet tubular flowers in summer. Zones 4 to 10.

P. smallii

p. SMALL-ee-eye. Small's Penstemon. Shrubby 1½- to 2-foot-tall perennial native to the eastern United States that spreads to about 2 feet. In late spring it produces spikes of tubular 1½-inch-long rose- to lilac-pink flowers that have white-striped throats. Zones 5 to 9.

❦ Perovskia

per-OFF-ski-uh. Mint family, Lamiaceae.

Seven species of subshrubs, all native to central Asia, belong to the genus *Perovskia,* one of which is a popular plant for perennial gardens. Commonly called Russian sage or simply perovskia, it produces airy spikes of tiny lavender-blue flowers that create a cloudlike haze of color above silver- to gray-green deeply cut leaves and silvery stems.

HOW TO GROW

Select a site in full sun with very well drained poor to average sandy or loamy soil. Plants grow well in dry soil and in alkaline soil and are good choices for seaside gardens. Well-drained soil is especially important in the winter. Newly planted specimens take a year or two to become established. After the first hard frost of fall, cut plants to within 1 foot of the ground. From the colder portions of Zone 5 north, plants are killed to the ground over winter but resprout in spring. In northern zones, cover them with evergreen boughs or straw over winter. For best results, do not divide Russian sage, because the woody crowns are hard to separate successfully. Propagate by taking cuttings from shoots that emerge from the base of the plants in spring or early summer. Or pot up small offsets that appear on the outside of established clumps.

P. atriplicifolia P. 175

p. ah-trih-plih-sih-FOE-lee-uh. Russian Sage. A 3- to 5-foot-tall subshrub, spreading from 3 to 4 feet, with silvery, deeply cut gray-green aromatic leaves. Bears showy panicles of small tubular violet-blue flowers from late summer to fall. 'Filagran' has very finely cut leaves. 'Blue Spire' is a heavy flowering selection with violet-blue flowers on 3-foot plants. Zones 5 to 9, to Zone 4 with winter protection.

❦ *Persicaria*

per-sih-CARE-ee-uh. Buckwheat family, Polygonaceae.

Commonly known as knotweeds or smartweeds, *Persicaria* species (formerly *Polygonum* species) primarily are annuals or perennials, although the genus contains a few subshrubs. Some spread by rhizomes or stolons, and a few are quite invasive well-known weeds, including common knotweed or doorweed *(P. aviculare)* and Pennsylvania smartweed *(P. pensylvanicum).* Still, the genus contains attractive and useful perennials. Typically, knotweeds have swollen leaf nodes, or "joints," simple leaves, and dense spikes or panicles of very small flowers that are funnel, bell, or cup shaped. Blooms come in shades of pink or red as well as white.

HOW TO GROW

Select a site in full sun or partial shade with average to rich, evenly moist soil. Plants struggle in areas with hot summers, so in the South, a site with afternoon shade is best. *P. bisorta* grows well in constantly moist, even wet soil. Divide the clumps in spring or fall either for propagation or to control their spread.

P. affinis
P. 176

p. ah-FIN-iss. Himalayan Knotweed. Formerly *Polygonum affine*. Mat-forming 10-inch-tall species with evergreen leaves that spreads to form 2-foot-wide mounds. Bears dense 2- to 3-inch-long spikes of cup-shaped rose-red ¼-inch-long flowers from midsummer to fall. 'Superba' bears pale pink flowers that turn dark red-pink above leaves that turn rich bronze-brown in fall. Zones 3 to 8.

P. bistorta
P. 176

p. bih-STOR-tuh. Bistort, Snakeweed. Formerly *Polygonum bistorta*. Vigorous 2½-foot-tall species that spreads to form 3-foot-wide mounds of semievergreen leaves. Bears dense, round 2- to 3-inch-long bottlebrush-like spikes of pink, bell-shaped, ¼-inch-long flowers from early summer to fall. 'Superba' bears pale pink flowers on 3-foot-tall plants. Zones 3 to 8.

❦ Petasites

pet-ah-SITE-eez. Aster family, Asteraceae.

Petasites species are vigorous perennials primarily grown for their large showy leaves. Commonly called butterburs or sweet coltsfoot, there are about 15 species in the genus native to Europe, North America, and Asia. All produce clumps of long-stemmed, heart- to kidney-shaped basal leaves and smaller scalelike leaves on the stems. *Petasites* species are dioecious, meaning plants are either male or female. They produce flower heads consisting of a mix of ray florets, disk florets, and threadlike florets, some of which are fertile and some of which are sterile. Flower heads are carried singly or in clusters.

HOW TO GROW
Select a site in partial to full shade with rich, constantly moist soil. A site in a bog garden or along a pond or stream is ideal; plants do not grow well in stagnant, wet conditions. Butterburs have thick, deep rootstocks and spread by rhizomes. They can become invasive, so select a site with care: a spot bordered on one side by water and contained on three sides by mown lawn or a wall is suitable. Propagate by dividing the clumps in spring or fall.

P. japonicus var. giganteus
P. 177

p. jah-PON-ih-kus var. jy-GAN-tee-us. A rhizomatous species forming 3½-foot-tall clumps of leaves that spread to 5 feet or more. Leaves are toothed, kidney-shaped, and from 2 to 3 feet across. Dense, conelike white or yellowish flower heads, each surrounded by a ruff of leafy bracts, appear in early spring before the leaves emerge. Zones 5 to 9.

ᴡ Phlomis

FLOW-mis. Mint family, Lamiaceae.

Four-sided stems and dense whorls, or tiers, of tubular, two-lipped flowers characterize *Phlomis* species. Sometimes referred to as Jerusalem sages, these are somewhat sagelike perennials, shrubs, and subshrubs native from Europe and northern Africa to Asia. Leaves are lance shaped to ovate, gray-green in color, and often covered with hairs. About 100 species belong to the genus.

HOW TO GROW

Select a site in full sun with average to rich, well-drained soil. *P. russeliana* will grow in light shade, and in the South, shade during the hottest part of the day is best for all species. Plants are fairly drought tolerant and also good choices for seaside gardens, as they tolerate salt. In zones where plants are not killed to the ground over winter, prune to shape immediately after flowering. Propagate by dividing the clumps in spring or fall, by cuttings of shoots taken in summer, or by seeds.

P. fruticosa

p. fru-tih-COE-suh. Jerusalem Sage. A mounding 3- to 4-foot-tall shrub that spreads from 4 to 5 feet. Bears gray-green leaves that are woolly underneath. Erect stems have dense whorls of golden yellow 1¼-inch-long flowers that appear from early to midsummer. Plants are killed to the ground north of Zone 7, and thus behave like perennials. Zones 4 to 8.

P. russeliana   P. 177

p. rus-el-ee-AH-nuh. Jerusalem Sage. A 3-foot-tall perennial with 3-foot-wide clumps of hairy, ovate leaves. Bears erect stems with dense whorls of butter yellow hooded 1- to 1½-inch-long flowers from late spring to early fall. 'Edward Bowles', a hybrid between this species and *P. fruticosa*, bears large gray-green leaves and whorls of sulphur yellow 1¼-inch-long flowers in early to midsummer. Zones 4 to 9.

P. tuberosa

P. 178

p. too-ber-OH-suh. A 4- to 5-foot-tall species that produces small tubers on its roots and spreads to form 3- to 4-foot-wide clumps. Bears whorls of purplish pink ¾- to 1-inch-long flowers in summer. Zones 5 to 8.

❦ *Phlox*

FLOX. Phlox family, Polemoniaceae.

This well-known genus contains 70 species, including a variety of handsome hardy perennials, popular annuals, and a few shrubs. Nearly all are native North American wildflowers — one species is from Siberia. They bear showy, rounded clusters of flowers. The individual blooms have a slender tube at the base, an abruptly flared and flattened face, and five lobes, or "petals." Leaves are simple and linear to ovate. The name *Phlox* is from the Greek word for flame, a reference to the fact that many species bear hot-colored flowers. Blooms come in crimson red, magenta-pink, white, pale pink, lavender, lavender-blue, and purple.

HOW TO GROW

There are phlox suitable for sun and shade and a wide range of soil conditions. The most commonly grown species can be divided into three groups based on both culture and bloom time. Give spring-blooming *P. bifida, P. douglasii,* and *P. subulata* full sun with average to rich, well-drained soil. *P. bifida* will grow in poor, very well drained soil. In areas with hot, dry summers, dappled afternoon shade is best. All three of these species thrive for years without needing to be divided unless they outgrow their space, die out in the centers of the clumps, or appear to be less vigorous. Propagate by dividing plants in spring or by taking cuttings in early to midsummer of new shoots that arise near the base of the plant.

P. divaricata and *P. stolonifera* both thrive in light to full shade in a site with rich, evenly moist, well-drained soil. Both spread into broad clumps via creeping stems that root where they touch the soil; *P. stolonifera* spreads more quickly and widely than *P. divaricata. P. divaricata* may be disfigured by powdery mildew; keep the soil evenly moist and thin out the stems to help prevent this disease. These species need dividing only if they outgrow their space. Propagate dividing plants in spring after the flowers fade, by digging up rooted plantlets that appear, or by taking cuttings in spring or early summer from shoots that arise near the base of the plant. Both self-sow.

Summer-blooming *P. carolina, P. maculata,* and *P. paniculata* all thrive in full sun or partial shade and rich, deeply prepared, evenly moist soil. All are best in areas with relatively cool summers. None tolerate drought, so water deeply in dry weather. In southern zones, a site with light shade during the hottest part of the day is best. Feed plants in spring with a topdressing of compost or well-rotted manure. Deadhead spent flowers to prolong bloom and prevent self-sowing. (Named cultivars do not come true from seeds, and seedlings, which generally have unattractive magenta-pink flowers, will overwhelm improved cultivars. Rogue out seedlings that do appear.) Tall phlox, especially *P. paniculata,* usually require staking. Dig and divide all of these species every 2 or 3 years in fall or spring to keep them vigorous. Propagate by division or by taking cuttings in spring or early summer from shoots that arise near the base of the plant. Powdery mildew is a problem on *P. paniculata,* causing large white blotches on the leaves, which eventually drop off. To prevent this, select a site with good air circulation, plant resistant species and cultivars (both *P. carolina* and *P. maculata* resist this disease), thin stems in spring so air can circulate through the clumps, and keep plants well watered during dry spells. Clean up and destroy all mildew-infected plant debris in late summer. To prevent the disease, spray wettable sulfur on the foliage weekly once the first patch of white appears on the leaves.

P. bifida P. 178

p. BIFF-ih-duh. Cleft Phlox, Sand Phlox. Mounding 6- to 8-inch-tall plant that spreads as far. Bears needlelike, evergreen leaves and fragrant, star-shaped ¾-inch-wide lavender to white flowers with deeply cleft petal ends in spring. Zones 4 to 8.

P. carolina

p. care-oh-LINE-uh. Carolina Phlox, Thick-leaved Phlox. A 3- to 4-foot-tall species that spreads from 1½ to 2 feet. Features glossy oval leaves and clusters of purple to pink ¾-inch-wide flowers in summer. Zones 4 to 9.

P. divaricata P. 179

p. dih-var-ih-KAH-tuh. Wild Blue Phlox, Woodland Phlox. A 10- to 14-inch-tall woodland native that spreads to 2 feet or more and has semievergreen leaves. Bears clusters of fragrant lavender, pale violet, or white flowers in spring. 'Fuller's White' has white flowers. 'Louisiana Purple' has purple flowers with magenta eyes. 'Clouds of Perfume' bears especially fragrant pale lavender-blue flowers. Zones 3 to 9.

P. douglasii

p. doug-LASS-ee-eye. Douglas's Phlox. Mounding 3- to 8-inch-tall plant that spreads to 1 foot. Bears white, lavender, or pink ½-inch-wide flowers singly or in very small clusters from late spring to early summer. 'Crackerjack' bears magenta-red blooms on 5-inch plants. Zones 4 to 8.

P. maculata
PP. 179–80

p. mac-you-LAH-tuh. Wild Sweet William, Meadow Phlox. An erect 2- to 3-foot-tall species that forms 1½-foot-wide clumps. Bears glossy leaves and elongated clusters of fragrant ¾- to 1-inch-wide mauve pink flowers in early to midsummer. 'Miss Lingard' (sometimes listed under *P. carolina*) has white flowers. 'Omega' is white with a lilac eye, and 'Rosalinde' is rose pink. Zones 4 to 8.

P. paniculata
P. 180

p. pan-ick-you-LAH-tuh. Garden Phlox. A popular, heavily hybridized 3- to 4-foot-tall species that forms 2- to 3-foot-wide clumps. Bears rounded clusters of fragrant ½- to 1-inch flowers in summer to early fall. Many cultivars are available with pale to rose pink, orange-red, crimson, purple, lilac, and white flowers. Bicolor blooms are also available. Several cultivars that resist powdery mildew are available, including 'David' (white), 'Katherine' (lavender), 'Pax' (white), and 'Sandra' (scarlet). 'Bright Eyes' is a popular compact selection from 2 to 2½ feet tall with pink flowers. 'Nora Leigh' has white-edged leaves and pale lilac flowers. Zones 3 to 8.

P. stolonifera
P. 181

p. sto-lo-NIFF-er-uh. Creeping Phlox. A 4- to 6-inch-tall species spreading by stolons to form 1- to 2-foot-wide drifts. Bears loose clusters of pink, lilac-blue, or white flowers in spring. Cultivars include 'Blue Ridge' (lilac-blue), 'Bruce's White' (white), and 'Pink Ridge' (mauve-pink). Zones 3 to 8.

P. subulata
P. 181

p. sub-you-LAH-tuh. Moss Phlox, Creeping Phlox, Moss Pink. Ground-hugging 2- to 6-inch-tall species that forms 1½- to 2-foot-wide mats. Has evergreen, needlelike leaves and bears masses of ½- to 1-inch flowers directly atop the leaves in mid- to late spring in shades of lavender, purple, pink, or white. Many cultivars with solid and bicolor blooms are available: 'Fort Hill' bears dark pink blooms, 'Apple Blossom', pale lilac-pink ones with darker eyes. 'Blue Hills' has dark purple-blue flowers with notched petals, 'Snowflake', white blooms. Zones 2 to 9.

❦ *Physalis*

fy-SAL-iss. Nightshade family, Solanaceae.

Physalis species are commonly known as ground cherries because their tiny bell-shaped flowers are followed by berries encased in an inflated calyx that resembles a papery, lanternlike husk. About 80 species of annuals and perennials belong to the genus. One hardy perennial species is grown for its showy, bright orange "lanterns," which are used in dried arrangements and other crafts.

HOW TO GROW

Select a site in full sun or partial shade with average, well-drained, evenly moist soil. Plants spread quickly by rhizomes and can become invasive, so select the site with care. Water during dry weather, especially as the "lanterns" are developing. Divide plants as needed to keep them in check or for propagation. Or sow seeds.

P. alkekengi   P. 182

p. al-keh-KEN-jee. Chinese Lantern. Rhizomatous 2- to 3-foot-tall perennial that spreads to 3 feet or more. Bears rounded, arrowhead-shaped leaves and ¾-inch-long creamy white flowers in midsummer followed by berries surrounded by red-orange 2-inch-wide "lanterns." 'Gigantea', also sold as 'Monstrosa', bears exceptionally large fruit. Zones 5 to 8.

❦ *Physostegia*

fy-so-STEE-juh. Mint family, Lamiaceae.

Physostegia species are native North American perennials that spread by rhizomes and bear showy racemes of tubular, two-lipped flowers. There are about 12 species in the genus — all perennials with square stems and lanceolate to somewhat oblong leaves. The species commonly grown in gardens, *P. virginiana,* is sometimes called false dragonhead, a reference to the shape of the flowers. Obedient plant is another common name that also refers to the flowers, which have uniquely jointed bases that allow them to be moved on the main stalk. Once moved, they obediently remain pointed in the direction selected.

HOW TO GROW

Select a site in full sun to partial shade with average, evenly moist soil. Plants tolerate wet conditions but will flop in very fertile soil. Compact cultivars, which range from 2 to 3 feet tall, usually stand without staking. Obedient plants spread quickly by rhizomes: divide the clumps every 2 to 3 years to keep them in bounds and for propagation. Or propagate by stem cuttings taken in early summer.

P. virginiana
P. 182

p. vir-jin-ee-AH-nuh. Obedient Plant, False Dragonhead. Rhizomatous 3- to 4-foot-tall perennial that easily spreads to 2 or 3 feet. Bears dense, erect spikes of two-lipped 1-inch-long lilac- to rose pink flowers from midsummer to early fall. 'Alba' and 'Summer Snow' have white flowers. 'Pink Bouquet' bears bright pink flowers, while 'Vivid' bears bright purplish pink flowers on 2- to 3-foot plants. 'Variegata' has white-edged leaves and magenta flowers. Zones 3 to 9.

❦ Platycodon

plat-ee-COE-don. Bellflower family, Campanulaceae.

A single species commonly known as balloon flower belongs to the genus *Platycodon*. It is a dependable, clump-forming perennial with inflated flower buds that split open into broad, shallow, bell-shaped flowers. The common name refers to the balloonlike buds, while the botanical name refers to the 3-inch-wide flowers themselves: *Platycodon* is from the Greek *platys*, broad, and *kodon*, bell.

HOW TO GROW
Plant balloon flowers in full sun or light shade and average to rich well-drained soil. In the South, a spot that receives afternoon shade is best. Plants in rich soil and partial shade are more likely to need staking. Deadheading spent blooms keeps plants blooming all summer long. Mark the location of clumps, as they are late to emerge in spring and thus easy to dig into by mistake. Established clumps seldom need dividing, and they resent disturbance, but they can be dug in spring or early fall for propagation or transplanting. Rooted shoots that sometimes appear at the base of the clump offer another propagation option. Most cultivars also come true from seeds, and plants self-sow.

P. grandiflorus
P. 183

p. gran-dih-FLOR-us. Balloon Flower. Long-lived 2-foot-tall species forming 1-foot-wide clumps. Bears attractive blue-green, oval- to lance-shaped leaves and 2-inch-wide purple, blue-violet, lilac-blue, pink, or white flowers from early to midsummer. *P. grandiflorus* ssp. *mariesii* (also sold as 'Mariesii') bears purple-blue flowers on 1- to 1½-foot plants. 'Sentimental Blue' has lilac-blue flowers on 10- to 14-inch plants. 'Shell Pink' bears pale pink flowers on 2-foot plants. Fuji Series plants are seed grown and have white, pink, or purple-blue flowers. 'Double Blue' bears double lilac-blue flowers on 1½- to 2-foot plants. Zones 3 to 8.

☙ *Polemonium*

poe-leh-MOAN-ee-um. Phlox family, Polemoniaceae.

Commonly called Jacob's ladders, *Polemonium* species are annuals or perennials bearing tubular or bell-, saucer-, or funnel-shaped flowers in spring or summer. Blooms are borne either in branched clusters or singly and usually come in shades of lavender-blue or white, but also purple, pink, or yellow. The plants produce clumps of leaves divided in a pinnate (featherlike) fashion. Some 25 species belong to the genus.

HOW TO GROW

For the species listed here, select a site in full sun or partial shade with rich, well-drained, evenly moist soil. *P. reptans* is best in partial shade. Neither species tolerates heat and humidity, and in areas with warm summers they require a site with shade during the hottest part of the day. Plants seldom need division, but can be divided in spring for propagation. They also self-sow and can be grown from seeds.

P. caeruleum   P. 183

p. see-RULE-ee-um. Jacob's Ladder, Greek Valerian. Clump-forming 1- to 3-foot-tall perennial native to western North America as well as Europe and northern Asia. Forms handsome 1-foot-wide mounds of leaves topped by clusters of bell-shaped lilac-blue flowers in early summer. 'Brise D'Anjou' bears leaves variegated with creamy to pale yellow. *P. caeruleum* var. *lacteum*, also listed as var. *album*, bears white flowers. Zones 4 to 7.

P. reptans   P. 184

p. REP-tans. Creeping Jacob's Ladder. Mounding species native to the eastern United States that reaches about 1 foot in height and spreads to 1½ feet. Bears clusters of bell-shaped sky blue ½-inch-wide flowers in late spring and early summer. 'Lambrook Mauve', also sold as 'Lambrook Manor', bears ½- to ¾-inch-wide lilac-blue flowers. 'Alba' bears white flowers. Zones 2 to 8.

❦ *Polygonatum*

poh-lig-oh-NAY-tum. Lily family, Liliaceae.

Grown primarily for their handsome foliage, *Polygonatum* species are rhizomatous perennials with unbranched, erect or arching stems that bear linear to ovate leaves. The foliage of most commonly cultivated kinds is feather- or plumelike in effect. Plants bear small, pendent, bell-shaped or tubular flowers beneath the leaves either singly or in small clusters. The flowers, which usually are creamy colored or white with green markings, are followed by round, usually black, berries. The plants grow from many-jointed rhizomes: the botanical name, from the Greek *polys*, much, and *gony*, knee, refers to this fact. The common name Solomon's seal refers to the joints as well, which resemble the wax seals sometimes applied to official documents.

HOW TO GROW

Plant Solomon's seals in partial to full shade with rich, moist, well-drained soil. They tolerate full sun in northern zones, but require shade during the hottest part of the day in the South. Most species tolerate dry soil. They spread steadily, but not invasively, to form handsome drifts. Divide plants in spring or fall to propagate or to keep them from outgrowing their space.

P. biflorum

p. bi-FLOOR-um. Solomon's Seal. A 1½- to 7-foot-tall species forming 2- to 3-foot-wide clumps. Bears pendent ½- to 1-inch-long greenish white flowers either singly or in clusters of two or four from late spring to early summer. The enormous 4- to 7-foot-tall plants commonly listed as *P. commutatum*, and sometimes called great Solomon's seal, are currently classified as forms of *P. biflorum*. Zones 3 to 9.

P. humile

p. HUME-ill-ee. Dwarf Solomon's Seal. Dwarf 8-inch-tall species forming loose 2-foot-wide clumps. Bears solitary or paired, pendent, ¾-inch-wide white flowers in spring. Zones 5 to 8.

P. odoratum   P. 184

p. oh-door-AH-tum. Fragrant Solomon's Seal. A 2½- to 3-foot-tall species with pendent white 1¼-inch-long flowers borne singly or in pairs. Blooms late spring to early summer. *P. odoratum* var. *thunbergii* 'Variegatum', which has leaves striped at the edges with white, is most often grown. Zones 4 to 8.

Polygonum. See *Persicaria*

❦ *Polystichum*

pol-ISS-tih-cum. Wood Fern family, Dryopteridaceae.

Commonly called shield or sword ferns, *Polystichum* species bear leathery, often evergreen fronds that are once-, twice-, or thrice-cut. Most are 1 to 4 feet or more in height. The plants usually form graceful, vase-shaped clumps.

HOW TO GROW

Select a site in partial shade with evenly moist soil rich in organic matter. Christmas fern *(P. acrostichoides)* also grows in dry soil, on slopes, or among rocks, making it an excellent ground cover for shade. The fronds of evergreen species usually become prostrate by early winter. Either leave them in place from year to year or remove them in late winter before the new fronds unfurl. *Polystichum* species grow from erect, branched rhizomes that form crowns. Propagate them by digging the plants in spring and carefully separating the rhizomes.

P. acrostichoides   P. 185

p. ack-row-stick-OY-deez. Christmas Fern. A 1½-foot-tall fern native to the northeastern United States that forms 3-foot-wide clumps with time. Bears once-cut, evergreen fronds that have stocking-shaped leaflets. Zones 3 to 9. Gardeners in the Northwest should grow western sword fern *(P. munitum)* instead of Christmas fern. Also evergreen, it ranges from 1½ to 5 feet tall. Although hardy in Zones 6 to 9 it does not do well in the East.

P. setiferum

p. seh-TIFF-er-um. Soft Shield Fern, Hedge Fern. A 4-foot-tall evergreen species native to Europe. It forms 3-foot-wide clumps of shiny, twice-cut fronds. Many cultivars with crested or heavily divided fronds are available. Zones 5 to 8.

❦ *Potentilla*

poe-ten-TILL-uh. Rose family, Rosaceae.

The genus *Potentilla* contains about 500 species of perennials, subshrubs, and shrubs along with a few annuals and biennials. All bear five-petaled, cup- or saucer-shaped flowers in shades of yellow, orange, red, pink, and white. Blooms usually are borne over a long season from spring or early summer to fall and are carried singly or in small clusters. Leaves are compound, meaning they have separate leaflets, and arranged in a palmate (handlike) or pinnate (featherlike) fashion.

HOW TO GROW

Select a site in full sun or light shade with poor to moderately rich, well-drained soil. Sandy to loamy soil is fine; soils heavy in clay tend not to drain quickly enough. In southern zones, a site with light shade during the hottest part of the day is best. Dig the clumps in spring or fall to divide them for propagation or if they outgrow their space.

P. atrosanguinea   P. 185

p. ah-trow-san-GWIN-ee-uh. Himalayan Cinquefoil. A 1- to 1½-foot-tall species that forms 2-foot-wide clumps of gray-green silky-hairy leaves. Bears branched clusters of 1¼-inch-wide flowers in shades of yellow, orange, or red from early summer to fall. 'Gibson's Scarlet' bears single scarlet flowers. 'Vulcan' bears double red flowers; 'Yellow Queen', bright yellow ones; and 'Firedance', salmon-red blooms. Zones 5 to 8.

P. nepalensis

p. nee-pal-EN-sis. Nepal Cinquefoil. A 1- to 3-foot-tall perennial that can be somewhat short-lived. Plants form 2-foot-wide clumps topped by clusters of dark red 1-inch-wide flowers in early summer and sporadically to fall. 'Miss Willmott' bears bright reddish pink blooms on 1- to 1½-foot-tall plants. Zones 4 to 8.

P. neumaniana   P. 186

p. new-man-ee-AH-nuh. Formerly *P. tabernaemontani*, *P. verna*. Creeping 4-inch-tall species that forms dense 1-foot-wide mats. Bears loose clusters of yellow ½- to 1-inch-wide flowers from late spring into summer. Compact 'Nana' is 2 to 3 inches tall. Zones 4 to 8.

P. recta

p. RECK-tuh. Sulfur Cinquefoil. Erect 1- to 2-foot-tall species forming 1½-foot-wide clumps. Bears gray-green to green leaves and clusters of ½- to 1-inch-wide pale yellow flowers from early to late summer. 'Warrenii', also listed as 'Macrantha', bears bright yellow flowers. Zones 3 to 7.

P. tridentata

P. tri-den-TAH-tuh. Three-toothed Cinquefoil. A tough, vigorous, woody-based perennial native to the eastern United States as well as Greenland. Plants range from 6 to 12 inches in height and spread as far. Bears ever-green three-leaflet leaves topped by clusters of ¼-inch-wide white flowers in early summer. Compact 'Minima' is 4 to 6 inches tall. Zones 2 to 8.

❧ Primula

PRIM-you-luh. Primrose family, Primulaceae.

This large genus of popular garden plants contains some 425 species of hardy and tender perennials commonly called primroses or primulas. They produce rosettes of narrow to broadly rounded leaves and clusters of flowers that usually are salverform, meaning they have a slender tube at the base and an abruptly flared and flattened face. Some species bear tubular, bell-shaped, or funnel-shaped blooms. The botanical name alludes to the early-blooming nature of many primroses — it is taken from the Latin *primus*, or first.

HOW TO GROW

For the most part, the species listed here need partial shade and rich, evenly moist, well-drained soil. They grow best in cool climates, and in areas with cool summers they can be grown in full sun provided the soil remains evenly moist — the Pacific Northwest is ideal for growing prim-roses. In areas with warm summers, look for a spot that is shaded during the hottest part of the day. Exceptions are listed in the species descriptions below. Mulch plants annually in spring with chopped leaves or shredded bark to keep the soil moist and cool. Water as necessary to keep the soil moist, especially during spring and early summer when the plants are blooming and actively growing. In most areas, plants look bedraggled by midsummer; cut off leaves after they have yellowed. Prim-roses seldom need to be divided, but dig them in spring or early summer if they become overcrowded, begin to lose vigor, or for propagation.

Some faster-growing Polyanthus Group primroses benefit from being divided every 3 to 4 years. Or propagate by severing individual offsets, or crowns, from the outsides of the clumps with a trowel, or start from seeds.

P. auricula

p. aw-RICK-you-luh. An 8-inch-tall species forming a low 8- to 10-inch-wide rosette of gray-green leaves. Bears umbels of ½- to 1-inch-wide fragrant yellow flowers in spring. Zones 3 to 8.

P. denticulata
P. 186

p. den-tick-you-LAH-tuh. Drumstick Primrose. Produces 1- to 1½-inch-wide rosettes of leaves topped in early spring with round clusters of flowers on 8- to 12-inch stalks. The bell- or trumpet-shaped ¾-inch-wide blooms come in lavender purple or white and have yellow eyes. Thrives in rich, constantly moist soil and also soil that is wet to boggy in spring and summer. Plants require better drainage in winter, however, when wet conditions can rot the plants. Self-sows. Zones 3 to 8.

P. elatior
P. 187

p. eh-LAY-tee-or. Oxlip Primrose. Evergreen to semievergreen species with a low, 10-inch-wide rosette of puckered leaves topped in early to midspring by dainty clusters of tubular 1-inch-long yellow flowers held on 10- to 12-inch-tall stems. Zones 4 to 8; to Zone 3 with winter protection.

P. japonica
P. 187

p. jah-PON-ih-kuh. Japanese Primrose. Striking candelabra-type species producing a 1½-foot-wide rosette of leaves topped by erect 1½- to 2-foot-tall flower stalks in midspring. The ¾-inch-wide flowers are carried in one to six tiers, or whorls, along the stems and come in red, white, and shades of pink. Plants require partial to full shade (but good light) and constantly moist to wet soil, but will not grow in stagnant conditions: plant them where there is at least gentle water movement. Set the crowns slightly above the water line. Plants self-sow. 'Miller's Crimson' bears bright red blooms; 'Rosea', pink blooms; and 'Potsford White', white blooms. Zones 5 to 8.

P. juliae

p. JUL-ee-eye. A diminutive species with 2- to 3-inch-tall rosettes of leaves that spreads slowly to form 10- to 12-inch-wide clumps. Bears solitary magenta-pink 1-inch-wide flowers in early spring. 'Wanda' is a robust selection with red-purple flowers. Zones 3 to 8.

P. Polyanthus Group
P. 188

These hybrids are also listed as *P.* × *polyanthus* and are crosses between various hardy primroses. Plants form low 8- to 12-inch-wide rosettes of evergreen to semievergreen, rough-textured leaves and, in midspring, clusters of showy 1- to 2-inch-wide flowers on 6-inch-tall stems in a wide range of colors, including pale to deep yellow, red, orange, violet-blue, white, and pink. They often have yellow eyes. Depending on the cultivar, they can be hardy to Zone 3, but florist's types are usually less hardy — to Zone 6. Zones 3 or 6 to 8.

P. sieboldii

p. see-BOL-dee-ee. Siebold Primrose. Produces 8- to 12-inch-wide rosettes of leaves topped in early spring by 1-foot-tall clusters of delicate, lacy-looking 1-inch-wide flowers. Flowers come in pale pink, rose, white, pale purple, and purple-red. Zones 3 to 8.

P. veris
P. 188

p. VAIR-iss. Cowslip Primrose. Produces low 5- to 6-inch-wide rosettes of evergreen or semievergreen leaves and 1-inch-tall clusters of fragrant, nodding 1-inch-wide yellow flowers in early to midspring. Zones 4 to 8.

P. vulgaris
P. 189

p. vul-GAIR-iss. English Primrose, Common Primrose. Formerly *P. acaulis.* Produces 6- to 8-inch-wide rosettes of evergreen to semievergreen 9- to 10-inch-long leaves and clusters of pale yellow 1- to 1½-inch-wide flowers in early spring. Many cultivars are available, with either single or double flowers, in white, orange, magenta, purple-pink, and yellow. Zones 4 to 8.

❦ Prunella

pru-NELL-uh. Mint family, Lamiaceae.

Seven species of semievergreen perennials belong to this genus of mint family plants. All bear dense spikes of two-lipped tubular flowers in shades of violet, pink, and white. Leaves range from linear to lance shaped or ovate and may be entire or lobed. Plants spread to form thick mats of foliage.

HOW TO GROW

Select a site in full sun or partial shade with average soil that remains evenly moist. They do not tolerate dry soil. Since plants root easily at the leaf nodes and also self-sow, they can be quite invasive: *Prunella vulgaris* is a common weed of lawns and waste places. Especially in areas with cool summers, select a site with care to keep them in bounds, and watch for and dig up plants that spread too far. Shear the plants to remove flowers as they fade to curtail self-sowing. Divide in spring or fall as needed for propagation.

P. grandiflora

P. 189

p. gran-dih-FLOOR-uh. Large Selfheal. Vigorous 6-inch-tall perennial that spreads to form 3-foot-wide mats. Bears rounded, slightly toothed leaves and upright spikes of 1¼-inch-long purple flowers in summer. 'Loveliness' bears pale lavender purple blooms; 'Pink Loveliness', pink flowers; 'White Loveliness', white flowers. Zones 5 to 8.

Pulmonaria

pull-mon-AIR-ee-uh. Borage family, Boraginaceae.

Commonly called lungworts, Bethlehem sages, or simply pulmonarias, *Pulmonaria* species are underappreciated perennials that add season-long interest to the garden. Among the earliest perennials to bloom, pulmonarias produce small clusters of dainty, bell-shaped flowers from late winter to late spring before or just as the leaves begin to emerge. Blooms come in shades of lavender- and violet-blue as well as white, pink, and red. Most cultivated pulmonarias produce mounds of broadly oval green leaves splashed with white or silver. The largest leaves are produced in a low rosette at the base of the plant, and smaller leaves are borne on the flower stems as well. The foliage remains attractive until early winter, and in mild-climate areas, some lungworts are evergreen. About 14 species belong to the genus.

HOW TO GROW

Grow lungworts in partial to full shade in a site with rich, evenly moist soil. A site with morning sun and afternoon shade also is suitable. Plants self-sow, and seedlings may be very attractive, although pulmonarias hybridize freely, so they will not be identical to the parents. Established plants tolerate drought, but watering during dry weather keeps the foliage looking its best. Plants thrive for years without needing to be divided, but for propagation the clumps can be dug in spring, after they flower, or in early fall.

P. angustifolia

p. an-gus-tih-FOE-lee-uh. Blue Lungwort, Blue Cowslip. A 10- to 12-inch-tall species that spreads by rhizomes to form 1½-foot-wide clumps. Bears unspotted dark green leaves and funnel-shaped ⅜-inch-wide blue flowers in early spring. *P. angustifolia* ssp. *azurea* bears rich blue flowers with red-tinted buds. Zones 4 to 8.

P. hybrids   P. 190

Many hybrid lungworts with outstanding foliage or spring-borne flowers are available. They are 9 to 14 inches tall and spread to 18 inches. 'Janet Fisk', with white-marbled leaves, has pink flowers that age to blue and is hardy in Zones 3 to 8. 'Spilled Milk', Zones 5 to 8, has leaves that are mostly silver-white and pink flowers that age to blue. 'Roy Davidson', also hardy in Zones 5 to 8, has mid-green leaves evenly blotched with silver and sky blue flowers. 'Sissinghurst White', Zones 4 or 5 to 8, is grown for its white flowers.

P. longifolia   P. 190

p. lon-jih-FOE-lee-uh. Longleaf Lungwort. Forms 9- to 12-inch-tall mounds of lance-shaped 18-inch-long leaves with silver spots and spreads by rhizomes to form 2½-foot-wide clumps. It bears showy clusters of purple-blue flowers in early spring. Zones 4 to 8.

P. rubra

p. ROO-bruh. Red Lungwort. A 1- to 1½-foot-tall species forming mounds of solid green leaves that reach 2 feet in length. Spreads by rhizomes to form 3-foot-wide clumps. Bears reddish pink flowers in early spring. Zones 5 to 8.

P. saccharata   P. 191

p. sack-ah-RAH-tuh. Bethlehem Sage. Produces 8- to 12-inch-tall mounds of silver-spotted leaves and spreads by rhizomes to form 2-foot-wide clumps. In early spring, bears pink flower buds that open to purple-blue or red-violet flowers. Evergreen in areas with mild winters. 'Mrs. Moon', with pink buds and bluish lilac flowers, is the most commonly available cultivar. 'Pierre's Pure Pink' has shell pink flowers. Zones 3 to 8.

❦ *Pulsatilla*

pul-sah-TILL-uh. Buttercup family, Ranunculaceae.

Commonly called pasqueflowers, *Pulsatilla* species are clump-forming perennials with very finely cut leaves that have a fernlike texture and cup- or bell-shaped flowers, which are borne in spring and early summer. The flowers are followed by silvery-hairy pomponlike seed heads that also are ornamental. About 30 species belong to the genus.

HOW TO GROW

Plant pasqueflowers in full sun with rich, very well drained soil. The plants go dormant in early summer, so mark their locations to avoid digging into the clumps by mistake. In general, they are slow to establish and resent transplanting, so select a permanent location. (Small plants often are easier to establish than large ones.) Avoid digging or dividing plants unless absolutely necessary, because the roots are easily damaged. Plants self-sow, and seedlings, which are easy to move when small, are a good propagation option. Or, take root cuttings in winter.

P. vulgaris   P. 191

p. vul-GAIR-iss. Pasqueflower. Formerly *Anemone vulgaris*. A 6- to 10-inch-tall species with feathery, silvery-hairy leaves that emerge after the plants have nearly finished blooming. Bears 1½- to 3½-inch-wide flowers in shades of rosy purple, blue-violet, and white in very early spring. Zones 5 to 8.

❦ *Ranunculus*

rah-NUN-cue-luss. Buttercup family, Ranunculaceae.

Best known as buttercups, *Ranunculus* species are primarily perennials, although there are some annuals and biennials among the 400 species in the genus. Most bear cup-, bowl-, or saucer-shaped flowers with five petals around a cluster of showy stamens. There also are garden-grown forms with double flowers, as well as species that lack petals altogether. Yellow is by far the most common flower color, although a few species feature white, pink, orange, or red blooms. Buttercups produce a rosette of leaves that vary greatly in shape: they range from deeply cut or lobed in a featherlike fashion to simple with entire or toothed leaf margins. There are buttercups suitable for a wide range of conditions, including boggy spots, rock gardens, shady moist woodlands, and spots with rich soil in sun or partial shade. Depending on the species, plants have fibrous or tuberous roots, and there are species that spread by rhizomes or runners. Some can be aggressive spreaders.

HOW TO GROW

All the species listed here thrive in full sun or partial to full shade with rich, moist, well-drained soil. *R. aconitifolius* is best in partial to full shade with constantly moist soil. Dig up spreading species, such as *R. repens*, if they outgrow their space, or dig portions of the clumps to keep them in bounds. Propagate by dividing clumps in spring or fall, separating and potting up small offsets, or starting from seeds. Most species self-sow.

R. aconitifolius

r. ack-oh-nye-tih-FOE-lee-us. Aconite Buttercup, Bachelor's Buttons. A 2-foot-tall clump-forming species that spreads to about 1½ feet. Bears white ½- to ¾-inch-wide flowers in late spring and early summer. 'Flore Pleno', with double flowers, is more often grown than the species. Zones 5 to 9.

R. acris   P. 192

r. AY-kris. Tall Buttercup, Meadow Buttercup. A 1- to 3-foot-tall species native to Europe that has naturalized in North America. Plants spread to 1 to 1½ feet and bear 1-inch-wide golden yellow flowers from early to midsummer. 'Flore Pleno', also sold as 'Plena' and 'Multiplex', bears double flowers and is more often grown than the species, which is fairly weedy. Zones 3 or 4 to 8.

R. montanus

r. mon-TAN-us. A low-growing 3- to 6-inch-tall species that spreads by rhizomes to form 1-foot-wide mats. Bears ¾- to 1-inch-wide yellow flowers in early summer. Spreads, but is not as invasive as *R. repens*. 'Molten Gold' bears 1- to 1¼-inch-wide golden yellow flowers. Zones 4 to 8.

R. repens   P. 192

r. REE-penz. Creeping Buttercup. Fast-spreading 1- to 2-foot-tall perennial that spreads by stolons to form drifts 6 feet or more across. Bears clusters of ½- to ¾-inch-wide yellow flowers from late spring to midsummer. Double-flowered 'Pleniflorus', sometimes sold as 'Flore Pleno', is somewhat less invasive and more commonly grown than the species. Zones 3 to 8.

❦ *Ratibida*

rah-tih-BID-uh. Aster family, Asteraceae.

Native to North America and Mexico, *Ratibida* species are woody-based biennials and perennials grown for their daisylike blooms. Commonly called Mexican hat or prairie coneflowers, they bear flower heads with long drooping ray florets, or "petals," surrounding prominent, conelike centers of disk florets. Ray florets are yellow, orange, or purple-brown; conelike centers are generally brown. The leaves are deeply cut in a pinnate, or featherlike, fashion. There are about five or six species of *Ratibida,* which are closely related to orange coneflowers (*Rudbeckia* spp.) and were once included in that genus.

HOW TO GROW

Select a site in full sun with average, well-drained soil. Plants tolerate dry soil as well as heat and humidity. Neutral to alkaline pH is best. Propagate by dividing plants in spring, but divide only young plants, as the roots and crowns become woody with age. Or start from seeds. Both species listed here are sometimes grown as annuals or biennials.

R. columnifera   P. 193

r. col-um-NIFF-er-uh. Prairie Coneflower. Formerly *Lepachys columnifera, Rudbeckia columnifera.* A 3-foot-tall native North American wildflower that spreads to about 1 foot. From early summer to fall it bears yellow daisylike 3-inch-wide flower heads with conelike 2-inch-tall centers that turn from green to brown. *R. columnifera* f. *pulcherrima* bears flower heads with purple- or red-brown ray florets. Zones 3 to 10.

R. pinnata

r. pin-AH-tuh. Drooping Coneflower, Gray-headed Coneflower. Formerly *Lepachys pinnata, Rudbeckia pinnata.* A 3- to 4-foot-tall species native to North America that forms 1½-foot-wide clumps. Has blue-green leaves and, from summer to fall, bears 5-inch-wide daisylike flower heads with yellow ray florets surrounding red-brown cones. Zones 3 to 10.

❦ *Rheum*

REE-um. Buckwheat family, Polygonaceae.

Of the 50 species that belong to this genus, common rhubarb (*Rheum* × *hybridum,* formerly *R. rhabarbarum)* is undoubtedly the best known, but there also are rhubarbs grown for their ornamental value. All rhubarbs are rhizomatous perennials native from Europe to Asia and China. They bear clumps of large, often coarsely toothed leaves that either are rounded or lobed in a palmate (handlike) fashion. While the individual flowers are tiny and petalless, they are borne in enormous, showy panicles that resemble huge astilbe (*Astilbe* spp.) blossoms.

HOW TO GROW

Select a spot in full sun or partial shade with deeply prepared, rich soil that remains evenly moist. Top-dress plants annually with compost, composted manure, or other organic matter to keep the soil rich. Plants do not tolerate drought or heat. Water deeply during dry weather. In the South, constant moisture and shade during the hottest part of the day are essential. Cut the bloom stalks to the ground after the flowers fade. Propagate by dividing the clumps in spring or severing small offsets that appear around the outside of the clumps.

R. palmatum — P. 193

r. pal-MAY-tum. Chinese Rhubarb. Enormous, bold, clump-forming plant producing 3- to 4-foot-tall mounds of 3-foot-long leaves that easily reach 6 feet in width. Bears 4- to 6-foot-tall panicles of tiny flowers in early summer that range from creamy green to red, and in bloom plants are 7 to 8 feet tall. 'Atrosanguineum' has leaves that are red-purple when young and reddish pink blooms. 'Bowles' Crimson' bears red flowers and leaves that are red underneath. Zones 5 to 9.

❦ *Rodgersia*

ro-JER-zee-uh. Saxifrage family, Saxifragaceae.

Rodgersia species, which are closely related to astilbes (*Astilbe* spp.), are grown for their handsome, bold foliage as well as their fluffy, branched panicles of tiny flowers. The individual flowers are petalless, star shaped, and quite small — about ¼ inch wide — but are borne in large branched panicles above the foliage. The leaves are compound, with leaflets arranged in a palmate (handlike) or pinnate (featherlike) fashion, and often distinctively textured. Some species feature foliage with a bronze or purple tint, and several exhibit excellent fall color. The genus contains six species native to China, Japan, and other parts of Asia. All are vigorous, rhizomatous perennials native to areas with moist soils.

HOW TO GROW

Select a site in light to full shade with rich, evenly moist — even constantly wet — soil. Plants tolerate drier conditions, provided they are planted in shade, and full sun, provided they receive ample moisture and are growing in an area where summers do not get too hot. They are best planted along a pond or stream, or in a bog garden, to ensure they receive ample moisture. To propagate, divide plants in early spring or fall or sow seeds.

R. aesculifolia

r. ess-cue-lih-FOE-lee-uh. Fingerleaf Rodgersia. Clumping species forming 3-foot-tall mounds of foliage that spread to 3 feet or more. Leaves, which are palmate and resemble those of horsechestnut (*Aesculus* spp.), have a corrugated or crinkled texture and can be 2 feet across. Plants bear 2-foot-long panicles of white flowers in mid- to late summer and reach 6 feet in bloom. Zones 5 to 8.

R. pinnata   P. 194

r. pin-NAH-tuh. Fingerleaf Rodgersia. A species producing 2- to 3-foot-tall mounds of heavily veined, rough-textured leaves that spread to 3 or 4 feet. The 3-foot-long leaves are pinnate but sometimes look palmate. Plants bear 1- to 2-foot-long panicles of yellowish white, pink, or red flowers in mid- to late summer and reach 3 to 4 feet in bloom. 'Superba' bears leaves that are bronze-purple when young and rose pink flowers. Zones 5 to 8.

R. podophylla   P. 194

r. poe-doe-FILL-uh. Bronze-leaved Rodgersia. Formerly *R. japonica*. A bold-leaved species forming 4-foot-tall mounds of leaves that spread to 6 feet. Leaves are 1 to 1½ feet long and turn bronze-red in fall. Plants bear 1-foot-long panicles of creamy flowers in mid- to late summer and reach 5 feet in bloom. Zones 5 to 8.

R. sambucifolia

R. sam-buke-ih-FOE-lee-uh. Elderberry Rodgersia. A species with pinnate 2½-foot-long leaves forming 2-foot-tall clumps of leaves that spread to 3 feet. Plants reach 3 feet in bloom and bear 1½-foot-tall panicles of white or pink flowers from early to midsummer. Zones 5 to 8.

❦ Rudbeckia

rude-BECK-ee-uh. Aster family, Asteraceae.

Commonly known as black-eyed Susans, orange coneflowers, or simply rudbeckias, these aster family plants are native North American wildflowers grown for their showy, summer-borne, daisylike flower heads. Some 20 species of annuals, biennials, and perennials belong to the genus, all of which bear flower heads consisting of ray florets, or "petals," surrounding spiny black, brown, or green centers of disk florets, which produce the seeds. Most have ray florets in shades of yellow to yellow-orange, but one popular species comes in a wider range of colors, including yellows as well as red-brown and rusty orange. Leaves may be lance shaped and simple or toothed, deeply lobed or cut in a pinnate (featherlike) fashion.

HOW TO GROW

Give coneflowers full sun to light shade and average to rich soil. While evenly moist soil is ideal, plants are drought tolerant once established. Most stand without staking, although *R. laciniata* may need some support. Coneflowers also don't need dividing regularly. Dig them in spring or fall if they outgrow their space, die out in the centers of the clumps, or for propagation. Or propagate by seeds. Plants self-sow.

R. fulgida   P. 195

r. FUL-jih-duh. Orange Coneflower. A 1½- to 3-foot-tall perennial that spreads to 1½ feet. Bears 2- to 2½-inch-wide daisies with orange-yellow ray florets and chocolate brown centers from midsummer to early fall. 'Goldsturm' (*R. fulgida* var. *sullivantii* 'Goldsturm') bears 3- to 4-inch flowers on 2-foot plants. Zones 3 to 9.

R. hirta   P. 195

r. HUR-tuh. Black-eyed Susan. An erect, well-branched biennial or short-lived perennial ranging from 1 to 3 feet in height and spreading from 1 to 1½ feet. Bears 3- to 6-inch-wide single or semidouble flowers from summer to early fall. (Many cultivars are available, and gloriosa daisies belong here.) They bear 3- to 6-inch-wide flowers in shades of red-brown, yellow, gold, bronze, and rusty orange; many flowers have bicolor "petals." 'Becky Mixed' is a dwarf mix, to 1 foot tall, that comes in similar colors. 'Indian Summer' bears golden yellow 6- to 9-inch-wide blooms. 'Toto' bears golden flowers on 10-inch plants. Zones 3 to 9.

R. laciniata
P. 196

r. lah-sin-ee-AH-tuh. Ragged Coneflower, Green-headed Coneflower, Cut-leaved Coneflower. Robust 3- to 6-foot-tall species that spreads by rhizomes to form 3- to 4-foot-wide clumps. Bears 3- to 6-inch-wide flower heads with yellow ray florets and green centers from midsummer to fall. 'Golden Glow' bears double flowers on 5- to 6-foot plants. 'Goldquelle', also double, stays between 3 and 4 feet. Zones 3 to 9.

R. maxima
P. 196

r. MAX-ih-muh. Giant Coneflower. A 5- to 9-foot-tall species with 2- to 3-foot-wide clumps of handsome gray-green 1-foot-long leaves. Bears 3- to 5-inch-wide flower heads in late summer with orange-yellow ray florets and cone-shaped 1½-inch-tall brown centers. Zones 3 to 9.

R. nitida

r. NIT-id-uh. Clump-forming 5- to 6-foot-tall species that forms 3-foot-wide clumps. Bears 4-inch-wide flower heads in late summer and early fall with yellow ray florets surrounding green centers. 'Autumn Glory' bears gold flowers on 5-foot plants. 'Herbstsonne', a 6-foot hybrid between this species and R. laciniata, bears yellow 4- to 5-inch-wide flower heads from midsummer to fall with green to yellow-brown centers. Zones 3 to 9.

❦ Ruta

ROO-tuh. Rue family, Rutaceae.

The genus Ruta contains about eight species of shrubs, subshrubs, and woody-based perennials native to the Mediterranean, northern Africa, and southwestern Asia. They bear aromatic leaves that are deeply cut in a pinnate (featherlike) fashion and clusters of yellow flowers with four or five fringed or toothed petals. Contact with the foliage of these plants can cause severe dermatitis in some people, especially in sunny, hot weather. One species — R. graveolens — is commonly grown in perennial gardens, where it is treasured more for its foliage than its flowers.

HOW TO GROW

Select a site in full sun or partial shade with average, moist, very well drained soil. Plants tolerate heat and drought. Clumps seldom need to be divided. The best propagation option is to root cuttings in summer. Wear gloves and long sleeves while working with these plants.

R. graveolens
P. 197

r. grav-ee-OH-lens. Common Rue. Shrubby 2-foot-tall perennial forming 2-foot-wide mounds of aromatic, handsome, fernlike blue-green leaves. Bears clusters of ¾-inch yellow flowers in summer. 'Blue Beauty' bears blue-green leaves and reaches 1½ feet tall. Zones 4 to 9.

❦ Salvia

SAL-vee-uh. Mint family, Lamiaceae.

The large salvia clan comprises some 900 species of widely distributed annuals, biennials, perennials, and shrubs. Commonly called sages as well as salvias — the popular culinary herb common sage *(Salvia officinalis)* belongs here — they bear erect spikes of tubular two-lipped flowers in shades of violet, purple, lilac, mauve purple, scarlet, pink, white, and rich true blue. Each flower has a tubular, bell-, or funnel-shaped calyx at the base, which in some species is quite showy in its own right. Like other mint family plants, most species feature square stems. Leaves are usually simple, ranging from linear and lance shaped to heart shaped and ovate. They are generally toothed or scalloped and are often aromatic and hairy.

HOW TO GROW

Grow salvias in full sun to light shade and average to rich, well-drained soil that is evenly moist. In areas with hot summers, a site with dappled afternoon shade is best. Most species are very drought tolerant once established. Good soil drainage is especially important in winter. Common sage *(S. officinalis)* needs very well drained soil and is best in full sun. In areas where salvias are marginally hardy, grow them against a south-facing wall for extra winter protection or take cuttings in late summer and overwinter them indoors. Hardy perennial salvias seldom need dividing, but can be dug in spring or early fall if they outgrow their space or for propagation. Propagate by division, cuttings taken from spring through early fall, or seeds. To keep *S. officinalis* healthy and vigorous, replace or propagate plants every 3 to 4 years.

S. azurea

s. ah-ZURE-ee-uh. Blue Sage, Azure Sage. Shrubby 3- to 4-foot-tall species that spreads from 2 to 3 feet. Bears dense racemes of ¾-inch-long blue or white flowers from late summer to fall. Zones 5 to 9.

S. officinalis

P. 197

s. oh-fish-in-AL-iss. Common Sage, Garden Sage. Shrubby 2- to 2½-foot-tall species that spreads to about 3 feet. Bears evergreen, aromatic leaves used in cooking that are woolly and gray-green. Produces branched racemes of ½-inch-long lavender-blue flowers in midsummer. Compact 1-foot-tall 'Aurea' has yellow leaves. 'Icterina' has leaves splashed with yellow and green. 'Tricolor' has variegated leaves marked with green, purple, pink, and cream. 'Purpurascens' bears leaves that are reddish purple when young. Zones 5 to 9, to Zone 4 with winter protection; cultivars may be less hardy than the species.

S. pratensis

s. pray-TEN-sis. Meadow Sage, Meadow Clary. Shrubby 1- to 3-foot-tall species that spreads as far. Bears oval, wrinkle-textured leaves and branched clusters of 1-inch-long violet flowers from early to midsummer. 'Haematodes' bears blue-violet flowers. 'Rosea' has rose pink blooms. Zones 3 to 9.

S. × sylvestris

P. 198

s. × syl-VES-triss. Hybrid Sage. A 2- to 3-foot-tall hybrid *(S. nemorosa × S. pratensis)* forming 1-foot-wide clumps. Bears dense racemes of ½-inch-long pinkish purple flowers from early to midsummer. 'Blue Queen', also sold as 'Blaukönigin', bears blue-violet flowers on 2-foot plants. 'May Night', also sold as 'Mainacht', has ¾-inch-long indigo flowers on 2-foot plants. 'Rose Queen' bears pink flowers and grayish green leaves on 2½-foot plants. 'East Friesland', also sold as 'Ostfriesland' and sometimes listed as a cultivar of *S. nemorosa,* bears violet-blue flowers on 1½-foot plants. Zones 4 to 9.

Sanguinaria

san-gwi-NAIR-ee-uh. Poppy family, Papaveraceae.

A single species of woodland wildflower native to eastern North America belongs to this genus. Commonly called bloodroot, it grows from a fleshy rhizome that exudes red bloodlike sap when cut. The dainty white flowers, which resemble daisies more than the poppies to which this plant is related, emerge in spring shortly before the leaves.

HOW TO GROW

Select a site in partial to full shade with rich, evenly moist, well-drained soil. Plants go dormant and disappear by midsummer, so mark the locations of clumps to avoid digging into them by mistake. Propagate by seeds or by dividing the clumps immediately after they flower. Double-flowered forms must be propagated by division.

S. canadensis   P. 198

s. can-ah-DEN-sis. Bloodroot, Red Puccoon. A slowly spreading, rhizomatous species that reaches 4 to 6 inches in height and spreads to 1 foot. Bears cup-shaped 2½- to 3-inch-wide flowers in spring that open before the scalloped, kidney-shaped leaves unfurl. 'Flore Pleno', also sold as 'Multiplex', bears long-lasting double white flowers. Zones 3 to 9.

❦ *Sanguisorba*

san-gwi-SOR-buh. Rose family, Rosaceae.

Commonly called burnets, these unlikely-looking rose family plants bear handsome pinnate (featherlike) leaves and bottlebrush-like spikes of tiny flowers on wiry, erect stems. Blooms come in white, pink, or red and lack petals but have prominent stamens. About 18 species belong to the genus, all of which are rhizomatous perennials.

HOW TO GROW

Plant burnets in full sun or partial shade and well-drained soil that is fairly rich in organic matter and remains evenly moist. In the South, a spot with shade during the hottest part of the day is best. *S. canadensis* is a vigorous spreader and can become invasive in wet-soil sites. Tall species require staking. Propagate by division in spring or fall or by seeds.

S. canadensis   P. 199

s. can-ah-DEN-sis. Canadian Burnet. A 6-foot-tall species native to North America that easily spreads by rhizomes to 3 or 4 feet. Bears fluffy 6- to 8-inch-long spikes of white flowers from midsummer to fall. Zones 3 to 8.

S. obtusa

s. ob-TOO-suh. Japanese Burnet. A 2-foot-tall species that forms 2- to 3-foot-wide clumps. Bears handsome 1½-foot-long gray-green leaves and 3-inch-long spikes of fluffy deep pink flowers from midsummer to fall. Zones 4 to 8.

S. officinalis

s. oh-fish-in-AL-iss. Great Burnet. A 4-foot-tall species that spreads to 2 or 3 feet. Bears nearly 2-foot-long leaves and maroon to purple-brown flowers that are carried in short, rounded 1-inch-long spikes from early summer to fall. Zones 4 to 8.

❦ Santolina

san-toe-LEE-nuh. Aster family, Asteraceae.

Santolina species are actually shrubs and subshrubs rather than herbaceous perennials, but most gardeners use them as perennials in sunny beds and borders as well as herb gardens. About 18 species belong to the genus, all evergreens native to the Mediterranean. They bear aromatic leaves usually finely cut in a pinnate (featherlike) fashion and petalless, rounded, buttonlike flower heads consisting of all disk florets.

HOW TO GROW

Select a site in full sun with poor to average, very well drained soil. Sandy soil is ideal. Plants tolerate heat but because of fungal diseases do not fare well in areas with wet, humid summers. Some gardeners shear off the flowers to highlight the foliage. Prune plants hard in spring to keep them compact, and/or cut them back hard immediately after flowering. Propagate by cuttings in late summer.

S. chamaecyparissus
P. 199

s. cam-ee-sip-ah-RISS-uss. Lavender Cotton. A 1- to 2-foot-tall shrub that forms 2- to 3-foot-wide mounds of finely cut, woolly gray-white leaves. Bears ½- to ¾-inch-wide yellow flowers from mid- to late summer. 'Lambrook Silver' has silvery gray foliage. 'Lemon Queen' is compact, to 2 feet tall and wide, with lemon yellow flower heads. 'Weston' is a dwarf form that reaches about 6 inches and spreads to 8 inches. Zones 6 to 9.

S. rosmarinifolia

s. rose-mah-rin-ih-FOE-lee-uh. Green Lavender Cotton. Formerly *S. viridis*. Mounding shrub reaching 2 feet in height and spreading to 3 feet. Bears fernlike bright green leaves and yellow ¾-inch-wide flower heads in midsummer. 'Primrose Gem' bears pale yellow flower heads. Zones 6 to 9.

❦ *Saponaria*

sap-oh-NAIR-ee-uh. Pink family, Caryophyllaceae.

Soapworts, as *Saponaria* species are commonly called, bear clusters of five-petaled flowers usually in shades of pink. Leaves are simple and usually lance shaped. Some 20 species — both annuals and perennials — belong to the genus. They are native from Europe to southwestern Asia and closely related to *Lychnis* and *Silene*, both commonly referred to as catchflies. *Saponaria* is from the Latin *sapo,* soap, and refers to the fact that the leaves of some species produce a lather when rubbed in water.

HOW TO GROW

Plant soapworts in full sun in average, well-drained soil, preferably with a neutral to alkaline pH. Plants do not do well in areas with very hot, humid summers. Sandy soil is fine, and too-rich soil causes plants to flop over. *S. officinalis* tolerates partial shade but is more likely to flop there. Cut soapworts, especially *S. ocymoides,* back hard after flowering to keep plants compact. The perennials spread readily to form broad clumps because they grow from fleshy white roots that creep, and stems sometimes root where they fall over and touch the soil. Except for double-flowered forms, plants also self-sow. Dig clumps in spring or fall to keep them in bounds or for propagation. Or propagate by rooting cuttings in summer. Plants can be grown from seeds, but double-flowered forms do not come true and must be propagated vegetatively.

S. × lempergii P. 200

s. × lem-PER-jee-eye. Soapwort. Sprawling hybrid that forms ½- to 1-foot-tall clumps that spread to 1½ feet. Bears clusters of hot pink 1-inch-wide flowers from midsummer to fall. 'Max Frei' bears paler pink flowers than the species. Zones 5 to 8.

S. ocymoides P. 200

s. oh-sih-MOY-deez. Rock Soapwort. Low-growing 3- to 6-inch-tall species that spreads to 1½ feet. Bears loose clusters of ½-inch-wide pink flowers in summer. 'Rubra Compacta' bears red flowers on low, dense plants. 'Alba' has white flowers. Zones 4 to 8.

S. officinalis

s. oh-fish-in-AL-iss. Bouncing Bet, Soapwort. Fast-spreading 1- to 2½-foot-tall perennial that spreads by rhizomes to form 2-foot-wide clumps.

Bears clusters of ¾-inch-wide white, pink, or red flowers from summer to fall. 'Alba Plena' has double white flowers. 'Rosea Plena' bears fragrant double pink flowers. 'Rubra Plena' has double red flowers that fade to pink. Zones 3 to 9.

❀ Satureja

sah-tur-EE-juh. Mint family, Lamiaceae.

Commonly known as savories, *Satureja* species are aromatic-leaved annuals, perennials, and subshrubs with spikes of tiny two-lipped tubular flowers. The pungent leaves are linear, lance shaped, or rounded. About 30 species belong to the genus, one of which is a popular perennial herb.

HOW TO GROW

Grow summer savory in full sun and loose, average to rich, well-drained soil. Neutral to slightly alkaline pH is best. Cut plants back in early spring. Plants become woody and need to be renewed every 2 to 3 years: propagate them by starting from cuttings taken in summer, by dividing in early spring, or by seeds.

S. montana   P. 201

s. mon-TAN-uh. Summer Savory. Shrubby 16-inch-tall perennial with lance-shaped leaves that spreads from about 8 inches to 1 foot. Bears upright spikes with whorls of tiny lavender-pink flowers in summer. Zones 5 to 8.

❀ Saxifraga

sacks-ih-FRA-juh. Saxifrage family, Saxifragaceae.

Saxifraga is a large, very diverse genus containing about 440 species and hundreds of cultivars. Leaves vary greatly in shape, but most plants produce only basal leaves. The individual flowers, which usually have five petals, are small, but most species bear them in abundance in racemes or panicles. Plants are semievergreen or evergreen and usually perennial, although the genus contains a few biennials and annuals. Most are mat- or cushion-forming plants — some are almost mosslike — native to mountainous regions in the Northern Hemisphere and are most often grown in rock gardens. The botanical name is from the Latin *saxum,* rock, and *frango,* break, and alludes to the fact that many saxifrages grow naturally in rock crevices.

HOW TO GROW

The cultural requirements of saxifrages vary widely: most species need rock garden conditions and grow well only in the Pacific Northwest, New England, and adjacent parts of Canada, because they do not tolerate summer heat and humidity. The species listed here are exceptions to that rule and, unless otherwise noted, grow well in partial to full shade with well-drained, moist soil that is rich in organic matter. Well-drained soil is essential to success. Propagate by dividing plants in spring, separating individual rosettes of foliage and rooting them, or by seeds.

S. stolonifera   P. 201

s. sto-low-NIFF-er-uh. Strawberry Geranium, Mother of Thousands. Formerly *S. sarmentosa.* Stoloniferous species that produces low 2- to 4-inch-tall mounds of hairy, kidney-shaped 1½- to 3½-inch-long leaves. Plant spreads to 1 foot or more. Bears loose panicles of small 1-inch-wide white flowers in summer. 'Tricolor' bears leaves variegated with pink, white, and green. Zones 6 to 9.

S. umbrosa var. *primuloides*

s. um-BRO-suh var. prim-you-LOY-deez. Dwarf London Pride. Formerly *S. primuloides.* An 8-inch-tall evergreen with rosettes of leathery, ovate to spoon-shaped leaves with scalloped edges. Bears loose panicles of starry, pale pink ¼- to ⅜-inch flowers in spring. Zones 4 to 7.

S. × urbium

s. × UR-bee-um. London Pride. Vigorous 12-inch-tall species that spreads to 2 feet. Bears rosettes of evergreen, spoon-shaped, leathery leaves and loose panicles of starry ⅜-inch-wide white flowers flushed with pink in summer. Zones 5 to 7.

❦ *Scabiosa*

scah-bee-OH-suh. Teasel family, Dipsacaceae.

Commonly known as pincushion flowers or scabious, *Scabiosa* species are annuals, biennials, or perennials. As their common name suggests, they bear rounded flower heads that somewhat resemble pincushions. The blooms, which can be single or double, also look somewhat like daisies or asters and actually are constructed in a somewhat similar fashion. They have small central florets that form the "pincushion" surrounded by larger petal-like florets. The leaves are either entire, lobed, or deeply cut in a featherlike fashion. About 80 species belong to the genus.

HOW TO GROW

Pincushion flowers thrive in full sun and average, well-drained soil. A neutral to slightly alkaline pH is best. Plants do not tolerate soil that is too moist, especially in winter. In the South, select a site that receives afternoon shade. Deadhead regularly to prolong bloom. Divide clumps in spring if they outgrow their space or become too crowded, or for propagation. Or propagate by taking cuttings from shoots that arise at the base of the plant in spring.

S. caucasica

P. 202

s. cau-CASS-ih-kuh. Pincushion Flower, Scabious. Clump-forming perennial that reaches 2 feet when in bloom and spreads as far. Bears featherlike leaves and rounded 3-inch-wide flower clusters in lavender, white, yellow, and rose-purple from summer to early fall. 'Miss Willmott' and 'Alba' both bear white flowers. Zones 4 to 9.

S. columbaria

s. col-um-BAR-ee-uh. Clump-forming perennial reaching 2 feet in bloom and spreading to 3 feet. Bears featherlike leaves and lilac-blue 1½-inch-wide flower heads from summer to fall. 'Butterfly Blue' and 'Pink Mist', also sold as 'Butterfly Pink', are outstanding, long-blooming cultivars sometimes listed under S. caucasica. Zones 3 to 8.

Sedum

SEE-dum. Orpine family, Crassulaceae.

Tough, drought-tolerant sedums are annuals, biennials, perennials, subshrubs, and shrubs with fleshy leaves that are either oval and somewhat flattened or rounded. Also called stonecrops, they produce tiny, star-shaped, five-petaled flowers carried in dense, showy clusters ranging from ½ to 8 inches or more across. Perennial species range from mat-forming 1-inch-tall ground covers to 2-foot-tall mounding specimens for beds and borders. Some species are evergreen, others deciduous. Many feature ornamental foliage. About 400 species belong to this genus.

HOW TO GROW

Plant sedums in full sun in well-drained, average to rich soil. They also grow in poor, dry soil. Wet soil leads to root or crown rot and death. Some low-growing sedums can become quite invasive and are best used alone as ground covers where they can spread as they will. Dig or cut back spreading types as needed to keep them in bounds. In late winter or early spring, cut clump-forming sedums such as 'Autumn Joy' to the ground. Dig the clumps if they outgrow their space or begin to look overcrowded, but otherwise the plants don't need regular division. Propagate by dividing the clumps in spring or fall or by taking cuttings any time the plants are not in flower. Some species self-sow.

S. acre

s. AY-ker. Gold Moss Sedum. Fast-spreading 2-inch-tall species that easily spreads to several feet. Bears evergreen leaves and small ½-inch-wide clusters of starry yellow-green flowers in summer. 'Aureum', with yellow leaves, is a more modest spreader. Zones 4 to 9.

S. aizoon

s. eye-ZOON. Aizoon Stonecrop. Rhizomatous 1½-foot-tall perennial that spreads as far. Bears flat 3- to 4-inch-wide clusters of ½-inch-wide yellow flowers in early summer. Zones 4 to 9.

S. album

s. AL-bum. White Stonecrop. Spreading 4- to 6-inch-tall species that forms 1½-foot-wide mats. Bears evergreen leaves and 1- to 2-inch-wide clusters of small white flowers in summer. 'Murale' has bronze-green leaves; 'Coral Carpet' has pink leaves on 4-inch plants. Zones 3 to 9.

S. hybrids   P. 202

By far the best-known hybrid sedum is 'Autumn Joy', also sold as 'Herbstfreude'. It produces 2-foot-tall, 2-foot-wide clumps with 8-inch-wide heads of densely packed flowers. The flowers start out as pale green buds in midsummer, open to dark pink and gradually age to red-brown from late summer through fall, and stand though winter. Zones 3 to 9. 'Ruby Glow', another excellent hybrid, is a 10-inch-tall plant with purplish green leaves and 2½-inch-wide clusters of pinkish red flowers from midsummer to early fall. Zones 5 to 9. 'Vera Jameson', also 10 inches tall, bears

2½-inch-wide clusters of rose pink flowers in late summer and fall and bears purplish to burgundy leaves. Zones 4 to 9.

S. kamtschaticum
P. 203

s. kamt-SHAH-tih-cum. A 4-inch-tall species that spreads modestly by rhizomes to form 1-foot-wide clumps. Bears 1- to 2-inch-wide clusters of golden yellow flowers in late summer. 'Variegatum' has white-edged leaves. Zones 4 to 9.

S. sieboldii

s. see-BOLD-ee-ee. October Daphne. A 6- to 9-inch-tall species with arching stems of fleshy blue-green leaves edged in pink. Bears 2½-inch clusters of pink flowers in fall. Zones 3 to 8.

S. spathulifolium

s. spath-you-lih-FOE-lee-um. A 4-inch-tall species that tolerates light shade and spreads modestly to form mats about 2 feet wide. Bears tiny fleshy, evergreen leaves and ½- to 1-inch-wide clusters of starry yellow flowers just above the foliage in summer. 'Cape Blanco' has silver-blue leaves; 'Purpureum' has red-purple and silver ones. Zones 5 to 9.

S. spectabile

s. spec-TAB-uh-lee. Showy Stonecrop. Clump-forming 1½-foot-tall species that spreads as far. Bears rounded 1½-inch-wide clusters of pink flowers in late summer. Hot pink–flowered 'Brilliant' is its best-known cultivar. 'Carmine' bears dark pink flowers. 'Variegata' has pale pink flowers and leaves with creamy yellow centers. Zones 3 to 9.

S. spurium
P. 203

s. SPUR-ee-um. Two-row Sedum. Fast-spreading 4-inch-tall species that rapidly forms mats 2 to 3 feet or more in width. Bears fleshy, evergreen leaves and loose 1½-inch-wide clusters of pinkish purple or white star-shaped flowers in late summer. 'Dragon's Blood', also sold as 'Schorbuser Blut', has purple-tinted leaves and dark pink flowers. 'Elizabeth' has bronze and maroon leaves; 'Tricolor' produces pink-, white-, and green-striped ones. Zones 4 to 9.

S. telephium

s. tel-EH-fee-um. Clump-forming 2-foot-tall species that spreads to about 1 foot. Bears gray-green 3-inch-long leaves and loose 3- to 5-inch-wide clusters of small starry purple-pink flowers in late summer and early fall. *S. telephium* ssp. *maximum* 'Atropurpureum' has dark purple stems and leaves and pink flowers; it reaches 1½ to 2 feet in height. Zones 4 to 9.

❦ *Sempervivum*

sem-per-VYE-vum. Orpine family, Crassulaceae.

Commonly known as hen and chicks or houseleeks, *Sempervivum* species are rosette-forming perennials with succulent, evergreen leaves. The plants spread slowly but steadily to form low, dense mats by producing new offsets at the ends of runners. In summer, full-grown rosettes produce a loose panicle of small pink, purplish, or white flowers that are star shaped or almost resemble small daisies. The rosettes, commonly referred to as the "hens" or mother plants, die after they flower, but new rosettes, or "chicks," quickly fill in the space they leave.

HOW TO GROW

Select a site in full sun or light shade with poor to average, well-drained soil. Plants are quite drought tolerant and will happily thrive with their roots in a crevice between rocks, in spots with only 2 to 3 inches of soil (provided the soil doesn't remain wet), in raised beds, and in containers. Extremely dry conditions cause plants to shrivel and become dwarfed. Pull up the mother plants after they bloom to make room for surrounding plantlets. To propagate, divide the clumps or pick off individual "chicks" and plant them any time during the growing season.

S. arachnoideum

s. ah-rack-NOY-dee-um. Cobweb Houseleek. Mat-forming species forming 2- to 3-inch-tall, ½- to 1-inch-wide rosettes of leaves that are covered with spider web–like hairs. Spreads to form 1-foot-wide mounds. Bears 1-inch-wide clusters of reddish pink flowers on 1-foot-tall stems in summer. Zones 4 to 8.

S. tectorum   P. 204

s. teck-TOR-um. Hen and Chicks, Roof Houseleek. Forms 2- to 4-inch-tall rosettes of succulent leaves that are green to blue-green and sometimes flushed with purple or maroon in summer. Rosettes are 2 to 4 inches across and plants spread to form 2-foot-wide mounds. Bears 12- to 15-

inch-tall stems topped by 2- to 4-inch-wide clusters of small red-purple flowers in summer. Many cultivars are available, with various-sized rosettes and leaves ranging from green with dark tips to maroon or red. Zones 4 to 8.

❦ *Sidalcea*

sid-AL-see-uh. Mallow family, Malvaceae.

Sidalcea species are native North American wildflowers closely related to hollyhocks (*Alcea* species) as well as a less well known genus, *Sida*. This relationship is commemorated by the botanical name, which combines the two names — *Sida* and *Alcea*. The genus contains between 20 and 25 species of annuals and perennials, all bearing erect racemes of five-petaled, hollyhock-like flowers. Blooms come in shades of pink, purple-pink, and white. The leaves are rounded and usually lobed or divided in a palmate (handlike) fashion.

HOW TO GROW

Select a site in full sun or light shade with average to somewhat rich, moist but well-drained soil. A spot with shade during the hottest part of the day is best in the South, as plants do not tolerate heat and humidity well. Plants thrive in a wide range of soils — from sandy to loamy — provided the soil is well drained. Cut the flowering stems back hard after the flowers fade to encourage compact growth and a second flush of blooms, as well as to curtail self-seeding. Dig and divide the clumps in spring or fall if they die out in the center, outgrow their space, or for propagation. Or propagate from seeds.

S. malviflora P. 204

s. mal-vih-FLOOR-uh. Checkerbloom. A 2- to 4-foot-tall 1½-foot-wide perennial with erect racemes of 2-inch-wide pink or lavender-pink flowers from early to midsummer. Most available cultivars are hybrids between this species and *S. candida*. 'Brilliant' bears carmine red flowers. 'Elsie Heugh' has purple-pink flowers. 'Party Girl' has gray-green leaves and pink flowers on 2- to 3-foot plants. Zones 5 to 8.

❦ *Silene*

sy-LEE-nee. Pink family, Caryophyllaceae.

Commonly known as campions or catchflies, *Silene* species are annuals, biennials, or perennials found mostly in the Northern Hemisphere, especially in the Mediterranean. About 500 species belong to the genus, all with flowers that have five notched or cleft petals in shades of pink, white, and red. The flowers are carried singly or in clusters and in many species have an inflated calyx at the base of the corolla (petals). Leaves are opposite and linear to rounded. *Silene* species are quite similar to *Lychnis* species, which are also commonly called campions and catchflies.

HOW TO GROW
Select a site in full sun or partial shade and average, well-drained soil. Neutral to slightly alkaline pH is best. Good drainage is essential. Plants tolerate dry soil and sandy or even rocky conditions. Perennials commonly are short-lived, especially in areas with hot, humid summers, but they do self-sow. Propagate by division in spring, by taking cuttings from shoots that arise from the base of the plants in spring, or by seeds.

S. acaulis
s. aw-CAUL-iss. Moss Campion. Mosslike 2-inch-tall species, native to the Arctic in North America, Europe, and Asia, that spreads to about 8 inches. Bears evergreen leaves and solitary ½-inch-wide pink flowers from late spring to summer. Zones 3 to 6.

S. caroliniana
s. care-oh-lin-ee-AH-nuh. Carolina Campion. An 8-inch-tall evergreen species native to North America. Forms 6-inch-wide clumps and bears clusters of 1-inch-wide pink flowers in early summer. Zones 5 to 8.

S. regia
s. REE-jee-uh. Royal Catchfly. A 2- to 5-foot-tall North American native wildflower that spreads to 1 foot and bears ½- to 1-foot-wide clusters of brilliant red 1-inch-wide flowers in spring and early summer. Zones 5 to 8.

S. schafta   P. 205
s. SHAFF-tuh. Schafta Campion, Shafta Pink. A 3- to 6-inch-tall species that spreads to 1 foot and bears clusters of ¾-inch-wide magenta-pink flowers from late summer to fall. Zones 5 to 7.

S. virginica

P. 205

s. vir-JIH-nih-kuh. Fire Pink. Short-lived 2- to 3-foot-tall perennial native to North America that forms 1-foot-wide clumps. Bears clusters of brilliant red ¾-inch-wide flowers in spring and early summer. Zones 4 to 7.

☙ *Silphium*

SIL-fee-um. Aster family, Asteraceae.

Silphium species are robust native North American wildflowers that bear branched clusters of flower heads that resemble sunflowers or yellow daisies. The common name rosinweed comes from the fact that when cut, the stems exude a rosinlike sap that smells like turpentine. Unlike most aster family plants, *Silphium* flower heads have sterile disk florets (the "eyes"): the seeds are produced by fertile ray florets, or "petals."

HOW TO GROW

Select a site in full sun or light shade with average, deeply prepared, evenly moist soil. Soil that is too rich encourages rank growth and plants that are likely to flop. These are tall, bold plants, best for wild gardens or the backs of borders; site them with care as they can take up considerable space and will thrive for years without needing to be divided. Propagate by dividing the clumps in spring or early fall or by sowing seeds. Plants self-sow.

S. laciniatum

s. lah-sin-ee-AH-tum. Compass Plant. A 5- to 10-foot-tall species forming 2- to 3-foot-wide clumps. The common name refers to the fact that the 1½-foot-long pinnately lobed (featherlike) leaves orient themselves north and south on the stems (flat sides facing east and west). From midsummer into fall, plants bear clusters of 5-inch-wide flower heads with yellow ray florets and darker yellow centers. Zones 5 to 9.

S. perfoliatum

P. 206

s. per-foe-lee-AH-tum. Cup Plant. Bold 5- to 8-foot-tall species forming 3-foot-wide clumps. The common name refers to the fact that older leaves are connate-perfoliate, meaning their bases join across the stems and form a "cup" that holds water. Bears branched clusters of 3-inch-wide yellow flowers with darker yellow centers. Blooms from midsummer to fall. Zones 5 to 9.

ꙮ *Sisyrinchium*

sis-ee-RINK-ee-um. Iris family, Iridaceae.

Commonly known as blue-eyed or golden-eyed grasses, *Sisyrinchium* species are clump-forming or rhizomatous plants native to North and South America. About 90 species of annuals and semievergreen perennials belong to the genus, all producing grassy clumps of linear to lance-shaped leaves that often are arranged in fans. They bear small star- or cup-shaped flowers in spring and summer. Blooms are carried singly or in clusters above the foliage and come in shades of purple-blue, yellow, mauve, and white.

HOW TO GROW
Select a site in full sun with poor to average soil that is well drained. Neutral to slightly alkaline pH is best. The plants will grow in evenly moist soil but require good drainage, especially in winter. Propagate by dividing the clumps in spring or fall or by seeds. Plants self-sow.

S. graminoides P. 206

s. gram-in-OY-deez. Blue-eyed Grass. Formerly *S. angustifolium*; plants grown as *S. bermudiana* and *S. birameum* also belong here. A ½- to 1½-foot-tall perennial forming grassy ½- to 1-foot-wide clumps of linear leaves. Bears starry purple-blue ¾-inch-wide flowers with yellow throats over a long period in summer. Zones 3 to 9.

ꙮ *Smilacina*

smile-ah-SEEN-uh. Lily family, Liliaceae.

Commonly called Solomon's plume or false Solomon's seal, Smilacina species are rhizomatous perennials producing erect or arching, un-branched stems. Plants bear ovate to lance-shaped leaves and large fluffy clusters of flowers at the tips of the branches. The individual flowers, which are star shaped and creamy white in color, are followed by clusters of round green berries that ripen to red.

HOW TO GROW
Select a site in partial to full shade with rich, moist, well-drained soil. Plants require shade during the hottest part of the day in the South and regular watering in dry weather to look their best. Plants spread steadily,

but not invasively, to form handsome drifts. Propagate by dividing clumps in spring or fall. Plants also self-sow, and seedlings are easy to move any time during the growing season.

S. racemosa P. 207

s. ray-sih-MOSE-uh. Solomon's Plume, False Solomon's Seal. A 1½- to 3-foot-tall native North American wildflower with arching stems that end in a 6-inch-long plume of tiny ¼-inch-wide creamy white flowers in spring. Red berries follow the flowers in late summer or fall. Zones 4 to 9.

☙ *Solidago*

sol-ih-DAY-go. Aster family, Asteraceae.

Classic harbingers of fall, *Solidago* species — better known as goldenrods — are well-known wildflowers that all too often are overlooked by gardeners. There are about 100 species in the genus, all woody-based perennials. Most are native to North America, but a few species are from South America and one is native to Europe. They bear undivided or toothed, lance-shaped leaves on stiff stems. Like other aster family plants, goldenrods bear flower heads consisting of tiny ray and disk florets. In this case, the individual flower heads usually are yellow and quite small. They consist of a cluster of disk florets that are bisexual, surrounded by a row of small ray florets that are all female, so all can produce seeds. (In many aster relatives, the ray florets, or "petals," are sterile.) Flower heads are carried in showy, plumelike panicles; racemes; or spikes from midsummer to fall. The flowers *do not* cause hay fever. Goldenrods bloom at the same time as ragweeds (the primary hay fever culprit), but their pollen is too heavy to be dispersed in the air.

H O W   T O   G R O W

Plant goldenrods in full sun with poor to average soil that is moist but well drained. Most tolerate dry soil, except *S. virgaurea.* Too-rich soil causes rank growth and plants that tend to flop, as well as rampant spreading. *S. caesia* grows in full sun or partial shade; *S. odora, S. sphacelata,* and *S. sempervirens* grow in poor, even sandy soil and also tolerate salt, making them good choices for seaside gardens. Select goldenrods with care, as many species spread quite quickly by rhizomes and become very invasive. The species listed here are well-behaved garden residents. Like asters, goldenrods are best divided every 2 to 3 years. Cut the seed heads off after the flowers fade if self-sowing becomes a problem. Propagate by dividing the clumps in spring or fall or taking cuttings in early summer. Species can be propagated by seeds.

S. caesia

s. SEE-see-uh. Wreath Goldenrod. Native 1- to 3-foot-tall species that spreads by short, thick rhizomes to 2 or 3 feet. Bears blue-green leaves on wandlike bluish purple stems. Yellow flower heads are borne in small tufts or clusters in the leaf axils all along the stems from late summer to fall. Zones 4 to 8.

S. odora

s. oh-DOOR-uh. Sweet Goldenrod. Native 1½- to 3-foot-tall species that forms 3-foot-wide clumps. Bears lance-shaped leaves that are anise-scented when crushed. Yellow flower heads are carried in late summer in a series of one-sided panicles that form a plumelike cluster. Zones 3 to 9.

S. rugosa   P. 207

s. rue-GO-suh. Rough-leaved Goldenrod, Rough-stemmed Goldenrod. Native 4- to 5-foot-tall species that spreads steadily, but not invasively, to form 2- to 3-foot-wide clumps. Bears wrinkled, hairy, toothed leaves and large plumelike panicles of golden yellow flowers in fall. 'Fireworks' has panicles with lacy, arching branches and is more compact than the species, to 3 or 4 feet. Zones 4 to 9.

S. sempervirens

s. sem-per-VYE-rens. Seaside Goldenrod. Native 4- to 6-foot-tall species forming 2- to 3-foot-wide clumps. Bears lance-shaped leaves and showy panicles of ¼-inch-wide flower heads from late summer to fall. Zones 4 to 9.

S. sphacelata   P. 208

s. sfay-sel-LAH-tuh. Dwarf Goldenrod. Native 2-foot-tall species that spreads 1 to 2 feet. Bears rounded leaves and arching, branched panicles of flowers in fall. 'Golden Fleece', a heavy-blooming, dwarf 1½-foot-tall cultivar, is more commonly grown than the species. Zones 4 to 9.

S. virgaurea

s. vir-GAR-ee-uh. European Goldenrod. A 2- to 3-foot-tall species that spreads to about 1½ feet. Bears lance-shaped, toothed leaves and dense spikelike racemes of golden flowers from late summer to fall. 'Cloth of

Gold' is a vigorous 1½- to 2-foot-tall cultivar with golden yellow flowers. 'Goldenmosa' also is a compact 2½-foot-tall selection. 'Crown of Rays' produces 2- to 3-foot stems and does not require staking. Zones 3 to 9.

❧× *Solidaster*

× sol-ih-DAS-ter. Aster family, Asteraceae.

This is a hybrid genus consisting of a single species, the result of a natural cross between upland white aster *(Aster ptarmicoides)* and a species of goldenrod — Canada goldenrod *(Solidago canadensis)* or perhaps Missouri goldenrod *(S. missouriensis)*. Although both parents are native North American wildflowers, oddly enough the cross occurred in a nursery in France. Plants bear large clusters of small yellow daisylike flower heads from midsummer to fall. Leaves are lanceolate to linear-elliptic.

HOW TO GROW
Select a site in full sun with average to somewhat rich, well-drained soil. Propagate by dividing the clumps in spring or fall or by taking cuttings from shoots at the base of the plant in spring.

× *S. luteus* P. 208

× s. LOO-tee-us. Also listed as *S.* × *hybridus*. A 2- to 3-foot-tall perennial that forms 1-foot-wide clumps. Bears branched clusters of daisylike ½-inch-wide flower heads with pale yellow ray florets surrounding darker yellow centers. Zones 5 to 8.

❧ *Spigelia*

spy-JEE-lee-uh. Logania family, Loganiaceae.

About 50 species of annuals and perennials native to North and South America belong to the genus *Spigelia*. They bear ovate, entire leaves and clusters of tubular to funnel-shaped flowers in shades of red, yellow, and purple. One species is sometimes grown in gardens.

HOW TO GROW
Select a site in partial shade with rich, moist, well-drained soil. A spot in full sun also is suitable, provided the soil remains moist. Propagate by dividing the clumps in spring or from seeds. *S. marilandica* is native to

the southeastern United States: when buying plants, be sure they are seed grown and not wild collected.

S. marilandica   P. 209

s. mair-ih-LAN-dih-cuh. Indian Pink, Maryland Pinkroot. A 2-foot-tall clump-forming perennial that spreads to 1½ feet. Bears clusters of erect 2-inch-long red flowers from spring to summer. Zones 6 to 9.

Stachys

STAY-kuss. Mint family, Lamiaceae.

Stachys contains about 300 species of annuals, perennials, and shrubs that have square stems and hairy, often aromatic, lance-shaped to ovate leaves. The leaves have entire, toothed, or scalloped margins and promi-nent veins. Plants bear small tubular, two-lipped flowers either in spikes or racemes, or in whorls in the leaf axils.

HOW TO GROW

Select a site in full sun or partial shade with very well drained, average soil. Lamb's ears (Stachys byzantina) grow well in sandy soil. A site with shade during the hottest part of the day is best in the South. In areas with hot, humid, rainy summers, plants are frequently subject to crown rot. Cut plants back in midsummer if the foliage looks diseased or the stems appear to be rotting. They will recover in fall when cooler weather arrives. Some gardeners consider the flowers unattractive and remove them as they appear. Cut plants to the ground in fall or early spring: fall is best in areas with wet winters, because it prevents the leaves from smoth-ering the crowns. Divide plants in spring if they outgrow their space, become overcrowded and die out in the middle, or for propagation.

S. byzantina   P. 209

s. bih-zan-TEE-nuh. Lamb's Ears, Woolly Betony. Formerly S. lanata, S. olympica. Mound-forming perennial primarily grown for its ½- to 1-foot-tall rosettes of white-woolly leaves that form clumps spreading to 2 feet or more. Bears woolly, erect 1½-foot-tall spikes of ½-inch-long pur-ple-pink flowers from early summer to fall. 'Countess Helene von Stein', also sold as 'Big Ears', has large 10-inch-long greenish white leaves with a feltlike texture. 'Primrose Heron' has yellow-gray leaves. 'Silver Carpet' has gray-white leaves and does not flower. Zones 4 to 8.

S. macrantha
P. 210

s. mah-CRAN-tha. Betony. Formerly *S. grandiflora*. A 1- to 2-foot-tall species that forms 1-foot-wide clumps of hairy green leaves with scalloped margins. Bears showy, dense spikes of pinkish purple 1¼-inch-long flowers from early summer to fall. Zones 3 to 8.

S. officinalis

s. oh-fish-in-AL-iss. Wood Betony, Bishop's Wort. A 2-foot-tall species that spreads to 1 foot. Bears nearly hairless, scallop-edged leaves and showy spikes of ½-inch-long flowers from early summer to fall in shades of purple, pink, and white. Zones 5 to 8.

✿ Stokesia

STOKE-see-uh. Aster family, Asteraceae.

Stokesia contains a single species of perennial native to the southeastern United States. Commonly called Stokes' aster, it bears rosettes of rounded, lance-shaped, evergreen leaves and cornflower- or asterlike flowers from midsummer to early fall.

HOW TO GROW

Plant in full sun or light shade in rich, evenly moist, well-drained soil. Poorly drained soil leads to crown rot and death. Plants generally require staking. Deadheading encourages plants to rebloom. Propagate by dividing the clumps in spring or fall, by root cuttings taken in late winter or early spring, or by sowing seeds.

S. laevis
P. 210

s. LEE-vis. Stokes' Aster. A 1- to 2-foot-tall species that forms 1½-foot-wide clumps. Bears 2- to 3-inch-wide flower heads with two rows of fringed ray florets, or "petals," around fuzzy centers of disk florets. Flowers come in shades of violet-blue, pink, and white. 'Blue Danube' bears showy 4-inch-wide lavender-blue flowers. 'Alba' has white flowers. Zones 5 to 9.

✿ Stylophorum

sty-LOFF-or-um. Poppy family, Papaveraceae.

Three species belong to this genus in the poppy family. All are perennials with pinnately lobed leaves, meaning the leaves are deeply divided into segments arranged in a featherlike fashion. They produce clusters of saucer-shaped, four-petaled, poppylike flowers in shades of yellow or orange.

HOW TO GROW

Select a spot in partial to full shade with average to rich, moist soil. Plants survive in full sun but generally have unattractive, scorched foliage there. Propagate by dividing the plants very carefully in spring, or better yet, start from seeds. Where happy, plants self-sow with enthusiasm.

S. diphyllum P. 211

s. die-FILL-um. Celandine Poppy. A 1- to 1½-foot-tall species native to the eastern United States that forms 1-foot-wide mounds. Bears deeply lobed 8- to 12-inch-long leaves with scalloped margins and clusters of golden yellow 1- to 2-inch-wide flowers from spring to summer. Zones 4 to 8.

❦ *Symphytum*

sim-FYE-tum. Borage family, Boraginaceae.

Commonly known as comfrey, *Symphytum* species bear clusters of nodding, tubular flowers that resemble bluebells (*Mertensia* species). Blooms have five lobes, or petals, and come in shades of blue, purple, pink, and white. The plants produce mounds of hairy, oblong to lance-shaped leaves with prominent veins and a wrinkled texture. Comfreys are rhizomatous perennials with fleshy roots and can become invasive. Between 25 and 35 species belong to the genus. Common comfrey *(S. officinale)* has traditionally been used in a variety of herbal preparations, but leaves and roots cause severe indigestion if ingested, and contact with the foliage can cause skin irritation. Both botanical and common names refer to the traditional herbal use for this plant, which was once used to heal broken bones: the botanical name is from the Greek *symphio,* to grow together, while comfrey is from the Latin word *conferva,* meaning join together.

HOW TO GROW

Select a site in full sun or partial shade with average to rich, moist soil. Even moisture is essential if the plants are to look their best in sun. Comfreys are very vigorous spreaders, so select a site with care. They make excellent ground covers in shade, but quickly overtake less robust companions, and even small sections of root left in the soil will give rise to new plants. Variegated forms tend to be less vigorous than green-leaved ones. Some gardeners remove the flowers of variegated forms as they appear to enhance the foliage. Taller species require staking. Propagate by dividing the clumps in spring, by taking root cuttings in late fall, or by seeds.

S. caucasicum

s. cau-CAS-ih-cum. Caucasian Comfrey. A 1½- to 2-foot-tall species that spreads to 2 feet. Bears clusters of bright blue ½-inch-long flowers from early to late summer. Zones 3 to 9.

S. hybrids

A variety of hybrids of uncertain parentage are available. 'Hidcote Pink' bears clusters of pale pink and white ½-inch-long flowers in spring on 1½-foot plants. 'Hidcote Blue', also 1½ feet tall, bears red buds that open into ½-inch-long pale blue flowers, also in spring. 'Goldsmith' bears leaves patterned with gold and creamy white with pale blue, pink, or cream flowers in spring on 1-foot plants. Zones 5 to 9.

S. officinale   P. 211

s. oh-fish-in-AL-ee. Common Comfrey. Vigorous 3- to 4-foot-tall species that spreads to form 5- to 6-foot-wide mounds. Bears branched clusters of ¾-inch-long flowers from late spring to summer in shades of violet purple, pink, and creamy yellow. The cultivar 'Variegatum' bears white-edged leaves. Zones 3 to 9.

S. × uplandicum   P. 212

s. × up-LAN-dih-cum. Russian Comfrey. A 4- to 6-foot-tall species that spreads to 4 feet. Bears clusters of pinkish blue buds that open into ¾-inch-long purple-blue flowers from late spring to late summer. 'Variegatum' has gray-green leaves with white margins on 3-foot-tall plants that spread to 2 feet. Zones 3 to 9.

❦ Tanacetum

tan-ah-SEE-tum. Aster family, Asteraceae.

Tanacetum contains some 70 species of annuals, perennials, and sub-shrubs with leaves that are entire, toothed, lobed, or deeply cut in a feathery fashion. The foliage often is aromatic. The flowers are daisy- or buttonlike and are carried singly or in clusters. The centers, or "eyes," which may or may not be surrounded by petal-like ray florets, consist of a dense cluster of yellow disk florets that produce the seeds. Over the years, members of this genus have been classified in various genera, including *Chrysanthemum, Pyrethrum,* and *Matricaria.*

HOW TO GROW

Select a site in full sun with average, well-drained soil. Sandy soil is ideal, although plants will thrive in any soil, provided it is well drained. Deadhead plants regularly to keep them neat and prevent an abundance of self-sown seedlings. (*T. parthenium* is especially prolific.) Cut back *T. coccineum* hard after flowering to encourage plants to produce a second flush of bloom. Divide plants in spring or fall if they outgrow their space or die out in the middle of the clumps. In addition to division, plants can be propagated by rooting cuttings of shoots that appear at the base of the plants in spring, taking cuttings in early summer, or by seeds.

T. coccineum P. 212

t. cock-SIN-ee-um. Painted Daisy, Pyrethrum. Formerly *C. coccineum, P. coccineum, P. roseum.* Bushy 1½- to 2½-foot-tall perennial spreading to 1½ feet. Bears deeply cut leaves and 3-inch-wide daisylike flowers in early summer with ray florets in shades of pink, red, yellow, and white. 'Eileen May Robinson' bears single pink blooms. 'James Kelway' produces single red flowers. Zones 3 to 7.

T. parthenium P. 213

t. par-THEN-ee-um. Feverfew. Formerly *C. parthenium, M. parthenium, P. parthenium.* Bushy 1½- to 2-foot-tall species that spreads to 1 foot. Bears aromatic, feathery leaves and small 1-inch-wide daisylike flowers in summer with yellow centers and white ray florets. 'Aureum' bears golden foliage and comes true from seeds. 'Flore Pleno', 'Snowball', and 'Tetra White' all bear double white flowers. Zones 4 to 9.

T. vulgare

t. vul-GAH-ree. Common Tansy. Vigorous 2- to 3-foot-tall perennial spreading to 1½ feet. Bears mounds of pinnately lobed (featherlike) or toothed leaves topped by clusters of bright yellow ½-inch-wide buttonlike flower heads in summer. Zones 3 to 8.

❦ Teucrium

TOO-cree-um. Mint family, Lamiaceae.

Commonly called germanders, *Teucrium* species are perennials, sub-shrubs, or shrubs with handsome, aromatic, simple or lobed leaves that can be evergreen or deciduous. They bear whorled clusters or racemes of small bell-shaped to tubular flowers that are sometimes, but not always, two lipped. About 100 species belong to the genus, most native to the Mediterranean. Germanders have a long history of medicinal use — the botanical name honors Teucer, the first king of Troy, who is believed to have been the first to use the plants medicinally.

HOW TO GROW
Select a site in full sun with poor to average, well-drained soil. Neutral to slightly alkaline pH is best. *T. chamaedrys* can be used as a low hedge. In this case, prune or shear the plants in spring to within about 2 inches of the ground to keep them compact. Propagate by taking cuttings in early or midsummer. Or start from seeds.

T. chamaedrys   P. 213

t. cam-EE-driss. Germander, Wall Germander. Evergreen or deciduous sub-shrub that ranges from 1 to 2 feet in height and spreads to about 1 foot. Bears dark green leaves and loose racemes of ½- to ¾-inch-long two-lipped flowers in shades from pale pink to purple. Blooms in summer and early fall. Zones 5 to 9.

❦ Thalictrum

tha-LICK-trum. Buttercup family, Ranunculaceae.

Although their relationship is not immediately apparent to the non-botanist, *Thalictrum* species are closely related to buttercups (*Ranunculus* spp.), clematis (*Clematis* spp.), and columbines (*Aquilegia* spp.). Commonly called meadow rues, *Thalictrum* species produce mounds of handsome, lacy-textured blue-green leaves that usually are divided several times in a pinnate (featherlike) fashion and have lobed or toothed leaflets. The flowers are petalless, but they create a showy, delicate effect because they are borne in large branched clusters above the foliage and usually have prominent clusters of stamens. About 130 species belong to the genus, all of which are perennials.

HOW TO GROW

Plant meadow rues in partial shade with rich, moist soil. They tolerate full sun provided the soil remains constantly moist, but a site with some shade is best. In areas with warm summers, site them where they receive shade during the hottest part of the day. Plants tend to be late to emerge in spring, so mark the clumps to avoid digging into the crowns by accident early in the season. Water during dry weather. Taller species generally need staking. Plants thrive for years without needing to be divided, but can be dug and divided if necessary in early spring or fall for propagation. Or propagate by seeds.

T. aquilegifolium   P. 214

t. ack-wih-lee-jih-FOE-lee-um. Columbine Meadow Rue. Rhizomatous 2- to 3-foot-tall species forming 1½- to 2-foot-wide mounds of columbine-like leaves with rounded leaflets. In early summer it bears 6- to 8-inch-wide clusters of fluffy ½-inch-long flowers with showy purple or white stamens. Zones 4 to 8.

T. delavayi

t. deh-LAH-vay-eye. Yunan Meadow Rue. A 2- to 4-foot-tall species that forms 2-foot-wide clumps. From summer to fall, it bears branched panicles of fluffy flowers with purple sepals and creamy yellow stamens. 'Hewitt's Double' has rounded mauve purple flowers consisting of many petal-like sepals. Zones 4 to 9.

T. dioicum

t. die-OH-ih-kum. Early Meadow Rue. A 1- to 3-foot-tall species native to North America that spreads to 2 feet. Bears panicles of yellow to yellowish green flowers. Male and female flowers are borne on separate plants, and male plants have the showiest blooms. Zones 4 to 9.

T. flavum   P. 214

t. FLAY-vum. Yellow Meadow Rue. Vigorous 1- to 3-foot-tall species that spreads by rhizomes to form mounds 2 to 4 feet wide. Bears panicles of lightly fragrant ¼-inch-long yellow flowers in summer. T. flavum ssp. glaucum, which has blue-green leaves and stems, bears large clusters of pale sulphur yellow flowers. Zones 5 to 9.

T. rochebruneanum 'Lavender Mist'   P. 215

t. roe-cheh-brew-nee-AH-num. Lavender Mist. A 3- to 5-foot-tall species forming 2- to 3-foot-wide mounds of foliage topped in summer by loose panicles of ½-inch-long lilac-pink or white flowers. Zones 4 to 7.

❦ *Thermopsis*

ther-MOP-sis. Pea family, Fabaceae.

Commonly called false lupines, *Thermopsis* species are rhizomatous perennials bearing erect racemes of flowers that resemble lupines (*Lupinus* spp.) or baptisias (*Baptisia* spp.). Most species bear yellow flowers, but some have purple ones. Leaves are palmate (handlike) and have three leaflets. Flat seedpods follow the petal-like flowers, and this is the main characteristic that distinguishes these plants from baptisias, which bear rounded, inflated pods. Some 20 species belong to the genus, all perennials native from North America, Russia, eastern Asia, and India. The botanical name is from the Greek *thermos*, lupine, and *opsis*, appearance.

HOW TO GROW
Select a site in full sun or very light shade with average, well-drained soil that remains evenly moist. In areas with hot summers, a site with shade during the hottest part of the day is best. Stake in early spring to keep them erect. These drought-tolerant plants have deep taproots and thrive for years without needing to be divided. Since they resent being disturbed and are slow to recover (digging breaks the deep roots), dig them only if necessary in early spring. Propagate by division — or by severing and potting up or replanting portions of the clumps that spread too far — taking cuttings in early summer, or starting from seeds.

T. villosa   P. 215
t. vil-LOW-suh. Carolina Lupine. Formerly *T. caroliniana.* Native North American wildflower, found from the Carolinas to Georgia, that ranges from 3 to 5 feet in height and, with time, spreads as far. Bears dense 8- to 12-inch-long racemes of ¾-inch-long yellow flowers in late spring and early summer. Zones 3 to 9.

❦ *Thymus*

TYE-mus. Mint family, Lamiaceae.

Handsome, useful thymes are valued as cooking herbs, ground covers, and ornamentals. About 350 species belong to this genus, including woody-based perennials, subshrubs, and shrubs. Rounded, lacy-looking clusters of pink, rose-purple, or white flowers cover the plants in late spring or early summer. The tiny individual flowers are two lipped and range from about ⅛ to ⅜ inch in length. Plants bear very aromatic, evergreen, oval to linear leaves that are small too, about ½ inch or less.

HOW TO GROW

Select a site in full sun or very light shade with well-drained soil. Plants prefer warm, dry, poor, sandy or gravelly soil, but also grow in rich soil or even in heavy clay, provided drainage is excellent. Moist soil or poorly drained conditions lead to fungal diseases and rot, while too-rich soil causes rampant growth and foliage that has less fragrance and flavor. A spot with good air circulation is best, especially for *T. pseudolanuginosus.* Mulch with gravel to control weeds but maintain soil drainage. Toward the northern part of their range, protect shrubby thymes in winter with evergreen branches placed over the plants after the ground freezes in late fall. Trim shrubby species in mid- to late summer after they flower to keep them neat looking. On variegated or golden-leaved forms, prune off or dig out any growth that reverts to all-green. Divide (or propagate and replace) shrubby thymes every 3 or 4 years, since they tend to become woody and less vigorous. Divide mat-forming thymes only if they die out in the centers of the clumps or for propagation. With either type, divide plants in spring or early fall. Or propagate shrubby thymes by cuttings taken in spring or summer or by mound layering in spring. Seed-grown thymes seldom resemble their parents.

T. × citriodorus   P. 216

t. × sih-tree-oh-DOOR-us. Lemon Thyme. Shrubby, rounded 10- to 12-inch-tall plant that spreads to about 2 feet. Mounds of lemon-scented leaves are topped by clusters of pale lilac flowers in summer. 'Aureus' bears yellow leaves while 'Argenteus' has silver-edged leaves. Zones 5 to 9.

T. pseudolanuginosus

t. SUE-doe-lah-nue-jih-NO-sis. Woolly Thyme. Mat-forming 1- to 3-inch-tall species that spreads from 1 to 3 feet. Bears silvery-hairy leaves and sparse pale pink flowers in summer. Requires perfect drainage. Zones 5 or 6 to 8.

T. pulegioides

t. pul-ed-jee-OY-deez. Mother of Thyme. A 3-inch-tall subshrub that spreads to a foot or more and bears mauve pink flowers in late spring and early summer and lemon-scented leaves. Zones 4 to 9.

T. serpyllum   P. 216

t. ser-PILL-um. Wild Thyme, Creeping Thyme. Ground-hugging subshrub ranging from 1 to 10 inches in height and spreading to about 1½ feet. Bears aromatic leaves and purple flowers in summer. Dwarf cultivars, such as 1-inch-tall 'Pink Chintz', are especially handsome as ground covers. *T. serpyllum* var. *coccineus* (formerly *T. praecox* 'Coccineus') is a 3-inch-tall creeper with purple-red flowers. Zones 4 to 9.

T. vulgaris

t. vul-GAIR-iss. Common Thyme, Garden Thyme. A 6- to 12-inch-tall subshrub forming a spreading 1½-foot-wide mound of twiggy branches covered with gray-green aromatic leaves. White or rose-purple flowers appear from late spring to early summer. Zones 4 to 8.

✿ *Tiarella*

tee-uh-RELL-uh. Saxifrage family, Saxifragaceae.

Tiarella species, commonly known as foamflowers, are shade-loving perennials native to North America as well as eastern Asia. About seven species belong to the genus, all of which produce mounds of toothed, primarily basal leaves that either are simple in outline or, more often, lobed in a palmate (handlike) fashion. The leaves have prominent veins and are covered with bristly hairs. Plants bear airy panicles or racemes of tiny ¼- to ½-inch-wide white or pinkish white flowers from spring to summer.

HOW TO GROW

Plant foamflowers in partial to full shade with rich, evenly moist, well-drained soil. A slightly acid pH is best. Plants grow naturally in damp woodlands and along streambanks, but constantly wet soil usually is fatal, especially in winter. Propagate by digging and dividing the clumps in spring or fall, by digging up individual plantlets that emerge at the end of runners, or by seeds.

T. cordifolia   P. 217

t. core-dih-FOE-lee-uh. Allegheny Foamflower. A 6- to 10-inch-tall native North American wildflower that spreads vigorously by runners and rhizomes to form 1- to 2-foot-wide clumps. Bears fluffy, spikelike racemes of white flowers in spring above attractive maplelike leaves. 'Brandywine' bears leaves with showy red veins. 'Tiger Stripe' also has red-veined leaves with a prominent central stripe. 'Slickrock' bears very deeply cut, dark green leaves. 'Eco Red Heart', sometimes listed as a cultivar of *T. wherryi*, has leaves with a reddish central blotch. Zones 3 to 8.

T. wherryi P. 217

t. WHERE-ee-eye. Wherry's Foamflower. Compact perennial, similar to *T. cordifolia*, that reaches 6 to 10 inches in height but spreads much more slowly, eventually forming 6- to 10-inch-wide clumps. Bears fluffy, spike-like racemes of white or pink-tinged flowers in spring above attractive maplelike leaves. 'Oakleaf' bears oakleaf-shaped foliage and pink flowers. 'Dunvegan' forms clumps of deeply lobed leaves topped by pink flowers. Zones 3 to 8.

❧ *Tradescantia*

trad-ess-CAN-tee-uh. Spiderwort family, Commelinaceae.

Commonly known as spiderworts, *Tradescantia* species are hardy and tender perennials bearing clusters of saucer-shaped flowers that have three petals and three sepals. While the individual flowers last only half a day, they are produced in clusters, each with a pair of boat-shaped bracts at the base, and appear over a long season. Leaves are usually strap to lance shaped, but also can be linear or ovate. They are attached to the stems by a sheath that clasps the stem. About 65 species of spiderwort native to North, South, and Central America belong to this genus. The hardy perennials commonly grown in gardens usually are hybrids.

HOW TO GROW

Select a site in light to full shade with rich, moist, well-drained soil. Cut plants to the ground after the main flush of flowers to discourage reseeding, encourage rebloom, and keep plants neat looking. In areas with cool summers, they regrow fairly quickly; in areas with warm summers, they re-emerge in fall. Plants spread vigorously to form dense clumps. For propagation and to keep plants in bounds, dig and divide them every 3 to 4 years in spring or fall. Spiderworts self-sow with enthusiasm, but hybrids do not come true from seeds.

T. Andersoniana Group P. 218

Spiderwort. Clump-forming hybrids that produce 1½- to 2-foot-tall mounds of lance-shaped leaves and spread from 2 to 3 feet. Bears clusters of saucer-shaped 1-inch-wide three-petaled flowers from early to mid-summer. Blooms come in violet, lavender-blue, pink, rose-red, and white. 'Iris Prichard' bears white flowers with pale lavender-blue shading. 'Red Cloud' has bright rose-red flowers. 'Purple Dome' bears violet purple blooms. 'Snowcap' has large white blooms. 'Purple Profusion' bears violet-blue leaves on 1- to 1½-foot-tall plants. 'Concord Grape,' also 1 to 1½ feet tall, bears rosy purple blooms. Zones 4 to 9, to Zone 3 with winter protection.

T. virginiana

t. vir-jin-ee-AH-nuh. Virginia Spiderwort. Native North American wildflower forming 1- to 2-foot-tall mounds of strap-shaped leaves that spread from 2 to 3 feet. Bears clusters of 1-inch-wide purple-blue flowers. Zones 4 to 9.

❦ *Tricyrtis*

tri-SIR-tiss. Lily family, Liliaceae.

Tricyrtis species, or toad lilies, as they are also called, are perennials native from the Himalayas to Japan and the Philippines. They form clumps of erect or arching stems clothed in ovate to somewhat oblong leaves. The leaves clasp the stems at the base. Toad lilies have unusual, waxy-textured flowers that are borne either singly or in clusters in the leaf axils or, less often, at the stem tips. Blooms have six tepals (petal-like segments of a flower that cannot be distinguished as either sepals or petals) and may be star, funnel, or bell shaped. About 16 species belong to the genus.

HOW TO GROW

Select a site in light to full shade with rich, moist, well-drained soil. Plants thrive for years without needing to be divided. Propagate by dividing plants in spring. Toad lilies self-sow in areas with summers that are long enough for the seeds to ripen.

T. formosana

t. for-mo-SAH-nuh. Formosa Toad Lily. Also listed as *T. stolonifera*. Rhizomatous 1- to 2-foot-tall species also spreading by stolons to form 2-foot-wide clumps with time. Bears glossy dark green leaves with purple-green spots on somewhat zigzagged stems. From late summer into fall, plants produce clusters of upward-facing, starry 1-inch-wide flowers in white, pinkish white, or pinkish purple with red-purple spots. Zones 4 to 9.

T. hirta

P. 218

t. HUR-tuh. Toad Lily. Also listed as *H. japonica*. A 2- to 3-foot-tall species that spreads by rhizomes to form 2-foot-wide clumps. Bears clusters of white, purple-spotted flowers in late summer and fall in the leaf axils along the stems. 'Variegata' bears leaves with yellow margins. 'Miyazaki' bears white flowers with lilac purple spots on 3-foot plants. Zones 4 to 9.

❦ *Trillium*

TRIL-ee-um. Lily family, Liliaceae.

Trilliums are spring-flowering perennials native to woodlands in North America as well as eastern Asia. They grow from tuberlike rhizomes and form clumps of erect stems, each topped by a single set of rounded to ovate or diamond-shaped leaves. The flowers are solitary and borne above the whorl of leaves. The botanical name *Trillium* is from the Latin *tres*, a reference to the normal number of leaves borne on each stem as well as the number of sepals and petals on each flower.

HOW TO GROW

Select a site in partial to full shade with moist, well-drained soil rich in organic matter. Soil with an acid to neutral pH is best for most species. Mulch plants annually with chopped leaves to keep the soil moist and replenish organic matter. Trilliums are spring ephemerals, meaning they die back after flowering, generally by early summer, so mark the locations of plants to avoid digging into them accidentally. *Do not* collect trilliums from the wild or purchase plants that have been wild collected. See page 6 for information on avoiding wild-collected plants. Propagate by dividing the rhizomes in spring after the plants flower. The divisions may be slow to re-establish. Trilliums also self-sow where happy, although plants take several years to bloom from seeds.

T. erectum

t. ee-RECK-tum. Stinking Benjamin. A 1- to 1½-foot-tall native North American wildflower that spreads to about 1 foot. Bears 2- to 3½-inch-wide flowers with foul-smelling maroon to maroon-brown petals in spring. Blooms are on long stalks and point up or out. Zones 4 to 9.

T. grandiflorum   P. 219

t. gran-dih-FLOOR-um. Great White Trillium, Wood Lily, Wake-robin. A 1- to 1½-foot-tall native North American wildflower that eventually forms 2-foot-wide clumps. In spring, bears showy, short-stalked 3-inch-wide white flowers that change to pink. Zones 4 to 8.

Trollius

TROLL-ee-us. Buttercup family, Ranunculaceae.

Trollius species, commonly called globeflowers, are perennials native to areas with damp to wet soils in Europe, Asia, and North America. The plants bear buttercup-like flowers that may be cup shaped, bowl shaped, or rounded and come in shades of yellow, orange, white, and pink. The flowers consist of showy, petal-like sepals: the petals resemble the stamens and form a small cluster in the centers of the flowers. The plants produce low mounds of mostly basal leaves that are palmately lobed (divided in a handlike fashion) and usually toothed.

HOW TO GROW

Select a site in full sun or partial shade with very rich soil that is constantly moist or wet. A site in a bog garden or along a pond or stream is ideal, and globeflowers prefer heavy, clayey soil rather than sandy conditions. Globeflowers are best in areas with cool summers. In Zones 6 and 7, give them a site with shade during the hottest part of the day. Water regularly in dry weather. Cut the plants back after the first flush of flowers and feed them to encourage a second flush of flowers. To propagate, divide clumps in spring or fall or start from seeds.

T. × cultorum

P. 219

t. × cul-TOR-um. Hybrid Globeflower. A group of hybrid cultivars ranging from 2 to 3 feet in height and forming 2-foot-wide clumps. They bear 1- to 3-inch-wide flowers from spring to midsummer. 'Alabaster' bears creamy yellow flowers in spring. 'Earliest of All' has orange-yellow blooms in spring. 'Goldquelle', also sold as 'Gold Fountain', bears 3-inch-wide yellow blooms. 'Orange Princess' has 2½- to 3-inch orange blooms. 'Golden Queen' bears 2-inch-wide orange flowers on 2-foot-tall plants. 'Pritchard's Giant' has yellow blooms on 3-foot plants. Zones 3 to 6.

T. europaeus

t. you-roh-PAY-us. Common Globeflower. A 2-foot-tall species that forms 2-foot-wide clumps and bears rounded 2-inch-wide yellow flowers from early to midsummer. 'Superbus' bears an abundance of 4-inch-wide sulphur yellow blooms. Zones 4 to 7.

❦ *Uvularia*

you-view-LAIR-ee-uh. Lily family, Liliaceae.

Commonly known as merry bells or bellworts, *Uvularia* species are spring-blooming wildflowers native to eastern North America. Five species belong to the genus, all rhizomatous perennials with pendent, bell-shaped flowers consisting of six tepals (petal-like segments of a flower that cannot be distinguished as either a sepal or a petal). The blooms are carried on erect branched or unbranched stems clothed with lance-shaped leaves. Both species listed here bear perfoliate leaves, meaning leaf bases have lobes that surround the stem, making it appear as if the stem is inserted through the leaf.

HOW TO GROW
Select a site in partial to full shade with rich, moist, well-drained soil. Mulch with compost or chopped leaves in spring. Water during dry weather. Plants spread by rhizomes to form handsome clumps with time, and they can grow for years without needing division. Propagate by dividing the clumps in spring or fall or by sowing seeds.

U. grandiflora   P. 220

u. gran-dih-FLOOR-uh. Large Merrybells, Great Merrybells. A clumping 1- to 1½-foot-tall perennial that spreads to about 1 foot. Bears yellow to orange-yellow 2-inch-long flowers, either singly or in pairs, in mid- to late spring. The flowers of this species have few, if any, granules inside (see *U. perfoliata*), stamens that are longer than styles, and leaves with downy undersides. Zones 3 to 9.

U. perfoliata

u. per-foe-lee-AH-tuh. Perfoliate Bellflower, Strawbell. A 1- to 2-foot-tall species with 1- to 1½-inch-long pale yellow flowers in spring. The flowers of this species have orange granules inside, stamens shorter than styles, and leaves that are smooth underneath. Zones 4 to 8.

❦ *Vancouveria*

van-coe-VAIR-ee-uh. Barberry family, Berberidaceae.

Close relatives of epimediums, *Vancouveria* species are perennial wildflowers native to western North America. Three species belong to the genus, all rhizomatous, spring-blooming perennials that form handsome mounds of delicate-looking, fernlike foliage. The leaves are twice or thrice divided into rounded, shallowly lobed leaflets. Blooms have 6 to 9 sepals that drop quickly once the flowers open plus 6 reflexed petals and 12 petal-like sepals that are reflexed like the true petals.

HOW TO GROW

Select a site in partial shade with rich, evenly moist, well-drained soil. Water during dry weather. Mulch annually with chopped leaves or compost to replenish soil and retain moisture. Propagate by dividing the clumps in spring or fall.

V. hexandra
P. 220

v. hecks-AN-druh. Vancouveria, American Barrenwort. Formerly known as *Epimedium hexandra*. A 10- to 14-inch-tall woodland wildflower native to the Pacific Northwest that forms 1-foot-wide clumps of fine-textured leaves. Bears white flowers in spring. Zones 5 to 7.

✤ Veratrum

ver-AH-trum. Lily family, Liliaceae.

Commonly called false hellebores, *Veratrum* species are vigorous perennials producing handsome clumps of bold, pleated, broadly ovate to nearly round leaves that have prominent veins. They produce erect panicles of small, densely packed, starry to bell-shaped flowers in summer. Blooms may be greenish, white, reddish, brown, or nearly black. About 45 species belong to the genus, all of which are perennials that grow from stout black rhizomes that are poisonous. The leaves and seeds are poisonous as well.

HOW TO GROW

Select a site in partial shade with deep, very rich, moist but well-drained soil. Plants tolerate full sun in constantly moist soil, but in areas with warm summers, select a site with shade during the hottest part of the day. Water as necessary during dry weather; if the soil dries out, the edges of the leaves become scorched and crispy. Propagate by dividing plants in early spring or fall.

V. viride
P. 221

v. VEER-ih-day. Indian Poke. A 2- to 6-foot-tall perennial native to North America that spreads to about 2 feet. Bears 2-foot-tall panicles of starry green to greenish yellow flowers from early to midsummer. Zones 3 to 8.

⚑ Verbascum

ver-BAS-kum. Figwort family, Scrophulariaceae.

Commonly known as mulleins, *Verbascum* species produce erect, spire-like bloom stalks covered with small flowers that have a short, tubular base and five spreading lobes or petals. About 360 species belong to this genus, and most are biennials, although the genus also contains some annuals, perennials, and subshrubs. Most species have hairy to woolly leaves borne in a large rosette at the base of the plant. Mulleins are native from Europe to northern Africa and Asia and are also widely naturalized in North America.

HOW TO GROW

Select a site in full sun with poor to average, well-drained soil. Neutral to slightly alkaline pH is ideal. Established plants tolerate dry soil. The species listed here are grown as biennials or perennials. Plants have deep taproots and are happiest if left undisturbed once planted. Propagate by division in spring, by taking root cuttings in late fall or winter, or by sowing seeds. Plants self-sow.

V. chaixii
P. 221

v. SHAKE-see-eye. Nettle-leaved Mullein. A 3-foot-tall perennial forming a low 1½-foot-wide rosette of gray-green 2- to 10-inch-long leaves. Bears narrow, branched panicles of densely packed 1-inch-wide yellow flowers from mid- to late summer. *V. chaxii* f. *album* bears white flowers with mauve purple eyes. Zones 4 to 8.

V. olympicum
P. 222

v. oh-LIMP-ih-cum. Olympic Mullein. A 6-foot-tall perennial with a 2-foot-wide rosette of silvery white woolly leaves and stems. Bears branched, candelabra-like bloom stalks that reach 3 feet in length with 1¼-inch-wide golden yellow blooms from early to late summer. Plants often die after flowering. Zones 6 to 8.

❧ *Verbena*

ver-BEE-nuh. Vervian family, Verbenaceae.

Some 250 species of annuals, perennials, and subshrubs, both hardy and tender, belong to the genus *Verbena*. Most are native to the Americas, although a few species are found in southern Europe. They have square stems and usually opposite leaves that range from toothed to deeply lobed. Their small flowers have a slender tube at the base and an abruptly flared and flattened face that has five lobes, or "petals." Blooms are carried in showy spikes or clusters over a long season and come in shades of purple, violet, pink, cream, scarlet, and magenta.

HOW TO GROW

Select a site in full sun to light shade with poor to average, well-drained sandy or loamy soil. Shade during the hottest part of the day is best in the South. Plants tolerate both heat and drought. *V. hastata* will grow in evenly moist, well-drained soil. Trim back creeping species to control their spread and keep them bushy. Deadhead or shear the plants after the main flush of flowers to encourage rebloom. Dig and divide the plants in spring if they outgrow their space or die out in the centers of the clumps, or for propagation. Or propagate from cuttings taken in late summer, or from seeds.

V. canadensis

v. can-ah-DEN-sis. Rose Verbena, Rose Vervian. A ½- to 1½-foot-tall perennial native to North America that spreads to 3 feet by stems that root where they touch the soil. Bears dense, rounded 2½-inch-wide clusters of rose pink flowers in early summer and then blooms sporadically until fall if spent flowers are removed. 'Homestead Purple' is a mildew-resistant, purple-flowered cultivar. Zones 6 to 10.

V. hastata   P. 222

v. has-TAH-tuh. Blue Vervain. A 3- to 5-foot-tall perennial with stiff, branched, 2- to 4-inch-wide clusters of flowers from early summer to early fall in shades of violet, purple, and sometimes white. Zones 3 to 7.

❦ *Vernonia*

ver-NO-nee-uh. Aster family, Asteraceae.

Vernonia is a vast genus containing about 1,000 species of annuals, perennials, vines, subshrubs, shrubs, and trees. Many of the species that belong here are tropical or subtropical, but about 19 species of fall-blooming herbaceous perennials are hardy and native to North America. The perennial species have erect stems clothed in simple leaves that are either toothed or toothless. They bear large branched flower clusters that are somewhat rounded and are made up of buttonlike flower heads in shades of purple, violet, reddish pink, and sometimes white. The individual flower heads consist of small tubular disk florets; they lack ray florets, or "petals."

HOW TO GROW
Select a site in full sun with average, evenly moist, well-drained soil. Plants tolerate drought. *V. noveboracensis* also grows naturally in damp to wet soil. Cutting the stems back hard once or twice early in the season encourages branching and keeps plants shorter and more compact. Clumps benefit from being divided every 3 or 4 years. Propagate by division in spring or fall or by seeds.

V. noveboracensis   P. 223

v. no-vay-boar-ah-SEN-sis. Ironweed. An East Coast native wildflower ranging from 3 to 7 feet in height and forming 2- to 3-foot-wide clumps. From late summer to fall, bears 6- to 8-inch-wide flower clusters consisting of many reddish purple ½-inch-wide flower heads. Zones 5 to 9.

❦ *Veronica*

ver-ON-ih-kuh. Figwort family, Scrophulariaceae.

Best known as speedwells, *Veronica* species are vigorous, easy-to-grow plants that offer flowers in a rich palette of colors including true blue, violet-blue, pink, and white. The genus contains about 250 species of annuals, perennials, and a few subshrubs native primarily to Europe. All bear linear to lance-shaped or rounded leaves and showy bottlebrush-like spikes of flowers. The individual blooms are tiny — from ¼ to ½ inch wide. While the most popular speedwells are upright plants, there also are low-growing, mat-forming species useful as ground covers or rock garden plants. Most speedwells are quite vigorous, though still well behaved enough for the garden, but creeping speedwell (*Veronica fili-formis*) is a mat-forming 2-inch-tall species with pale blue flowers that becomes a serious weed in gardens and lawns.

HOW TO GROW

Plant speedwells in full sun or partial shade and average to rich soil that is moist but well drained. Plants will not tolerate constantly moist conditions, especially in winter, but since they are fairly shallow rooted they also are not particularly drought tolerant. Water during dry weather. Taller-growing speedwells may need staking — very rich soil increases the likelihood they will flop. Cut plants back after they flower, as some species may rebloom. Most benefit from being divided regularly — about every 3 or 4 years. Propagate by dividing the clumps in spring or fall, by taking cuttings in late spring or early summer, or by sowing seeds.

V. austriaca ssp. teucrium   P. 223

v. aw-stree-ACK-uh ssp. TOO-cree-um. Hungarian Speedwell. Formerly *V. teucrium* and *V. latifolia*. A ½- to 2-foot-tall species that spreads to 2 feet. Bears rich, deep blue flowers in 4- to 6-inch-long spikes from late spring to early summer. 'Crater Lake Blue', from 1 to 1½ feet tall, bears intensely blue flowers in early summer. Zones 3 to 8.

V. gentianoides

v. jen-shan-OY-deez. Gentian Speedwell. A ½- to nearly 2-foot-tall species that forms dense mats of foliage about 1½ feet wide. Bears loose 10-inch-long spikes of pale blue to white flowers in late spring to early summer. Zones 4 to 8.

V. longifolia   P. 224

v. lon-jih-FOE-lee-uh. Long-leaved Speedwell. A 2- to 4-foot-tall species that spreads to 2 feet. Bears dense 10- to 12-inch-long clusters of small lilac-blue flowers in late summer and early fall. 'Icicle' bears white flowers, and 'Rosea' has pink blooms. 'Blauriesen', sometimes sold as 'Foerster's Blue', bears deep blue flowers. Zones 3 to 8.

V. prostrata

v. pros-TRAH-tuh. Harebell Speedwell. Low-growing 3- to 6-inch-tall species that spreads to 1½ feet. Produces short spikes of starry blue flowers in late spring or early summer. 'Heavenly Blue' bears intensely blue flowers on 3-inch plants. Zones 5 to 8.

V. spicata

v. spy-KAH-tuh. Spike Speedwell. A 1- to 3-foot-tall species that spreads as far. Bears dense, foot-long spikes of flowers from early to late summer in shades of purple, blue, pink, and white. 'Blue Charm' bears pale lavender-blue flowers on 3-foot plants. 'Red Fox', also sold as 'Rotfuchs', has deep pink flowers and reaches 1 foot. 'Icicle' bears white flowers on 2-foot plants. 'Goodness Grows' bears dark violet-blue flowers on 1- to 1½-foot plants. Woolly speedwell (*V. spicata* ssp. *incana*, formerly *V. incana*) features spikelike flowers borne over densely hairy gray-green leaves. Woolly speedwell does not do well in areas with hot, wet summers: give it especially well drained conditions and avoid getting the leaves wet when watering. Zones 3 to 8.

V. 'Sunny Border Blue'

A 1½- to 2-foot-tall hybrid that spreads to 1 foot or more and bears showy violet-blue 7-inch-long spikes of flowers from early summer to late fall. Zones 4 to 8.

V. virginica. See Veronicastrum virginicum

❦ Veronicastrum

veh-ron-ih-KAS-trum. Figwort family, Scrophulariaceae.

Two species belong to this genus in the figwort family, one native to Siberia and the other to North America. Both are perennials with whorls of simple, toothed leaves and spikes of small flowers that resemble those of speedwells (*Veronica* species). The individual blooms have a long slender tube at the base that opens into flared lobes, or "petals." (*Veronica* species have short-tubed flowers with petal lobes that are longer than the tube, while *Veronicastrum* flowers have a tube longer than the petal lobes.) The botanical name marks this resemblance: it is derived from the name *Veronica* and the suffix *-astrum,* which indicates an incomplete resemblance.

HOW TO GROW

Select a site in full sun to partial shade with average to rich, moist soil. Plants usually have a laxer habit in shade and need staking. Water in dry weather, and feed annually. Divide clumps every 4 years or so to keep them from becoming overcrowded. Propagate by division in spring or fall, by cuttings taken from nonflowering stem tips in early summer, or by sowing seeds.

V. virginicum P. 224

v. vir-JIH-nih-kum. Culver's Root, Culver's Physic. Formerly *Veronica virginica.* Robust 4- to 6-foot-tall perennial native to North America that forms 2- to 4-foot-wide clumps. Fom midsummer to early fall, bears fluffy, bottlebrush-like racemes of densely packed ¼-inch-long flowers that can be white or pinkish or pale bluish purple. Zones 3 to 8.

❧ *Vinca*

VINK-uh. Dogbane family, Apocynaceae.

The seven species that belong to the genus *Vinca* are hardy or tender subshrubs native from Europe and northern Africa to central Asia. Commonly called periwinkles or vinca, they bear opposite, ovate to lance-shaped leaves and flowers that have a slender tube at the base and an abruptly flared and flattened face. The flowers have five lobes, or "petals."

HOW TO GROW
Select a site in full sun or partial shade with average to rich, well-drained soil. *V. minor* grows best in partial shade. The plants have slender stems that spread widely and root at the nodes wherever they touch the ground. Cut back plants hard in spring to shape them and control their spread. Propagate by taking cuttings in summer or dividing the clumps in spring or fall. Another option is to separate and dig up small plants that arise where stems have touched the soil and rooted.

V. minor P. 225

v. MY-nor. Common Myrtle, Lesser Periwinkle, Common Periwinkle. Spreading 4- to 6-inch-tall subshrub that forms mats of foliage several feet wide. Bears oval leaves and lavender-blue ¾- to 1-inch-wide flowers in spring and sporadically later in the season. *V. minor* f. *alba* bears white blooms. 'Bowles' Variety' has 1¼-inch-wide lavender flowers. 'Alba Variegata' has leaves with creamy white edges. 'Atropurpurea', also sold as 'Purpurea' and 'Rubra', bears red-purple flowers. Zones 4 to 9.

ꙍ *Viola*

vy-OH-luh. Violet family, Violaceae.

Viola is a large genus of beloved garden plants commonly known as violets, violas, and pansies. The genus contains some 500 species of annuals, biennials, and perennials (both hardy and tender), along with a few subshrubs. They bear flowers with five petals: a spurred lower petal that is the lower "lip," two petals that point up, and two more that point sideways. Leaves range from rounded and toothed or lobed to heart-shaped but also can be cut in a pinnate (featherlike) fashion.

HOW TO GROW

Select a planting site in partial to full shade with rich, moist, well-drained soil. Violets tolerate full sun with consistent soil moisture, but generally are happier with some shade. *V. pedata* is an exception: it requires very well drained, sandy soil that is high in organic matter and has an acid pH. All violets grow best during seasons when temperatures are cool, from late winter to early summer and again in fall. Plants spread by creeping rhizomes and also self-sow: they can become quite weedy and invasive, but make a dense, weed-smothering ground cover in the right site. Pull up unwanted seedlings wherever they appear. Propagate by division in spring or fall or by seeds. The species hybridize readily, so self-sown seedlings may not resemble their parents. Many perennial species also can be propagated by stem-tip cuttings taken in spring or summer.

V. canadensis

v. can-ah-DEN-sis. Canada Violet. Native 6- to 12-inch-tall wildflower that forms 1-foot-wide mounds of heart-shaped leaves. Bears white ½- to ¾-inch-wide flowers with yellow eyes in spring. The backs of the petals are blushed with purple. Zones 3 to 8.

V. cornuta   P. 225

v. core-NEW-tuh. Horned Violet. A 4- to 12-inch-tall species that spreads by rhizomes to form 12- to 14-inch-wide mounds of evergreen, oval, toothed leaves. From spring to summer, plants bear 1- to 1½-inch-wide lilac-blue flowers that look like small pansies. 'Chantreyland' bears apricot flowers; 'Jersey Gem', purple-blue blooms; 'Alba' and 'White Perfection', white flowers; and 'Blue Perfection', sky blue blooms. Zones 6 to 9.

V. labradorica

v. lab-rih-DOOR-ih-kuh. Labrador Violet. Native 1- to 4-inch-tall species that spreads via prostrate stems to form mounds 1 foot or more wide. Bears kidney- to heart-shaped leaves and pale purple ½-inch-wide flowers in spring and summer. Zones 2 to 8.

V. odorata

v. oh-door-AH-tuh. Sweet Violet, English Violet, Garden Violet. Rhizomatous 2- to 8-inch-tall species that spreads to 1½ feet. Bears rounded to heart-shaped leaves and ¾-inch-wide lavender-blue or white flowers in spring. Cultivars include 'Czar', which bears dark violet flowers, and 'White Czar', which bears white blooms. Zones 6 to 8.

V. pedata

v. peh-DAH-tuh. Bird's-foot Violet, Crow-foot Violet. Native 2- to 6-inch-tall wildflower that spreads by rhizomes to form 1-foot-wide mounds of deeply cut leaves with very narrow lobes. Bears 1¼-inch-wide pale lavender blooms in late spring and early summer. Zones 4 to 8.

V. sororia

v. sor-OR-ee-uh. Woolly Blue Violet. Native 3- to 6-inch-tall species that spreads by rhizomes and forms 8-inch-wide mounds of rounded, scalloped, densely hairy leaves. In spring and summer, bears ¾-inch-wide white flowers speckled and streaked with purple. Some forms have violet-blue flowers. Zones 4 to 8.

❦ Waldsteinia

wald-STINE-ee-uh. Rose family, Rosaceae.

This small genus in the rose family contains about six species that bear three-parted leaves and yellow saucer-shaped, five-petaled blooms that reveal a close relationship to potentillas or cinquefoils (*Potentilla* spp.). The common name barren strawberry refers to the fact that the flowers, which are borne singly or in small clusters, are followed by small dry, inedible fruits. While *Waldsteinia* species are vigorous, they are not to be confused with *Duchesnea indica,* a closely related, similar species commonly called mock strawberry. It is a very invasive weed that spreads quickly by runners.

Select a site in partial to full shade with average to rich soil. Even soil moisture is best, although plants tolerate drought and are useful ground covers for dry shade. They also will grow in full sun, provided the soil remains moist. Propagate by dividing the clumps in spring or fall.

W. fragarioides
w. fray-gair-ee-OY-eye-deez. Barren Strawberry. Rhizomatous 4- to 10-inch-tall native wildflower that spreads to form 2-foot-wide mats. Bears clusters of saucer-shaped ¾-inch-wide golden yellow flowers in spring and summer. Zones 3 to 8.

W. ternata   P. 226
w. ter-NAY-tuh. Barren Strawberry. Rhizomatous, semievergreen species native to Siberia, China, and Japan that reaches 4 inches and spreads to 2 feet. Bears bright yellow ½-inch-wide flowers in late spring and early summer. Zones 3 to 8.

❧ Yucca

YUCK-uh. Agave family, Agavaceae.

Rugged, adaptable yuccas are perennials, shrubs, and trees native to North and Central America. Some 40 species belong to the genus, and the perennials grown in gardens are tough, woody-based plants that produce large dense clumps of bold, linear to lance-shaped evergreen leaves. The clumps are topped in summer by showy, erect spikes of creamy white flowers that are waxy textured, nodding, and bell shaped. Bloom spikes rise to a height of 5 to 10 feet or more, well above the 2- to 2½-foot-tall mounds of sword-shaped leaves.

HOW TO GROW
Plant yuccas in full sun or very light shade. They grow in a wide range of soils, including average to rich, well-drained soil, and dry, sandy soil. Plants do not tolerate wet conditions but will grow in clay soil, provided it is well drained. Cut off the flower stalks at the base after the blooms fade. The individual crowns die after they flower, so cut them out of the clumps when the leaves begin to fade. Clumps can be left for years without needing division and form broad mounds with time. They are quite deep rooted and difficult to dig, so give them plenty of space at planting

time. Divide plants in spring or fall if they outgrow their space or for propagation. Or propagate by severing and replanting new plants, called pups, that appear around the outside of the clumps.

Y. filamentosa P. 226

y. fil-ah-men-TOE-suh. Adam's Needle. North American native species with stiff blue-green 2½-foot-long evergreen leaves. Forms 2½-foot-tall clumps of foliage that spread to 4 or 5 feet wide. Bears 5- to 6-foot-tall panicles of 2-inch-wide green or cream flowers in summer. Variegated cultivars, which add year-round color to the garden, include 'Bright Edge' and 'Color Guard', which have leaves with yellow margins, and 'Golden Sword' and 'Garland Gold', which have yellow-centered leaves. *Y. flaccida* resembles *Y. filamentosa* but has leaves that are less rigid and tend to droop at the tips. Both species are hardy in Zones 4 to 10.

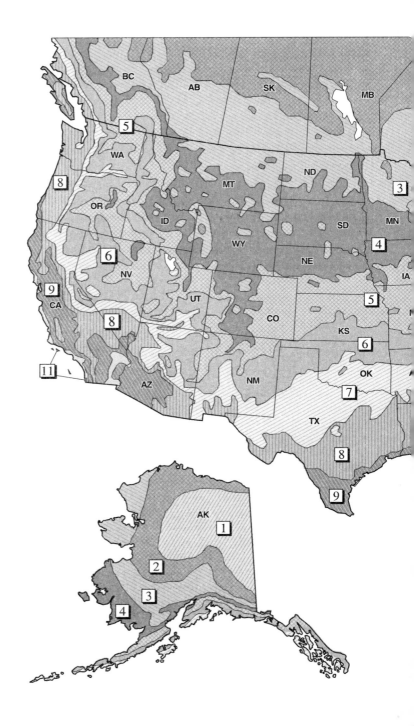

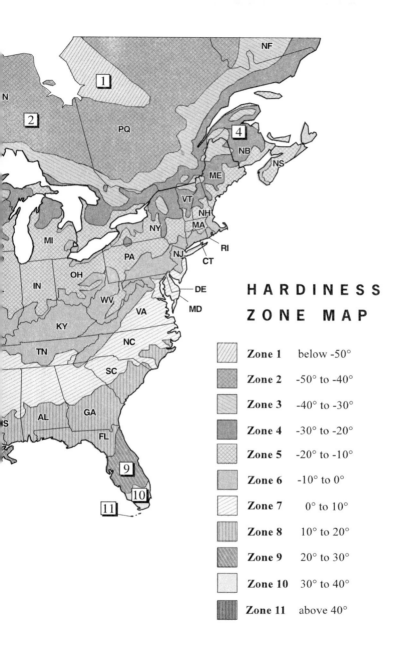

HARDINESS ZONE MAP

	Zone	Temperature
	Zone 1	below -50°
	Zone 2	-50° to -40°
	Zone 3	-40° to -30°
	Zone 4	-30° to -20°
	Zone 5	-20° to -10°
	Zone 6	-10° to 0°
	Zone 7	0° to 10°
	Zone 8	10° to 20°
	Zone 9	20° to 30°
	Zone 10	30° to 40°
	Zone 11	above 40°

✿Photo Credits

BLOOMS OF BRESSINGHAM NORTH AMERICA: 128 top

STEPHANIE COHEN: 182 top, 221 top

R. TODD DAVIS PHOTOGRA-PHY: 28 bottom, 30 top, 36 bottom, 45 top, 47 top, 59 bottom, 60 top, 63 bottom, 80 top, 82 top, 93 top, 98 bottom, 129 top, 134 top, 134 bottom, 135 top, 137 top, 141 top, 143 top, 148 bottom, 150 top, 155 top, 156 top, 156 bottom, 159 top, 159 bottom, 164 bottom, 169 top, 177 top, 178 bottom, 179 top, 180 bottom, 181 top, 183 top, 186 top, 188 top, 205 bottom, 206 bottom, 207 top, 211 top, 218 top, 222 bottom

BARBARA W. ELLIS: 31 top, 61 bottom, 97 top, 131 top, 131 bottom, 140 top, 174 top, 198 bottom, 215 bottom, 219 top

DEREK FELL: 204 bottom

CHARLES MARDEN FITCH: 31 bottom, 52 top, 61 top, 64 bottom, 79 top, 81 top, 87 top, 96 top, 110 bottom,
125 bottom, 127 bottom, 149 bottom, 165 bottom, 167 bottom, 187 bottom, 191 top, 217 top

MARGE GARFIELD: 34 top, 35 top, 36 bottom insert, 37 top, 38 bottom, 55 top, 73 top, 88 top, 89 bottom, 94 bottom, 106 bottom, 107 top, 109 top, 110 top, 111 bottom, 115 top, 122 top, 132 top, 133 bottom, 139 top, 146 top, 168 bottom, 171 bottom, 176 top, 179 bottom, 184 top, 188 bottom, 190 top, 191 bottom, 199 top, 200 top, 204 top, 219 bottom, 220 top, 221 bottom, 225 top, 226 top

CHARLES MANN: vi–1, 3, 4, 26, 27, 28 top, 29 top, 29 bottom, 35 bottom, 36 top, 41 top, 42 bottom, 44 bottom, 46 bottom, 47 bottom, 48 top, 48 bottom, 50 top, 50 bottom, 51 top, 53 bottom, 55 bottom, 56 top, 56 bottom, 62 bottom, 66 bottom, 68 top, 68 bottom, 69 top, 70 bottom, 74 bottom, 75 bottom, 76 bottom, 77 top, 77 bottom, 83 top, 84 top, 85 top, 85 bottom, 89 top, 90 bottom, 91 bottom, 92 top, 92 bottom, 93 bottom, 95 top, 95 bottom, 96 bottom, 98 top, 99 top, 99 bottom, 101 bottom, 102 bottom, 106 top, 108 bottom, 111 top, 119 top, 120 top, 120 bottom, 121 top, 122 bottom, 123 bottom, 125 top, 126 top, 126 bottom, 127 top, 132 bottom, 135 bottom, 138 top, 138 bottom, 142 bottom, 144 top, 144 bottom, 145 top, 146 bottom, 149 top, 150 bottom, 152 top, 153 top, 160 bottom, 162 top, 163 bottom, 165 top, 169 bottom, 170 top, 170 bottom, 173 top, 173 bottom, 174 bottom, 175 top, 175 bottom, 176 bottom, 177 bottom, 182 bottom, 183 bottom, 185 bottom, 193 top, 195 top, 197 top, 199 bottom, 202 top, 203 top, 203 bottom, 212 bottom, 213 bottom, 216 bottom

NEW ENGLAND WILD FLOWER SOCIETY (L. NEWCOMB): 72 bottom

NANCY ONDRA: 39 bottom

JERRY PAVIA PHOTOGRAPHY, INC.: ii–iii, 11, 30 bottom, 32 top, 32 bottom, 33 top, 33 bottom, 34 bottom, 37 bottom, 38 top, 39 top, 40 top, 40 bottom, 41 bottom, 42 top, 43 top, 43 bottom, 44 top, 45 bottom, 46 top, 49 top, 49 bottom, 51 bottom, 52 bottom, 53 top, 54 top, 54 bottom, 57 top, 57 bottom, 58 top, 58 bottom, 59 top, 60 bottom, 62 top, 63 top, 64 top, 65 top, 65 bottom, 66 top, 67 top, 67 bottom, 69 bottom, 70 top, 71 top, 71 bottom, 72 top, 73 bottom, 74 top, 75 top, 76 top, 78 top, 78 bottom, 79 bottom, 80 bottom, 81 bottom, 82 bottom, 83 bottom, 84 bottom, 86 top, 86 bottom, 87 bottom, 88 top, 90 top, 91 top, 94 top, 97 bottom, 100 top, 100 bottom, 101 top, 102 top, 103 top, 103 bottom, 104 top, 104 bottom, 105 top, 105 bottom, 107 bottom, 108 top, 109 bottom, 112 top, 112 bottom, 113 top, 113 bottom, 114 top, 114 bottom, 115 bottom, 116 top, 116 bottom, 117 top, 117 bottom, 118 top, 118 bottom, 119 bottom, 121 bottom, 123 top, 124 top, 124 bottom, 128 bottom, 129 bottom, 130 top, 130 bottom, 133 top, 136 top, 136 bottom, 137 bottom, 139 bottom, 140 bottom, 141 bottom, 142 top, 143 bottom, 145 bottom, 147 top, 147 bottom, 148 top, 151 top, 151 bottom, 152 bottom, 153 bottom, 154 top, 154 bottom, 155 bottom, 157 top, 157 bottom, 158 top, 158 bottom, 160 top, 161 top, 161 bottom, 162 bottom, 163 top, 164 top, 166 top, 166 bottom, 167 top, 168 top, 171 top, 172 top, 172 bottom, 178 top, 180 top, 181 bottom, 184 bottom, 185 top, 186 bottom, 187 top, 189 top, 189 bottom, 190 bottom, 192 top, 192 bottom, 193 bottom, 194 top, 194 bottom, 195 bottom, 196 top, 196 bottom, 197 bottom, 198 top, 200 bottom, 201 top, 201 bottom, 202 bottom, 205 top, 206 top, 207 bottom, 208 top, 208 bottom, 209 top, 209 bottom, 210 top, 210 bottom, 211 bottom, 212 top, 213 top, 214 top, 214 bottom, 215 top, 216 top, 217 bottom, 218 bottom, 220 bottom, 222 top, 223 top, 223 bottom, 224 top, 224 bottom, 225 bottom, 226 bottom, 227 top

✦Index